You are cordially invited to the

BEST CHOICES IN ATLANTA

Published in the U.S.A.

I

Best Choice Series:

Best Choices on the Oregon Coast
Best Choices off Oregon's Interstates
Best Choices in Central and Eastern Oregon
Best Choices in Portland and the NorthWillamette Valley
Best Choices in Northern California
Best Choices In Northern California/Bay Area Edition
Best Choices in Western Washington
Best Choices in Orange County
Best Choices in Arizona
Best Choices in Colorado
Best Choices in San Diego
Best Choices in Sacramento
Best Choices in San Francisco
Best Choices in the Tampa Bay Area
Best Choices in Central and Southeast Texas
Best Choices in the Seattle-Tacoma Area
Best Choices in Eastern Washington
Best Choices in New Mexico
Best Choices in Alaska
Best Choices in Idaho
Best Choices in British Columbia
Best Choices in Los Angeles
Best Choices in Western Pennsylvania
Best Choices along the California Coast
Best Choices in St. Louis
Best Choices in Atlanta
Best Choices in Utah

**For additional copies, write or call:
Gable & Gray, The Book Publishers
PO Box 880
Medford, Oregon 97501-0063
1-800-627-7753**

Director of Editing	Doreen Ambrosio Johnson
Managing Editor	Joseph R. Kiefer II
Editor	T. Jefferson Reeder
Editorial Staff	John Cunningham
	Sally Duhaime
	Genevieve Renée Getreu
	Debra Grande
Editorial Assistant	Stephanie Paris
Senior Staff Writer	Gary Corwin
Area Information Writer	Merritt Scott Miller
Contributing Writers	Geraldine Baldassarre
	Patrick C. Claflin
	Joseph G. Follansbee
	Mark Forrest
	Bobbi Guthert
	Richard Hacker
	Bill Hagle
	Joan Lovitt
	Tam Moore
	C. Anders Nilsson
	Roy Scarbrough
	Sky
	Joan Wood
Area Analyst	Tonya Nygren-Powell
Art Department Manager	Scott McKay
Staff Artist	Don Bissell
Contributing Artists	John C. Benson Jr.
	Sarah Cribb
Cover Designer	Laura Kay
Cover Photograph	Tourist Div. GA. Dept. Industry & Trade
Print Coordinator	Debbie Wager

Copyright © 1988 by Gable & Gray, The Book Publishers.
All rights reserved. No part of this book may be reproduced in any form or by an electronic means, including information storage and retrieval systems, without permission in writing from the publisher, except by a reviewer who may quote brief passages in a review.

Library of Congress Catalog Card Number: 88-81777
ISBN: 0-944729-19-3   First Edition: 1988

FOREWORD

Welcome to *Best Choices In Atlanta*. I invite you to join me in the adventure of discovering the best attractions, parks, museums, events, businesses and geographical regions this magnificent area has to offer. The stories, maps and business reviews within this complete guide have been designed for several reasons: for shopping and dining tips, an itinerary planner, and an informational guide to let you know more of the area you're visiting.

My life has been filled with challenging excursions in almost every state within our richly diverse nation and beyond. Each area offers something special that sets it apart from the others. For example, the Oregon Coast is one of the most beautiful coastlines I have ever seen, Colorado offers the splendor of the Rocky Mountains, while Florida has its warm waters and year round vacation land. Seattle's Space Needle caps the city's picturesque skyline, and the famous hydroplane races provide entertainment for all. My adventures have taken me on a cruise past the White Cliffs of Dover, I have walked through the markets of Bangkok, marveled at the grand castles of Germany, and ridden a burro along the country roads of Mexico. My feet love to travel, my eyes love to see the world and my mind loves to remember all of those places as I pass my discoveries on to others.

But enough about me! You purchased this guide to explore the *Best Choices In Altlanta*. So without further ado, here's how to use this book:

In focusing on Atlanta, I have divided the book into three major sections, or chapters: Atlanta and its vicinity; Day Trips (short, worthwhile excursions to outlying areas); and, finally, cities of interest outside of Atlanta. Each section begins with an introduction to the region, highlighting helpful facts, major highways, population, attractions, local events and history, which will provide you with enlightened opportunities and ideas for exploration. Within the text certain especially interesting locations and attractions have been singled out with feature articles. Cities and towns are listed alphabetically by region in the Table of Contents. Then, within the text, each business is listed alphabetically within its corresponding category. The guide's description of the businesses and services will give you an idea of the "Best Choices" you may look forward to as you encounter them on your travels. To find specific businesses, as well as area features, turn to the index in the back of the book.

We certainly have not found every "Best Choice" in Atlanta, and would love to hear about it when you encounter a "Best Choice" that merits mention and is not included in this book. If your contribution is interviewed and selected for the next edition, Gable & Gray will happily ship you any one "Best Choice book" you desire as a "Thank you." Simply select the book from the list of already published editions at the front of this guide and mention your preference in your letter.

The editors and writers who have contributed their creative vitality to the compilation of this guide trust you will find it a valuable addition to your travels.

Join me now as we visit the *Best Choices In Atlanta.*

MYLES MONTGOMERY

TABLE OF CONTENTS

CHAPTER 1: Atlanta and Vicinity 1
    Georgia on My Mind 2
    Acworth/Lake Allatoona 7
    Alpharetta 7
    Six Flags Over Georgia 12
    Atlanta 16
    Atlanta During the Civil War 159
    Sweet Auburn 164
    Avondale Estates 169
    Buford 171
    Chamblee 172
    College Park 175
    Hartsfield Atlanta International Airport 177
    Conyers 182
    Decatur 184
    Duluth 190
    Dunwoody 193
    East Point 196
    Forest Park 197
    Jonesboro 199
    The Chattahoochee Recreation Area 208
    Kennesaw 211
    The Battle of Kennesaw Mountain 222
    Lawrenceville 227
    Lilburn 232
    Marietta 233
    Morrow 245
    Norcross 246
    Roswell 253
    Sandy Springs 264
    Smyrna 267
    Stone Mountain 269

CHAPTER 2: Day Trips from Atlanta 276
    Andersonville National Historic Site 276
    Athens and Augusta 284
    Callaway Gardens-A One of a Kind Resort 293
    Chickamauga and Chattanooga National
        Military Park 296
    Cleveland: Home of Babyland Hospital 305
    Columbus 306
    Dahlonega: A Little City Big on Fun 310
    Helen: Georgia's Bavarian Mountain Town 314
    Macon 316
    The State Park Loop 321
    Unicoi State Park/Chattahoochee National Forest 333

CHAPTER 3: Areas of Interest Outside Atlanta 336
    Cartersville 337
    Fayetteville 339
    LaGrange 343
    Behold the "Lowly" Peanut 353
    Newnan 356
    Pine Mountain 361
    Warm Springs 369
    So You'd Like to be a Tourist? 374

INDEX 381

CHAPTER ONE: ATLANTA AND VICINITY

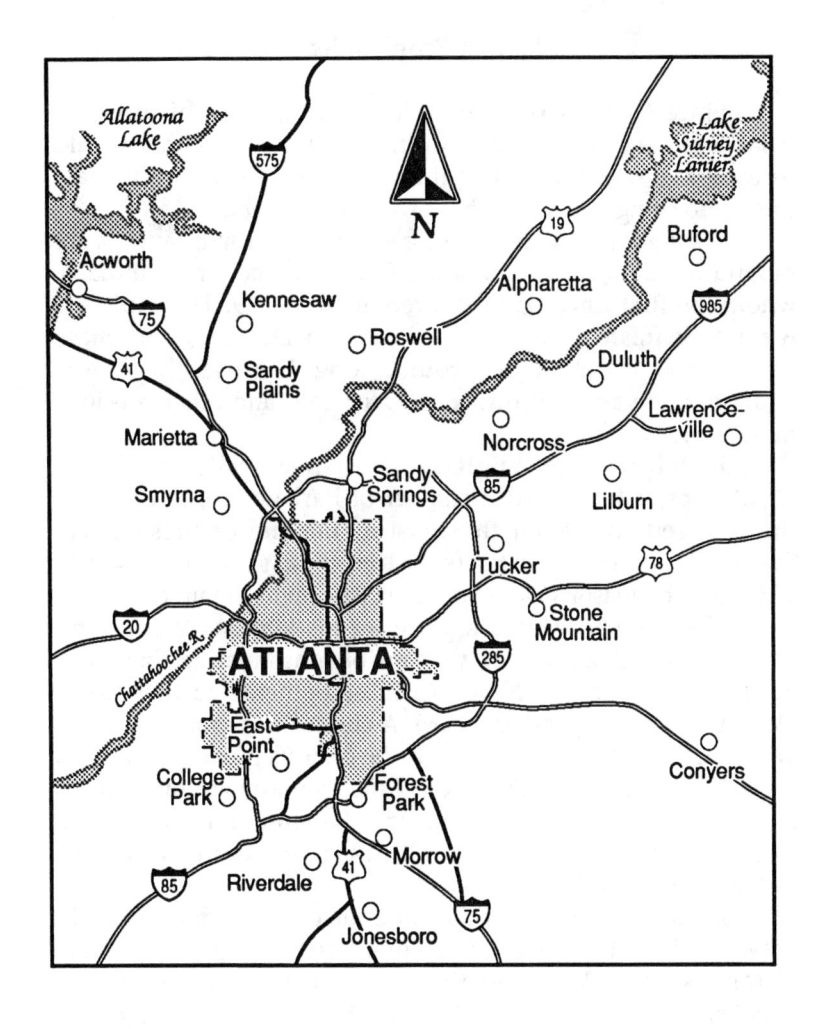

Atlanta and Vicinity

GEORGIA ON MY MIND

By

Merritt Scott Miller

Since Georgia is so abundantly steeped in history and Atlanta is the center of much of it, no writings on either would be complete without a brief glimpse at how this beautiful state came into being and how it has grown since its birth.

It's believed that Georgia's original inhabitants were mound builders, ancestors of the Cherokee and Creek Indians, whom the first European explorers met in 1539. The explorers were a Spanish party under Hernando De Soto, and these hardy men didn't stick around long because they were searching, in vain as it turned out, for gold and other precious metals.

It fell to the English, and specifically to James Oglethorpe, a British MP (member of Parliament), to establish the first settlement, on the coast at the site of present day Savannah, under a charter from King George II. This was in 1733, and the reasons were both altruistic and economic.

His Majesty wanted a place for his kingdom's poor and disenfranchised, as well as a means of consolidating England's growing hold on the New World settlements further north along the New England seaboard. A charter was granted in 1752 and some twenty-five years later, the castoffs of King George II repaid the Crown by joining the American Revolution. Britain, in turn, responded by capturing Savannah in 1778 and maintaining its hold on most all of Georgia until Cornwallis surrendered at Yorktown.

Expansion into Georgia's interior occurred most heavily between 1770-1840, with movement from Virginia and the Carolinas. It took a long time because the Cherokees and Creeks, who had the territory first, expressed a vigorous unwillingness to give it up. Their resistance was fierce and is honored most appropriately by an expression which lingers today and reveals the enduring admiration the descendants of

Atlanta and Vicinity

those early white settlers felt for those they dispossessed. When the Cherokees were relocated far to the west, the route was called the "Trail of Tears."

It was during this same period that cotton became king and slavery became an economic mainstay as northern Georgia grew to be a major supplier of the growing cotton markets in an equally industrializing England. The invention of the cotton gin by Eli Whitney allowed farmers to quickly separate the fiber from the seed and made cotton an economically effective crop. Cotton grew to become a major force in social, economic, political and industrial life. Both the maintenance of slavery and the plantation system were, in large part, due to the dependence of the Southern states on cotton for their livelihood. Thus it could be said that this useful plant also helped bring about the Civil War.

The southern part of the state remained largely wilderness until after the War Between the States. Few places below the Mason-Dixon line evoke as many memories of the Civil War as Georgia, and for many, it is best summed up in a two word term that yet sounds like a single epithet—"damned Yankees." Much of this came about in 1864 when, after years of bloodshed which eventually cost both sides more than a half million dead, President Abraham Lincoln ordered General William Tecumseh Sherman to march across Georgia and destroy the ability of this major source of Confederate resistance to continue to occupy the state.

Historians from both sides of the Mason-Dixon have debated for years about the necessity of Sherman's measures, but the fact remains that he and his 60,000 troops burned

Atlanta and Vicinity

Atlanta in November and reached Savannah a month later. By the end of 1864, valiant Georgia was brought to her knees.

Ironically enough, the Civil War and the notorious Reconstruction which followed did not eradicate the state's fundamental economic system or way of life for nearly ninety years after. Emancipated Blacks joined impoverished whites in a tenant farming system which bore a striking resemblance to the antebellum era. Instead, what did impact Georgia was a small insect with more devastating power than all the Union armies ever assembled under Abe Lincoln's command.

In song and in story, you'll still hear this little critter memorialized with a bitter irony so typical of the 1920s. The boll weevil virtually destroyed Georgia's cotton crop and forced thousands of families off the land and either to the state's major metropolitan areas or to the big cities of the north. In 1900, for example, Blacks comprised forty-seven percent of the state's population. By 1970, that figure was reduced to twenty-six percent. That those who remained triumphed through the civil rights movement, which affected primarily the urban areas, is evident in Atlanta today. The birthplace of Dr. Martin Luther King, Jr., its mayor is Andrew Young, one of Dr. King's most effective aides and United Nations ambassador under another Georgia boy made good, President Jimmy Carter. Black progress has been complemented by post-war industrialization, primarily in the Atlanta area, and the influx of a great many white professionals from other parts of Dixie and from north of that famous line. Georgia boasts many notable achievements, which have impacted not only the South, but the entire nation. A few of them include:

1733—The first Black Baptist Church was established at Silver Bluff.

1735—The first agricultural experimental farm and station was established in the Savannah area.

—The first silk was sent from Savannah and made into a dress for the Queen.

—Georgia's reputation for religious freedom was dramatically demonstrated when General Oglethorpe donated 600 acres of land to the Moravian Church.

Atlanta and Vicinity

1736—The first Protestant Sunday School in America was founded by John Wesley in Savannah.

1775—The first American warship, a Georgia schooner under dual command of Captain Bowen and Major Joseph Habersham, struck out at Her Majesty's Navy.

1788—The fourth state in the nation and the first in the South, Georgia ratified the United States Constitution.

1793—The cotton gin was invented by Eli Whitney.

1802—The first American woman to publish and edit a newspaper launched *The Washington Gazette*.

1819—The first steamship in the world to cross the Atlantic Ocean, *The Savannah*, sailed from its namesake on May 20, enroute to Liverpool, England.

1820—The first railroad in America, built by Henry McAlpin, went into operation on his plantation.

1821—The first Indian alphabet was created by a Cherokee scholar, Sequoyah. Seven years later, the first Indian newspaper, *The Cherokee Phoenix*, was launched.

1828—The first American gold rush occurred when the mineral was discovered near Dahlonega.

1834—The first ocean going ship made of iron, *The John Randolph*, was built.

1836—The first college in the world to grant degrees to women, Wesleyan, was founded in Macon; Catherine Brewer was the first woman to receive her degree, in 1840. Eleven years later, the first two sororities, Alpha Delta Pi and Phi Mu, were organized.

1842—Ether was first used as a surgical anesthetic by Dr. Crawford W. Long.

—The sewing machine was created by Georgia inventor Dr. Francis Goulding.

1866—Georgia became the first state to grant full property rights to married women.

1877—Georgia became the first state to create its own Department of Agriculture. Three years later, Georgia created the first state railroad commission.

1881—The first certificate granted to a Black nurse was awarded by Atlanta's Spelman College.

1886—Coca Cola was invented and sold.

Atlanta and Vicinity

  1887—The first American deposits of aluminum ore were discovered in Floyd County.
  1912—The Girl Scouts of America were formed by Georgian Juliette Low.
  1922—Georgian Rebecca Felton was elected the first woman United States senator.
  1945—Georgia became the first state to lower the voting age from twenty-one to eighteen.
  1977—Georgia became the ranking location site for film making and third in total film production in the United States.
  —The second busiest airport in the nation, Atlanta's Hartsfield International Airport, served 14,978,872 passengers.
  1979—The first transit rail system of its kind in the world was established in Atlanta.

  Georgia has much of which to be proud, then, and a legacy which dates back to the dawn of the "New World." Its state seal depicts an arch supported by three pillars, atop which is a banner bearing the state's motto, "Wisdom, Justice and Moderation." Over this, and symbolic of the state's colonial roots, is the word "Constitution." The other side portrays a ship being loaded with tobacco and cotton, while in the left foreground is a man plowing and a flock of sheep. The motto on this side is "Agriculture and Commerce. 1776."
  Georgia's state flag has its state seal on the flagstaff third of blue background. The remainder of the background is red and upon it are crossing bands of blue, bordered in white, containing the thirteen white stars of the Confederate States of America. These remind all born under it or who come to live

here that she is both a member of the greater Union and very much the master of her own destiny.

ACWORTH/LAKE ALLATOONA

This community of 4,500 lies ten miles northwest of downtown Atlanta on Interstate 75, about five miles north of Marietta. Situated on an arm of Allatoona Lake, Acworth serves travelers as a 12,000 acre playground surrounded by 25,000 wooded acres.

Like all of Cobb County, which includes the communities of Marietta and Kennesaw, the most appropriate adjectives to describe this community are mellow and relaxed. History and the pastoral beauty of the northern Georgia countryside intertwine romantically, creating a sincere illusion of timelessness as irresistible as it is unforgettable.

ATTRACTION

• **Lake Acworth**, an arm of Allatoona Lake which reaches into Cobb County, features **Acworth Beach**, which is 400 feet of sandy shore complete with a fishing pier, waterslide and picnic pavilions. This, in turn, is but an aspect of an extensive system of parks and other recreational facilities which have for years lured golfers, swimmers, tennis enthusiasts and all those who know what it is to relax and enjoy life under the warm Georgia sun. For more information, contact the Cobb Chamber of Commerce, P.O. Box Cobb, Marietta, GA 30065; (404) 980-2000.

ALPHARETTA

This thriving community of about 12,496 in the Blue Ridge foothills of North Fulton County lies on the other side of the Chattahoochee River, north of Atlanta. It is part of a

Atlanta and Vicinity

demographic region which includes the larger town of Roswell to the immediate west and the smaller community of Mountain Park just north of Roswell.

As with this 136 square mile region at large, history has played a major role in Alpharetta. Originally established as a trading post on a Cherokee Indian Trail leading from the North Georgia mountains to the Chattahoochee River, Alpharetta was initially known as New Prospect Campground. Its name was subsequently changed to Alpharetta, meaning, in Greek, "first town." Incorporated in 1858, it was one of the major cotton producing regions of North Georgia, until Sherman's March through the area in 1864. The region offers rolling hills, deep woods, clear streams and pristine pastures along with antebellum tree lined streets and the modern office complexes of major corporations such as AT&T, Herman Miller and Kimberly Clark.

ATTRACTIONS

- **North Fulton County** is "horse country" and the **Wills Park Equestrian Center** is the best way to arrange tours of the thoroughbred farms. The center itself hosts horse shows almost every weekend from early spring through late fall in its covered arena.
- **The Providence Park Outdoor Recreation Center**, north of Alpharetta, offers backpacking, rock climbing and rappelling and was designed specifically to appeal to all ages.
- **North Fulton County** is a recognized center for antique shops, boutiques and art galleries. This area stretches from the Roswell Historic area up Canton Street, to Crabapple and through downtown Alpharetta.

For more information, contact North Fulton Chamber of Commerce & State Local Welcome Center, 1025 Old Roswell Road, Suite 101, Roswell, GA 30076; (404) 993-8808.

Atlanta and Vicinity

ANTIQUE SHOP

THE RAVEN'S NEST, INC./THE FRIENDLY TOAD
780 Mayfield Road
Alpharetta, GA 30201
Tel. (404) 475-3647
Hrs: Tue. - Sat.   10:00 a.m. - 5:00 p.m.
          Sunday   1:00 p.m. - 5:00 p.m.
Visa, MasterCard, AMEX and Discover are accepted.

The mysterious phenomenon of the friendship which has developed between the haughty raven and the impish toad appears to have something to do with their mutual love of antiques and Folk Art. This symbiotic duo has managed to combine their personalities and interests and have achieved a true creative endeavor. Some suspect it has something to do with the remnants of the cotton gin which has been a part of The Raven's Nest since the 1800s.

For thirteen years, The Raven's Nest has been treating its customers to a wide range of antiques with an emphasis on pre-1840 American and English pieces, high-style country and formal period items. Shopping for such treasures is a joy in the spacious rooms with beautiful displays throughout. It seems as though every antique collector has at least one piece of porcelain or art that would truly be magnificent if only reconditioned. At The Raven's Nest you can have art and porcelain restoration done, as well as repair your favorite lamp. Recently, the quaint, warm and cheerful country cottage located next door, The Friendly Toad, has added its bit of charm to the environment. The Toad displays interesting Folk Art and folklore displays.

For southern hospitality at its best, stop by for a cup of coffee or tea and homemade cookies. You'll be surprised at the congeniality of your two unusual hosts, as well as the

Atlanta and Vicinity

assortment of antiques and art. These two rascals will even provide free delivery and arrange for shipment out of state. It's always a pleasure to see unusual relationships develop over tea and art.

HARDWARE STORE

SMITH ACE HARDWARE, 8560 Holcomb Bridge Road, Alpharetta, GA Tel. (404) 587-1800. They offer the very best in hardware, service and gifts with more than 30,000 items in stock. This includes lawn furniture, plants, picnic supplies and sophisticated gifts.

PHOTOGRAPHY

CLAYTON CAMERACRAFT
28 North Main Street
Alpharetta, GA 30201
Tel. (404) 475-0022
Hrs: Mon. - Fri. 10:00 a.m. - 6:00 p.m.
Visa and MasterCard are accepted.

"You name it, we frame it," is the slogan of Clayton Cameracraft. Through the lens of Forrest Clayton's camera you will see beautiful pictures of people, animals and the world itself.
Clayton's specializes in weddings and commercial photographs anywhere in the world. Mr. Clayton has taken pictures in Europe and throughout the United States. Once he has captured the perfect picture on film he then develops and prints the images. To complete the effect he frames the picture in wood, brass and other ornamental material. If you care to have your portrait taken in the Cameracraft studios, a lovely

dressing room is provided for you; and, you have a choice of backdrops in various moods and colors.

Clayton Cameracraft has a reputation for quality work and courteous service. No job is too big, too small or too difficult for Clayton Cameracraft.

Atlanta and Vicinity

SIX FLAGS OVER GEORGIA

by

Merritt Scott Miller

If you thrill to the heart stopping action of a roller coaster, laugh until you ache at the antics of Bugs Bunny, Daffy Duck, Elmer Fudd, Porky Pig and the rest of the Looney Tunes crowd, or if you just plain like to have fun and don't mind having a tremendous amount of it, Six Flags Over Georgia is the place for you.

This is Dixie's premier amusement park and it's spread over 331 acres. It includes over 100 separate facets of entertainment and it all adds up to one gem of a park. Its one price admission includes all rides, shows and attractions. Here, roller coasters are king.

Because of Georgia's mild weather, this park operates an average of 165 days annually and since it opened in 1967,

Atlanta and Vicinity

48,000,000 people have passed through its gates, for an average of 2,289,333 folks a year.

What draws them? Hang on, and heeere we go: It's called Z Force and it is the only coaster in the world which duplicates the dive bombing sensation fighter pilots know so well. Built of nearly 130 tons of steel supported by five main columns, it covers half a football field, reaches close to 75 feet at its highest point and runs a total of 1,900 feet up and through six curving dives. Computer controlled, it was built by Intamin AG of Switzerland, the company which also created Free Fall and Thunder River. That's for starters.

The Mind Bender is a triple loop roller coaster which catapults passengers at speeds up to fifty miles per hour. The Great American Scream Machine rises 105 feet at its highest peak and extends over 3,800 feet, for a classic wooden roller coaster ride which reaches fifty-seven miles per hour at its hair raising fastest.

For a wet and wild trip in a twenty passenger boat down a roaring fifty foot waterfall, it's Splashwater Falls, and if that doesn't satisfy your need for thrills, try Thunder River and ride a twelve passenger raft through roaring rapids and deep rock canyons. If you've ever wanted to leap off a ten story building but also wanted to survive to tell your friends about it, take the Free Fall. And for the nostalgia air buffs among you, thrill to the days of flying in an open cockpit biplane with Air Racer. It looks like a Ferris wheel but one somebody tilted on its side. Twenty-one gondola cars on the fifty-one foot Wheelie spin like a centrifuge, then rise to the full vertical. And for those who recall those eternal bumper cars so popular at county fairs throughout Dixie and the North, it's Dodge City Bumper Cars, which are reputed to be the best of their kind in the country. And there are fifty of them, folks.

Six Flags is a midway to end all midways. It is divided into eight areas:

• **The British Area** contains Hanson cars, for the touring grace of early roadsters, and the Maypole circular swing called the Highland Swing.

Atlanta and Vicinity

- **The Confederate Area** is famous for the Great Six Flags Air Racer, and it is here that visitors can catch the Six Flags Railroad for a tour of the entire park. Those who may have visited the famous Dahlonega gold mining village will find a runaway mine train for a hang on ride.
- **The Looney Tunes Area** includes the Yosemite Sam Playfort and Buccaneer Boats.
- **The Lick Skillet Area** is the home of the Wheelie, Thunder River, Splashwater Falls and the Lick Skillet Skybuckets.
- **The Cotton States Area** is where you'll find the famous Z Force, the Great American Scream Machine, the Dodge City Bumper Cars and more. It is here, as well, that a portion of the park's incredible arcade is located.
- **The French Area** is another boarding place for the Six Flags Railroad.
- **The Modern Area** has The Great Gasp, a twenty story parachute drop; the Free Fall, the Mind Bender, and a giant suspended swinging pirate ship called, appropriately enough, The Flying Dutchman.
- **The Georgia Area** is host to a variety of water rides, including the Log Flumes.

Of course, that's not all. For those who enjoy the more sedate side of thrill seeking, Six Flags has some of the best entertainment in the South as well.

Music and magic, starring the Looney Tunes characters, is available in the Looney Tunes Theatre. In Looney Tunes Land, you'll find that swampy sleeper, The Bullfrog Revue. The Southern Star Amphitheatre hosts some of the biggest names in the music industry. And what would any Atlanta area amusement park be without Coca Cola's prestige? Naturally enough, then, Graffiti's is considered one of the hottest spots for those who love to dance to the latest sounds.

All this excitement is bound to work up quite an appetite and Six Flags hasn't neglected its cuisine, either. Do you like pizza? You'll find it in rapture at Tondee's Tavern, in the British area. How about tacos, or barbecued pork sandwiches, or down home country cookin'? Yep, you guessed it. All on the

Atlanta and Vicinity

grill in the Lick Skillet area. And for those who long for the aura of the antebellum (and what true son or daughter of Dixie doesn't?) stroll to the Confederate area and try the Plantation House.

Although Six Flags actually came into being as recently as 1967, its carousel, hand carved for the opening of Riverview Park by the Philadelphia (PA) Toboggan Company, dates back to 1908 and while at Riverview was ridden by such diverse American figures as Al Capone, William Randolph Hearst and President Warren G. Harding.

Other facts you might enjoy about Six Flags:

- It is the second largest producer of ice in Georgia.
- Over forty former Six Flags performers are presently on Broadway or in television.
- The park is the largest single location employer of youth in Georgia.
- The Crystal Pistol is a replica of the Anthenaeum, that famous pre-Civil War theater in Atlanta.
- During an average season of 165 operating days, guests consume more than ninety-six tons of hamburger meat; thirty-eight tons of hot dogs; seventy-one tons of chicken; five million drinks; 432,000 fruit juice sippers; eighty-one tons of nachos; forty-nine tons of cheese; thirty tons of cotton candy; twenty-two tons of chili; 235,000 pizzas and 189,000 giant pretzels.

Bon appetit!

Six Flags Over Georgia is located about twelve miles west of Atlanta on Interstate 20 West and Six Flags Road. For more information, contact Six Flags Over Georgia, P.O. Box 43187, Atlanta, GA 30378; (404) 948-9290.

Atlanta and Vicinity

ATLANTA

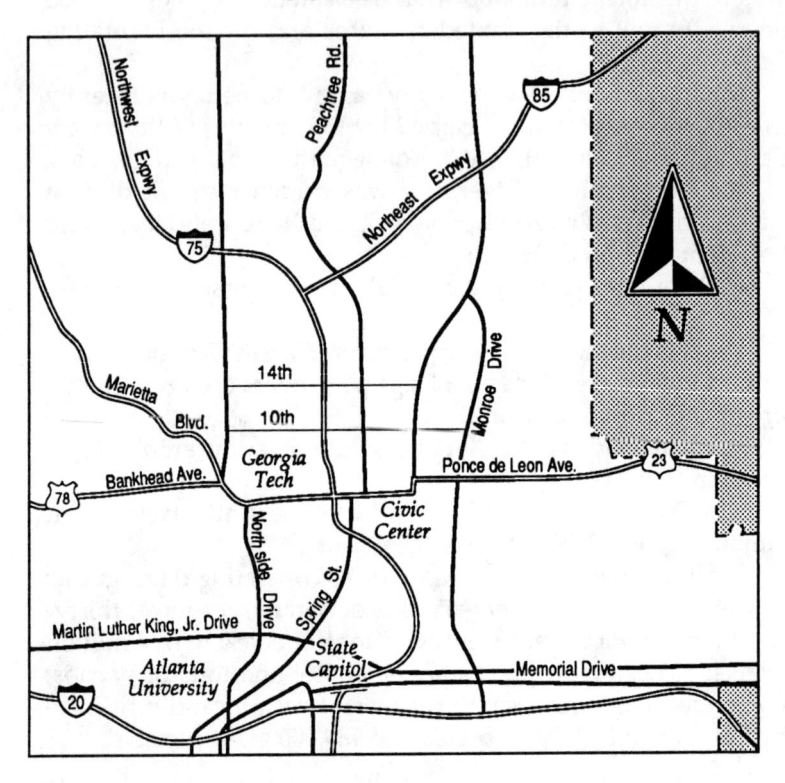

Atlanta is a thriving community of approximately 426,100 within the 132 square miles defined by its city limits and a total of 2,029,600 in its 4,374 square mile greater metropolitan area. Situated on the Piedmont Plateau at about 1,050-feet elevation, it is blessed with a generally mild climate. Temperatures average forty-five degrees Fahrenheit in January and seventy-nine degrees Fahrenheit in July; rainfall totals about forty-seven inches per year. Its population is approximately fifty percent black, and includes citizens of British, German and Polish ancestry.

Truly a city of the Old South and the New, Atlanta has many preserved mansions and is redolent with the aroma of dogwood blossoms. A mighty industrial and commercial center, it is home for over 2,000 plants which manufacture 4,000 different items. These include aircraft, automobiles, furniture, cloth, chemicals, grocery items, wood pulp products, iron and steel. Renowned as the birthplace and national headquarters of Coca Cola, it is also home for more than 400 Fortune 500 companies.

Atlanta's growth potential was demonstrated rather dramatically in two surveys conducted by the Louis Harris organization in 1986-87. The city was ranked first over twenty-nine others for its business climate. Another study done during the same period by the Massachusetts Institute of Technology found Atlanta the second fastest growing office market in the nation. In terms of tourism, the downtown area contains more than 12,000 rooms, with additions planned each year.

An idea of the flavor of the city can be gleaned from a study released in 1986 by *The Atlanta Journal and Constitution*. Among those employing more than 8,000 people are Atlanta City Schools, City of Atlanta, Delta Air Lines, Inc., General Motors, Lockheed-Georgia and the U.S. Department of Defense. Eastern Airlines, Emory University, Georgia Power Company, IBM, Norfolk Southern, Sears, and the Postal Service employ 5,000-7,999. *The Atlanta Journal and Constitution*, Coca-Cola, First National Bank of Atlanta, Food Giant Stores, Ford Motor Company, Georgia Institute of Technology, Grady Memorial Hospital, Macy's, MARTA, Scientific-Atlanta, Waffle House, Inc., and Winn-Dixie Stores are among those with 2,500-4,999 workers. The city has nine television stations, thirty-three radio stations, seven daily newspapers, a national league baseball team, a national football league team, a national basketball team and a major sports stadium. Its airport is the second busiest in the world and its Metropolitan Atlanta Rapid Transit Authority (MARTA) is rated one of the best in the country. AMTRAK has a morning train to New Orleans and an evening train each to Washington, D.C. and New York City. Along with Greyhound and Trailways bus services, ten limousine services, two handicapped transportation services and a host of taxi companies service the area. The importance of education to Atlanta is evidenced in its twenty-nine colleges

Atlanta and Vicinity

and universities, which include Georgia Tech, Oglethorpe University, Clark Atlanta University, Spelman, Morehouse, Morris Brown and the Interdenominational Theological Center.

Atlanta is administered by a mayor and eighteen council members, and its greater metropolitan area covers ten counties, each with its own distinct identity and several of whose cities predate Atlanta herself. Her suburbs include East Point, College Park, Decatur, Forest Park, Marietta, Roswell and Smyrna, and the city proper is divided into six districts: downtown; midtown; Little Five Points and Inman Park; Buckhead; Southside and the Airport; and Virginia and Highlands. Atlanta was not designed as a grid, which can be trying for newcomers but adds to the special quality of the city.

The downtown area spreads out from Woodruff Park and includes many of the major convention centers, hotels, and government buildings. The nineteenth and twentieth centuries blend here to include such outstanding attractions as the state capitol, the *Cable Network News* (CNN) center, the Georgia-Pacific Center portion of the High Museum of Art, the Atlanta Historic Society and the Martin Luther King, Jr. Historic District in the old black commercial area of "Sweet" Auburn Avenue. It is here that many of the city's former warehouses are being transformed into charming rentals, shops, and pubs.

The midtown district is roughly defined by Ponce de Leon Avenue and Pershing Point, and it is here that turn of the century Victorian buildings stand beside the skyscrapers of IBM and Southern Bell. Midtown is home to the world's largest drive-in, the Varsity, along with the Fox Theatre, the Woodruff Arts Center and that section of Peachtree Street which, in addition to almost predating the town, has become famous as the South's "Broadway" for all its theatrical and other cultural offerings. Joggers frequent the area because of Piedmont Park. The park hosts the Dogwood Festival in the spring and the Atlanta Arts Festival in autumn.

Inman Park, Atlanta's first suburb, was planned in the 1890s by business promoter Joel Hurt, and here you'll find Callanwolde, the mansion of the Candler family of Coca Cola fame, and the Jimmy Carter Presidential Center. The neighborhood literally radiates antebellum charm and a sense

Atlanta and Vicinity

of timelessness reminiscent of Margaret Mitchell's *Gone With the Wind*. Situated on the DeKalb-Fulton line and bordered by Austin, Euclid, McLendon, Moreland and Seminole avenues, Little Five Points takes its name from the intersection of Peachtree, Marietta, Decatur, Edgewood and Whitehall streets. Once best known for its 1960s counterculture ambiance, with the maturation of the Baby Boomers who gave Atlanta a reputation contrasting with its sixty-six year history, the city has become a delightful and interesting blend of boutiques, "Off Broadway" style theaters, dance studios, art galleries and other displays of Atlanta's fascinating and occasionally eccentric creative sector. Buckhead is where the creme de la creme of Atlanta society live. Imposing mansions and modern homes are the order here. The Atlanta Historical Society offers a mansion tour through Buckhead, and includes the Swan House and the Tullie Smith House. Atlanta's nightlife flourishes in the district. The Buckhead's restaurants, clubs and shopping are world famous. Lenox Square, the Southeast's largest shopping center, and the chic Phipps Plaza are typical. Lenox Square is well worth the trip. Considered by many to be the anchor of Buckhead, it is the home of a twenty-story office complex, a four-hundred room luxury hotel, Macy's, Neiman-Marcus, an impressive 1.4 million square feet of shopping malls, and more than 200 other shops, restaurants, night clubs and theaters, as well as a MARTA station and 7,000 parking spaces.

The Southside is perhaps best known as the home of the Hartsfield International Airport, the Georgia International Convention and Trade Center, and the community of Jonesboro, of *Gone With the Wind* fame. Forest Park hosts one of the world's largest farmer's market; and much of Atlanta's rail history is still evident in East Point, College Park and Hapeville, which are also noted for their antique shops and Southern cooking.

The neighborhood around the intersection of Virginia and North Highland avenues is where you'll find Atlanta's avant garde. The bookstores, art galleries, pottery studies and art deco antiques have made the area one of the city's hottest new attractions. This is also a restaurant connoisseur's paradise, whether one's palate leans toward the offerings of Taco Mac's

Atlanta and Vicinity

and its 175 varieties of beer, or toward the more sedate cuisine of George's Deli and Capo's Cafe. Nightlife abounds here, also. For years, Atlantans have enjoyed the friendly rivalry between this neighborhood and Buckhead for the best in contemporary jazz, vocal artists, and the latest trends in the music business.

HISTORY OF ATLANTA

A look at the history of Atlanta is a look at Atlanta itself. A city mindful of its heritage and building for the future, Atlanta is a unique juxtaposition of the modern and the long ago. Its origins begin long before the advent of the Spanish, led by Ponce de Leon in search of the legendary Fountain of Youth, and certainly pre-date the European colonists who ultimately settled all of what is now the state of Georgia. As nearly as anthropologists and archaeologists have been able to determine, Atlanta's Piedmont area, through which flows the hauntingly beautiful Chattahoochee River, was the site of an ancient Creek Indian village known as Standing Peachtree. According to legend, the village was named for a magnificent tree which stood at the spot where Peachtree Creek joined the Chattahoochee. The name also gave Atlanta its unofficial motto, "Meet me on Peachtree."

Colonial settlement began in the early 1700s and was sporadic but consistent well through the Revolutionary War. The consolidation of Georgia's independence from England added impetus to a restless search for timber, furs, farmland and other resources necessary to build a growing America. By the early nineteenth century, there were enough pioneers in the area to warrant the establishment, in 1814, of a U.S. military outpost at Standing Peachtree. Named Fort Gilmer, the post kept war between settlers and Native Americans at bay, and a trading post flourished. Immigration to what is now metropolitan Atlanta is historically noted as beginning in 1821. In 1833, "downtown Atlanta" was settled by Hardy Ivy, the original Atlantan.

But it was the advent of the railroads which determined the nature of Atlanta. In 1837, a New Hampshire engineer

Atlanta and Vicinity

drove a stake into the spot marking the southern end of the Western and Atlantic Railroad, and the railhead was officially designated Terminus. Passenger train service from the village started on Christmas Eve of 1842 with a run to Marietta and back. The next year, Terminus was incorporated and its name changed to Marthasville, in honor of the daughter of former Georgia governor Wilson Lumpkin.

The railroad continued to dominate the town. The chief engineer for the Western and Atlantic reported to his superiors that the site "would be a good location for one tavern, a blacksmith shop, a grocery store and nothing else." Because the name Marthasville was too long to conveniently write on freight orders, a railroad executive changed it in 1845 to Atlanta. Historians believe it represented the feminine form of Atlantic. Whether that is true or not, it became popular to refer to the city in the feminine gender.

Religious freedom and diversity, a major theme in the founding of the original thirteen colonies, played a key role in the growth of Atlanta, along with the Revolutionary War and both the national and Georgia state constitutions. Catholic and Episcopal parishes were formed in 1846, followed in 1848 by Baptist, Methodist and Presbyterian.

An indication of how rapidly the city was growing was evident in 1846. The Atlanta Hotel and Washington Hall became the city's first hostelries. A third railroad, the Macon and Western (now Central of Georgia), completed its line from Macon. Near the middle of the century, in 1847, approximately 2,000 people lived in the city and its first bank was established. A year later, the newly chartered City of Atlanta elected its first city council and Moses W. Formwalt became its first mayor. In 1848, telegraph service began at the Macon and Western depot, and Atlanta's first successful newspaper, *The Intelligencer*, was founded. A year later, the city purchased the original acreage of Oakland Cemetery and the first fire company was formed. These volunteers now looked after the welfare of a community of 2,569.

Politics were much in evidence in 1851 as the "Moral Party" trounced the "Free and Rowdy Party" in what one historian termed "a spirited city election." A year later, a

Atlanta and Vicinity

fourth railroad, the Atlanta and West Point, completed its Atlanta terminus. In 1853, Edward A. Vincent drew up the first city map and the city limits described a circumference one mile from the center of town.

The suburbs were growing during that period as well. In 1854, Fulton County was organized from portions of DeKalb County. Fulton County's combination city hall and county courthouse was built on the spot where the state capitol now stands, and Atlanta Medical College was chartered.

By late 1855, Atlanta showed every indication of shedding much of its Piedmont frontier heritage. On Christmas Day, her streets became gas lit, and the next year The Atlanta Gas Light Company became the city's first official corporation. Atlanta's importance as a rail center continued to dominate economics and the news. In 1857, she was designated the "Gate City" as a tribute to the role transportation was playing in her development.

On January 19, 1861, Georgia seceded from the Union and the following four years were tragic ones for Atlanta, as they were for the South and for the entire nation. In 1862, the city became a major Confederate military post, supply base, and hospital and relief center. (At one time, 60,000 wounded Confederate troops inhabited the city.) While this brought increased prosperity to the city's commercial and agricultural sectors, it also precipitated the destruction of the city, the first indication of this doom manifesting itself in 1863 when, under the supervision of Lemuel P. Grant, the city's defense lines were constructed.

In July of 1864, Sherman's Union forces crossed the Chattahoochee. Throughout August, Atlanta was pounded by an artillery bombardment the likes of which had never before been seen in the entire world. During this period, Atlantans took refuge in cellars, in backyard trenches known as "gopher holes," and in dugouts built near a water supply and equipped with non-perishable food stuffs. Those who could fled south on foot, horseback, in wagons, and in any other way possible. The exodus ceased when Sherman's army seized the railroad at Jonesboro on September 1. That same night, Confederate

Atlanta and Vicinity

General Hood evacuated the Atlanta garrison and the mayor surrendered the city the next day.

Sherman promised protection of life and property, then changed his mind and ordered the final evacuation of Atlanta. In a controversial decision generally conceded as necessary to shorten the war, he ordered the dismantlement and burning of any resources which could possibly be used by the Confederacy. His battle weary veterans, many historians claim, vented their rage against the Confederacy by torching anything that would burn, and before Sherman's command regained control the city was razed. Between the bombardment and the torching, all but 400 of Atlanta's 4,500 houses and commercial buildings were destroyed. As Medora Field Perkerson notes in *White Columns in Georgia*:

"*It was an extremely cold winter. While the bodies of soldiers had been buried in shallow graves—later to be reinterred in cemeteries—the frozen carcasses of horses, mules and dogs killed in combat littered the late battlefields around the city.*

The city itself was a rubble heap. Wells and cisterns covered over with debris were among the many hazards encountered by those who sought to rebuild their homes. More than one citizen had to be rescued from these deathtraps when the earth apparently gave way beneath him."

Atlanta and Vicinity

In 1865, by order of the federal government that now presided again over North and South, Atlanta became a U.S. military post. The gradual return of its citizens continued and that year witnessed the beginning of a miracle, the rebirth of a city which refused to die. Buildings and businesses sprang up, and new foundations for black society developed. James Tate and Grandison B. Daniels organized the first school for blacks, which eventually became Atlanta University. A grocery store on Walton Street in the central business district became the first black-owned business in the city. In 1867, Atlanta University was chartered as a center of higher education for black students. Within a year, Atlanta had replaced Milledgeville as the state capital, and by 1869 the city, whose population a decade before numbered 9,554, had grown to 21,789. The first railed streetcars, drawn by horses and mules, soon began operations and in 1872, radical reconstruction formally came to an end.

Rebuilding, however, did not. By 1873, a public school system was in full operation and the city's first uniformed police force was organized. The Church of Immaculate Conception completed its new building and it stands today as Atlanta's oldest existing church structure.

Cotton, an antebellum mainstay, re-emerged as a dominant economic factor after reconstruction. Morehouse College moved to Atlanta from Augusta, and Morris Brown College was founded in the basement of Big Bethel Church, becoming the first black college in Georgia. Spelman Seminary was also established. By now the population stood at 37,409, and in 1882, The Atlanta Journal was founded.

1884 saw the introduction of Coca Cola, still headquartered in Atlanta. In 1886, Ebenezer Baptist Church was established, the church where, seventy-four years later, the Reverend Dr. Martin Luther King, Jr. would preach his first sermon.

As the calendar turned the first page of the new century, 89,872 citizens resided in Atlanta. Auburn Street, the black commercial district, by then boasted ten businesses and two professionals. A year later, many Atlantans stood amazed at the sight of the first locally owned automobile, a Locomobile

Atlanta and Vicinity

steamer. In 1902, the Carnegie Library was dedicated and the federal penitentiary opened.

By 1910, high culture again came to Atlanta in the form of what immediately became annual visits of the Metropolitan Opera Company. Population had rocketed to more than 150,000. The venerable old black-owned Silver Moon Barber Shop was soon giving haircuts and shoeshines on Auburn Street.

In 1917, along with the entry of the United States into the First World War, a second fire came to Atlanta, this one leaving nearly 10,000 people homeless. But the city continued to grow and rebuild, and the same year the NAACP established its Atlanta branch. By the end of the war, Atlanta laid claim to 200,000 residents.

1936 shot Atlanta into the hearts and minds of Americans nationwide with the publication of Margaret "Peggy" Mitchell's immortal novel *Gone With the Wind*. Three years later, in 1939, David O. Selznick's screen adaptation of *Gone With the Wind* premiered in Atlanta. World War II saw major growth in the city, and as technology industrialized agriculture, those agrarian workers who found employment in defense plants stayed on.

By 1950, the city had grown from a near village of 2,569 a century before to an incredible 331,314. Two years later an eighty-one square mile annexation added 100,000 new citizens to the census, which by the end of the decade registered 487,000. The 1960s brought tremendous industrial expansion to Atlanta. Fifty apartment complexes, hotels and office buildings went up in the downtown area and the completion of the $18,000,000 Atlanta Stadium brought professional teams to the city. It was during this decade that Atlanta earned its reputation as one of the most racially integrated metropolitan areas in the South. From 1962 to 1969, her public schools were integrated and in 1969, voters elected a Jewish mayor and a black vice mayor.

Major downtown construction continued into the 1970s and in 1973, vice mayor Maynard Jackson was elected mayor, the first such black official in a major Southern city. The Omni International complex, home of the 1988 Democratic National Convention, opened, followed in 1976 by the Peachtree Center

Atlanta and Vicinity

Plaza Hotel, one of the tallest buildings in the world, and the same year, the George L. Smith II Georgia World Congress Center.

In 1981, former United Nations ambassador Andrew Young was elected mayor. For more information, contact the Atlanta Historical Society, Inc., 3099 Andrews Drive, N.W., Atlanta, GA 30355; (404) 261-1837.

ATTRACTIONS

• **The Academy Theatre**, home of Georgia's oldest resident performing company, has shows October through June. Each year, the theater presents Charles Dickens' immortal classic A Christmas Carol. The Academy Theatre is the home of Jomandi Productions, Inc., a professional black theater company specializing in original plays by black authors. Broadway and film stars, as well as nationally acclaimed directors are often featured. This is also an excellent theater for new works. **The Carl Ratcliff Dance Theatre** performs here as well. This modern dance troupe is most active in spring and fall. For more information, contact Academy Theatre, 173 14th Street (at Juniper), Atlanta, GA 30309; (404) 892-0880.

• One of the nation's largest non-profit theaters is the **Alliance Theatre**. Established in 1968 in the Woodruff Arts Center, the 800 seat mainstage theater and the 200 seat **Studio Theatre** have been the scene for an impressive range of productions from Shakespeare to current Broadway and off Broadway shows. A recent offering, and representative of the Alliance season was the smash hit End of the World with Symposium to Follow, an entertaining mystery thriller by Arthur Kopit. Sandra Deer's acclaimed hit So Long On Lonely Street also premiered here. For more information, contact The Alliance Theatre, 1280 Peachtree Street, Atlanta, GA 30309; (404) 892- 2414.

• **The Atlanta Botanical Garden**, spread across sixty-three acres in Piedmont Park, includes herb, rose, vegetable and

Atlanta and Vicinity

Japanese gardens, as well as a hardwood forest. Considered one of the best examples of its kind, it offers free tours Sunday at 3:00 p.m. For more information, contact Atlanta Botanical Garden, 1345 Piedmont Ave., N.E., Atlanta, GA 30309; (404) 876-5858.

• For Broadway musicals with major stars the caliber of Shirley MacLaine and Ann-Margret, it's the **Atlanta Civic Center's** 4,000 seat auditorium. This is also the home of the famed **Atlanta Ballet**, an established professional company whose season runs from October through May and features classical and new works. Robert Barnett is the artistic director. The Atlanta Civic Center also receives an annual visit from the New York Metropolitan Opera. For more information, contact The Atlanta Civic Center, 395 Piedmont Avenue, Atlanta, GA 30308; (404) 523-6275.

• Those who enjoy chamber music will be thoroughly delighted with the **Atlanta Chamber Players**. This versatile group performs music from all eras, including at least one new work per season. That season runs from September through May. For more information, contact Atlanta Chamber Players, 1132 West Peachtree Street, N.W., Atlanta, GA 30309; (404) 872-3360.

• **The Atlanta College of Art** offers a one hour tour of the facilities and an opportunity to glimpse some of tomorrow's talent on the rise. For more information, contact Diane Meyers, Atlanta College of Art, 1280 Peachtree Street, Atlanta, GA 30309; (404) 898-1164.

• **The Atlanta-Fulton Public Library** houses one of the nation's largest collections of *Gone With the Wind* memorabilia, and other special exhibits and archives, including an impressive mass of material by and about William Shakespeare. A gourmet cafeteria with indoor and outdoor seating makes this one a cultural experience with pronounced culinary overtones. For more information, contact the Atlanta-Fulton Library, One Margaret Mitchell Square, Atlanta, GA. 30303; (404) 688-4636.

• Atlanta's oldest corporation, **Atlanta Gas Light**, has an interesting historical collection tracing the city from the antebellum days to the present. For more information, contact

Atlanta and Vicinity

Atlanta Gas Light, 235 Peachtree Street, N.E., Suite 500, Atlanta, GA. 30303; (404) 572-0850.

• **The Atlanta Historical Society** maintains quite an impressive collection of antebellum exhibits, displays and artifacts on its twenty-seven acres. These include two restored homes from the period. **McElreath Hall**, the society's actual headquarters, houses both permanent and rotating collections, including "Atlanta and the War," "Atlanta Resurgens," and others. In conjunction with the research library, these displays and exhibits offer as dramatic a recreation of that tragic war as one can find outside Atlanta's famed Cyclorama.

• **The Tullie Smith House**, an 1840s plain plantation house, was built in DeKalb County around 1835. This two story structure, with its detached kitchen, represents the practical lifestyle of the early Piedmont Georgia pioneers. Vegetable and herb gardens, a yard with flowers, displays of period plantings, an orchard, field crops, barn, corncrib, smokehouse and slave cabin complete this faithfully re-created plantation. Demonstrations include spinning, quilting, open hearth cooking and blacksmithing. Tours are offered.

• **The Swan House**, built in 1928, is a rich example of Italian Renaissance (Palladian) architecture, and gives visitors a glimpse of the life of a wealthy Atlanta family during the 1930s The swan motif is used consistently throughout, both in architectural details and period furnishings. Formal gardens, terraced lawns, and massive stairs with water cascades complete the grounds.

• **The Victorian Playhouse**, next to the boxwood gardens of the Swan House, should delight the children. It's a faithful re-creation from the turn of the century, replete with furniture, dolls, toys and games.

For more information, contact the Atlanta Historical Society, 3101 Andrews Drive, N.W., Atlanta, GA 30305; (404) 261-1837.

• **The Atlanta International Raceway**, a 1.5 mile paved oval track, is one of the best places north of Dayton to catch major motor sports. The facility has two Grand National Race events annually. It is NASCAR and FIA sanctioned, and features Indy car races and motocross. It also hosts the Atlanta

Atlanta and Vicinity

Journal 500 and Coca-Cola 500, as well as NTPA tractor-pulls, four-wheel-drive racing and Bobtail 200 truck races. It is located twenty-five miles south of Atlanta at Interstate 75 South and Hampton. For more information, contact Atlanta International Raceway, Hampton, GA 30228; (404) 946-4211.

• For sports action at its finest, it's **Atlanta-Fulton County Stadium**, home of the **Atlanta Braves** baseball team and the **Atlanta Falcons** football team. It is also the site for a host of meetings and concerts. There are 6,500 parking spaces and MARTA operates a shuttle bus from downtown. For more information, contact the Atlanta-Fulton County Stadium, 521 Capitol Avenue, S.W., Atlanta, GA 30312; (404) 522-1967. For more information on the Braves, call (404) 577-9100; on the Falcons, (404) 588-1111.

• **The Atlanta Jazz Theatre** offers contemporary jazz dance and performs from September through May. For more information, contact Atlanta Jazz Theater, 5544 Chamblee-Dunwoody Road, Atlanta, GA. 30338 (404) 393-9519.

• The lobby of the *Atlanta Journal and Constitution* **Building** on 72 Marietta Street houses historic front pages, a linotype machine and displays featuring Ralph McGill, Margaret Mitchell and others who worked for the paper. For more information, call (404) 526-5286.

• **Atlanta Newspapers** offers a one hour tour of editorial and production facilities. For a fascinating behind the scenes glimpse at big city news production and distribution, contact Denise Grant, Atlanta Newspapers, 72 Marietta Street, Atlanta, GA 30303; (404) 526-5691.

• One of the best tributes to black corporate progress is on exhibit in the atrium of the **Atlanta Life Insurance Company**, one of the largest black owned insurance companies in the nation. Located now on Herndon Plaza, 100 Auburn Avenue, it was founded in 1905 by Alonzo F. Herndon, a former slave, and has a collection of family memorabilia and a rotating exhibit of the corporation collection. For an appointment, call (404) 659-2100.

• **The Atlanta Museum**, constructed in 1938, has more than 2,500 local and international historical items. For more

Atlanta and Vicinity

information, write Atlanta Museum, 537 Peachtree Street, N.E., Atlanta, GA. 30303; or call (404) 872-8233.

• One of Georgia's more recent "favorite sons" is honored by the **Carter Presidential Center**, at One Copenhill. Dioramas include the "Oval Office," "Town Meeting" and display of gifts given to the former Annapolis Naval Academy graduate, peanut farmer, governor and national chief executive. Sited on approximately thirty acres, the Library contains over 27,000,000 photographs and documents chronicling his administration alone. The museum also has a major multimedia exhibit exploring the highlights of the thirty-eight presidents who preceded him. A restaurant and Japanese garden, the **Carter Center of Emory University**, **Global 2000** and the **Carter-Menil Human Rights Foundation** are also located here. For more information, contact the Carter Presidential Center, 1 Copenhill, Atlanta, GA 30307; (404) 331-3942.

• For the young and the young at heart, and particularly those to whom the names "Howdy Doody," "Kukla, Fran and Ollie," "Lambchop," and "the Muppets" have special significance, the **Center for Puppetry Arts** will prove fascinating. Performances for children run from September through May and a summer festival is staged in July and August, featuring both day and evening performances. The museum contains the largest private collection of puppets in America. One exhibit traces the history of puppetry and the art of puppet making, with figures from around the world. For more information, contact the Center for Puppetry Arts, 1404 Spring Street, N.W., Atlanta, GA 30309; (404) 873-3391.

• **The Center Stage Theatre**, located in the heart of the midtown Atlanta theater district, offers not only local, regional and national theatricals, but jazz arts and modern dance showcases as well. For more information, contact Center Stage Theatre, 1374 West Peachtree Street, Atlanta, GA 30309; (404) 874-1511.

• **The Atlanta Preservation Center** in Room 401 of the Flatiron Building on 84 Peachtree Street, N.W. serves as the starting point for walking tours of six of Atlanta's historic districts. These include: the Capitol area, featuring the government buildings; the Fairlie-Popular area, featuring commercial buildings; the Fox Theatre district, featuring urban development; the Inman Park tour, a Victorian residential district; Oakland Cemetery, a Victorian cemetery and park; and West End and the Wren's Nest tour, which includes the Joel Chandler Harris home and surrounding area. For more information, call (404) 522-4345.

• **Black American heritage** is preserved in a permanent collection of exhibits designed to provide a complete walk through the Afro-American experience. The APEX uses state of the art multi-media displays to trace Black roots from early Africa to contemporary America. For more information, contact The APEX, 135 Auburn Boulevard, N.E., Atlanta, GA 30312; (404) 521- APEX.

• *The Cable News Network Center*, headquarters of *CNN* and *Headline News*, offers daily tours of this most impressive national news network. Housed in a dramatic atrium complex adjacent the **Georgia World Congress Center and Omni Coliseum**, it's a definite Atlanta focus of interest. For more information, contact CNN Center, One CNN Center, Marietta Street at Techwood Drive, Atlanta, GA 30335; (404) 681-2161.

• One of the nicest things Coca-Cola Company founder Asa G. Candler ever did for Atlanta was to have a son named Charles Howard Candler, because the home of that son, built in 1920, houses the **Callanwolde Fine Arts Center**.

Roughly translated, the name means Candler Woods and it is appropriate. Designed by Emory University architect Henry Hornbostle, the entire 27,000 square foot mansion is centered around a large open courtyard. These, in turn, are surrounded by twelve acres (originally twenty-seven) of sculptured lawns, formal garden, nature trails and rock garden. The architectural detail of the mansion is exquisite, consisting of walnut paneling, stained glass, bronze balustrades, and the delicate artistry of the ceiling and fireplace reliefs.

One of the most unique features of the house is its music system, the heart of which is the remarkable Aeolian organ with its 3,752 pipes. The largest of its kind in working condition, its outlets reach from the tone chamber to every major room in the mansion.

Atlanta and Vicinity

This remarkable cultural and arts facility schedules performances, artists, lectures and exhibits throughout the year. It contributes, in a major way, to the culture of the community as well, with day and evening classes in crafts, writing, painting, dance, photography and other techniques.

A gallery on the second floor features one man shows by local painters, and the art shop, established in 1975, has available for purchase some of the region's finest paintings, prints, sculpture, weavings, handmade jewelry, and pottery. The inventory is judged every ninety days by the Callanwolde Guild.

Groups performing on a regular basis include the Callanwolde Concert Band, Callanwolde Poetry Committee, The Young Singers of Callanwolde, the Southern Order of Storytellers, and The Apprentice Dance Company.

For information on tours, performances and other aspects of this marvelous cultural center, contact Callanwolde Fine Arts Center, 980 Briarcliff Road, Atlanta, GA 30306; (404) 872-5338.

- **The Coca-Cola Bottling Company**, one of Atlanta's oldest and richest corporate citizens, offers a half hour tour of its main bottling room. For more information, contact Cliff Coker, The Coca-Cola Bottling Company, 864 Spring Street N.W., Atlanta, GA 30308; (404) 897-6949.

- One of the finest African-American museums in the nation is located in Atlanta. **Collections of Life and Heritage** contains exhibits on local black history; the life and times of Atlanta educator Benjamin E. Mays; dioramas depicting "Sweet Auburn" Street; and rotating exhibits by local and national black artists. This is also the home of the famed Paul Jones **Collection of African Art**. For more information, contact Collections of Life & Heritage, 135 Auburn Avenue, N.E., Atlanta, GA 30303; (404) 521-COLH.

- **The Cyclorama** is one of the most unique historical preservation experiences in the world. It consists of a century old cylindrical oil painting and multi-media presentation depicting the Battle of Atlanta. The mural, which appears three dimension, stands forty-two feet high, is 358 feet in circumference and weighs over 9,334 pounds. It is the combined effort of a group of German and Polish artists brought to America in 1885-86 by Mr. William Wehner, owner of a Milwaukee, Wisconsin, studio. First exhibited in Detroit in 1887, the painting toured the entire country and was brought to Atlanta in 1891, where it was first shown in a building on the north side of Edgewood Avenue, near Piedmont Avenue. It was subsequently bought in auction by Mr. George V. Gress, an Atlanta citizen, in 1893. Mr. Gress donated it to the City of Atlanta in 1898.

In 1921, it was transferred from an old wooden building in Grant Park to its present marble museum on a hillside in Grant Park. It achieved its three-dimensional quality in 1936, when funds from Warm Springs resident and president Franklin Delano Roosevelt's Works Projects Administration paid for the addition of blasted tree stumps, bushes, shrubbery, broken rails and cross-ties, realistic plaster figures of Confederate and Federal figures and the other fragments which form the battlefield's foreground. Special lighting and sound effects were added later, giving the entire painting a chillingly realistic effect.

The Cyclorama is also the home of the "Texas", the locomotive used to pursue the stolen "General" during The Great Locomotive Chase. An additional museum contains even more artifacts and exhibits from the period and an extensive bookstore provides a most impressive range of texts on the Civil War. For more information, contact The Cyclorama, 800 Cherokee Avenue, S.E., Grant Park, Atlanta, GA 30315; (404) 658- 7625 or (404) 624-1071.

• **Delta Airlines** offers two tours; the first is of the **Hartsfield Atlanta International Airport** terminal and includes a visit aboard a Delta aircraft; the second includes a museum room and maintenance facility. For more information, contact Tour Coordinator, Delta Airlines, Hartsfield Atlanta International Airport, Atlanta, GA 30320; (404) 765-2554.

• **Emory University's Museum of Art and Archaeology**, in Michael C. Carlos Hall (the Old Law Building), is dedicated to ancient art and archaeology from the Mediterranean and Near East, the Americas and Asia. Examples of European and

Atlanta and Vicinity

American art reach from the Thirteenth Century and extend through contemporary times.

The University started a general collection in 1875, at its original campus in Oxford, Georgia. In 1919, after moving to Atlanta, the University Museum was dedicated to antiquities. Specific archaeological activities have been pursued by the faculty since the 1920s, while the establishment of the collection of drawings and prints dates back to the 1960s. The Old Law Building itself was erected in 1916 as part of the campus master plan of Beaux-Arts architect Henry Hornbostle. Now on the National Register of Historic Places, the interior of the building was re-designed in 1985 by renown post-modernist architect Michael Graves.

The permanent collection focuses on the ancient cultures of the Near East and Mediterranean and, in the Egyptian gallery, includes a mummy dating from 300 B.C.; decorated pottery from Abydos, which goes back to 3,000 B.C.; and an illustrated papyrus fragment from the Book of the Dead.

Cuneiform tablets, some still in their original envelopes, come from Mesopotamia. Stamp and cylinder seals give scholars a glimpse of aspects of life in the Near East, and there is also Persian pottery and Luristan bronzes. Ancient Palestine's Bronze Age is represented by artifacts from Jericho, and glass vessels dating to the Roman period complement a collection tracing the evolution of oil lamps from about 3000 B.C. to the Islamic period.

Other artifacts from underwater excavations of the Sea of Galilee and the ancient harbor of Caesarea are also on display. The museum houses a collection of Greek pottery from the Geometric through the Hellenistic period, terra-cotta figurines, commemorative coins and outstanding examples of Roman period sculpture.

Traveling exhibitions from other major galleries and universities are also featured. For more information, contact

Atlanta and Vicinity

Michael C. Carlos Hall, Emory University, 1380 South Oxford Road, Atlanta, GA 30322; (404) 727-7522 or (404) 727-4282.

• Money makes the world go around, and there is a most impressive fiscal review housed in the headquarters of the **U.S. Sixth District Federal Reserve Bank**. Exhibits and subjects include the evolution of money, money in America, and a special numismastic section. This is also an excellent place to learn about how the private banking system developed in this country. For more information (tours are by appointment), contact the Federal Reserve Bank Monetary Museum, 104 Marietta Street, N.W., Atlanta, GA 30303; (404) 521-8747.

• **The Fernbank Science Center** will prove to be of great interest for anyone visiting Atlanta or the surrounding suburbs. Located at 156 Heaton Park Drive, N.E., it contains a sixty-five acre forest, exhibits on the Apollo space program, dinosaur models, a planetarium, and an observatory.

The planetarium and observatory are marvels in their own right. The brainchild of Jim Cherry, DeKalb County Superintendent of Schools, they comprise a vast science education complex with a professional staff of educators and scientists.

Dedicated on December 3, 1967, its 1987-88 programs, typical of its incredible array of offerings, included "Death of the Dinosaurs" which addressed one of the great planetary mysteries. "Star of Bethlehem" is a Christmas perennial and re-creates, with all the awe, mystery and profound implications, the sky over Bethlehem the night Christ was born, and the "star" itself.

"Celestial Clockwork" examines time and answers such questions as "Why is our year about 365 days long? Why is a month about 30 days long? Is the day longer now than it was in the distant past? Why are there really thirteen constellations in the Zodiac? Why wasn't George Washington born on Washington's birthday?"

Atlanta and Vicinity

"Moon Madness" explores how the heavens really influence us and speculates on whether the moon actually controls the birth or crime rate. Myths, legends, tales and superstitions regarding the mysterious universe are explored.

There is also a range of children's holiday programs, films, lectures and multi-media presentations. For more information, contact Fernbank Science Center, 156 Heaton Park Drive, Atlanta, GA 30307; (404) 378-4311.

• One of the more dramatic representations of Atlanta's earliest post-colonial history is **Fort Peachtree**, a fortification and trading post established in the early 1800s as a defense against the resident Creek Indians. Today, a replica of a log cabin occupies the site and houses Indian artifacts and historic documents. Tours conducted by docents are available upon reservation. For more information, write Fort Peachtree, 2630 Ridgewood Road, N.W., Atlanta, GA 30327; or call (404) 355-8229.

• One of the more venerable of Atlanta's institutions is the famous **Fox Theatre**. This a fine example of the opulence of movie house architecture during the 1920s. Distinguished by its minarets, onion domes and crenellated parapets, it houses a 4,600 seat auditorium with an Egyptian-Art Deco design motif consistent throughout. It is listed with the National Register of Historic Places. The Fox Theatre hosts a wide range of live performances and a summer movie series. Tours are available April through October, in conjunction with the Atlanta Preservation Center. For more information, contact Fox Theatre, 660 Peachtree Street, N.E., Atlanta, GA 30365; (404) 881-1997 or (404) 892- 5685.

• No finer collection of Georgia historical and genealogical records and maps exists than the one housed at the **Georgia Department of Archives and History**. This seventeen story building just southeast of the State Capitol, has an

Atlanta and Vicinity

auditorium whose stained-glass windows depict the rise and fall of the Confederacy. Records here date back to 1733, and it is here that historians and genealogists generally begin their research. For more information, contact Georgia Department of Archives and History, Ben W. Fortson, Jr., State Archives and Records Building, 330 Capitol Avenue, S.E., Atlanta, GA 30334; (404) 656-2393 or (404) 656-2350.

- Certainly no trip to Atlanta would be complete without a tour of the **Georgia State Capitol**. One of its distinctions is its dazzling dome of gold leaf. This brilliant white building, constructed in 1889, houses natural science displays, a Hall of Flags, and a Hall of Fame commemorating Georgians of distinction. For more information, contact Georgia State Capitol, Capital Hill at Washington Street, Atlanta, GA 30334; (404) 656-2844.

- A fine example of the Greek Revival style of architecture can be seen at the **Georgia Governor's Mansion**, at 391 West Paces Ferry Road, N.W. Finished in 1968, it offers a tour of the first floor and a fine collection of Federal period furniture. For more information, call (404) 261-1776.

- **Grant Park**, bounded by Atlanta Avenue, Sidney Street, Cherokee Avenue and the Boulevard, is one of Atlanta's most beautiful areas. It has 144 scenic acres which include Old Fort Walker, some Civil War breastworks, the Atlanta Zoo, Cyclorama and miles of scenic trails. This alone would make a memorable excursion lasting the entire day.

- Black business is honored with a personal glimpse into the life of one of its truly great leaders. The **home of Alonzo F. Herndon**, founder of the Atlanta Life Insurance Company, dates back to 1910 and is on the National Register of Historic Places. Open for tours, it features original family furnishings and a collection of Venetian and Roman glass. For more information, contact The Herndon Home, 587 University Place, N.W., Atlanta, GA 30314; (404) 581-9813.

Atlanta and Vicinity

• Acclaimed architect Richard Meir designed the **High Museum of Art**. The brilliant, white tiled building has won him a host of prestigious awards. Since the museum opened in 1983, it has been a premier attraction on Atlanta's sight seeing circuit. Its interlocking galleries feature American, European, Modern and African art, American decorative arts, European porcelain and a variety of traveling exhibitions. Vistas stretch from one viewing area to another and ramps connect each level. A four story atrium is considered the centerpiece of an institution which has, in the short time it has been in existence, captured national attention with such exhibits as, "Masterpieces of the Dutch Golden Age"; "The Advent of Modernism"; "China: 7000 Years of Discovery"; "Jacob Lawrence: American Painter"; and "The Machine Age in America". There is a Junior Gallery for the kids and a rich program of varied daytime and evening tours, lectures, films, workshops and concerts. The museum shop contains a wide range of catalogues, art books, posters, postcards, stationery and special gift items. Cafe Pentimento is open daily for lunch, Sunday brunch and pre-performance dinners. The downtown location contains the museum's permanent collection and other exhibits can be viewed at the Georgia-Pacific Center, 133 Peachtree Street. For more information, contact the High Museum of Art, 1280 Peachtree Street, N.E., Atlanta, GA 30309; (404) 892-4444.

• **The High Museum at Georgia-Pacific Center** offers 4,500 feet of gallery space for such traveling exhibits as: "N.C. Wyeth: The Met Life Murals"; "The Art of The New Yorker: A 60-Year Retrospective"; "American Illustration, 1890-1925: Romance, Adventure, & Suspense"; "The Grand Manner: Historical and Religious Painting in France, 1700-1800"; "Arts in America: The Turn of the Century, 1885-1917"; "Southern Expressions: Michael Brakke"; and "Yasuo Kuniyoshi, Paintings and Drawings". The Museum also offers the High Noon Series of free films, lectures, concerts and gallery talks. Its shop has a wide selection of books, posters, notecards and stationery, jewelry, toys and gift items. The Museum itself is available for receptions, private parties, and private viewing of the exhibitions. Also within the Georgia- Pacific Center are a conference and training center, a 250-seat auditorium, and two restaurants. For more information, contact the Georgia-Pacific Center is located at 133 Peachtree Street, N.E., Atlanta, GA 30303; (404) 577-6940.

• One of Atlanta's oldest existing buildings, constructed in 1889, is the **Inman Park Trolley Barn**. It once housed the trolley cars of the Atlanta and Edgewood Street Railroad Company. Recently restored, it is now scheduling various events and is open to the public. Set in Atlanta's oldest suburb, it's well worth the visit. For more information, contact the Inman Park Trolley Barn, 963 Edgewood Avenue, N.E., Atlanta, GA 30307; (404) 242-2300.

• **The Martin Luther King, Jr. Center** houses the most complete memorial to this Nobel Peace Prize winner and national civil rights leader ever assembled. Located at 449 Auburn Avenue, N.E., (Auburn Avenue between Jackson and Randolph streets), the entire two block area has been designated a historic site and is operated by the National Park Service. It includes his birth home, restored to its 1929 condition, and the Ebenezer Baptist Church, where he first began his ministry, and where Sunday services are still held.

His gravesite, with his crypt and the eternal flame, are located next door, within the grounds of the M.L. King, Jr. Center for Nonviolent Social Change.

The historic complex offers a film presentation, an exhibit chronicling his life, displays of his personal effects, and a gift shop. The buildings and the store fronts in the surrounding neighborhood of "Sweet Auburn" Avenue are being renovated to restore them to the turn of the century, when Auburn Avenue was the economic heart of black Atlanta.

For more information, write The Martin Luther King, Jr. Center, 449 Auburn Avenue, N.E., Atlanta, GA 30312; (404) 524-1956.

• For one of the best tours of a major public transportation system and for an outstanding presentation of how it works, the **Metropolitan Atlanta Rapid Transit Authority** (MARTA) offers a one and a half to three hour tour tailored for specific interests. Included are rail stations, direct connections, rail shops, bus garages, transit police, communications and train

Atlanta and Vicinity

centers. For more information, contact Lindy Welch, 2200 Summit Building, 401 West Peachtree Street, N.E., Atlanta, GA 30365; (404) 586-5167.

• A good opportunity to see education in action in Atlanta is offered by **Mercer University**, a college with a student body of 1,750 students. Its half hour tour includes classrooms and other facilities. For more information, contact Mercer University in Atlanta, 3000 Flowers Road South, Atlanta, GA 30341; (404) 451-0331.

• **Morris Brown College** offers a two-hour tour of educational facilities and the Atlanta University Center. For more information, contact M. Paulyne Morgan White, Morris Brown College, 643 Martin Luther King, Jr. Drive, Atlanta, GA 30312; (404) 525-7831, Ext. 126.

• One of the most profound of Atlanta's attractions spreads across eighty-eight peaceful acres and dates back to 1850. Now operated by the Bureau of Parks, Recreation and Cultural Affairs, the **Oakland Cemetery** is the final resting place of golfing legend Bobby Jones, Gone With the Wind author Margaret Mitchell, Morris Brown College founder Bishop Wesley Gaines, several Georgia governors and other Georgians of distinction. Buried here, as well, are hundreds of Federal and Confederate soldiers killed during the Battle of Atlanta. Complementing the cemetery's historical significance is a wealth of Victorian statuary, making this one of the better aesthetic experiences Atlanta has to offer. For more information, contact Oakland Cemetery, 248 Oakland Avenue S.E., Atlanta, GA 30312; (404) 577- 8163.

• **The Nexus Gallery** offers a comprehensive range of contemporary art in a variety of media including video, photography, painting, sculpture and multimedia installations. For more information, contact Nexus Contemporary Art Center, 608 Ralph McGill Boulevard, Atlanta, GA 30312; (404) 688-2500.

• For basketball action at its best, it's the **Omni Coliseum**, home of the NBA **Atlanta Hawks**. This 16,000-seat indoor sports palace also hosts circuses, ice extravaganzas, boxing, horse shows, concerts, conventions and a myriad of other events. For more information, contact Omni Coliseum, 100

Atlanta and Vicinity

Techwood Drive, N.W., Atlanta, GA 30303; (404) 681-2100. For more information on the Atlanta Hawks, call (404) 681-3600.

• As busy Atlantans have discovered, one of the best places to take a break from the cares and concerns of city living is the **Outdoor Activity Center**, located at 1442 Richland Road, S.W. Three miles of trails meander through twenty-six acres of towering oaks, beeches, poplars and pines. Located just three miles from downtown Atlanta, it is definitely worth the visit. For more information, call (404) 752-5385.

• No shopping or dining experience would be complete without a visit to Atlanta's famed **Peachtree Center**. There, you'll find a vast complex containing some of the city's finest hotels, restaurants, arcades and office towers. This is one of the finest examples of a controlled environment in existence. Architectural marvels such as an atrium lobby and revolving rooftop lounge made their first appearances there in the **Hyatt Regency Atlanta**. The Westin Peachtree Plaza is the tallest hotel in the western hemisphere. And to top it all off, a fantastic skybridge connects with the **Atlanta Market Center**. It is bounded by Baker, Ellis, Williams and Courtland streets, Northeast, and more information can be obtained by contacting Peachtree Center, Atlanta, GA 30303; (404) 659-0800.

• **The Peachtree Playhouse** is the home of **Just Us Theatre**, a professional black troupe specializing in the avant-garde with contemporary themes. The season is from September through April. For more information, contact the Peachtree Playhouse, 1150 Peachtree Street, N.E., Atlanta, GA; (404) 876-2350.

• Those who fell in love with the Uncle Remus tales, either in the original or translated with unforgettable charm by Walt Disney and his brilliant team of animation artists, will no doubt enjoy paying homage to the creator of Brer Rabbit, Brer Fox and Brer Bear with a tour of **The Wren's Nest**, the historic Victorian home of author and journalist Joel Chandler Harris. This one features original furnishings, family memorabilia, and first editions of Harris' works. And for your information, the estate was named for a family of wrens which nested in the mailbox. For more information, contact The Wren's

Atlanta and Vicinity

Nest, 1050 Gordon Street, S.W., Atlanta, GA 30310; (404) 753-8535.

• More than 900 animals, including mammals, birds of prey and reptiles, are on display at **Zoo Atlanta**. Located at 800 Cherokee Avenue, S.E., Grant Park, this great adventure features an Animal Contact zoo for children and the incredible Flamingo Plaza. For more information, write Zoo Atlanta, 800 Cherokee Avenue, S.E., Atlanta, GA 30315 or call (404) 624-5600.

• Constructed of Stone Mountain granite and decorated with elaborate plasterwork, murals and woodwork, the great Victorian mansion at 1516 Peachtree Street contains **Rhodes Hall**, which, in turn, houses the offices of the Georgia Trust, the largest non-profit historical preservation organization in the country. For more information, contact **Georgia Trust** for Historic Preservation, 1516 Peachtree Street, Atlanta, GA; (404) 881-9980.

• **The Roswell Historical Society**, founded in 1830, features fifteen structures which survived the Civil War. The group has established a walking tour which, over the decades, has become acclaimed as one of the better ways to appreciate the history of this fascinating city. For more information, contact the Roswell Historical Society, 227 South Atlanta Street, Atlanta, GA 30075; (404) 992-1665.

• To see how electronic equipment is manufactured, tested and marketed, **Scientific Atlanta, Inc.** has evolved a tour for business groups which covers production, earth stations and electronics. For more information, contact John Feight, Scientific Atlanta, Inc., P.O. Box 1005600, Atlanta, GA 30348; (404) 441-4000.

• No implement or instrument in the world today perhaps more epitomizes our society than the telephone. **The Southern Bell Center's Telephone Museum**, at 675 West Peachtree Street, N.E. houses vintage phones, switchboards, a record of Alexander Graham Bell's assistant, Thomas Watson, and other fascinating memorabilia. For more information, call (404) 529-7334.

• Atlanta—perhaps more than any other major city in the southeast except Chattanooga—owes its birth, existence

Atlanta and Vicinity

and growth to the railroad. One of the best ways to see Atlanta, then, is to climb aboard the **New Georgia Railroad**. You'll ride the train pulled by the 1910 vintage steam engine Old 750, which made its maiden run on the Florida East Coast. You'll begin this one at the Zero Milepost of the Western and Atlantic Railroad, erected in 1850 and located near the Georgia Railroad Freight Depot at Underground Atlanta. The Depot itself is an attraction, the oldest standing building in Atlanta and completed in 1869. On Saturdays, the train steams out from the Zero Milepost on an eighteen mile loop past the Oakland Cemetery, Atlanta's oldest burial ground. From there, the train huffs and toots through the Martin Luther King Historic District, then through the Hulsey Yards of the Georgia Railroad, future site of the CSX Piggyback Facility, a state of the art intercontinental freight shipping facility.

From there, the train moves on to **Inman Park**, a district fashionable when the engine was in its first years of operation, and the home of Coca-Cola's founders. Nearing the halfway point, the engine chuffs over the trestle near Emory University, past the Station and Egleston Hospital for Children. Circling under Piedmont and Peachtree Roads, then along the banks of Peachtree Creek, Old 750 passes markers which point out the sites of the Battle of Atlanta.

In all, it takes an hour and a half to complete the circle, and it's well worth the trip.

As a note of interest, in her prime, Old 750 could steam up to eighty miles an hour. Her tender carries eighteen tons of coal and 7,500 gallons of water. It takes a half ton of coal to reach fifty miles per hour from a standstill. (On the tour, she stays within the legal twenty-five mile an hour speed limit.) Old 750 has a contemporary partner, a backup engine used when the old steamer needs a break for maintenance or repair. Engine 6901 is a diesel veteran which pulled the famous Southern Crescent. Both trains are operated by the Atlanta Chapter of the National Railway Historical Society, in conjunction with the CSX Rail Transport and Norfolk Southern. For more information, contact The New Georgia Railroad, The Georgia Building Authority, One Martin Luther King, Jr. Drive, Atlanta, GA 30334; (404) 656-3253.

Atlanta and Vicinity

- Contemporary civil rights history is preserved in the original conference room in which Dr. Martin Luther King and the **Southern Christian Leadership Conference** put together that movement. Located in the SCLC headquarters at 334 Auburn Avenue, it includes Dr. King's office, now occupied by Reverend Joseph Lowrey. For more information, call (404) 522-1420.

- **The Theatrical Outfit** is the place to go for Atlanta's Off-Broadway plays. Located in the heart of the midtown theater district, its eleventh anniversary season included The Mystery Corpse, the one-person show Together at Last, and Rashomon. The season runs October through May, and includes an abbreviated summer stock. For more information, contact Theatrical Outfit, 1012 Peachtree Street, Atlanta, GA 30309; (404) 872-0665.

- For those who have never seen the film Gone With the Wind, or for those who have and would enjoy seeing it again, the **CNN Cinema 6**, at Marietta Street and Techwood Drive, screens it daily. For more information, call (404) 577-6928.

- **The Woodruff Arts Center**, since 1968, has joined such Marthasville mainstays as the Fox Theatre to insure Atlanta's international reputation for high culture and art. The 1,800-seat Symphony Hall each year witnesses the winter concert series of the acclaimed Atlanta Symphony Orchestra. The Center is also home of the Atlanta Children's Theatre, Atlanta College of Art, and the High Museum of Art. For more information, contact Woodruff Arts Center, 1280 Peachtree Street, N.E., Atlanta, GA 30309; (404) 892-2414.

- If you enjoyed a behind the scenes look at the print media, **WSB Radio and Television's** forty-five minute tour of electronic media news room and studio facilities should just about make you an expert. For more information, contact Beth Wright, WSB Radio and Television, 1601 West Peachtree Street, N.E., Atlanta, GA 30309; (404) 897-7369.

- **The Yellow River Wildlife Game Ranch**, located ten miles east of Interstate 285 on the Stone Mountain Freeway (Highway 78) between Stone Mountain and Snellville, features more than 600 species in a park consisting of thirty-seven acres of gently rolling hardwood forests and the beautiful Yellow

Atlanta and Vicinity

River. Deer, buffalo, bear, mountain lions, fox, raccoons, rabbits and other creatures call this preserve home. Yellow Springs also features a petting zoo for the youngsters. For more information, contact Yellow River Wildlife Game Ranch, 4525 Highway 78, Lilburn, GA 30247; (404) 927-6643.

- **Stone Mountain Carving Museum's** curator, Roy Faulkner, is the sculptor of Stone Mountain, Georgia's Mount Rushmore. He narrates a film on his feat. Other exhibits include the tools used and additional artifacts. This attraction makes a fascinating complement to the Stone Mountain Park experience and provides a rare opportunity to meet perhaps America's greatest living historical sculptor. For more information, contact Stone Mountain Carving Museum, 6080 Memorial Drive, Stone Mountain, GA 30083; (404) 498-8042.

- One of the largest outdoor markets in the world is located in Forest Park. **The Atlanta State Farmers' Market** retails fresh vegetables and fruits, poultry, smoked meats, plants, floral items and other unique food and greenstuffs. Open seven days a week, it is situated on 146 acres approximately ten miles south of Atlanta. For more information, contact Atlanta State Farmers Market, 16 Forest Parkway, Forest Park, GA 30050; (404) 366-6910.

- Atlanta's **Chastain Park** features an outdoor amphitheater and program of events the likes of which is seldom seen anywhere in the United States. The Atlanta Symphony performs here, as do top names in rock, popular, country western, jazz and bluegrass. For an updated schedule and additional information, contact Chastain Park, 140 West Wieuca Road, Atlanta, GA 30342; (404) 252-8866.

- Believed by many to be the burial sheet of Jesus Christ, the **Shroud of Turin** has been the subject of a raging controversy since it was first displayed in Turin, Italy. At **Omni International**, a host of exhibits subjects the Shroud to comprehensive scientific examination and analysis. The exhibit includes a narrated tour. For more information, contact Omni International, (404) 577-5590.

Atlanta and Vicinity

EVENTS

• Early April witnesses the world famous **Atlanta Dogwood Festival**. Included in the celebration are tours, concerts, parades, art and craft shows and demonstrations, a fashion show, various sporting events, a hot air balloon race and a host of other events.

• Marietta hosts the **Atlanta Golf Classic** at the Atlanta Country Club on Paper Mill Road. This PGA tour highlight is held in June.

• Summer sees the **Georgia Renaissance Festival**, and this one is as good as any found in the nation. Plays, crafts, music and a host of other related events make this May-June festivity one of the highlights of the season.

• Atlanta's Piedmont Park hosts the **Arts Festival of Atlanta** in the fall. Graphics, crafts, architecture, paintings, concerts, drama and every other aspect of the arts is featured in this one.

In all, Atlanta hosts several hundred celebrations and events each year. The dates of these vary by year, and admission prices, guest artists and other relevant aspects change as well. For an updated list, contact the Atlanta Convention and Visitors Bureau, 233 Peachtree Street N.E., Atlanta, GA 30343; (404) 521- 6600.

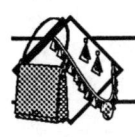

ACCESSORIES

E. ROOKS
6039 Sandy Springs Circle
Atlanta, GA 30328
Tel. (404) 252-0687
Hrs: Tue. - Sat. 10:00 a.m. - 6:00 p.m.
Call for late appointments.
Visa, MasterCard and AMEX are accepted.

E. Rooks will pamper and indulge you in grand style. Known throughout Atlanta for its selection of fine reproduction jewelry, E. Rooks lives up to the slogan, "E. Rooks Completes Your Fashion Statement." E. Rooks has the looks and the high style of a Beverly Hills Rodeo Drive shop. With help available at the snap of her finger, a woman can have accessories she has always dreamed of, and at affordable prices.

"Travel jewelry" are the pieces celebrities and socialites carry on trips to avoid taking their more costly gems. These fabulous pieces include reproductions of the jewelry of the Duchess of Windsor. They are hand cut gem designs of superb craftsmanship. E. Rooks carries pieces in the style of Tiffany's, David Webb, Harry Winston and Cartier. The treasure chests of E. Rooks spill out the special line of Swarovski, Ciner earrings, Majorica Pearls, unique silver pieces, gorgeous silk scarves, fabulous belts by Christopher Ross and bags by Balenciaga. You'll see still more sophisticated booty, such as reveal glasses by Ted Lapidus, purses in the style of Chanel, lovely sweaters, hats and skirts.

Licensed aestheticians offer a full line of beauty services, including a Day-Spa using only the finest products. Exclusive to the Atlanta area is the complete line of René Guinot skin care products. E. Rooks' staff will serve you tea in a porcelain cup while they ready your pedicure in a private room. E. Rooks encourages you to bring in your own outfit to help the staff accessorize you from head to toe. E. Rooks can copy your pieces or design a one of a kind piece to your order. E. Rooks is conveniently located in Sandy Springs, well away from the hubbub of Roswell Road.

> **KLEINBERG SHERRILL**
> 55 Bennett Street
> Atlanta, GA 30309
> Tel. (404) 355-2778
> Hrs: Mon. - Fri. 9:30 a.m. - 6:30 p.m.
> Personal checks are accepted.

The Kleinberg Sherrill boutique in Buckhead is the first company owned and operated store carrying exclusively Kleinberg Sherrill designer label accessories. The renowned line of belts, handbags and small leather goods is available nationally at specialty stores such as Martha, I Magnin, Bergdorf Goodman, and Neiman Marcus. The Atlanta boutique boasts the most comprehensive selection of merchandise from the different collections.

Crafted on the premises, the couture collection of handbags and belts is made with luxurious American alligator skins. Customers in the boutique are permitted to visit the adjacent workrooms and select the skin of their choice. In addition to alligator, other popular skin choices are ostrich, lizard and French calf. A recent addition to the Kleinberg Sherrill line is the Signature collection of handbags in French calf with alligator trim. Sportier in style, these bags are nice for daytime wear. Evening bags are now available as well in exotic skins with sculpted metal handles or in all over beading with faceted stones.

Perhaps the most recognized look of the Kleinberg Sherrill line is the gold vermeil and sterling silver belt buckle. Detachable and interchangeable, these buckles make an unforgettable statement. Two of the designer pieces are on permanent display at the Costume Institute of the Metropolitan Museum of Art. Published in limited editions, and cast like pieces of fine jewelry, these buckles are collected by customers the world over.

Kleinberg Sherrill accessories appear frequently in *Vogue, Harper's Bazaar, Elle* and *W* and continue to live up to the tradition of style and elegance.

ACCOMMODATIONS

ATLANTA CABANA HOTEL, 870 Peach Street Northeast, Atlanta, GA. Tel. (404) 875-5511, (800)235-3261. The Atlanta Cabana Hotel features lovely rooms, a great restaurant and an inviting pool. Omni Stadium, Georgia Tech and the World Congress Center are all nearby.

ATLANTA HILTON AND TOWERS, 255 Courtland Street, Atlanta, GA. Tel. (404) 659-2000. The Hilton offers 1250 luxurious rooms and eight international restaurants. Tennis courts, a pool, a jogging track and a health club are available for guests who would like to continue their fitness programs while away from home.

DOUBLETREE HOTEL, 7 Concourse Parkway Northeast, Atlanta, GA. Tel. (404) 395-3900. The Doubletree Hotel offers 371 guest rooms and the award winning Acacia Restaurant. Banquet and meeting facilities are available for conventions and private occasions.

EMBASSY SUITES HOTEL
2815 Akers Mill
Atlanta, GA 30339
Tel. (404) 984-9300
    (800) EMBASSY
All major credit cards are accepted.

Located four blocks from Cumberland Mall and across the street from Atlanta Galleria, the Embassy Suites Hotel is close

Atlanta and Vicinity

to everything that is important in Atlanta. Within a twelve mile radius you can visit Six Flags over Georgia, Atlanta Stadium, White Water Park and Chattahoochee River National Forest and Wild Life Park.

All 261 suites contain a luxurious living room/work area, a private bedroom, wet bar, refrigerator with icemaker, two telephones, two TV's with remotes, a sofabed and an indoor whirlpool and sauna. Ideal for the business traveler, the Embassy Suites Hotel also provides complete audio-visual equipment, flip charts, blackboards, easels and meeting rooms to suit all your business needs.

Jamies Restaurant, located off the plush, plant filled atrium, offers Continental/American cuisine in an elegant setting. Also offered is a complementary cooked to order breakfast and complimentary two hour cocktails in Jamies Restaurant and Lounge. At the Embassy Suites you can enjoy a plush two-room suite for no more than the cost of a typical hotel "single." In company with regular visitors to Atlanta, who know the best places, you'll want to make a delightful habit of staying at Embassy Suites.

EMBASSY SUITES HOTEL
1030 Crown Pointe Parkway
Atlanta, GA 30338
Tel. (404) 394-5454
　　　(800) EMBASSY
All major credit cards are accepted.

Centrally located in the center of the Atlanta Perimeter Center, the Embassy Suites Hotel offers the ultimate in luxurious accommodation for either the business or leisure traveler. Within a twenty mile radius you can take advantage of excellent shopping facilities, Stone Mountain Park, White Water Amusement Park, and Six Flags over Georgia. Hartsfield Airport is twenty-five minutes away with bus transport to the hotel via Northside Airport Express.

The 241 elegantly appointed rooms overlook a lush, plant filled atrium complete with granite floors and a one story waterfall. The rooms themselves combine elegance with efficiency. Spacious two room suites, softly decorated in mauve tones, contain a private bedroom with remote control TV, telephone, and your choice of either two full size beds or one king size bed, a private living room with a queen size sofa bed, mahogany dinette set, refrigerator with ice maker, microwave, console TV and telephone. For the business or conference person there are meeting rooms with capacity for 150 people, executive meeting suites and four boardrooms. Also included for your convenience are non-smoking suites, Alexander's Restaurant and lounge, a gift shop, gameroom and gym complete with an indoor pool, sauna, whirlpool and exercise room.

For the ultimate holiday or business meeting, let the Embassy Suites Hotel take care of you with their friendly and efficient staff. Alexander's Restaurant and lounge also provides a casual, yet elegant, environment in which to sample the excellent Continental/American cuisine. Come and let the Embassy Suites Hotel show you why it was picked as a "Best Choice" for Georgia.

EXECUTIVE VILLAS HOTEL, 5735 Roswell Road, Atlanta, GA. Tel. (404) 252-2868. The Executive Villas Hotel boasts suites with full kitchens, as many as three bedrooms, cable television and HBO. A complimentary breakfast and newspaper are available. Other amenities include courtesy transportation, a pool and a library.

FRENCH QUARTER SUITES, 2780 Whitley Road Northwest, Atlanta, GA. Tel. (404) 980-1900. One of the reasons the French Quarter Suites has a reputation as the "jazziest hotel in Atlanta" is that each suite in this all-suite, luxury hotel features an oversize whirlpool bath. Other reasons for their reputation include the live jazz entertainment in the Bourbon Street Cabaret and the classic "Cafe Orleans" cuisine in the restaurant.

HOTEL IBIS, 101 International Boulevard, Atlanta, GA. Tel. (404) 524-5555. The Hotel Ibis is one acre of France in downtown Atlanta. A free buffet is served and a restaurant,

Atlanta and Vicinity

lounge and sidewalk cafe are all on the grounds. A short walk will take you to the World Congress Center or shopping areas.

LANIER PLAZA HOTEL, 418 Armour Drive Northeast, Atlanta, GA. Tel. (404) 873-4661, (800) 554-8444. The Lanier Plaza Hotel will pick you up at the airport and take you to one of their 350 spacious rooms or thirteen decorator suites. Two restaurants, and a lounge which features live music, are on the grounds. An Olympic size pool with a large sundeck is available for your relaxation.

MARRIOTT SUITES - ATLANTA /PERIMETER
6120 Peachtree-Dunwoody Road
Atlanta, GA 30328
Tel.   (404) 668-0808
         (800) 228-9290
Visa, MasterCard, AMEX, Discover and Diners Club are accepted.

For a complete home away from home, reserve your place at the Marriott Suites - Perimeter Center. Whether you're on business or pleasure, the 224 luxury suites will provide for your every need. A suite includes a living room with a pull out sofa bed, a king sized bedroom and luxurious marbled bathroom with separate shower and tub. Two remote controlled TV's with HBO, CNN, ESPN, the Disney Channel, express check out and video message service are available to facilitate both business and entertainment, as are the two dual line telephones, the oversized work desk, wet bar and refrigerator stocked with complimentary juices, sodas and snacks. The house restaurant, Windows, is available for formal dining, with an adjoining lounge and complimentary breakfast buffet. There is also a private dining room, an indoor/outdoor pool, whirlpool, health club and saunas.

But the most outstanding feature of the Marriott Suites is the friendly staff. Additional conveniences include a bell staff, evening room service, valet, safe deposit boxes and a sundry shop.

Atlanta and Vicinity

Travelers to the Marriott Suites - Atlanta/Perimeter can take in numerous attractions such as the Civic Center, Stone Mountain, sports events at Fulton County Stadium, Six Flags, the Georgia World Congress Center, Cyclorama, White Water Park, Omni, the Perimeter Mall and more. Marriott Suites - Perimeter offers all the appeal of residential design with all the convenience of a full service hotel. In addition there are meeting rooms, the Conference Center (for up to 210 people), and executive Board rooms to accommodate all your business activities while you reside at the Marriott Suites.

MAYFAIR SUITES HOTEL, 7000 Roswell Road Northwest, Atlanta, GA. Tel. (404) 394-6300. The Mayfair Suites Hotel offers one, two and three bedroom suites on fourteen beautifully landscaped acres. Among the many amenities available are airport pickup, courtesy shuttles to nearby restaurants and entertainment, an exercise center and a library.

PIERREMONT PLAZA HOTEL, 590 West Peachtree Street Northwest, Atlanta, Ga. Tel. (404) 881-6000, (800) 446-1762. The Pierremont Plaza Hotel offers 505 guest rooms, convention space for 1200, five swimming pools, a restaurant and a lounge. The hotel is conveniently located in downtown Atlanta.

RAMADA RENAISSANCE HOTEL, 4736 Best Road, Atlanta, GA. Tel. (404) 762-7676, (800) 228-9898. The Ramada Renaissance Hotel has received the highest ratings for its rooms and services. Located five minutes from the airport, the hotel offers complimentary shuttle service, a ballroom for 500 and full health club facilities.

THE RESIDENCE INN, (five locations), Atlanta, GA. Tel. (800) 331-3131. Each Residence Inn features one or two bedroom suites with fully equipped kitchens. A complimentary breakfast buffet is available or you can take advantage of the grocery service. The pool and whirlpool spa are a great way to relax after a meal.

Atlanta and Vicinity

TERRACE GARDEN INN, 3405 Lenox Road Northeast, Atlanta, GA. Tel. (404) 261-9250. The Terrace Garden Inn boasts 371 beautiful rooms and suites, two restaurants, two lounges and a hair salon. A full range of exercise facilities is available for fitness-conscious guests.

THE WESTIN PEACHTREE PLAZA, Peachtree at International Boulevard, Atlanta, GA. Tel. (404) 659-1400. The Westin Plaza, "Atlanta's landmark hotel," was completely renovated in 1987. The luxurious rooms and suites, three restaurants, five lounges and twenty-four hour room service have earned the highest ratings.

ANTIQUE SHOPS

THE ATLANTA ANTIQUES EXCHANGE
1185 Howell Mill Road Northwest
Atlanta, GA 30318
Tel. (404) 351-0727
Hrs: Mon. - Sat. 10:00 a.m. - 5:00 p.m.
Visa, MasterCard, AMEX and Discover are accepted.

Collectors, interior designers, dealers and everyone who loves the timeless beauty known only to antiques, here is a place just for you: The Atlanta Antiques Exchange. The antiques establishment is filled to capacity with captivating eighteenth and nineteenth century English, Oriental and continental furniture, porcelain and decorative accessories. Glass enclosed shelves reaching up to the high ceiling and surrounding the room, display the largest collection of fine porcelains in the Southeast. Here, you will find a remarkably extensive assemblage of varied porcelains—the showroom specialty—as well as furniture, chandeliers, bronzes, boxes cloisonne, candlesticks and majolica. There is also a large collection of Straffordshire figurines as well as a sizeable selection of tureens, platters, vases and generally decorative items.

The Atlanta Antiques Exchange has been in business for more than 12 years, and is a direct importer. The showroom is centrally located in an in-town antique section of Atlanta, and offers you the quality and quantity you expect from a fine establishment. All who come to the Atlanta Antiques Exchange are seerved by experienced, accommodating, courteous staff who reflect the Exchange's concern for satisfying each individual customer's needs.

BYGONE ERA ARCHITECTURAL ANTIQUES, 4783 Peachtree Road, Atlanta, GA. Tel. (404) 458-3016. A wide selection of quality residential and commercial antiques are offered in a seemingly limitless display. Bygone Era handles everything from saloon decor to bathroom fixtures.

THE WRECKING BAR
292 Moreland Avenue
Atlanta, GA 30307
Tel. (404) 525-0468
Hrs: Mon. - Sat. 9:00 a.m. - 5:00 p.m.
Visa, MasterCard and AMEX are accepted.

The Wrecking Bar is founded on the desire to "rescue the past from the future." The Wrecking Bar is one of only a few firms in existence created solely for the preservation and restoration of the ornamental and decorative heritage of old buildings. Dedicated to gathering authentic architectural details from both domestic and imported sources, the collection of items within the three story building is incomparable to any in the nation.

The first time visitor to The Wrecking Bar will be astounded at the quantity and quality of the items displayed in the firm's showrooms and warehouse. The firm's three level building is equivalent to approximately 18,000 square feet of storage area and displays about two million dollars worth of inventory. Individual antique collectors and design professionals come from all over the globe to search through the beautiful and intriguing items. Because the inventory is constantly changing, a catalogue is not available. However, if you have a specific item or area of interest, the staff will photograph appropriate pieces and mail the images to you. The list of items rescued from buildings marked for destruction is long and detailed. You can view wood carvings, statuary, newel posts, paintings, columns, carousel horses, mantles, andirons, stained glass windows and a legion more of articles of the past.

The Wrecking Bar was founded by Wilma Stone and is Atlanta's pioneer firm in the architectural antique business. An extensive restoration, design and installation service is also available. A staff of skilled artisans can assist you in the creation and assembling of architectural components for private or commercial use. The Wrecking Bar is housed in the Victor Kriegshaber Home, itself a showcase of splendid architecture that is listed in the National Register of Historic Places.

APPAREL

AUSTRALIAN BODY WORKS, 4385 Roswell Road, Atlanta, Ga. Tel. (404) 252-7990. You will find a distinguished line of aerobic wear at Australian Body Works, as well as a fine selection of accessories.

BOUTIQUE PHYSIQUE
Phipps Plaza
3500 Peachtree Road
Atlanta, GA 30326
Tel. (404) 231-3262
Hrs: Mon. - Sat. 10:00 a.m. - 6:00 p.m.
Visa, MasterCard, AMEX and Discover are accepted.

With a bolt of energy and a jolt of color, Boutique Physique is a store offering the finest in women's exercise outfits, dance wear and accessories in the Atlanta area.

Owner Boots Strauss, devoted to exercise herself, has built a fantastic shop offering an expanded selection of the best in action wear including hard to find lines such as Dance France and Changes by Theodore. For fashion forward women looking for the non-traditional in a traditional city you can choose from a wide selection of California casual clothing in natural fibers designed to be worn year round, all hand picked by Ms. Strauss herself. Accessories to be found at the Boutique Physique include belts, fashion leg warmers, and head bands as well as a large selection of AVIA athletic shoes and swimsuits. Their exceptional collection of earrings, including both costume and genuine, ranges from Lunch at the Ritz to Katherine Palmer's exquisite gold designs.

You'll enjoy the boundless enthusiasm of Ms. Strauss and her staff. They are always ready to help you with any question you might have, from help in selecting the right aerobic shoes to assisting you in obtaining a complete sports wardrobe. "From workin' out to steppin' out," Boots Strauss and her fine staff look forward to assisting you with your sports fashion needs at the Boutique Physique.

CUSTOM CLOTHING BY H. STOCKTON, INC.
8735 Dunwoody Place, Suite 3
Atlanta, GA 30350
Tel. (404) 594-9668
Hrs: Tailoring by appointment.
Visa, MasterCard and AMEX are accepted.

A successful image, like any wise investment, is achieved through careful planning. Gentlemen, let Custom Clothing by H. Stockton develop a wardrobe for you that complements your individual style and taste. The professional staff of this unique business will meet with you at your home, office or hotel suite. You arrange the time, at your convenience, day or evening.

Custom Clothing by H. Stockton was conceived of as a way to provide the ultimate in gentlemen's clothing services, more service than even the finest clothing stores could provide. Their motto is: "We bring our store to you." They offer impeccable hand-sewn tailoring of the finest fabrics by old

Atlanta and Vicinity

world craftsmen who set the standards for quality, style and comfort and fit. They not only tailor superb, classical business clothing, but will make anything a gentleman may require, including golf and casual slacks. They will create dress and sport shirts in any style, as well as a wide range of other menswear.

At Custom Clothing by H. Stockton, service, quality, fit and total satisfaction are 100 percent guaranteed. Call for more information or to schedule an appointment. They will be happy to assist you with all of your clothing needs.

>**FANCY DELANCEY**
>Chastain Square
>4279 Roswell Road, Suite 602
>Atlanta, GA 30342
>Tel. (404) 252-9555
>Hrs: Mon. - Sat. 9:30 a.m. - 6:00 p.m.
>Open by appointment as well.
>Also,
>1401 Johnson Ferry Road
>216 Merchants Festival
>Marietta, GA 30062
>Visa, MasterCard and AMEX are accepted.

"Come, let us put you together," is the invitation offered to you by Fancy Delancey. Clothing which is easy to wear but sophisticated and different is what you will find at Fancy Delancey. "We offer unique clothing but not at special occasion prices," explains owner Susan Krisch.

The merchandise mix includes belts, hosiery, scarves, jewelry, sportswear, dresses, after-five and special hand-knits from such lines as Rialto, Karen Kane, Sybil, Barbara Barbara and Adrienne Vittadini. "Our style is fashion forward," says Susan, who is always shopping for new lines. Fancy Delancey is contemporary, but not junior, and features beautiful merchandise with excellent service and reasonable prices. Susan specializes in giving her customers the "total look."

Fancy Delancey has three locations and each has a warm and inviting feel to it. Big sofas and hot coffee are offered to your shopping companions. The East Cobb store highlights daywear and casual clothes, while the Chastain Square shop caters to a more "in town" life style with dressier clothes. For the woman who is a born shopper and wants a "one stop" store, Fancy Delancey is the place to go. Fancy Delancey stores are located on well-traveled streets in neatly kept shopping centers with convenient parking.

GRETCHEN'S CHILDREN'S SHOP
1246 West Paces Ferry Road at
West Paces Ferry Shopping Center
Atlanta, GA 30327
Tel. (404) 237-8220
Hrs: Mon. - Sat. 10:00 a.m. - 5:30 p.m.
Visa, MasterCard and Discover are accepted.
Also,
3356-B Chamblee-Tucker Road, Atlanta, GA 30341
Tel. (404) 458-5549
2472 Jett Ferry Road Atlanta, GA 30338
Tel. (404) 399-5383

Gretchen's is a full service children's store where you'll find everything you need for boys and girls from birth through pre-teen. The owners have revived the art of providing a full service specialty children's shop.

For babies, Gretchen's has layettes, basic baby items, underwear and a large selection of lovely clothing. For older children, sports clothing is in large supply as well as the hard to find, special occasion clothing. You'll find a wonderful selection of unusual toys, party favors, custom printed calling cards, gifts, shoes, an exclusive line of hand made finger puppets, custom blankets, youthful jewelry and everything or anything to complete an outfit. Clothing brands range from Oshkosh to Malley. The owners travel to New York to make sure they get the best clothing available to sell to their customers. They stock seasonal merchandise such as Halloween costumes, stocking stuffers, camp needs, winter coats and spring clothing. It's not unusual to find a group of pre-teens on their own, hovering over the earring display and locating the trendy

Atlanta and Vicinity

accessories they crave. Three generations often shop Gretchen's at the same time, and it's not unusual to find one of the staff people carrying the store owner's baby while she finds something special the shopper wants.

Upon entering the shop, it's easy to tell this is a homey and comfortable place, a welcome respite from impersonal department store shopping. The feel is upbeat and pleasant, with lovely balloon curtains and a separate alcove in the rear, which houses just babies' items. A toy box filled with "Cindy's toys" keeps youngsters playing happily while Mom discovers the fullness of Gretchen's service and selection.

GUFFEY'S OF ATLANTA, INC.
3340 Peachtree Road Northeast
Atlanta, GA 30326
Tel. (404) 231-0044
Hrs: Mon. - Sat. 10:00 a.m. - 6:00 p.m.
　　　Thursday　10:00 a.m. - 8:00 p.m.
Visa, MasterCard and AMEX are accepted.

Guffey's of Atlanta, Inc. is a businessmen's clothier which places the emphasis on service and fine American made clothing. The quiet and elegant shop is adjacent to the gleaming, twenty-two story, multifaceted and mirrored Tower Place Building. Don Guffey oversees the Tower Place store and Michael Ross facilitates the Galleria store.

Men who are looking for a classic, timeless style rendered in the finest of fabrics will find it at Guffey's of Atlanta, Inc. Suits are by Hickey-Freeman, ties are by Talbott and shoes are from the Cole-Haan and Allen Edmonds collections. The shop specializes in personalized service. Expertly made to measure shirts are tailored to fit out of the ordinary sizes. Fine casual slacks are by Barry Bricken; shirts are by Kenneth Gordon. Imported fabrics of British woolens, cashmeres and Italian silks are used by U.S. tailors in the making of the suits, slacks, jackets and shirts. Mr. Guffey and Mr. Ross hand select all of the fabrics used in their clothing. Jewelry and accessories of traditional style are offered.

Atlanta and Vicinity

Guffey's of Atlanta, Inc. is classically styled much like an Englishmen's club with comfortable furniture, brass fixtures and a low key atmosphere. It is a shop for the businessman needing the finest in apparel and service. For the executive too busy to come in, the stores offer outside salesmen. Guffey's of Atlanta, Inc. never forgets that the customer is the most important element in their business. They do more than their share to uphold their conviction that the Southern gentleman is one of the most elegantly dressed and up to date individuals in the entire country.

IBIS
Lenox Square
3393 Peachtree Road Northeast
Atlanta, GA 30326
Tel. (404) 264-9258
Hrs: Mon. - Sat. 10:00 a.m. - 9:30 p.m.
      Sunday   12:00 noon - 6:00 p.m.
Also,

Galleria Specialty Mall	Town Center
One Galleria Parkway	400 Earnest Barrett Pky.
Atlanta, GA 30339	Kennesaw, GA 30144
Tel. (404) 951-0570	Tel. (404) 426-7973

If you are the type of woman who likes to make a statement with her clothing, this is the store for you. Likened to wearable art, these fun, funky and affordable clothes are definitely for people who want something a little different.

While teaching in St. Croix, owner Jan Michaelis became taken with the tropical clothing she saw, and upon her return to the states she opened her own shop to present her favorite styles in clothing and accessories. Mostly casual, Jan says her clothes can be transformed into evening wear with a little creativity. Most items are made from natural fibers and have been hand painted, sewn, crocheted and batiked and imported from all over the world, mostly from Indonesia, China and Mexico. To accompany these originals is a wide variety, over 200 lines, of jewelry and other accessories. Items such as belts, scarves, shoes, socks, purses, bolo ties, earrings, necklaces and

Atlanta and Vicinity

pins are either imported or from well known local artists such as Katherine Dahl or Jeff DeVoor.

Located in a tri-level, oak paneled shop complete with tropical plants and upbeat music, this shop provides for the contentment of their customers, right down to a comfortable couch and beer for the man while his partner chooses her clothes or jewelry. With friendly and encouraging staff that work closely with customers to create an original look, combined with a great selection and a general atmosphere of "go for it!," you can't help but see why this shop was picked as a "Best Choice" for Atlanta.

JEANNE'S BODY TECH, 3160 Peachtree Road, Atlanta, GA. Tel. (404) 261-0227. Jeanne's Body Tech offers a fine line of aerobic wear such as Dance France.

THE JUNKMAN'S DAUGHTER
1130 Euclid Avenue
Atlanta, GA 30307
Tel. (404) 577-3188
Hrs: Mon. - Sat. 11:00 a.m. - 7:00 p.m.
      Sunday   12:00 noon - 6:00 p.m.
Visa, MasterCard and AMEX are accepted.

The Junkman's Daughter is more than a store—it is a lifestyle which, beginning with its opening in 1982, almost singlehandedly established Atlanta's in-town shopping district, Little Five Points. The style has crept steadily toward the burbs. The merchandise is eclectic. J.D. carries old toys, costumes, jewelry, and clothing, clothing, clothing, from Great Aunt Minnie's most chic muff to red hot NY/LA spandex.

If you want to change your image, freshen your London look, or play late at the hottest clubs, the clothes and accessories at J.D.'s are what you are looking for. But if it is retro-night and you feel romantic, Miss Scarlett is lurking in the jumbled racks with Rhett in the ample men's department. A downstairs skateboard shop keeps the youngest customers busy.

Owner Pam Mills-Majors is a third generation junkperson who's father bought out stores for thirty years and a lot of bits and pieces from long closed emporiums jumped across town to change from left-overs to retro-chic. Ms. Mills-Majors can't resist anything that is fun or a bargain so the store grew and in 1986 the Junkman Daughter's Brother opened in Athens, at 285 Broad Street. The whole thing finally hit *Glamour* magazine, *Women's Wear Daily* and the movies, from *The Big Chill* to *No Holds Barred*. So even if you're *not shopping*, the Junkman's Daughter is a must see.

MITZI AND ROMANO
1038 North Highland
Atlanta, GA 30306
Tel. (404) 876-7228
Hrs: Mon. - Thu.   11:00 a.m. - 9:00 p.m.
     Fri., Sat.   11:00 a.m. - 10:00 p.m.
     Sunday   12:00 noon - 6:00 p.m.

Mitzi and Romano was chosen "best womens fashion" by Atlanta Magazine, and the secret of their success lies in a dazzling array of unusual fashion designs which blend the charm of old Italy with contemporary U.S.A. There are no clothes on racks and a customer "could walk in the store with her hands behind her back," says owner Mitzi Ugolini.

Mitzi and Romano is situated among cafe-lined streets and the jazz clubs of the Virginia Highland district. This spacious store with it's tall archways invites customers to browse through the arrangements of uncluttered clothing. Mitzi and Romano is well known for their unique accessories. The fact is, Mitzi and Romano offers one of the most diverse and unusual collections of accessories in Atlanta. Mitzi Ugolini demonstrates uncanny ability to capture hard-to-find design lines. Top fashions from New York and Los Angeles find their way into Mitzi's shop. The unusual apparel expands on each client's individual taste to create a very personal style.

Atlanta and Vicinity

Weekend and evening wear consist of interchangeable separates and two-piece combinations which make for flexible wardrobes with long lasting appeal.

Mitzi and Romano provides "catering to your personal style with remarkable fashions and unparalleled accessories." Mitzi and Romano offers a complete array of sophisticated styles to embody the confidence of a woman who knows where she is going and what she hopes to find. Be sure to ask them about their exciting new store in the heart of Buckhead.

MOONCAKE
1025 Virginia Avenue
Atlanta, GA 30306
Tel. (404) 892-8043
Hrs: Mon. - Wed.   11:00 a.m. - 7:00 p.m.
      Thu. - Sat.   11:00 a.m. - 10:00 p.m.
      Sunday   1:00 p.m. - 5:00 p.m.
Visa, MasterCard and AMEX are accepted.

The kind of a shop that discriminating women love to discover, Mooncake has something for everyone. There are whimsical fashions, eclectic apparel and accessories for any mood. The shop was featured in *The Atlanta Journal and Constitution* as "boutique of the week." It is Atlanta's answer to every woman's quest for a shop that carries unique, fanciful clothing.

Mooncake will not buy anything, whether it is a New York or Paris design, unless it meets their exacting standards. The buyer's tastes are dramatic, exotic, romantic and fun. Choose from luscious lingerie, cotton casualwear, frilly tea-length gowns, ethnic styles or contemporary fashions. This is *the* place to find *the* dress, and every finishing touch detail. Accessories range from delicate French ballet slippers to hand-fused glass earrings. The shop carries both originals and reproductions of antique clothing. Future plans include an entire section devoted to wedding attire. The wide variety of clothing and accessories attracts an equally diverse cross section of customers. It's no wonder Mooncake has developed a reputation as the best place in the Atlanta area to shop for something different.

Find out how much fun shopping for clothing can be. Mooncake's artistic, unusual apparel and treasure chest array of jewelry, lingerie and gift items await your discovery.

POPPY'S
56 East Andrews Drive
Andrews Square
Atlanta, GA 30305
Tel. (404) 237-7015
Hrs: Mon. - Sat. 9:30 a.m. - 5:00 p.m
Also,
Vinings Jubilee Shopping Center
4200 Paces Ferry Road
Atlanta, GA
Tel. (404) 434-0568
Hrs: Mon. - Sat. 10:00 a.m. - 6:00 p.m.
Visa, MasterCard and AMEX are accepted.

Poppy's offers you a wonderful selection of updated classic clothing and a full line of compatible accessories from earrings to shoes, all at reasonable prices. A woman looking for versatility in her costuming from day wear to evening wear will find a tasteful variety of garments and accessories at Poppy's.

Designers such as Adrienne Vittadina, Ralph Lauren and Marissa Christina are displayed next to new designers who are continually being added to Poppy's lines. Buying is done with an awareness of new trends but with the eye for classic durability. Poppy's buyers travel from Dallas to New York in search of fresh designs. Poppy's garments are the kind of outfits which will become the "mainstays" in your wardrobe, clothing which is never out of fashion and always up to the minute. Poppy's accessories are attractive and complementary to their accompanying outfit. The staff of Poppy's is readily available to help "put it all together" for you.

Poppy's has recently opened a new store in Vinings Jubilee Shopping Center. The merchandise and staff of Poppy's are

Atlanta and Vicinity

lively and refreshing. Poppy's is a "one stop" shop for the busy working woman or the woman who wants to find a complete outfit all in one store. Whether you are searching for an elegant evening gown or a breezy sports outfit, Poppy's is sure to have something to meet your fancy.

> **REXER-PARKES**
> Brookwood Square
> 2140 Peachtree Road Northwest
> Atlanta, GA 30309
> Tel. (404) 351-3080
> Hrs: Mon. - Sat. 10:00 a.m. - 6:00 p.m.
>   Thursday Until 9:00 p.m.
> Visa, MasterCard and AMEX are accepted.

There's a blend of classic style and chic in the clothing offered at the Atlanta location for this well known New York store. The selection is designed for women who feel youthful, whatever their age. Rexer-Parkes stands out among the fine shops in the newly opened Brookwood Square development on Peachtree Road.

Part of the store's charm comes from the interior, with its soft colors, fresh flowers and cheerful staff. But there's also something about the way this shop presents its merchandise. Selections are displayed so you don't have to finger through the racks to put together an outfit. The custom designed display fixtures of pale oak and shining white let you see many selections. Their shop places an emphasis on putting together a total outfit of comfortable clothing. The fabrics tend toward natural fibers, appropriate for office or sport wear. The jewelry and accessories feature work of local artisans. Co-owners Marie Rexer and Ginny Feltus make frequent trips to New York and will find that special dress for clients as part of their unique service.

With the expertise of the staff and the combination of clothing and accessories, you can be assured of a complete look when you shop at Rexer-Parkes.

SNAPPY TURTLE
Cates Center
110 East Andrews Drive
Atlanta, GA 30305
Tel. (404) 237-8341
Hrs: Mon. - Sat. 10:00 a.m. - 5:30 p.m.
Visa, MasterCard and AMEX are accepted.

When you enter the Snappy Turtle, you enter a world of old style southern grace and hospitality, touched with just the right amount of sophistication and urbanity. Known for her cordial nature, graciousness and helpfulness, owner Blair Mann has created a classic shop for women who want to wear the best, whether it be sportswear, evening wear or casual dress.

Along with such lines as Berek, Albert Nippon, Barry Bricken, Paula Saker and Ronnie Heller, comes an assortment of smart accessories that really make the clothes. No run of the mill accessories here; all are created by artisans who obviously care for their work. If you need that something special, the Snappy Turtle has it in their line of scarves, jewelry, purses and belts. Known as a great source of resort wear, the Snappy Turtle also carries those hard to find cotton bathing suits and a large selection of sweater/skirt outfits, any of which will help you make your personal fashion statement.

Helped along by a fine word of mouth reputation and an eighty percent return customer list, the Snappy Turtle has a special wardrobing flair complete with special ordering for customers. Browsers are welcome, so come in and take a look at these fun, pretty and romantic items and see why the Snappy Turtle is a "Best Choice" for Georgia.

Atlanta and Vicinity

>
> **STEFAN'S INC.**
> 1160 Euclid Avenue Northeast
> Atlanta, GA 30307
> Tel. (404) 688-4929
> Hrs: Mon. - Sat. 11:00 a.m. - 7:00 p.m.
>   Sunday   12:00 noon - 5:00 p.m.
> Visa, MasterCard, AMEX and Discover are accepted.

   Whether your next role is Elliot Ness or Auntie Mame, you'll find just the right costume, to rent or buy, at Stefan's Inc., located in the heart of the quaint village within a city, Little Five Points. The shop will be easy to spot with its theatrical window display, capturing the mood of an era of the past.
   Appropriately, this vintage clothing store is housed in a turn of the century building with wood floors, oak wood cabinets and arched walls, the perfect setting to choose an outfit from days gone by. You'll feel right at home with the staff who wear vintage clothing themselves. They'll be happy to outfit you from head to ankle—they don't sell shoes—in clothing that hails from the era of the 1920s, 30s, 40s or 50s. Many of the clothes are purchased from estate sales which owner Rebecca Birdwhistell and business manager Sonya Scott love to attend. Stefan's is a practical place to shop if you like quality clothing at yesterday's prices. Whether you're going to a black tie dinner party or a costume ball, Stefan's will have something just right for you. It's a pleasure selecting clothing and accessories for men and women, all neatly arranged in the 2,000 square foot spacious area.
   The next time you're in the Little Five Points area don't forget to stop by Stefan's for your rhinestones, furs, satins and silks that will make you feel like a star who has just received the part.

Atlanta and Vicinity

VIVIAN GRAY OF ATLANTA
3820 Allen Court
Atlanta, GA 30328
Tel. (404) 252-0662
Hrs: Mon. - Fri. 10:00 a.m. - 6:00 p.m.
　　　Saturday　10:00 a.m. - 2:00 p.m.
Evenings by appointment.
Visa, MasterCard and AMEX are accepted.

　　　Vivian Gray of Atlanta specializes in creating exquisite custom designed pageant gowns, competition gowns, special costuming, wedding and debutante gowns. Vivian Gray has won many awards on local and national levels for her designs. Ms. Gray has achieved, through years of working in both the retail market and her own business, the reputation of being a designer and consultant par excellence. Vivian has designed clothes, gowns and costumes for competition in nine national pageants. She is a certified judge for the Miss Georgia preliminary pageant program and a frequent judge of local and state pageants. Many professional organizations have relied on Vivian's expert opinions and keen designs.
　　　Vivian works with the smallest of women to the tallest to create fantasy gowns. Vivian's designs are made from the "stuff of dreams." A small trusted staff produces detailed sewing, for your convenience, in the same location. The bead work is breathtaking. Vivian and her staff can repair or remodel your antique gowns. Alterations to your present gown can be done by appointment or on an emergency basis. Children also will delight in a dress made especially for them by Vivian.
　　　Vivian's twenty-six years of design and wardrobe coordination experience gives you the assurance of the best in service and product. The design drawn for you will consider all aspects of your needs from hair and skin color to personality and budget. Look and feel your best in a gown from Vivian Gray of Atlanta. Parking and access to Vivian Gray is troublefree.

Atlanta and Vicinity

ART GALLERIES

ABSTEIN GALLERY, 558 14th Street Northwest, Atlanta, GA. Tel. (404) 872-8020. The Abstein Gallery displays fine art by Atlanta and regional artists with a variety of styles ranging from the contemporary to the eclectic. Consultations and custom framing are offered.

ATLANTA ART GALLERY, 262 East Paces Ferry Road, Atlanta, GA. Tel. (404) 261-1233. The Atlanta Art Gallery offers American and European paintings of the last two centuries from private and corporate collections. The gallery specializes in restorations, framing and appraisals.

CARLSON & LOBRANO GALLERIES LTD.
55 Bennett Street
Atlanta, GA 30309
Tel. (404) 351-9897
Hrs: Mon. - Sat. 10:00 a.m. - 6:00 p.m.
Visa and MasterCard are accepted.

Knowledgeable collectors of fine art in the Atlanta area are quick to seek help from the Carlson & Lobrano Galleries, Ltd. Owner Nancy Carlson A.S.I.D., with a background in fine art, knows how to match her clients with art acquisitions. Whether one is looking for a Picasso original or a large sculpture for a commercial installation, Nancy will draw upon her wide range of resources to make an appropriate connection.

Nancy, currently chairholder of the Color Marketing Group, recently moved her gallery from the Atlanta Decorative Arts Center to her current Bennett Street location to work more directly with her clients. The large, renovated warehouse is ideal for displaying the broad variety of art that Nancy has carefully selected to please her customers. At Carlson & Lobrano Galleries, Ltd. one can find everything from evolving art of the Southeast to signed original New Yorker cartoons.

Atlanta and Vicinity

Contemporary ceramics complement antique Chinese furniture. Lovely tapestries woven on 300 year old Belgium looms are attractively displayed. A complete custom framing service is available, specializing in unique French and museum mattings

Carlson & Lobrano is a serious gallery with an eclectic collection of tasteful fine art. And Nancy Carlson A.S.I.D. is proud of her reputation for being able to solve difficult design problems. In fact, if she can't find just the right piece of art for your home, she can have it created. Five "house" artists do original works on commission.

FRANCES ARONSON GALLERY, 56 East Andrews Drive Northwest, Atlanta, GA. Tel. (404) 262-7331. The Frances Aronson Gallery offers investment-quality paintings and sculpture by American and European artists of the nineteenth and twentieth centuries. Master prints of traditional and contemporary impressionists are included in the collection.

GALLERY SOUTH, 265 Commerce Drive, Atlanta, GA. Tel. (404) 631-0500. Gallery South features original fine art, antique prints, graphic posters and airation art. Custom framing is available.

LOVETT MARIE GALLERY, 5223 Roswell Road, Atlanta, GA. Tel. (404) 252-7766. Lovett Marie Gallery offers investment graphics representing great works of art. Some of the artists featured are Chagal, Rockwell, Miro and Dali.

PATRICIAN GALLERIES SOUTH, 1649 Sands Place Southeast, Suite A, Atlanta, GA. Tel. (404) 955-2637. Patrician Galleries South is one of the largest and most complete galleries in the South. They specialize in corporate, designer and investment art by Miro, Rockwell and Delacroix, among others. The Patrician is also the exclusive dealer for works by Neiman, Dali and Kelly.

TRITT GALLERY, 2573 North Decatur Road, Atlanta, Ga. Tel. (404) 373-3544. Tritt Gallery features original oils,

Atlanta and Vicinity

sculpture, limited editions and water colors. Art purchased may be exchanged at the time of purchase, at the full price.

TULA SHOWROOMS/STUDIOS
75 Bennett Street
Atlanta, GA 30309

TULA brings a fresh approach to the world of art. Since 1984 it has offered an exciting mixture of working artists and art related businesses in both the fine and decorative arts. Housing both galleries and artists' studios, this renovated, contemporary facility, complete with a skylighted atrium, allows the browser to see works in progress as well as the finished pieces. There are artists working in a wide variety of media, including jewelry, ceramics, pottery, painting, sculpture, fiberglass, weaving and more. With a life and energy of its own, this unique cooperative environment attracts art collectors, designers and tourists alike.

TULA is a challenge to find, even for Atlantans. But it is well worth the effort. Heading north on Peachtree Street, pass Piedmont Hospital; look for Benihana on your right, then turn left into the driveway, which is Bennett Street.

SUSAN MARPLE, Studio H-1, Tel. (404) 351-8329 or (404) 351-3065. Susan is a designer of accessories and sweaters.

MARCY TURK, Studio L-1, Tel. (404) 352-5754. Marcy creates functional and sculptural works in ceramics.

JUDIE JACOBS, Studio L-1, Tel. (404) 352-5754. Judie designs clay-white earthenware plates and porcelain jewelry.

SIDNEY GUBERMAN, Studio C-1, Tel. (404) 355-0005. Sidney is a well-known painter and sculptor.

BITTY HERLIHY, Studio H-1, Tel. (404) 351-8329. Bitty is a fiber artist. She was the designer for Elizabeth Claire original jackets, sweaters and accessories, wall pieces and window treatments.

Atlanta and Vicinity

K. HARTWIG DAHL, Studio P-1 (rear), Tel. (404) 351-5477. Ms. Dahl is a well-known porcelain jewelry artist. She also creates abstract sculpture and paintings.

DAVID WESTMEIER, Studio D/E-1, Tel. (404) 351-6724 David is a master potter of thrown forms. He exclusively uses the raku method, incorporating bright iridescent color.

ADELINE TURMAN, Studio K-1, Tel. (404) 351-6642. Adeline works in pastel and charcoal, with a concern for color, space and form.

CHRISTA FRANGIAMORE, Studio N-1, Tel. (404) 351-3456. Christa, a glass artist, works with a layered glass technique incorporating sand-etched images. She also does architectural installations and accepts private commissions.

ARIEL GALLERY, Studio M-2, Tel. (404) 352-5753. Artist owned and operated, the Ariel Gallery shows works by its members in painting, clay, drawing, fiber, photography and glass.

DIANE McPHAIL, Studio L-2, Tel. (404) 352-5754. Diane's work is concerned with color, pattern, visual symbolism and ritual. It takes such diverse forms as geometric shaped canvases, experimental books and jewelry.

CAROLYN WICHER, Studio H-1, Tel. (404) 351-8329. Carolyn works on handmade paper, utilizing semi-abstract, loose fluid imagery. She has many two and three dimensional pieces. She will accept commissions.

CAMERON-COBB, LTD., Studio N-2, Tel. (404) 355-5676. This is a contemporary fine arts gallery specializing in original painting, fiber, sculpture and clay.

KATHERINE PANHORST SMITH, Studio G-1, Tel. (404) 351-6642. Katherine works on canvas and paper collaged with hand stained oriental papers and mylar film. Current series

Atlanta and Vicinity

about interior gardens—gardens of the heart. Collections include: Alembik, Fine and Callner, Atlanta; Omni Hotel, St. Louis, MO.; Alabama Power Co., Birmingham, AL.; President and Mrs. Jimmy Carter, Carter Center, Atlanta.

LYN PERRY, Studio I-1, Tel. (404) 351-0278. Lyn creates custom designed woven rugs, wall hangings, handbags and mobiles using a combination of natural fibers.

MARGO OWENS, Studio L-1, Tel. (404) 352-5754. Margo works in acrylic and oil on canvas. She also stylizes different periods of antique furniture and interiors, using line, shape and color to create visually pleasing images.

KATE PENDLETON, Studio L-1, Tel. (404) 352-5754. Kate creates designs of handmade felt for pillows and jackets. Her weavings include baby blankets and shawls.

SANDI GROW, Studio L-1, Tel. (404) 352-5754. Sandi works in black and white charcoal drawings, large oils and pastel drawings. She is best known for her "Holding on to the Dream" series.

PHYLLIS ALTERMAN FRANCO, Studio L-1, Tel. (404) 352-5754. Phyllis specializes in narrative and figurative drawing and painting. She is a charter member of Ariel Gallery.

Atlanta and Vicinity

BAKERIES

THE DESSERT PLACE
279 East Paces Ferry Road
Atlanta, GA 30305
Tel. (404) 233-2331
Hrs: Sun. - Thu. 11:00 a.m. - 11:30 p.m.
     Fri., Sat.   11:00 a.m. - 1:00 a.m.

Also,	In Macy's Dept. Store
1000 Virgina Avenue N.E	180 Peachtree Street N.E.
Atlanta, GA 30305	Atlanta, GA 3030
Tel. (404) 892-8921	Tel. (404) 524-4023

The aroma of baking cream cheese brownies is a lure few people can resist. The Dessert Place bakes brownies and numerous other irresistible delectables right under your nose. The Dessert Place bakes goodies so well it has won the *Atlanta Magazine* Award for "Best Desserts."

The Dessert Place is actually three places. All the shops offer pies and cakes and assorted goodies, plus Häagen-Dazs ice cream. Each store is slightly different in atmosphere. The Macy's store is primarily a retail store and offers a twelve stool counter. The Virginia Avenue shop is small, intimate and bustling and the East Paces Ferry shop is spacious with quiet music.

Each of these "sweeteries" brings the best in decadent delights to your table. If the cream cheese brownies don't get you, the Kentucky pie with its chewy, chunk chocolate and nuts will! On any given day you might find fresh blueberry muffins, Italian cream cake, Charleston Coconut Cake or a fresh fruit cobbler. The apple pie is always fresh from the oven.

Owners Sheryl Meddin and Ann Johnson create or are given all the recipes used in their shop. They will create one of

Atlanta and Vicinity

a kind wedding cakes or baked goods for special events. The Dessert Place offers the finest quality desserts and an engaging atmosphere in which to enjoy them.

HENRI'S BAKERY
61 Irby Avenue
Atlanta, GA 30305
Tel. (404) 237-0202
Hrs: Mon. - Sat. 7:30 a.m. - 6:00 p.m.
　　　Sunday　　 10:00 a.m. - 5:00 p.m.
Also,
999 Peachtree Street　　　6289 Roswell Rd.
Suite 130　　　　　　　　Atlanta, GA 30328
Atlanta, GA 30309

The same dedication to quality which Grandfather Henri instilled is found at Henri's Bakery today. Henri Fiscus came from Alsace Lorraine in the 1920s, first working in a New York hotel as a pastry chef and then in Atlanta as pastry chef for the Biltmore Hotel on Peachtree. He opened the first Henri's in downtown Atlanta, adding deli sandwiches during the slow months.

Today, original French recipes, created by Henri, are served to customers in a popular free standing building, built especially for Henri's in 1969. Dancers from the neighboring Atlanta School of Ballet, business people and local residents can be seen munching on Henri's famous sandwiches: ham and swiss, roast beef, corned beef, roast and smoked turkey, pastrami and the famous Henri's Po Boy, made with ham, roast beef, Swiss, salami and dill pickles on French bread. The bakery has an attached lunch room which seats fifty, where your luncheon can be topped off with the item Henri's is most famous for, an eclair. Before leaving you'll enjoy perusing the glass cases filled with delicious pastries such as French and Danish pastry cakes, cream filled confections, wonderful cookies and exquisitely decorated cakes.

Grandfather Henri, who worked seven days a week at the bakery, 'til the ripe old age of seventy nine, lives on at Henri's through his grandchildren. They continue Henri's insistence on the highest quality bakery and deli products. It's a tradition well worth preserving.

JOLI-KOBE
5600 Roswell Road at the Prado
Atlanta, GA 30342
Tel. (404) 843-3257
Hrs: Mon.-Sat.　10:00 a.m. - 6:00 p.m.
　　　Lunch　　　11:00 a.m. - 3:00 p.m.

It really is a small world when a Japanese style bakery and cafe becomes well-known for its French pastry. Such is life in the cosmopolitan city of Atlanta where the Joli-Kobe bakery has become one of the most popular lunch spots.

From the people who brought you Kobe Steaks, Atlanta now has the kind of bakery-cafe that has enjoyed enormous popularity all over Japan. It offers what must be the lightest and freshest French pastries in town, exquisite salads, breads and soups. The pastries include chestnut mousse, fresh fruit shortcake, Black Forest cake and the wildly popular chocolate mousse cake. The Rare Cheesecake features layers of sponge cake filled with cheese and topped with whipped cream. Lunch guests enjoy a wide selection of salads and sandwiches, each as carefully put together as a Japanese garden. Try the almond curried chicken salad. The teriyaki chicken sandwich will keep your taste buds in tune with the surroundings. The selection of domestic and imported beers will also please the palate, as well as the wine, juices and hot beverages.

The interior is exactly as one would find it in Tokyo. It is a neat, uncluttered place where you can watch the bakers at work behind the glass partitions. The smell of baking bread permeates the air as efficient and courteous waitresses scurry from table to table. No matter what you select at the Joli-Kobe it will do you a world of good.

Atlanta and Vicinity

BALLOONS

BALLOONS BY THE BUNCH
2484 Briarcliff Road, Suite 26
Atlanta, GA 30329
Tel. (404) 321-1004
Hrs: Mon. - Fri. 8:30 a.m. - 6:00 p.m.
  Saturday 10:00 a.m. - 3:00 p.m.
Visa, MasterCard, AMEX and Discover are accepted.

The next time your doctor writes a prescription for smile therapy, head down to the Balloons by the Bunch pharmacy to get it filled. They've been meeting the needs of smile enthusiasts in the Atlanta and Marietta areas for the past nine years.

Everyone deserves the thrill of answering their front door and being greeted by two shiny mylar balloons with an uplifting message, surrounded by nine big, bright and colorful latex balloons secured into a clay flower pot filled with Jolly Rancher candy. Deliveries can be customized to suit the occasion. You may want to send a smaller bunch to a hospital, or balloons that will float a long time to a small child. Creative customizing is done with the use of such props as stuffed animals: Gund, North American Bear and Steiff, coffee mugs and baskets, not to mention an assortment of colorful twelve inch rubber balloons which will float for up to eighteen hours. You can pick out the appropriate card to go with your "bunch"; they have one of the largest selections in Atlanta. This shop is sometimes known as "Bears by the Bunch" because of its immense selection of the lovable, furry creatures.

Balloons by the Bunch can make your next party an extravaganza with its unique, personalized decorations. Give yourself the experience of saying "I Love You," "Congratulations," or "Good Luck" in a way you've never said it before.

Atlanta and Vicinity

BOOKSTORE

OXFORD BOOK STORES, 2345, 2395 Peachtree Road, Atlanta, GA. Tel. (404) 262-3332. Oxford Book Stores has a computerized inventory of over 110,00 titles ranging from children's to foreign language books. Maps, posters, paperbacks and rare or collectible items are offered at reasonable prices.

COLLECTIBLES

WORLD WIDE COIN INVESTMENTS, 3145 Peachtree Road Northeast, Atlanta, GA. Tel. (404) 262-1810. World Wide Coin Investments buys, sells and trades valuable coins, bullion and gold or silver scrap. Coin books, albums and other accessories are offered to the serious investor along with free counseling.

COMEDY

THE NEXT CITY COMEDY THEATRE
Ponce de Leon and North Highland
696 A Cleburne Terrace
Atlanta, GA 30306
Tel. (404) 876-NEXT
Hrs: Showtime
    Thu. - Sat. 8:30 p.m. - 10:30 p.m.
Visa, MasterCard and AMEX are accepted.

"The Laughter of one Person is the laughter of 10,000." The Next City Comedy Theatre is a place where people learn how to be safe enough to risk going through the change that

Atlanta and Vicinity

happens when we laugh, so believes Robert Lowe, creator of The Next City Comedy Theatre.

The Next City Comedy Theatre features a Comedy Theatre Sports night. The competition, one of several weekly presentations, places four teams of comedians of marked extremes of experience and talent in a free-for-all of improvisational wits. Judges rate the teams on entertainment value and technical skill during a forty-five minute "first half" of short performances. The top two scorers then meet in a second half showdown of longer sessions. Creator Lowe acts as emcee. There is no handicapping, so amateurs are thrown against more experienced comedians.

Ongoing events include Saturday night Comedy Theatre Sports and open mike stand-up comedy. Friday night brings Comedy Showcase and The Best of Atlanta stand-up comedy. Thursday's shows include comedy works in progress and amateur comedy theatre sports. Workshops on creativity and comedy theatre sports are offered on Wednesday nights. The Next City Comedy Theatre is located in the Plaza Drugs Shopping Center at Ponce de Leon at North Highland.

EDUCATION

CLARK COLLEGE
240 James P. Brawley Drive Southwest
Atlanta, GA 30314
Tel. (404) 681-8000
      (404) 681-8093

For almost 120 years, Clark College has provided an academic atmosphere adhering to only the highest standard. Centrally located near downtown Atlanta, Clark offers a mix of liberal arts and career oriented programs, designed to optimize the students potential in the professional marketplace.

Among its many offerings, Clark College has one of the most advanced micro-computer equipped instructional centers for a college of its size, and a multi-use Mass Communication Center, which houses Cable Channel 3 and WCLK-FM radio station. To complement the academic program, Clark offers a full spectrum of professional, Greek, social and cultural organizations and activities.

Clark is one of seven member institutions in the Atlanta University Center. Its 2,000 plus students have the benefit of sharing resources and fellowship with more than 8,000 students who attend other A.U. Center schools.

With a faculty committed to excellence, a curriculum designed to accentuate the strengths of the student, and a campus replete with the most modern facilities, Clark College provides all the best aspects of college life.

In 1988, Clark College and Atlanta University, the oldest graduate institution in America serving a predominantly black student body, consolidated to form Clark Atlanta University. Through consolidation, a blending of the best of both schools has been accomplished and a stronger, more versatile institution will emerge.

ENTERTAINMENT

CENTER STAGE THEATRE
1374 West Peachtree Street
Atlanta, GA 30309
Tel. (404) 873-2500
Hrs: Box Office Mon. - Fri. 10:00 a.m. - 6:00 p.m.
Visa, MasterCard and AMEX are accepted.

Center Stage Theatre is filled with the energy and excitement of midtown Atlanta. This popular facility features an eclectic range of live entertainment on a near nightly basis, drawing crowds that span all age groups. Two full service bars, the Encore Restaurant and a lounge are also located within the complex, providing everything you need for a complete evening of dinner and entertainment.

Mrs. Frania T. Lee constructed Center Stage Theatre as a memorial to her daughter, Helen Lee Cartledge. Although the hall is little more than twenty years old, it has an Old World elegance that reminds one of the venerable European concert halls. The building contains an amphitheater with a seating capacity of 775 to 1000 persons that slopes at an angle of thirty-five degrees, providing an unobstructed view from every seat. The acoustics are excellent, making this an ideal location for video and audio work in addition to concerts, shows, plays and other live performances. The parade of artists who perform at Center Stage ranges from the intimate nightclub style of bluesman B. B. King to the big stage sounds of name rock bands.

Center Stage Theatre is available for small conventions and other bookings; the restaurant is available for banquets, receptions, private parties and meetings. Call or check the current entertainment listings in the Atlanta newspapers for the artists and shows that are currently playing here.

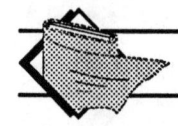

FABRIC SHOP

WALTER J. PENNY FINE FABRIC
4920 Roswell Road
Atlanta, GA 30342
Tel. (404) 255-2429
Hrs: Mon. - Sat. 9:30 a.m. - 6:00 p.m
Visa and MasterCard are accepted.

The post war period found Walter Penny heading for Atlanta with his car full of satins and taffeta. Walter had been a weaver in his youth and he knew his fabrics well. He wanted to expand his business beyond selling materials to casket companies. Walter approached an Atlanta store and before long created his own business which flourished. Walter J. Penny Fine Fabric store is an Atlanta institution now.

Atlanta and Vicinity

Recently, the well known store has made another move for the better. The shop has a new location in the Fountain Oaks Square shopping center.

The bright new store offers a comfortable space for sitting and choosing patterns from the many pattern books available. The staff is a well seasoned team who knows how to combine patterns and fabric for the best possible effect. The selection of materials is outstanding. You can choose from silks, raw silks, fine cotton and wools. Sewing notions of all varieties are available. The bridal section of the shop includes lace from France, materials for headpieces and readymade headpieces. Unusual buttons abound.

The service at Walter J. Penny Fine Fabric store hasn't changed in over forty years. Assistance is straightforward, honest and unpretentious. The quality of merchandise is the highest available. Walter J. Penny Fine Fabric will special order any fabric you wish and can refer you to competent dressmakers of the area. Remember, Walter J. Penny Fine Fabric has a new location in the Fountain Oaks Shopping Center.

FLORIST

FANTASIA FLOWERS LIMITED
856 St. Charles Ave. Northeast Suite 10
Atlanta, GA 30306
Tel. (404) 876-2055
Hrs: Mon. - Fri. 9:00 a.m. - 5:00 p.m.
Visa, MasterCard and AMEX are accepted.

No cliches are found at Fantasia Flowers Limited. Designer/artist David Cooke creates visually stunning floral arrangements for individuals and special events. He provides a full florist's service to the public and a complete floral service for special events such as weddings and corporate occasions.

Atlanta and Vicinity

David's innovative designs bloom as fresh as the flowers he uses.

The location of Fantasia Flowers Limited is as surprising as its unusual floral arrangements. Nothing of the studio is visible from the street. Fantasia Flowers Limited is a working studio, open and with no boundaries. This is a hands-on environment. David moves unrestricted through the myriad of colorful blooms choosing textures, fragrances and hues as if his workfloor was a giant painter's palette.

David builds rapport with his clients, listening carefully to their needs and desires. Then in concert with his client he creates an exceptional floral arrangement. David's favorite designs are free form and surprising. Fantasia Flowers Limited offers a garden of floral arrangements uncommon in beauty.

FURNITURE STORE

SCAN DES
2140 Peachtree Road
Brookwood Square
Atlanta, GA 30309
Hrs: Mon. - Sat. 10:00 a.m. - 6:00 p.m.
Visa, MasterCard and AMEX are accepted.

Owner Marianne Trull has combined her fashion background, her interest in interior design and her lifelong love of antiques to create the unique Scan Des furniture shop. For that distinctive Swedish look in home interior design, there's no better place to find furniture. The shop specializes in Gustavian style handpainted designs. This painstaking process results in soft and subtly colored furniture highlighted with delicate flowers and other decorations. The wood seems to magically shine through the hand rubbed finish.

Marianne has imported fine pieces from Sweden which are up to 150 years old. Marianne also designs reproduction pieces, some of which are handcrafted in Sweden, while others are finished by specially trained Atlantan artists. The pieces available at Scan Des have been written up in *House Beautiful*, *Southern Homes*, and *Better Homes and Gardens*. You'll enjoy the Swedish atmosphere of the shop, and the lilting Swedish accents of Marianne and her staff. In addition to furniture, Scan Des also stocks all sorts of design accessories and fabric to complete your interior design. Painted boxes from Scan Des' artists in residence may be custom ordered, as can custom painting of your chosen designs, on your previously owned or newly purchased pieces of fine furniture.

GARDEN

ATLANTA BOTANICAL GARDEN
1345 Piedmont Road
Atlanta, GA 30309
Tel. (404) 876-5858
      (404) 876-5859
Hrs: Tue. - Sat.   9:00 a.m. - 6:00 p.m.
      Sunday   12:00 noon - 6:00 p.m.

Escape the hustle and bustle of the city and relax in the quiet beauty of the Atlanta Botanical Garden. Located on sixty acres in Midtown's famous Piedmont Park, the Garden is a showcase for the wide variety of flora that thrives in the southern region.

A peaceful stroll through these magnificent gardens gives one a great feeling of wonder and appreciation for the captivating beauty of nature and extraordinary diversity of life. In a pleasant afternoon walk, you'll see superb herb gardens, fragrant rose gardens, perennial and camellia gardens to delight the senses, and matchless Japanese gardens to delight the mind. There are fifteen acres of an enchanting hardwood forest complete with walking trails where one can allow the cares of the world to slip quietly away. Opening in March of 1989, The Dorothy Chapman Fuqua Conservatory will feature 16,000 square feet of tropical, desert and endangered plants from around the world under glass. A full schedule of horticulture, flower arranging and gardening classes are offered for adults and children throughout the year, and free guided tours are available to the public every Sunday at 3:00 p.m.

The Garden's Gift Shop features a wide variety of unusual gifts and souvenirs, all with a floral theme. Lunch is available every Tuesday through Friday from 11:30 a.m. to 1:30 p.m., April through October. A truly delightful place to visit year round, the Atlanta Botanical Garden offers a seldom seen view of the beauty and grandeur of the living world around us.

GIFT SHOPS

ABBADABBA'S
421 B Moreland Avenue Northeast
Atlanta, GA 30307
Tel. (404) 588-9577
Hrs: Mon. - Sat. 11:00 a.m. - 7:00 p.m.
  Sunday 1:00 p.m. - 6:00 p.m.
Visa, MasterCard and AMEX are accepted.

Nestled between Atlanta's turn of the century residential neighborhoods of Candler Park and Inman Park, Little Five Points has been called Atlanta's "Village" for its unique array of businesses, events and people. "Little Five" is the place where people from every venue can come see and be seen; where Atlanta's past meets its future.

One of the landmark shops in Little Five Points is Abbadabba's, where Janice Abernethy has been providing comfort footwear, fine gifts, and designer jewelry since 1979. The emphasis on comfort started with Birkenstock sandals in the beginning, and has grown to include Rockport, Clarks and others. The trained sales staff can assure proper fit, an important part of making sure your feet will be as comfortable in the footwear as they can be.

Atlanta and Vicinity

The comfort shoes are complemented with an array of fashion and style, such as knee-high Zodiac boots, Victorian laced grannies, and chunkier, mod styles. This unusual footwear demands unusual clothes and scarves, leggings, hose and socks, along with the latest "NY/LA" styles in tops, skirts and dresses, and Abbadabba's has it all.

For years the store brimmed with a wild array of other products, leaving little room for customers to make their way through it all. Last year, a long-planned expansion was made downstairs, into what is now known as the "Wizard's Cellar." Here you can find the cards, toys, fantasy gifts, kaleidoscopes, star globes, chimes and "wonderstuff" which once cluttered the upstairs store. Visitors to the cellar can touch "magic stones," feel the Wizard's pet iguana, and wander in a fantasyland environment.

Stop in and visit both stores. Watch for the popular feline security director, Wo Shi-huan Ma, who may let you pet him if he's off duty. And while you are here, check out the other stores, clubs, bars and restaurants and find out for yourself why Little Five Points is the best little time in Atlanta!

FOLK•ART IMPORTS
25 Bennett Street
Atlanta, GA 30309
Tel. (404) 352-2656
Hrs: Mon. - Fri.   11:00 a.m. - 6:00 p.m.
　　　Saturday   11:00 a.m. - 5:00 p.m.
Visa and MasterCard are accepted.

Folk•Art Imports, a part of the Bennett Street group of shops, is like a tiny museum in which you are free to touch everything. Much of the folk art comes from South and Central America, collected by Veronica Kaplan during her travels.

You will see many possible gifts among the shelf pieces and clothing accessories as you wend your way through the fascinating displays of Folk•Art Imports. Take your time exploring this comprehensive collection of pottery, baskets, textiles, hammered copper and jewelry from other cultures. There are groups of miniatures which replicate aspects of other civilizations. Every piece in the store has a story. If you wish, Ms. Kaplan will add a detailed written description of the origin and crafting of the piece to go along with it as it leaves the store for a new home. Many of the items here are used in current home-decorating in what is called the "Southwestern" style of interiors. There are Zapotec rugs and Guatemalan "huipiles" which are visually stunning.

There's a trip to other cultures in store for you when you enter the Folk•Art Imports shop. It offers the cream of what many countries have to offer in the visual arts, assembled by a collector who wants to share with you what she has found.

FRAGILE
175 Mt. Vernon Highway
Atlanta, GA 30328
Tel. (404) 257-1323
Hrs: Mon. - Sat   10:00 a.m.- 6:00 p.m.
Evening Bridal Registry by Appointment.
MasterCard, Visa and AMEX are accepted.

Once you walk into this shop you won't be able to stop moving as you try and take in the vast array of fine gifts available. In this carefully lit, well organized setting all pieces, whether china, crystal or silver, are shown to their best advantage.

Begun as the owners' desire to run a small, independent business where the customer could be well served, this shop has grown into exactly that. Whether it is crystal, china, or flatware, there is a wide variety of traditional and contemporary designs. China includes Classic Rosenthal, Fitz and Floyd, Lenox, Villeroy and Boch and Andre Putnam, and many more. Crystal, encompassing a full range of prices, includes Orrefors, Gorham and Costa Bode, just to name a few. In addition to stemware there are vases, bowls, decanters, candlesticks and serving pieces. One wall holds a display of 120 patterns of flatwear including stainless, silverplate and silver from such artists as George Jensen, Ricci and Reed and Barton. If it is giftware you are after there is a wide range including china and silver baby gifts, picture frames in lucite, silver and leather and an extensive group of lucite serving pieces.

Along with all of these items, the warm and inviting staff offer free gift wrap and local delivery as well as UPS mailing service. Whether it is a late evening appointment for a bridal registry or a telephone order for one teacup, this staff will do anything they can to help you. Come, browse and be excited by this gift store; you'll soon see why it was picked as a "Best Choice" for Georgia.

GABBIES FASHION AND GIFT BOUTIQUE, 965 Main Street, Atlanta, GA. Tel. (404) 469-1995. Gabbies Fashion and gift Boutique offers Victorian elegance in the form of hat boxes, eyelet curtains and white iron beds. Displayed amid collectible dolls and Black Hills gold are Tom Clark's Gnomes and Woodspirits from the Cairn Studios.

GIFTS EXTRAORDINAIRE, LTD., 1026 Perimeter Mall, Atlanta, GA. Tel. (404) 395-9575. This gift shop offers a wide assortment of decorative accessories such as metal sculpture, tapestries, paintings and prints. You'll find exceptional pottery, statuary and museum reproductions.

HOSPITALITY HOUSE
Sandy Springs Plaza
6255 Roswell Road Northeast
Atlanta, GA 30328
Tel. (404) 255-0262
Hrs: Mon. - Sat. 9:30 a.m. - 6:00 p.m.
Visa, MasterCard and AMEX are accepted.

Style and Southern hospitality combine in this gift shop, which has operated for almost two decades in Sandy Springs Plaza. The variety of gift and paper items is large, with selections ranging from fine crystal to inexpensive but tasteful tokens to mark an occasion.

Hospitality House greets you with potpourris and fragrances that change with the season, its bright, well lit aisles lined with open displays that invite browsing. The staff

Atlanta and Vicinity

is obviously proud of their store, and what it carries, sharing that enthusiasm with the customers as they seek the right gift for the occasion. Perhaps one third of the floor space is devoted to paper items, including cards and things for party decorations. There is an engraving department which handles stationery, wedding invitations and similar special orders. You can contemplate the beauty of Astral and Miller Rogoska crystal, look at many porcelain pieces crafted in Europe and the Orient, or examine Royal Worcester Spode cookware. There is a gallery for Virginia Metalcrafters brass and many other items including a large selection of picture frames.

The variety and excellence of the selections make it a joy to shop at Hospitality House, where ideas for gracious living and gifts for special people come to fruition. The shop offers gift wrapping and shipping to complement the cheerful personal service you will receive in the sales area of the store. There is a second location for Hospitality House in the Buckhead area.

HOUSE OF DENMARK'S BUTIKKEN
GIFT GALLERY
1919 Piedmont Road Northeast
Atlanta GA, 30324
Tel. (404) 876-4815
Hrs: Mon.-Sat. 10:00 a.m. to 6:00 p.m.
   Thursday Open until 9:00 p.m.
Visa, Mastercard, AMEX and personal checks are accepted.

When you appreciate art, it's one thing to visit it in a museum, but it's quite another affair to live with it every day. Discover House of Denmark's Butikken Gift Gallery and see how easy it is.

For close to twenty years the House of Denmark has been a major source for fine contemporary Scandinavian furniture. The Butikken Gift Gallery shows how everyday objects can and should be works of art. Here, you can see the hand of the artist in tableware, decanters, candlesticks, pepper mills, spice racks, and jewelry. It's an absolute treat to visit this shop, where everything has been hand picked as a distinct work of beauty. Many of the items have been displayed in the Museum of Modern Art, but are truly timeless in their design. An example is the Alvar Aalto vase, an ageless design created in 1936. You'll find similar quality in the many limited edition art pieces and collectors' items from Rosenthal. Featured are designers such as Marcello Morandini, Michael Boehm and Dorothy Hafner, whose works are internationally known and sought by discriminating collectors. Famous Danish artist Björn Windblad stops by now and then to sign his work.

The style and presentation in this beautiful department resemble the respected Den Permanente gallery of Copenhagen. The delicate sound of water flowing from a fountain is just one of the environmental touches that make Butikken so special. From museum quality collectibles to kitchen utensils and gifts, you always find something extraordinary at Butikken.

HAIR SALON

BACKSTAGE LTD.
861 Oak Street Southwest
Atlanta, GA 30310
Tel. 404 758-CURL.
Hrs: Mon. - Fri. 10:00 a.m. -7:00 p.m.
     Saturday   9:00 a.m. - 4:00 p.m.
Visa and MasterCard are accepted.

Personal attention and skill always make the difference in hair salons, and the high degree of both at Backstage Ltd. is the reason so many women keep coming back. If you are not happy with your hair style, give the skilled stylists at Backstage a try.

Backstage features precision hair cutting by four master barbers. Backstage has built quite a reputation for itself in the five years it has been operating. It is known for its participation in an annual hair care show. Busy customers can

Atlanta and Vicinity

get in and out quickly, but for those who have time to indulge, there are also available pedicures, sculptured nails and facials. An expert color technician is on duty and there's always someone around who can do hair weaving and braiding with flair. You can also take home fine hair care products. As a technician for Avlon "Affirm" hair care products, owner Sylvia Wright can attend to every hair care need. The atmosphere is relaxing and pleasant. The comfortable waiting area is separate from the work station area. A special air filtration system keeps permanent wave solution odors out of the air. The ample parking is another nice touch.

Students and senior citizens can take advantage of a fifteen percent discount Monday through Wednesday. Another bonus is that Backstage will gladly direct you to the best restaurants in the area. Head to toe, the Backstage means beauty.

HARDWARE STORE

HIGHLAND HARDWARE
1045 North Highland Avenue Northeast
Atlanta, GA 30306
Tel. (404) 872-4466
    FAX 876-1941
Hrs: Mon. - Sat. 8:30 a.m. - 6:00 p.m.
    Sunday   12:30 p.m. - 4:30 p.m.
Visa, MasterCard and Servistar Card are accepted.

It's not every hardware store that is recommended by former President and woodworking expert Jimmy Carter as his store of choice. When owners Chris and Sharon Bagby, both graduates of Georgia Tech, founded Highland Hardware in 1978 they began adding little things, such as woodworking tools and supplies, the newsletter *Wood News*, workshops and seminars, top of the line tools, and a thriving mail order business. The list of accomplishments goes on and includes moving across the street from the original store into larger quarters with architecture and heritage befitting a most unusual hardware store.

The interior of the 5200 square feet of retail space is highlighted by skylights, hardwood floors, two oak staircases and a 1000 square foot mezzanine with an old fashioned wooden spindle railing. The atmosphere is that of an old fashioned hardware store. The two major foci are woodworking supplies, including a broad range of imported and domestic tools, a good selection of native hardwoods, and traditional hardware supplies. The Bagbys believe the more people they introduce to the hobby of woodworking, the more their business will flourish. They offer workshops and seminars during the spring and fall led by well known experts in the woodworking field, including Tage Frid, Irish woodturner Liam O'Neill and Japanese master Toshio Odate.

Customers also receive help from the staff including Product Engineer Zach Etheridge who teaches a series of basic skills workshops, Tool Sales Manager Brad Packard, horticulturist Phil Colson and Tony DiLeo whose specialties are turning and carving. If you're in need of tips on woodworking, hardware supplies or if you just want to sightsee in a unique, old fashioned store which has been officially inducted into the "Hardware Hall of Fame" by *Mother Earth News*, stop by Highland Hardware.

Atlanta and Vicinity

JEWELRY STORES

JODY
110 East Andrews Drive, Suite 112
Atlanta, GA 30305
Tel. (404) 233-3226
Hrs: Mon. - Sat. 10:00 a.m. - 6:00 p.m.
Visa and MasterCard are accepted.

Native Atlantan Jody Weatherly has traveled nationally and internationally to get special novelty pieces for her unusual shop. The Manhattan style boutique is crammed full, with an enormous variety of costume, fashion jewelry and accessories. You'll find the unusual as well as established lines. Jody likes to give young designers an opportunity. Well over 250 lines of jewelry are represented, including earrings, necklaces, bracelets, pins, scarves, pocketbooks, etc.

Designer lines of work encompass names like Ciner, Carolee, Swarovski, Katrina, Nash & Nash and Lunch at the Ritz. Accessory lovers will revel in the variety of Christopher Ross belts and handcast buckles, gift pieces from Kirks Folley from France, hand painted shirts by Nancy Dubin and Julie Hawks, and animal prints from Janet Cowart. Smashing leather purses are imported from Australia, as are other gift items, hairbows and artsy barrettes.

Jody's staff takes a personal interest in helping you discover the accessories that can perfect your favorite outfits. You are even invited to bring in your wardrobe combinations to find the best accessories for your needs. You can take your time, trying on everything that strikes your fancy. You'll find a whimsical something for every holiday and seasonal event, as well as items such as the solid brass earrings and native designed pieces with semi-precious stones. Everything is fairly priced.

MIDDLETON AND LANE JEWELERS, INC.
6027 Sandy Springs Circle
Atlanta, GA 30328
Tel. (404) 256-0253
Hrs: Tue. - Sat. 10:00 a.m. - 6:00 p.m.
Visa, MasterCard, AMEX and Discover are accepted.

Ancient techniques of metal working come alive in this little shop, where two artisans turn out contemporary jewelry and restore old pieces. The work of Middleton and Lane is often breathtaking in its beauty.

The artists are Ron Middleton, who has a broad background in jewelry work, and Norma Lane, a metalsmith and a jewelry designer. A large part of their business is done on commission, so the contents of the display cases are rather modest. In the same way, the outside of the shop looks like a neighborhood store, but you will find a vast difference inside when you enter and begin looking through the volumes of photos of past custom work. With access to the best quality diamonds, and to fine silver and gold, the artists can turn out whatever you desire, from the most avant garde of designs to traditional or even antique pieces with just a nuance of the contemporary. They also use some new alloys, such as a striking combination of stainless steel and silver. This is a quality repair shop as well as a place for the creation of jewelry.

A specialty of Ms. Lane is design of neck pieces in sterling silver, pendants and earrings in fourteen karat gold, and raised silver pieces which are one of her design features. Middleton does much of the wax and casting work, specializing in rings and pendants. Whatever you would like done in this shop, whether it be the design and execution of a new piece of jewelry, or the repair of an heirloom, you will find the design distinguished and the repair perfect.

Atlanta and Vicinity

KITCHEN SUPPLIES

KITCHEN FARE
2385 Peachtree Road
Peachtree Battle Shopping Center
Atlanta, GA 30305
Tel. (404) 233-8849
Hrs: Mon. - Thu.   10:00 a.m. - 8:00 p.m.
     Fri., Sat.   10:00 a.m. - 6:00 p.m.
Plus an evening cooking school.
Visa, MasterCard and AMEX are accepted.

"I should have come here first!" This is the phrase which is so often said by new customers of Laura and Gert Shapiro's Kitchen Fare. The Shapiro's sleek, contemporary shop is for the serious cook. It offers over 10,000 culinary products and expert advice to accompany each item. Kitchen Fare is a haven for those seeking quality kitchen tools and accessories.

    Kitchen Fare carries an extensive selection of bakeware, Magnalite Professional Cookware, Robot-Coupe and all of the accompanying accessories. The Cuisinart accessories are stocked for all models. The sought after French line of Jean Couzon stainless steel serving pieces, including table settings, are available. Beauty and function go hand in hand in these products. A mind boggling array of pepper mills line the shop shelves. Exotically shaped molds, fish poachers, cappuccino machines, battery operated flour sifters and 100% cotton towels are but a few of the many items available to meet your every need at Kitchen Fare.

    Cooking classes are held four nights a week, taught by Atlanta area food professionals. The classes are in tune with the times, offering simple, hearty and delicious recipes. The classes begin at 7:00 p.m. at Kitchen Fare and run until approximately 9:30 p.m. with one break. Each cooking class includes printed recipes and a tasting session. On class night, students are given a 10% discount on regularly priced merchandise. Ample parking is available. Kitchen Fare truly is "Your full-service Kitchen Shop."

MARKET

SEVANANDA
1111 Euclid Avenue
Atlanta, GA 30307
Tel. (404) 681-2831
Hrs: Mon. - Sat. 10:00 a.m. - 9:00 p.m.
       Sunday   12:00 noon - 8:00 p.m.

In order to live up to its name, Sevananda (a Sanskrit word meaning "service is bliss") provides the highest degree of service to its customers and members in a spirit of cooperation. Sevananda, the oldest and largest food cooperative in the Southeast, has been providing wholesome food and grocery items at reasonable prices since 1975.

The staff of Sevananda operates the store in an efficient and helpful manner, while offering a complete selection of products for natural living. You'll find the largest selection of organic produce and grains in Atlanta, as well as hundreds of herbs and spices; nuts, seeds and dried fruits; natural teas and juices and a wide variety of soy products. In addition to food items, you'll discover the latest in alternative books and magazines. If you'd like to look, smell and feel the way it was intended, you'll be pleased to experience the natural cosmetics and body products section of this spacious store. Cookware, utensils and household supplies for your log cabin—or to make your condo feel like one—are available. Sevananda offers all this at reasonable prices because of its collective purchasing practices. This store, conveniently located in the heart of the idyllic Little Five Points community, also provides an avenue

Atlanta and Vicinity

for treating the earth in a positive way through its newspaper and glass recycling center.

You can join the 2,000 others and become a member of the cooperative, entitling you to a 10% discount on all items purchased, or become a work member and receive a discount of 30% in exchange for working three hours per week. Whatever your connection, it will be a blissful one at Sevananda.

MUSEUM

ATLANTA HISTORICAL SOCIETY
3101 Andrews Dr. Northwest
Atlanta, GA 30305
Tel. (404) 261-1837
Hrs: Mon. - Sat.   9:00 a.m. - 5:30 p.m.
      Sunday   12:00 noon - 5:00 p.m.

Join a city wide family of people who know that Atlanta's exciting future is a reflection of its glorious past when you visit the Atlanta Historical Society.

Walk through Walter McElreath Hall and view two permanent exhibits: Atlanta and the War: 1861-1865; and Atlanta Resurgens, a tour of Atlanta from Reconstruction to the present. McElreath Hall also features an extensive library and archives and museum gift shop. Another important place to visit is Swan House. Listed in the National Register of Historic Places, this house was designed by Philip Trammell Shutze and is complete with the furnishings of the original owners. If you have the time, visit the Tullie Smith Farm restoration, a restored 1840s plain-style Georgia farmhouse, with separate kitchen, smoke house, barn, corn crib, log cabin, working blacksmith shop and flower, vegetable and herb gardens. Tour the house and see spinning, weaving and open hearth cooking. Included in admission is an unguided tour of the thirty-two acres of historical gardens, woodland trails and Garden for Peace.

You can join in celebrating Atlanta's past, present and future by visiting the Atlanta Historical Society. If you happen to be downtown, there is a convenient Information Center at 140 Peachtree Street in Margaret Mitchell Square, (404) 238-0655. This facility provides downtown visitors with community information about historic sites and programs. An original video of Atlanta history and special exhibits are available in the Information Center, housed in the restored Hillyer Building, built in 1911.

MUSIC

WAX 'N' FACTS
423 Moreland Avenue Northeast
Atlanta, GA 30307
Tel. (404) 525-2275
Hrs: Mon. - Sat. 12:00 noon - 7:30 p.m.

Record collectors love to browse in every record store they can find, especially the ones with personality. Wax 'n' Facts fits into this category, as well as into the category of having the most extensive collection of used recordings in Atlanta.

Located in the bohemian neighborhood of Little Five Points, Wax 'n' Facts began in 1976 as the dream of Harry DeMille and Danny Beard. Danny was a disc jockey for a local radio station in Atlanta, while Harry worked in a coffee house. Both loved music and wanted to make something out of that love. So they pooled their record collections together, shopped flea markets and opened their store. As time passed, they dropped the store's book collections (the "facts") and kept the records (the "wax"). Today, the store fills 1,800 square feet of space in a older building. The store is packed with records, tapes and compact discs in easily accessible boxes and crates. Sixty percent of the stock is used, forty percent is new. The store carries just about every kind of music, including rock, jazz, new wave, punk, country, Western and classical.

Atlanta and Vicinity

Wax 'n' Facts carries one of the largest collections of import recordings and 45 rpm records on the East Coast, with its specialty being English pressings. But if you can't find what you want, the store's employees will special order it or you. If you have a record for trade, bring it into the store. You can even purchase a t-shirt at Wax 'n' Facts. When you're in Atlanta, listen to Georgia State University's WRAS radio, where you'll hear many of the records Wax 'n' Facts offers.

NIGHTCLUB

JOHNNY'S HIDEAWAY
3771 Roswell Road
Atlanta, GA 30342
Tel. (404) 233-8026
Hrs: Mon.-Sun. 11:00 a.m. - 4:00 a.m.
Visa, MasterCard and AMEX are accepted.

If you enjoy the sounds of Benny Goodman, Billie Holiday and Elvis, you'll thank "Mr. E." for creating a place where you can "cut a rug" every night of the week. Owner Johnny Exposito has been running clubs since the 1960s, when he hosted acts such as Sonny & Cher, Tina Turner and the Beach Boys.

Five nights a week, those of you who were in high school during the 1930s and 40s will reminisce to the sounds of the Big Bands, jitterbugging until you drop, against a background of Gable and Gloria Swanson slides. On Wednesday and Sunday nights, you can rock around the clock with Elvis Presley, Bobby Darin and the Shirelle's to the tunes of the 1950s and 60s. You'll think you're back in the good old days surrounded by photos of Arlene Dahl, Count Basie and Johnny Maestro and the Crests. True nostalgia buffs will want to take advantage of the chance to celebrate their next anniversary or a wedding in an atmosphere Betty Boop would have chosen.

It's a relief to know that after you drop the kids off for a night of slam dancing, there is still somewhere to go where

Atlanta and Vicinity

memories are respected. All your senses will come alive at the cozy haven known as Johnny's Hideaway. You'll want to check the changing monthly calendar for special events, such as Casino Night, Free Pasta Dinner or live shows, such as The Four Freshmen and The Four Aces.

POTTERY

DONATELLI
Brookwood Square
2140 Peachtree Road
Atlanta, GA 30309
(404) 350-9154
Hrs: Mon. - Sat. 10:00 a.m. - 6:00 p.m.
Visa, MasterCard and AMEX are accepted.

If you appreciate the quality of ancient Italian craftsmanship, handed down from father to son for generations, you'll be irresistibly drawn to Donatelli. Owners Cynthia and Michael Davis have searched out the best artisans in old Italy and hand picked a fabulous array of colorful Italian pottery, conveniently available for you now at reasonable prices. The cherished tradition of skill and artistry is evident in every piece, from a dinner plate, to a vase, to the simplest teapot.

The small European style shop with its columns, archways, cherubim and softly playing classical music, charms shoppers as they browse through the collection of all imaginable pottery pieces. Umbrella stands, huge urns, statues, tiles, little bells and paperweights, plus a collection of hand-blown glassware from Spain, Mexico and Italy will captivate and delight you while you endeavor to narrow down your purchase. The pottery has a unique appeal that fits in the most traditional settings, as well as the most contemporary.

The Brookwood Square location is one of Buckhead's newest, most accessible spots. Only minutes from Midtown, it's also close to the Bennett Street shops and galleries, as well as the Atlanta Decorative Arts Center. Also for your convenience, the following services are available: bridal registry, free giftwrap, out of state orders, layaway and U.P.S.

PUBS

COUNTY CORK PUB
56 East Andrews Drive, Suite 16
Atlanta, GA 30305
Tel. (404) 262-A-BAR
Hrs: Mon. - Sat. 3:00 p.m. - 2:00 a.m.
Closed on Sunday.
Visa, MasterCard, AMEX and Carte Blanche are accepted.

County Cork Pub, 'tis a fine place to draw a yard of ale and play a game of darts while singing your favorite Irish tune. The father and daughter team of Cynthia and Art Fessenden have brought a little bit of Ireland to Dixie. The pub serves Guinness Stout on tap and a terrific bowl of Irish stew with a slab of soda bread.

Looking like an Irish second hand store, the pub's walls are laden with Irish memorabilia donated by the watering hole's many regulars. A shillalah headers the door, a sign by the entrance says "a hundred thousand times welcome" in Gaelic and a set of bag pipes rests in the corner. The booth benches are old pews from St. Joseph's in Athens and a Cork City Hall flag flies over the piano. The food is simple and simply delicious. Irish stew is served with an order of "spotted dog", that is, Irish soda bread with currants. The pub's sandwiches and salads are also tasty and hearty.

Native music plays from opening to last call. Live entertainment is from 9:00 p.m. to 1:00 p.m. Tuesday through Thursday, and there is open mike night every Monday night starting at 8:30. Whether you are Irish or not, you will be welcomed a "hundred thousand times" at the County Cork Pub.

SCRUB-A-DUB PUB
2480-2 Briarcliff Road
Atlanta, GA 30329
Tel. (404) 633-3886
Hrs: Every Day 8:30 a.m. - 11:00 p.m.

It's never been much fun to air your dirty laundry in public, but now, thanks to twenty-six year old Haris Lender, it can be. Just bring your laundry down to Scrub-A-Dub Pub and do your laundry while you partake of a beer or two and play pool, watch videos or listen to live entertainment.

Haris, who had worked part time in a pub/laundromat before moving to Atlanta and opening her own, wanted a place where people could do their laundry and relax at the same time. Fitted with large, heavy duty modern washing equipment, the laundromat section is clean, bright and filled with plants.

The pub itself is very separate from the laundromat even though the machines are just a few steps away. Decorated in cool green and mauve tones, with laundry memorabilia covering the walls, the pub boasts TV's, videos, live entertainment and a wide variety of drinks and snacks. While snacking on some of the hot, New York style pretzels, steamed quarter pound hot dogs or pizza, sample the imported beers such as Amstel, Corona, Guinness, Fosters or Heineken. Bud and Bud Lite are offered on tap and wine and wine coolers are also available. Wednesday night is free dryer night, so come down and have some fun while you do your laundry.

Atlanta and Vicinity

RACEWAY

ROAD ATLANTA
Racetrack location:
Route 1-Highway 53
Braselton, GA 30517
Tel. (404) 967-6143
      (404) 881-8233 in Atlanta
Call for the current schedule of events.

Known as the Southeast's premier road racing facility, and one of the busiest tracks in the U.S., Road Atlanta offers 2.52 miles of asphalt track for cars, motorcycles, and go-karts. It hosts a wide variety of major professional and amateur racing events, including the International Motor Sports Association's Camel GT series for sports prototype racing cars, the Sports Car Club of America's National Championship Valvoline Runoffs, the American Motorcycle Association's Camel Pro series, and numerous other events for vintage, exotic and high performance sports cars.

The Road Atlanta Driver Training Center offers numerous curriculums of defensive driving, advanced handling, and IMSA and SCCA approved road racing schools, along with custom designed driver training programs. Thousands of drivers have improved their skills and learned important safe driving techniques at the center. Road Atlanta's amenities include a meeting room with a seating capacity of 200, catering for special events and corporate outings, recreational and playground areas for kids and a scenic picnic area. A gift shop carries a complete selection of racing paraphernalia.

Come and enjoy the thrill of roadracing at this first class facility. Road Atlanta is located in Braselton on Highway 53, ten miles south of Gainesville, less than an hour North of Atlanta on Interstate 85; take Exit 49.

RESTAURANTS

ACACIA
7 Concourse Parkway
Atlanta, GA 30328
Tel. (404) 395-3900 Ext. 6603
Hrs: Lunch
   Mon. -Fri.   11:30 a.m. - 2:30 p.m.
   Dinner
   Mon. - Sat. 6:00 p.m. - 11:00 p.m.
All major credit cards are accepted.

    The Acacia has bloomed like the sweet flower chosen as a namesake. In the short time Acacia has been open it has accumulated award after award for its fine food. The Acacia is fast becoming known for outstanding preparation of food and excellent service.
    The full attention of the Acacia staff is given to you from the time you enter until you step out the door. Your host will bring a crock of marinated olives and a basket of crisp cheese toast for your first flavors while you consider the menu. Black Bean Soup with sour cream and chopped onion or Chicken and Sausage Gumbo are good choices for starters to your meal. The seviche of Sea Scallops Salad comes highly recommended with its marinade of lemon and lime juice, fresh peppers, olive oil and fresh herbs. Grill Specialties include fresh garden vegetables and Acacia distinctive rice which combines sautéed rice, red peppers, asparagus tips and black olives. The fish selections are outstanding, with grilled coho salmon in lemon butter topping the list. Grilled Georgia mountain trout with toasted almond butter is a favorite. The House Specialty is Veal Acacia.
    The desserts of Acacia are an experience in themselves. The Frozen Melon Souffle with sliced fresh lemon and The Perfect Lemon Souffle are to be savored. The hot souffles are to be remembered and reordered. Consider Acacia's hot

Atlanta and Vicinity

Cappuccino Souffle, Strawberry Souffle or Orange Souffle. The final detail of Acacia's attention to your dining pleasure is presented to you as a chocolate dipped strawberry which accompanies your check.

ADDIS ETHIOPIAN RESTAURANT, 453 Moreland Avenue Northeast, Atlanta, GA. Tel. (404) 523-4748. Discover the mystery of an ancient culture at the Addis Ethiopian Restaurant. Perfectly seasoned beef, chicken and lamb are featured on a menu which also includes a variety of vegetarian dishes.

ALFREDO'S
1989 Cheshire Bridge Road Northeast
Atlanta, GA 30324
Tel. (404) 876-1380
Hrs: Mon. - Thu.   5:00 p.m. -11:00 p.m.
     Fri. - Sat.   5:00 p.m. - 11:30 p.m.
     Sunday   5:00 p.m. - 10:00 p.m.
Visa, MasterCard, AMEX, Discover and AirPlus are accepted.

The atmosphere is *trattoria*, a relaxed, homey neighborhood place. The food is superb Italian. The waiters wear tuxedos and joke as only Italians do. Alfredo's began in 1974 as a little known neighborhood restaurant but soon became one of Atlanta's finest Italian restaurants. Many people still consider it their "home away from home."

Although the setting is formal, with white tablecloths, glittering candles, intimately grouped tables and waiters in evening clothes; the atmosphere is friendly. The food is as good as home cooked, too. Begin your meal with one of the eight appetizers offered including: Roast Peppers & Anchovies or the Mozzarella alla Marinara. Dinners include the Specialty of the House, veal served eleven different ways; Steak Pizzaiola, strip steak sauteed in spices, tomato sauce and mushrooms; eight types of pasta; seafood; pork; poultry and vegetables, including Eggplant Parmigiana. All meals are served with a dish of "Italian baked potato," a side of spaghetti with sauce.

Everyone's favorite, homemade Italian Cheesecake made with Ricotta cheese, is one of the fine desserts offered.

Although Alfredo's has grown in reputation over the years, the clientele remains eighty percent locals who keep coming back for more.

ATKINS PARK
794 North Highland Avenue
Atlanta, GA 30306
Tel. (404) 876-7249
Hrs: Mon. - Fri.   11:00 a.m. - 4:00 a.m.
      Saturday   10:30 a.m. - 3:00 a.m.
      Sunday   10:30 a.m. - 4:00 a.m.
Visa, MasterCard, AMEX and Diners Club are accepted.

Diners enjoy the remnants of a turn of the century community, Atkins Park, in the tree shaded sidewalks and stone gateposts still visible from the windows of Atkins Park Restaurant. The site of the present restaurant began its metamorphosis in 1922 when the house was raised by the owner, a traveling salesman, and Atkins Park Deli was built underneath. It became a popular tavern. Today the restaurant serves quality food at reasonable prices in a friendly and historic atmosphere.

Nostalgic surroundings, free use of dartboards, videogames and contemporary music set the stage for an experiential dining encounter. Featured entrees include pasta, seafood, poultry and beef, accompanied by your choice of soup or a fresh dinner salad and vegetables. House specialties include the classic Phoenix Chicken: stir fried sesame chicken and seasonal vegetables served with wild rice pilaf. The perfect way to top off your meal is with a Grand Marnier and Chocolate Mousse, a house favorite, prepared with only the finest ingredients.

Atkins Park also features a bar menu with munchies: Stuffed Spuds filled with chili and cheese; fried Cheese Sticks and Steak Fingers; a wide array of salads and sandwiches; hot dogs; simmered in dark beer and grilled, and half pound burgers. Soup lovers will be delighted with a cup or bowl of

Atlanta and Vicinity

Cioppino which may be served with fettuccine and is also on the regular menu. For an unusual dining experience stop by Atkins Park. You'll be ever grateful to the traveling salesman who started the series of events which led to such a warm, nostalgic and interesting place to dine.

AUNT CHARLEY'S
3107 Peachtree Road Northwest
Atlanta, GA 30305
Tel. (404) 231-8503
Hrs: Mon. - Fri. 11:30 a.m. - 4:00 a.m.
      Saturday   11:30 a.m. - 3:00 a.m.
      Sunday   12:30 p.m. - 4:00 a.m.
Visa, MasterCard, AMEX, Diners Club, Carte Blanche, Discover and Optima are accepted.

Aunt Charley's has been through many changes during the past thirteen years, including an expansion, more seating and Bocce Ball court outside. What hasn't changed is the friendly relaxed atmosphere, warm courteous service and terrific food. Management and staff continue to treat customers like family, one of the qualities which has given Aunt Charley's the nickname of "Buckhead's authentic neighborhood bar."

Whether you eat inside among trophies of teams sponsored by Charley's or outside on the patio, you'll enjoy lunch or dinner at this unique dining spot. Where else can you get a Bruno Burger, Buffalo Wings or a steaming bowl of award winning chili. Even the finest gourmet hot dogger has rarely been treated to such a wide variety of dogs as featured on the menu, all steamed in beer and served on a toasted bun. Sensational sandwiches and burgers can be washed down with a wide selection of domestic and imported beers. Don't forget to check the chalkboard for the daily specials. A visit to your Aunt Charley's for dinner will be met with scrumptious salads, simmering soups and international entrees: Oriental Stir Fry, Lasagne, New York Strip Bordelaise or the Chef's Special.

Atlanta and Vicinity

If you want to do something fun, check out the sports events and group trips hosted by Aunt Charley's: skiing, ball games and raft excursions. You're guaranteed good food, fun and friends.

AVANZARE
265 Peachtree Street Northeast
Atlanta, GA 30303
Tel. (404) 588-4135
Hrs: Lunch   Mon.-Fri.   11:30 a.m.-2:00 p.m.
     Dinner   Mon.-Sun.   6:00 p.m.-11:00 p.m.
Visa, MasterCard, AMEX and Diners Club are accepted.

As an Avanzare guest you will have a quality dining experience with a twist of fun added. When was the last time you scooped up a fork full of home style pasta under the watchful eye of a carnival colored clown fish? Or, when have you enjoyed a free form pizza, while sea life and fish dart about in an aquarium next to your table? Avanzare is the innovative new restaurant located on the Terrace Level of the Hyatt Regency Atlanta.

Avanzare is full of delightful surprises. An eat in or take out antipasto buffeteria features a daily changing menu of fifteen items. A salt-water aquarium fills one whole wall of the restaurant and is the third largest of its kind in the Southeast. From the Italian motif tile floor to the glazed cementitious pots of bright flowers, Anvanzare is refreshing and innovative.

Under the skillful hand of chef Antonello Bertoni of Varese, Italy, Avanzare offers contemporary Italian cuisine featuring a selection of unique pasta, seafood, veal and beef dishes. First tastes of the menu include Avanzare's drink of the gods, chilled asti spumante and fruit nectars. You may choose a main entree from delicious seafood, veal or beef and special pasta dishes such as Pennette All'Ortolana, a quill tube pasta with sun dried tomatoes, artichokes, parcini mushrooms and pesto. Avanzare's signature dessert is Ambrosia Truffle Torte, a flourless, rich chocolate torte made with ambrosia dark sweet

Atlanta and Vicinity

chocolate. Become friends with Avanzare, Atlanta's innovative new Italian restaurant and Antipasto Buffeteria.

BABY DOE'S MATCHLESS MINE, 2239 Powers Ferry Road, Atlanta, GA. Tel. (404) 955-3637. Enter the 1800s for a panoramic view of modern Atlanta. The dining at Baby Doe's is as matchless as it is hearty; steaks, seafood, and roast duckling are served for lunch and dinner.

BONES STEAK AND SEAFOOD, 3130 Piedmont Road Northeast, Atlanta, GA. Tel. (404) 237-2663. Bones Steak and Seafood offers award winning dining in Atlanta's entertainment and restaurant center. *The New York Times* recommended Bones for the "best steaks and lamb chops in the Southeast."

BOSCO'S
2293 Peachtree Road
Atlanta, GA 30309
Tel. (404) 351-3600
Hrs: Open every night at 6:00 p.m.
Also,
HEMINGWAY'S TERRACE
3081 East Shadowlawn
Atlanta, GA 30305
Tel. (404) 231-0900
Hrs: Open every night at 6:00 p.m.

Bosco's Ristorante Italiano is one of Atlanta's most exciting and popular restaurants. Chef Luigi Bosco and Maitre d' Enzo Menghini offer Atlantans and visitors alike an entertaining evening of superb dining in a warm and romantic atmosphere.

Hemingway's Terrace is a fine dining seafood restaurant, also located in Buckhead. Popular among Atlanta's elite, Hemingway's Terrace is a very exciting restaurant which features fresh fish and shellfish with other interesting specialties.

Atlanta and Vicinity

Located in Buckhead, Bosco's offers elegant dining without requiring jackets and ties. Both Bosco's and Hemingway's Terrace are located within 10 minutes of all major hotels in the area. For true excellence in Italian cuisine and the best in seafood, don't miss Bosco's and Hemingway's Terrace while you're in Atlanta.

BOSTON SEA PARTY
3820 Roswell Road
Atlanta, GA 30342
Tel. (404) 233-1776
Hrs: Mon. - Thu.   6:00 p.m. - 10:00 p.m.
     Fri., Sat.   5:30 p.m. - 11:00 p.m.
     Sunday   5:30 p.m. - 9:00 p.m.
Visa, MasterCard, AMEX and Diners Club are accepted.

It's about time for you to experience the Boston Sea Party, a reenactment of the buffet spread before our founding parents at the Green Lantern Tavern, immediately following the Boston Tea Party in the late 1770s. The slogan "A restaurant who's time has come again" makes one curious to find out what's behind the conceptual doors of an historical nautical dining establishment.

Bricked archways adorned with stained glass, candlelight and an immense open fireplace warmly welcome customers to one of the most unusual dining experiences they'll encounter. But the main attraction is the buffet tables or boat shaped piers of the best all-you-can-eat feast you've ever laid eyes on. The upscale buffet features Pier1, a cold appetizer with a six foot salad bar, eight feet of cold appetizers, and shrimp, oysters on the half shell, caviar, smoked salmon and pickled herring. And that's just the beginning. Pier 2 is the place where you'll dig in to seventeen different items including snow crab legs, barbecue baby back ribs, clam chowder and more. If you've a hearty appetite you'll have room for the main entree of your selection; fresh whole Maine lobster, filet mignon or fresh seafood catch are examples which are served table side. Hold on to your hats for Pier 3, the dessert buffet, which is

Atlanta and Vicinity

laden with tasty treats, such as chocolate mousse, cheescake, carrot cake and a variety of fruits and cheeses.

The Boston Sea Party is a wonderful and very reasonably priced place to go for a festive occasion with a group of friends. It also offers a great way to get a true flavor for our historical roots. It is a popular place to dine, so please make reservations in advance.

BUSY BEE CAFE
810 Martin Luther King Jr. Drive
Atlanta, GA 30314
Tel. (404) 525-9212
Hrs: Mon.-Sat.   11:15 a.m.-7:00 p.m.

Back in the days when the cry for civil rights was met by snarling police dogs and water cannons, the Busy Bee Cafe often hosted Martin Luther King, Jr., and other leaders who regularly came in to enjoy a meal. Today, the Busy Bee holds a prominent place in history, and it is also a standout in the realm of good soul food.

Sports figures such as Hank Aaron and Pedro Guerrero, political leaders such as Mayor Maynard Jackson and a variety of prominent musicians return from time to time to savor the soulful Busy Bee cooking that has been an Atlanta tradition for thirty-seven years. Everyone is welcome. Guests can dive into a steaming plate of ham hocks and chitterlings like they've never tasted anywhere else. The menu changes daily and ranges from meat loaf to something as exotic as a pig ear sandwich. Try the ham hocks with fried corn, collard greens and candied yams. The vegetables are always fresh, which makes the string beans, blackeye peas and fried corn extra tasty. The lemonade is always freshly squeezed. For dessert, you'll want to be sure to taste the special sweet potato pie.

The original location was next door, but even at the second location it is a relatively small restaurant with seating for only sixty people. The interior is homey, clean and very soulful. No matter what your roots are, if you have memories of being in your grandmother's kitchen just before Sunday dinner, this place will feel like home to you.

CAFÉ DE LA PLACE

2140 Peachtree Road Northwest, Suite I
Atlanta, GA 30309
Tel. (404) 351-3792
Hrs: Lunch (Brunch on Sat., Sun.)
       Mon. - Sun. 11:30 a.m. - 2:30 p.m.
       Dinner
       Mon. - Sat. 5:30 p.m. - 11:00 p.m.
       Sunday   5:30 p.m. - 10:00 p.m.

All major credit cards are accepted.

The Café De La Place, a recently opened country French restaurant, with moderate prices, has become the new chic place to be seen. Although reservations are not required by the management, it behooves dinner customers to make them because of the café's growing popularity.

Located in Buckhead's newest upscale shopping center, the restaurant is easily accessible and provides ample parking for its customers. The description of outdoor café fits, even indoors! One is immediately impressed with the light and airy atmosphere which transforms into a cozy evening spot for intimate rendezvous. You may want to order a beverage from the well stocked bar before beginning your meal with an appetizer of soup de jour or the favorite Huitres Helena á la Cream, oysters dipped in milk and flour and topped with a white cream sauce. Cold appetizers include a country style duck pâté. Entrées, served with salad, potatoes and vegetables, include veal, beef, lamb, chicken, duck, rabbit and seafood selections. All desserts are made fresh daily in the exhibition kitchen, including the superb Creme Caramel.

Large parties are welcomed. The high ceilinged interior, with its twenty-four foot mural of Toulouse-Lautrec scenes, has a seating capacity of eighty. After tasting the exquisite food and meeting the friendly staff you'll know why the Café De La Place has become a favorite of natives and visitors alike.

Atlanta and Vicinity

CAFÉ INTERMEZZO
1845 Peachtree Road Northeast
Atlanta, GA 30309
Tel. (404) 355-0411

Hrs:	Mon. - Thu.	1:30 a.m. - 2:00 a.m.
	Friday	11:30 a.m. - 3:00 a.m.
	Saturday	10:00 a.m. - 3:00 a.m.
	Sunday	10:00 a.m. - 1:00 a.m.

Visa, MasterCard and AMEX are accepted.

It's a descendant of the traditional European coffeehouse, a breath of Europe on Atlanta's Peachtree Road where you can linger to talk, read or just relax and think as you sip fine coffees and enjoy European pastries and light classical music. As the focal point of this renovated old Atlanta building stands "the world's largest espresso/cappuccino machine", a massive polished brass structure over six feet high and wide.

An English bust of Beethoven looks over the relaxed habitués of Café Intermezzo, as classical music plays softly among the sounds of a steam jet frothing milk on the machine, people talking in animated conversation, and footsteps on the dark pine floor. The premise of this European café, like its predecessor and the first of the tradition, Koschitsky's in seventeenth-century Vienna, is to provide a place for people to enhance and contemplate the fine art of living.

The menu offers a tremendous list of coffees, both filtered American-style and espresso-based, as well as the Turkish "broth" which brought coffee into its popular use. Eight different teas, freshly-brewed, and over forty-two different pastries which change in variety daily in their enchanting glass European display, enhance the possible choices for your experience. The entrée menu includes Jaffles, a wonderful Australian sandwich which is grilled similarly to a waffle and which has a variety of fillings, such as broccoli, cheese and mushrooms. The new menu also includes a variety of freshly-made Italian dishes, including fresh pasta entrées with the pasta made on-premise using an ABC pasta extruder. Café Intermezzo also offers wines, imported beers and liquers with a full bar.

You'll feel Café Intermezzo's warmth as you step through the doors, like stepping into Europe of another time. Tables clothed in white under glass tops, soft classical music, high, arched ceilings with large fabric banners welcome you to Café Intermezzo, and invite you again and again.

CAFE LAWRENCE
2888 Buford Highway
Atlanta, GA 30329
Tel. (404) 320-7756

Hrs:	Lunch	Mon. - Sat.	10:00 a.m. - 3:00 p.m.
	Dinner	Mon. - Thu.	5:00 p.m. - 10:00 p.m.
	Dinner	Fri., Sat.	5:00 p.m. - 11:00 p.m.

Visa, MasterCard and AMEX are accepted.

Cafe Lawrence is a beautiful Arabic restaurant with excellent food, entertainment and service. The rich aroma of foreign spices, the exotic sounds of middle Eastern music and the graceful movements of the belly dance will transport you into a world far beyond Atlanta.

As you enter the Cafe Lawrence you will notice a blackboard chalked with the night's specials. Take note of it as many of the delicious dishes served at Cafe Lawrence will be written only on this board. You may see an entree of Cabbage Rolls listed on the board. There's not a dish like it in any other area restaurant. Young, tender leaves of cabbage are wrapped firmly around lean forcemeat formed into long cylinders. A yogurt sauce is served with the rolls making a sassy, tantalizing dish. Another speciality to be found only at Cafe Lawrence is the Seafood Tahini made with large shrimp, scallops, garlic, lemon and rice. The Kibbi and Grape Leaves comes highly recommended. This dish consists of a mixture of bulgar wheat, ground sirloin, diced onions and spices, kneaded together then filled with ground beef, onions and pine nuts. You will be served one baked kibbi, one fried kibbi which is served with six grape leaves, yogurt sauce and salad. Desserts include Harissa, a cake of honey, raisins and walnuts. Finish your meal with a cup of strong Turkish coffee.

Atlanta and Vicinity

A belly dancing room provides relaxing entertainment at Cafe Lawrence. You will be seated on couches low to the floor and under a big tent. A fireplace is in the center of the room. The feeling of being in a Middle Eastern house is very real. Cafe Lawrence will cater large parties.

CAPO'S CAFE
992 Virginia Avenue Northeast
Atlanta, GA 30306
Tel. (404) 876-5655
Hrs: Mon. - Thu.   5:30 p.m. - 10:45 p.m.
      Fri., Sat.   5:30 p.m. - 11:00 p.m.
      Sunday   5:00 p.m. - 10:30 p.m.
Visa, MasterCard and AMEX are accepted.

Reviewed as a "Best Place To Eat For Under $10.00," Capo's Cafe is a restaurant where your satisfaction means everything. Both the owner and his excellent staff have engendered a loyalty from their customers that has kept some returning for over ten years.

From the two vintage park benches placed in front of the restaurant, giving the air of a sidewalk cafe, to the dark green interiors creating an intimate, warm atmosphere, good food and a friendly, courteous staff make dining at Capo's a pleasurable experience. Homemade bread is baked daily, and the Chicken Diable is the most frequently requested entree. Two boneless breasts of chicken are the base for this luscious dish, which are then stuffed with mushrooms and cream cheese, topped with Dijon mustard, walnuts and brown sugar. Jacob Stew is another excellent choice, with its chunks of sirloin beef and potatoes in a sour cream and dill sauce. Scallops Parisienne is a tantalizing dish of bay scallops in a Parisienne sauce, lightly seasoned with tarragon and baked with a mild Swiss cheese. Fresh boned Georgia trout is also on the menu, baked with a walnut and herb stuffing. Salads and vegetables are also served; an excellent Ratatouille is offered with homemade sauce served hot over buttered noodles. Salad dressings are outstanding, and the Curry Cream, Blue Cheese and Poppy Seed are sold by the bottle.

Atlanta and Vicinity

Originally opened as a neighborhood cafe mainly serving local residents through word of mouth, their clientele has spread to include residents throughout Atlanta and beyond. Capo's Cafe has endeavored to maintain a friendly and personal atmosphere at the restaurant, and if a line of people waiting to be served on the weekend is any indication of success, they have surely achieved their goal.

CAST OCEAN, 6319 Jimmy Carter Boulevard, Atlanta, GA. Tel. (404) 446-1588. The Cast Ocean is recognized as one of the finest seafood restaurants in Atlanta featuring Szechwan and Mandarin cuisines. An elegant atmosphere is carried through into the large banquet facilities. Reservations are recommended.

CHANTILLY'S UPTOWN GRILL, 418 Armour Drive Northeast, Atlanta, Ga. Tel. (404) 873-5213. Chantilly's Uptown Grill offers creative American cuisine in a casually elegant atmosphere. Chantilly's is located in the Lanier Plaza Hotel and serves lunch and dinner seven days a week.

CHEFS' CAFE
2115 Piedmont Road
Atlanta, GA, 30324
Tel. (404) 872-2284

Hrs:			
Dinner	Tue.-Thu.	5:00 p.m.-10:00 p.m.
Lunch	Tue. - Fri.	11:30 a.m. - 2:30 p.m.
Dinner	Fri. - Sat.	6:00 p.m. - 11:00 p.m.
Dinner	Sunday	6:00 p.m. - 10:00 p.m.
Brunch	Sunday	10:00 a.m. - 3:00 p.m.

Visa, MasterCard and AMEX are accepted.

Chefs' Cafe is a casual restaurant with a serious kitchen! Diners at Chefs' Cafe are discriminating people who want to eat well and be comfortable. The Chefs' Cafe menu is fun, eclectic and complements the Cafe's whimsical original art decor, which is guaranteed to bring a smile.

The service is excellent, the food delicious and the ambiance full of fun at Chefs' Cafe. Menu items are served with

Atlanta and Vicinity

flair. Appetizers include the universally popular Sauteed Crab Cakes with tomato butter and jalapeño tartar sauce and the Grilled Yellow Fin Tuna marinated in olive oil, crushed garlic, fresh basil and served on watercress with roasted sweet peppers, then sprinkled with tomato and basil vinaigrette. Entrees include Pasta of the Day, using fresh pasta, fresh fish; Free Range chicken from California and certified Black Angus New York Strip with roasted garlic and fresh herb butter or black pepper, shallot and cabernet butter. The Alaska tops the dessert list, consisting of white chocolate mousse, genoise and white chocolate with raspberry sauce. The Chefs' Cafe wine list is terrific and includes twenty-five premium selections of wine, served by the glass.

Ask about Chefs' Cafe's arrangements for private parties. Reservations are suggested. Chefs' Cafe is conveniently located at Piedmont and I-75 at the foot of La Quinta Inn. The parking is good and you are only minutes from mid town theaters and concerts.

CHEQUERS BAR & GRILL, 236 Perimeter Center Parkway, Atlanta, GA. Tel. (404) 391-9383. The freshest seafood in Atlanta is flown in from all over the country, and mesquite broiled to perfection at Chequers. They also feature prime rib and steaks with live jazz Tuesday through Saturday.

CHOPSTIX
4279 Roswell Road
Atlanta, GA 30342
Tel. (404) 255-4868
Hrs: Dinner   Mon.-Sun.   6:00 p.m. 11:00 p.m.
     Lunch   Mon.-Fri.   11:00 a.m. - 2:30 p.m.
Visa, MasterCard and AMEX are accepted.

No matter how much you like chow mein and won ton, Chopstix is the kind of Chinese restaurant where you'll want try something new and exotic. That's due partly to the stylish surroundings and partly to the staff which encourages its guests to make each visit a unique one.

Each visit may be unique, but customers return for the dependably delicious food. Chopstix has become the darling of the Atlanta restaurant reviewers. The restaurant is an artful blending of contemporary atmosphere and beautiful Chinese cuisine. Every dish appears to have been garnished by an artist. The menu is large and ambitious, but you'll also find a huge variety of specials. Among the special appetizers are black pepper oysters, Chinese pasta, calamari, mussels and clams. Main dishes include Birds Nest Shrimp, a Chopstix original, Spicy Lamb, and a number of fresh fish dishes, including a remarkable fresh bass. The chef is successful in blending delicate flavors and offering a fresh approach to many old favorites.

The decor is elegant and romantic. The etched glass panel with its graceful bamboo design tells you immediately this is a restaurant with a difference. Soft gray carpet, pink linens and ultra contemporary furniture are appealing in the glow of candlelight. Chopstix is still small and intimate, so its popularity often requires making reservations.

COACH AND SIX
1776 Peachtree Street Northwest
Atlanta, GA 30309
Tel. (404) 872-6666
Hrs: Dinner   Sun. - Fri.   6:00 p.m. - 11:00 p.m.
               Saturday   6:00 p.m. - 12:00 midnight
     Lounge   Mon. - Fri.   4:30 p.m. - until closing.
Visa, Master Card, AMEX, Diners Club and Discover are accepted.

What do Coretta King, Ted Turner, the Atlanta Falcons or Jimmy Carter have in common? They are all regulars at The Coach and Six Restaurant. Known throughout the world as a first class restaurant, The Coach and Six has garnered dozens of fine dining awards. Its success was in a large part created by its owner, Beverlee Soloff Shere. Plunging into leadership of the restaurant after the death of her husband, Hank Soloff, in 1974, Ms. Shere has brought The Coach and Six into national and international stature as a world class restaurant.

Atlanta and Vicinity

The Coach and Six posted receipts in excess of four million dollars in 1986. Ms. Shere's ability to keep up with public awareness and changing tastes has kept her restaurant at the leading edge of fine dining houses. She says, "Restaurants come and go, so few survive. When The Coach first opened, the business was eighty-five percent beef. Today, it's fifty-five percent fish and seafood." The Coach's extensive menu is translated in English, Japanese, Spanish, French and German. The American Heart Association has recognized The Coach for it's "healthy heart" dishes.

The Coach and Six has a warm, clubby, New York atmosphere and unrestrained elegance. Oil paintings of over 600 regular customers, many of whom are world famous, decorate the walls of the cocktail lounge. Everywhere Beverlee Shere's outgoing personality and philosophy are writ large on the surroundings. Her message is "come on in and enjoy one of America's finest, The Coach and Six."

CROSSROADS SEAFOOD AND LOUNGE, Peachtree at Spring Street, Atlanta, GA. Tel. (404) 875-2288. The Crossroads offers the casual dress atmosphere of a yacht club and a traditional menu featuring steak, burgers and seafood. Located just five minutes from downtown, the restaurant is convenient to the hotels of the Buckhead district.

DON JUAN'S SPANISH AND CONTINENTAL RESTAURANT
1927 Piedmont Circle Northeast
Atlanta, GA 30324
Tel. (404) 874-4285
Hrs: Mon. - Sat. 5:00 p.m. - 11:30 p.m.
Visa, AMEX and Diners Club are accepted.

Take a little vacation from the trouble of the everyday world and visit the spirit and flavor of old Spain. Don Juan's Spanish and Continental Restaurant gives you a chance to taste great Spanish cuisine without leaving the city. Located in an historical stucco building with a breathtakingly panoramic view of Atlanta, Don Juan's offers an extensive menu filled with many popular Spanish dishes. Open your meal with a Tapas Caliente (hot appetizer) such as Mejillones Gaditanas, mussels sauteed in white wine or marinera. Then try the restaurant's delicious gazpacho. Your choice of entrees includes Grouper á la Vasca style; grouper with lemon, butter, herbs, white wine and tomato sauce; Ternera Don Juan, a tender veal dish prepared right at your table; or the famous Paella Don Juan, a sumptuous seafood dish with king crab legs, shrimp, oysters, mussels and clams served on saffron flavored rice dotted with green peas. Owner Don Juan Moran suggests that first time diners might want to try their five course, delightfully tempting dinner, offering a splendid sampler of Spanish cuisine.

Wednesday through Saturday, you can enjoy the music of a live guitarist strolling around the tables. Don Juan's also offers complete banquet facilities for private parties of fifteen to 100 guests. Featuring "The Best Spanish Feast in Atlanta," Don Juan's Spanish and Continental Restaurant invites you to "Dream like Don Quixote and eat like Sancho Panza."

DUSTY'S BARBECUE
1815 Briarcliff Road
Atlanta, GA 30329
Tel. (404) 320-6264
Hrs: Sun. - Thu.   11:00 a.m. - 11:00 p.m.
     Fri. - Sat.   11:00 a.m. - 10:00 p.m.

Dusty's Barbecue was voted the best barbecue in Atlanta by *Creative Loafing*. And it richly deserves the praise. Linda Thornston opened this fifty-seat Southern barbecue restaurant in 1982, as a result of friends' enthusiastic response to her North Carolina style barbecue cooking. Since then, this casual restaurant has continued to serve up some of the best barbecue found anywhere.

Dusty's motto boasts, "We serve no swine before its time." Pork, beef and chicken barbecues at Dusty's are basted with a pepper ginger sauce and special pork blend. Another specialty is the Brunswick stew, which comes from an old Virginia wild game recipe. The baby back ribs are lean, tender and juicy. To

Atlanta and Vicinity

accompany your lunch or dinner, choose a side order of hush puppies, fried okra, sauerkraut, potato salad or applesauce. For dessert, there is a selection of pies and cobblers. Prices are moderate. Beer and wine are available.

Patrons come from long distances for the warm Southern hospitality and impressive North Carolina style cooking they find at Dusty's. Several items are available to go, including Dusty's hot, regular or sweet sizzlin' barbecue sauce. They will cater any size group, from 10 to 10,000.

EAT YOUR VEGETABLES
438 Moreland Avenue Northeast
Atlanta, GA 30307
Tel. (404) 523-2671
Hrs: Lunch   Mon. - Fri.   11:30 a.m. - 2;00 p.m.
     Dinner Mon. - Thu.   6:00 p.m. - 10:00 p.m.
             Fri. - Sat.   6:00 p.m. - 11:00 p.m.
     Brunch Sunday   11:00 - 3:00 p.m.
Visa and MasterCard are accepted.

Eat Your Vegetables provides an alternative to restaurants that feature foods that may compromise your healthy attitudes about food. The unusual eatery, located in the neighborhood of Little Five Points, makes a specialty out of serving the healthiest food in Atlanta.

The simple charming decor is coupled with a casual ambiance. White linen napkins complement the quaint tables and chairs and interesting art from local artists decorates the walls. Customers come back again and again to try items such as Eat Your Veggies Salad, with lettuce sprouts, carrots, mushrooms, avocado, tabouli and feta cheese. This dish is topped with sesame and sunflower seeds. Vegetable Wellington is a vegetarian treat; a delicate puff pastry stuffed with a grain and vegetable filling and topped with mushroom sauce. Eat Your Vegetables offers several delicious seafood and chicken entrees, including Tempura Chicken with Sesame Sauce, a boneless breast of chicken dipped in crisp batter and fried, then served with a sesame tamari sauce. The Seafood Special features one of the many seafoods from gamefish to shellfish selected and delivered daily to the kitchen. Look for the day's choice on the specials board. All entrees include baked rolls, salad, and vegetables.

For dessert, try a sinfully healthy chocolate cheesecake, a tofu carob pie, or Gorin's ice cream. All desserts are freshly baked. Eat Your Vegetables has become an preferred meeting place of the health conscious and one of Atlanta's best restaurants.

EMPRESS OF CHINA III, 4251 North Peachtree Road, Atlanta, GA. Tel. (404) 451-1216. The Empress of China III offers "the royal treatment" in cuisine and service. Reservations for groups of six or more guests are recommended by this highly-rated restaurant.

ENCORE RESTAURANT, 1374 West Peachtree Street, Altanta, GA Tel. (404) 897-1548. The restaurant boasts quality dining, excellent service and affordable prices. Return to nineteenth century San Francisco when one steps through the Tiffany designed archway from the original B & O Railway Headquarters.

56 EAST RESTAURANT AND DESSERTS
56 East Andrews Drive
Atlanta, GA 30342
Tel. (404) 364-WINE
Hrs: Lunch
      Mon. - Fri.   11:30 a.m. - 2:30 p.m.
      Dinner
      Mon. - Thu.   5:30 p.m. - 11:00 p.m.
      Fri. - Sat.   5:30 p.m. - 12:00 midnight
Visa, MasterCard and AMEX are accepted.

Gastronomes are encouraged to visit 56 East Restaurant and Desserts for an opportunity to sample all the gourmet delights that have ever tempted them. If the saying "pretty is as pretty does" ever came true, it was at "56" where the American contemporary cuisine delights the eye and the

Atlanta and Vicinity

palate, enhanced by suggested wines to match with any of the foods of the often up dated menu.

56 East has over 350 wines on the master list. Each day 50 or so are offered by the taste, glass or bottle starting with Champagnes, continuing with Chardonnay, Cabernet, classic wines from Bordeaux, Burgandy and California, rounding off with Ports, Sauternes and other dessert wines. Wines are suggested to match with Caviar Trio of Beluga, Salmon and American golden caviars on toast rounds with traditional garnish; or try Oriental Oysters sauteed with just a hint of curry served on julienned vegetables. One might sample a chilled soup of fresh California strawberries with blueberry coulis. To encourage you to explore flavors, a variety of light courses are offered such as Chicken Georgia, a sauteed breast of chicken with pecans and peaches, or Catch of the Day, or a Trio of Baby Filets with a medallion of veal, lamb and beef with wild mushrooms and Cabernet Sauvignon glaze. 56 also prepares full dinners for those who prefer a more traditional approach.

All of these delicacies are served in an atmosphere especially suited to encourage experimentation. The decor starts with a sophisticated series of cartoons and framed wine label posters, continuing with parquet floors, corian tabletops and arched glass doors. You may be seated in the dining room , the "wine shop," on a sunny patio or a fountainhead courtyard, or cluster near the piano in the dessert room. Desserts express the latest culinary trends: philo packets of truffles, lacy almond baskets brimming with fresh berries, apple roulade, dessert cheeses, and chocolate done white or dark but always rich and memorable.

As a new concept in dining, 56 East Restaurant and Desserts will have you returning again and again for the most delightful education you have ever experienced.

FISHERMAN'S COVE, 201 Courtland Street, Atlanta, GA. Tel. (404) 659-3610. Fisherman's Cove features a selection of "favorites" and house creations of every imaginable dish. Daily fresh fish specials are offered in this restaurant located between the Radisson and Hilton hotels.

GRAND CHINA
2975 Peachtree Road
Atlanta, GA 30305
Tel. (404) 231-5415
Hrs: Mon. - Fri. 11:30 a.m. - 10:45 p.m.
 Sat. - Sun. 12:00 noon - 11:00 p.m.
Visa, MasterCard and AMEX are accepted.

People who love good Chinese food will be thrilled to discover Grand China. Mr. and Mrs. Chang, the owners of this comfortable restaurant, happily embrace each opportunity to shower exotic delights on welcome guests.

The incredible menu offers over 200 delicious choices. Traditional favorites include steamed fish, Ginger Duck, Mu Shu Pork, and fried dumplings. Hunan and Szechuan meals are specialties for diners who prefer spicy cuisine. Appetizers, soups, fish, duck, chicken, seafood, vegetable, beef and pork selections offer something for every appetite. Try the Crabmeat and Corn Soup, Pineapple Fried Rice or Szechuan Cold Noodle appetizer. In addition, Grand China offers a variety of delectable house specialties, including Chicken with Pecans, Spare Ribs, Prawns with spicy sauce and Chinese vegetables, Orange Beef, Scallops in Black Bean Sauce and Eight Delight Duck.

For those who prefer to dine at home, Grand China offers free delivery within a four mile radius. Make your next party or banquet special with catering provided by Grand China. For fine service and authentic Chinese cuisine, Grand China is your "Best Choice" in Atlanta.

INDIGO COASTAL GRILL, 1399 North Highland Avenue, Atlanta, GA. Tel. (404) 876-0676. A restaurant specializing in seafood from Cape Cod to the Caribbean. The casual, laid back dining area is a hot spot in town, its key lime pie a dessert of exceptional flavor.

Atlanta and Vicinity

JOHNNY ROCKETS
6510 Roswell Road
Atlanta, GA 30328
Tel. (404) 257-0677
Hrs: Sun. - Thu.   11:00 a.m. - 12:00 midnight.
     Fri. - Sat.   11:00 a.m. - 2:00 a.m.

Where can a hungry traveler find a really juicy hamburger and an extra thick shake? Johnny Rockets answers the question with a flair that seems to have come from the 1940s.

Johnny Rockets makes a business of serving what it calls the "original" hamburger, amid a world of neon signs, nickel jukeboxes and all the rest of the atmosphere of times gone by. Travelers may know of the chain, which began in Los Angeles a few years back. It's nostalgia, with lots of good food and fun. The menu is simple. There are two basic hamburgers, both big and juicy, with a choice of extras including grilled onions, bacon, chili and more. A half dozen sandwich choices and fries and chili by the cup complete the eating part of the offering. The fountain has bottled soda pop including a distinctive root beer which reaches back over the decades. Coca Cola from the fountain can be ordered in several flavors. Thick shakes, hand dipped malted milk and ice cream floats are at the fountain with its classic appearance. Also offered are apple and peach pies, with or without a scoop of ice cream. It's the menu that just about every soda fountain relied on in the days before fast food. Seating is at the counter, just like the good old days. A second location has just opened in Buckhead at West Paces Ferry and Peachtree.

Part of the magic of Johnny Rockets is the jukebox, belting out songs that are quite danceable. There's a Seeburg selector in reach of just about everyone, playing records for a nickel. And, when the beat is right, you just may put down your malt and swivel around to the floor to dance with your honey. That's part of Johnny Rockets and the old soda fountain, too.

La GROTTA
2637 Peachtree Road
Atlanta, GA 30305
Tel. (404) 231-1368
Hrs: Mon.-Sun. 6:00 p.m. - 10:30 p.m.
Reservations are required.
Visa, MasterCard, AMEX, Diners Club, Carte Blanche and Discover are accepted.
Also,
647 Atlanta Street
Roswell, GA 30075
Tel. (404) 998-0645

The war is over and the Italians have won. In Atlanta, that fabled city of fine dining, the Italian food at La Grotta has overcome the French fare once ruling this Georgian capital. In business since 1978, La Grotta's reputation as the best Italian restaurant in the city is well deserved.

Dishes that originated in Northern Italy are available for your dining pleasure. Begin your meal with a selection from the antipasti menu, such as Vitello Tonnato, thinly sliced veal with tuna, lemon and caper Sauce, or Carpaccio, thinly sliced filet of beef marinated in Lemon Dressing. La Grotta features a wide variety of freshly made pasta entrees, including Black and White Linguini with Calamari, olive oil, garlic and fresh tomato, Tortellini served with a creamy tomato and basil sauce, and Spaghetti Carbonara, a tasty mixture of spaghetti, prosciutto ham, eggs, cream and parmesan cheese. Sauteed fillet of grouper, butterfly shrimp, Dover sole and mussels are available for fish fanciers. Veal, beef and chicken Grotta Specialties include tantalizing dishes such as loin of veal with a white wine sauce topped with fresh Scottish smoked salmon, Veal Scallopini with wild mushrooms in a creamy Marsala sauce, and medallions of Beef Filet topped with shrimp and served with a light brandy sauce.

To complement your meal, select a fine wine from the extensive wine list, considered the best in Georgia. "The Sweet End" to your dining experience is a La Grotta dessert. Italian favorites include an assortment of pastries, Italian ice cream,

Atlanta and Vicinity

cheesecake and other tempting treats. For an authentic Italian meal in an atmosphere of comfort and elegance, La Grotta is your "Best Choice."

THE LARK AND THE DOVE
5788 Roswell Road
Atlanta, GA 30328
Tel. (404) 256-2922
Hrs: Lunch
    Mon. - Fri.   11:30 a.m. - 2:30 p.m.
    Dinner
    Mon. - Thu.   6:00 p.m. - 11:30 p.m.
    Fri., Sat.   6:00 p.m. - 12:00 midnight
    Sunday   6:00 p.m. - 10:00 p.m.
Visa, MasterCard, AMEX, Diners Club and Carte Blanche are accepted.

Elegant service, superior cuisine and quietly sophisticated surroundings combine to make The Lark and The Dove a distinctive dining experience. The Lark and The Dove is famous for its prime rib and equally praised for its fresh seafood, Veal Francaise, South African lobster tails and the marvelous Caesar Salad.

Beginning with delicious appetizers, The Lark and The Dove offers everything from Shrimp Scampi and Spinach Souffle to Crab Crépes Gratinee and Escargots Bourguignonne. Closely accompanying the appetizers are the garden fresh salads with selections from The Lark and The Dove's famous Caesar Salad prepared at your table by the Maitre d'. The Hearts of Palm Salad, with its exotic center cut hearts of palm, is served in the classic manner. Prime rib of course commands the entrée selection, followed closely by aged New York strip steak. Or perhaps your palate would prefer seafood such as grilled tuna, broiled grouper or blackened redfish. Special treats for dessert include Bananas Foster, prepared with flair at your tableside. The Lark and The Dove houses an excellent wine cellar.

Nightly, light piano classics, contemporary and jazz entertainment is provided in the upstairs lounge. You can dance

Atlanta and Vicinity

or simply relax and enjoy the music. The Lark and The Dove will cater the most intimate party to the grandest gathering. Valet parking is available at The Lark and The Dove.

LINDY B's
3057 Peachtree Road
Atlanta, GA 30305
Tel. (404) 365-8600
Hrs: Brunch   Sat., Sun.   11:30 a.m. - 3:00 p.m.
      Lunch   Mon. - Fri.   11:30 a.m. - 2:30 p.m.
      Dinner   Mon. - Sun.   5:30 p.m. - 11:30 p.m.
Visa, MasterCard and AMEX are accepted.
Also,
LINDY'S
10 King Circle at Peachtree Hills
Atlanta, GA 30305
Tel. (404) 231-4113

Lindy B's is the third restaurant for successful Atlanta restaurateur Linda Capozzoli-Beigh. Lindy's, a neighborhood Italian cafe, is located three miles south of Lindy B's in Peachtree Hills at 10 King Circle. This fabulous new restaurant in Buckhead serves "American Fare with New England Charm." Lindy B's offers innovative American Cuisine in an atmosphere reminiscent of a Nantucket summer home.

Among the most popular offerings are Pasta Crab Cakes, peppered prime rib, pasta dishes, lobster and corn fritters and the famous Chicken Diablean Atlanta tradition of chicken stuffed with mushrooms and cream cheese, topped with dijon mustard, walnuts and brown sugar.

Desserts are made daily on the premises and are as original as Lindy B's itself. Toll House Cheesecake, White Chocolate Pound Cake, Hot Gingerbread Sundae and Maple Walnut Bread Pudding are among the favorites. The drinks are no less original. Betty Connecticut, the house specialty, is a concoction of hot apple cider and vanilla liqueur, topped with mounds of whipped cream and white chocolate shavings. The all-American wine list, featuring wines from New England, adds to the uniqueness of Lindy B's. Meals are served with a

Atlanta and Vicinity

basket of hot homemade muffins and fresh whipped apple butter.

The setting goes hand in hand with the wonderful food. Lindy B's is homey yet sophisticated and you'll feel like you're dining in someone's Cape Cod cottage. There is a white Victorian porch and patio for outdoor dining. The inside dining area is filled with nooks and crannies. Window seats and booths offer privacy, and every surface displays the comfortable little items that make a home. You'll see family photos, cupboards with china tea cups, wooden roosters, lacy trimmings and hooked rugs. The bar area is like a living room complete with day bed, trompe l'oeil bookshelves, wicker furniture and a blue and white hand painted floor.

Lindy B's offers a pleasant oasis in bustling Buckhead. Dine here for dinner and then do the Buckhead scene. Lindy B's is the place for Saturday and Sunday brunch and weekday lunch.

LONE STAR STEAKS, 4233 Roswell Road, Atlanta, GA. Tel. (404) 256-6366. Relax and enjoy lunch or dinner at "America's Best Steakhouse." Lone Star is open for lunch six days a week, and dinner seven days, in the Buckhorn district of Atlanta.

MA MAISON RESTAURANT
2974 Grandview Avenue
Atlanta, GA 30305
Tel. (404) 266-1799
Hrs: Lunch   Tue. - Sun. 11:30 a.m. - 1:30 p.m.
       Dinner   Tue. - Sun. 6:00 p.m. - 10:00 p.m.
Visa, MasterCard, AMEX and Air Plus are accepted.

If you want the feeling of being in a small chateau in the countryside of France and dining on a succulent meal while being attended to by a superb staff, then Ma Maison is the restaurant to mark in your appointment book. Ma Maison has won a wealth of accolades for its Nouvelle Continental cuisine and impressive wine list.

The *Atlanta Business Chronicle* comments on Ma Maison's wine list, "There is an impressive wine list offering a wide selection of California and imported brands." The wine list consists of 130 plus wine selections including twenty-two choices by the glass. Ma Maison also features vintage ports and cognacs. Many of the vintages date back as far as 1904.

The *Atlanta Magazine* writes, "Ma Maison in Buckhead offers Nouvelle Continental cuisine at its freshest and most appealing!" Ma Maison's menu features fresh Norwegian salmon, swordfish, grouper, giant sea scallops, orange roughy, Mahi Mahi and much more. Ma Maison receives fresh fish deliveries twice daily. Red meat dishes are equally fresh and appealing. A favorite entrée is the Filet of Beef with cream morels and truffles.

MARRA'S
1782 Cheshire Bridge Road Northeast
Atlanta, GA 30324
Tel. (404) 874-7347
Hrs: Mon. - Fri. 11:30 a.m. - 2:30 p.m.
     Sat. - Sun. 6:00 p.m. - 11:00 p.m.
Visa, MasterCard, AMEX and Diners Club are accepted.

What is now one of the most popular methods of preparing seafood in the Atlanta area, grilling, began at Marra's Seafood Grill in 1981. After eleven years experience in the restaurant business, owner Gene Marra opened Marra's where he cooks the very freshest seafood, shipped in daily, over peach, apple and cherry wood fires.

Whether you come to Marra's for an intimate lunch or dinner in one of the three semi-private dining rooms or for a gala affair in the upstairs loft, you'll enjoy Gold Medal wines and simply prepared grilled fish with special sauces in an atmosphere of simple sophistication. The restaurant is housed in a renovated home which seats 106 and is decorated with white linen, oak paneling and Georgia art. The two head chefs have been at Marra's since it opened its doors, serving appetizers such as Steamed Mussels Mariniere, Clams Amalfi and Fried Calamari. Meals at Marra's usually begin with

Atlanta and Vicinity

specially made thick crusted peasant bread called Boule, served with Marra's signature appetizer spread, taramasalada, and a bowl of soup such as the house bisque. House specialty entrees include Cioppino San Francisco style, Frog Legs Cacciatore or the sauteed Dover sole flown in from Belgium three times a week. Charcoal grilled entrees include Georgia rainbow trout, swordfish steak, grouper and an eight ounce centercut filet mignon. All entrees are served with a choice of homemade pasta or house potato and vegetable of the day. Desserts are tasty at Marra's. They offer key lime pie, Ricotta Cheesecake, English Trifle and Chocolate Mousse pie.

Marra's Seafood Grill is not only the first, it is the best. For one of the only places in Atlanta where you can enjoy the freshest grilled seafood cooked over fruitwood coals try Marra's. After managing eighteen restaurants and owning five, Gene Marra has the business down to a science.

MC KINNON'S LOUISIANE AND THE GRILL ROOM AT MC KINNON'S
3209 Maple Drive Northeast
Atlanta, GA 30305
Tel. (404) 237-1313
Hrs: Mon. - Thu.   6:00 p.m. - 10:00 p.m.
      Fri. and Sat.   6:00 p.m. - 10:30 p.m.
      Closed on Sundays.
Reservations are suggested.
All major credit cards are accepted.

Nestled in a little alcove right off Peachtree near Piedmont is Mc Kinnon's Louisiane, a class act restaurant which has become an Atlanta institution. Wonderfully spicy Cajun and delicate Creole dishes are expertly prepared and served up by attentive tuxedoed waiters who provide a warm and welcome atmosphere to make you feel at home. Nothing is too good for the guest of Beth and Billy McKinnon. Oil and watercolor prints grace the walls and the tables are elegantly set for intimate dining with sparkling tableware and crisp white linen tablecloths.

If it's your first visit, you're in for an experience which won't be your last. Once you've tried the Snapper Patout, a broiled red snapper with crawfish and cream sauce, you're hooked. You'll return to sample the hot peppered shrimp, the fabulous shrimp romaulade or the stuffed eggplant which should be called Eggplant Surprise with its delectable shrimp and crab filling. There's always a full house at Mc Kinnon's where ninety-five percent of the dishes prepared are composed around fish and shellfish. House favorites please the regulars and convert the newcomers. But Mc Kinnon's keeps up with the times by gradually changing the menu to interest the discerning clientele.

The Grill Room is a separate dining room at Mc Kinnon's, with a personality all its own. The menu and cooking techniques differ from the main dining room and here you don't need reservations. You can walk right in and feast on fresh tuna, sword salmon cooked on a chargrill and served plain, blackened or with a creamy sauce such as spicy corn butter or jalapeño beurre blanc sauce.

After dinner in the main room or The Grill Room, you are invited to retire to the piano bar in the back and enjoy the relaxing music where you can sip an Irish coffee or perhaps indulge in a sinful dessert. One never dines at Mc Kinnon's without a genuine welcome from host and owner Billy Mc Kinnon. He's there to greet you on your arrival and see to your personal comforts as you enjoy a delightful evening at Mc Kinnon's Louisiane.

THE MELTING POT
857 Collier Road
Atlanta, GA 30318
Tel. (404) 351-1811
Hrs: Sun.-Thu.   5:30 p.m.-10:00 p.m.
      Fri.-Sat.   5:30 p.m. - 12:00 midnight
Visa, MasterCard and AMEX are accepted.

All fine restaurants are supposed to be intimate and romantic, but there's something especially romantic and intimate when the food is fondue. Perhaps it's the sense of

Atlanta and Vicinity

sharing that comes with dipping tasty tidbits into a shared fondue pot. As the cheese melts, so might a few inhibitions.

At The Melting Pot one can step into a bit of Switzerland, where the aroma of cheese wafts through the air in a chalet-like atmosphere. The ambiance is casual. Another special feature of the Melting Pot are the wines. The well thought out wine list includes everything from a fine Bordeaux to California Chardonnay. Thirteen different wines are available by the glass, which makes your fondue experience a wine tasting event as well. Guests have a choice of cheeses. The cheddar cheese fondue is made with a beer base, and a blend of sharp cheddar and emmenthaler cheeses all seasoned with garlic and spices. The Swiss cheese fondue contains a wine base. Dippers include chunks of pumpernickel, French bread, apples and vegetables. There's a seafood fondue that offers fresh shrimp, scallops and seasonal fish. The Melting Pot also offers beef and chicken dinners as well as a vegetarian fondue dinner. All dinners come with a choice of chef or mushroom salads. Your dessert may include a milk chocolate or white chocolate-Amaretto fondue with morsels of pound cake, bananas and fruit as dippers.

So if you have not fondued since the 1960s, The Melting Pot can soothe any pangs of nostalgia. Add a glass of wine and be ready for romance.

MINOO FINE BAKERY AND RESTAURANT
Leahmann's Plaza at Executive Park
2484 Briarcliff Road
Atlanta, GA 30329
Tel. (404) 320-9522
Hrs: Lunch   Mon. - Sat. 11:00 a.m. - 2:30 p.m.
     Dinner   Mon. - Sat. 10:30 a.m. - 2:30 p.m.
     Brunch   Sunday   10:00 a.m. - 2:30 p.m.
Visa, MasterCard and AMEX are accepted.

Few have ever seen Paradise, but those who have equate it with Minoo Fine Bakery and Restaurant, which features wonderful French and Continental cuisine. After one taste of the incredible selection of fine pastries and gourmet specialties, you'll know what Minoo means. It means, in fact, "paradise" in the native language of owners Khalil and Minoo Gorji.

More than a year ago, the pair opened a new restaurant in Atlanta, planning a menu and pastry selection unbeatable in Georgia. With its shining, modern look, the bakery impresses the eye as well as the palate with elaborate cakes, huge cookies, and pastries such as cream cheese Danish. The Napoleans are especially tempting with their feathery light crust, delicious cream filling and smooth, creamy icing. The restaurant invites you to a special meal in an intimate, candlelit dining room. Its rich, yet simple look comes from the pale gray and dark red decor, accented by the delicate flower designs on the china. Items that grace the menu include New York Strip Steak, Veal Minoo, a veal cutlet in creamy cognac sauce with mushrooms, and mesquite grilled swordfish.

On Friday and Saturday nights, Minoo Fine Bakery and Restaurant offers an Iranian specialty. For example, "fesenjan," a variety of sweet and sour chicken cooked with ground walnuts and pomegranate sauce and served with rice. Such a delight will send you into seventh heaven.

MODO SUSHI, Cobb Parkway at Spring Road, Atlanta, GA. Tel. (404) 438-2636. Modo Sushi is a beautiful sushi bar featuring 100 original recipes. Lunch and dinner are served seven days a week.

THE OLD SPAGHETTI FACTORY, 249 Ponce de Leon, Atlanta, GA. Tel. (404) 872-2841. The Old Spaghetti Factory features an atmosphere of rich wood and stained glass. Spaghetti with five delicious sauces and crisp salads are served at family prices.

THE ORIGINAL PANCAKE HOUSE, 1937 Peachtree Road Northeast, Atlanta, GA Tel. (404) 351-3533. Apple-Pancake, Dutch-Baby, egg omelettes, business breakfasts, and more grace the breakfast table at The Original Pancake House. Only the highest quality fresh ingredients are prepared and served in this casual and comfortable atmosphere.

Atlanta and Vicinity

PARTNERS MORNINGSIDE CAFÉ
1399 North Highland Avenue
Atlanta, GA 30306
Tel. (404) 875-0202
Hrs: Tue. - Sat.   6:00 p.m. - 11:00 p.m.
         Fri.- Sat.   6:00 p.m. - 11:30 p.m.
Visa, MasterCard and AMEX are accepted.

It's a happy, small restaurant, built as a neighborhood bistro, that quickly earned a reputation reaching far beyond the neighborhood. Food is superior and the menu changes daily, leading to surprises even for regular diners at the Café.

Folks wait for tables sitting on benches or stand sipping wine amid the aroma of basil and rosemary bushes planted in tubs outside. Original art work decorates the walls. The menu is hand lettered daily to present new creations of Jules Paulk, a chef well known in Atlanta. Any day you may find Italian, Thai, or American Southwestern entrées. Specials of fresh seafood are posted on the blackboard. Among the best entrées is a boneless chicken rolled in cornbread and pecans with a Jack Daniels sauce. Stirfry dishes reflecting an Asian influence are popular. Sometimes there are spicy Szechwan dishes. Of desserts, two favorites are a torta built with mascarpone cheese, macaroons and shaved chocolate topped with berries. Another is Georgia Peach poundcake, served with ice cream and a topping created from Jack Daniels whiskey and peach purée. Espresso and a special blend of Colombian coffee are offered, along with a wide selection of wines from California and Australia.

Partners Morningside Café has been featured in the *New York Times* and its walls are decorated with local and regional honors. Despite the Cafe's wide renown, it remains a friendly neighborhood place where good food at moderate prices is combined with a casual atmosphere.

PARTNERS PANTRY, 1399 North Highland Avenue, Atlanta, GA. Tel. (404) 873-0676. It's a gourmet take out restaurant operated by the same folks who run the Partner's Morningside Cafe and Indigo Coastal Grill. Wine, salad dressing and desserts featured at both restaurants are sold along with many entrees and complete meals to go.

THE PATIO BY THE RIVER
4199 Paces Ferry Road Northwest
Atlanta, GA 30339
Tel. (404) 432-2808.
Hrs: Lunch   Mon. - Fri. 11:30 a.m. - 2:30 p.m.
       Dinner   Mon. - Sat. 6:00 p.m. - 10:30 p.m.
Visa, MasterCard, AMEX and Diners Club are accepted.

Located in a beautiful setting overlooking the Chattahoochee river, the Patio by the River reminds one of the many wonderful restaurants in France situated on the river. In fact, once you've tasted the fabulous cuisine you'll realize that Chef-owner Mary Hataway has worked in some of the finest restaurant kitchens in France.

You'll make a grand entrance through antique French doors, into an inviting sitting area with tasteful artwork. The old brick in the main dining room combined with lace and sparkling crystal lends elegance and warmth. Have a drink on the patio in warm months, or enjoy the cheerful, glowing fire in winter. The ambiance in all seasons is special.

An unusual Butternut squash soup in the winter or a crisp Cucumber soup in the summer will start your meal off right. Classic French dishes, often with Southern overtones, include herbed oysters, Crabmeat Mornay, grilled salmon steak and triple cut loin lamb chops. For dessert, the chocolate mousse is famous.

Large parties down by the river, inluding barbecues, are a specialty for groups and entertaining. Private dining in a cozy room called The Library is also available.

Atlanta and Vicinity

RIO BRAVO
3172 Roswell Road
Atlanta, GA 30305
Tel. (404) 262-7431
Hrs: Lunch   Mon. - Sun. 11:30 a.m. - 3:00 p.m.
     Dinner   Mon. - Fri. 5:30 a.m. - 11:00 p.m.
     Dinner   Sat., Sun. 5:30 a.m. - 12:30 a.m.
All major credit cards are accepted.

Rio Bravo cantina is famous for fajitas and fiestas. Fresh Mexican food is prepared on the premises using only the finest of ingredients. Enchiladas are hand rolled, and poblano peppers are air freighted in from the West Coast. Icy cold margaritas are made from fresh squeezed fruits, and the taste of the guacamole, beans and sauces will tease your taste buds for more.

Rio Bravo's famous fajitas come marinated, charbroiled and served with rice and grilled vegetables. A Tex-Mex Feast is an event by itself. This banquet consists of fajitas, chicken fajitas, pork fajitas, half a barbecued chicken, ribs and spicy chicken wings served with French fries, guacamole, sour cream and pic-de-gallo. Daily specials feature fajitas made with a variety of delicious ingredients such as plump, tender shrimp sauteed with veggies in Rio Bravo's spicy jalapeno butter and ready to roll in fresh, hot tortillas.

The mood is festive at Rio Bravo. Strolling mariachis serenade the crowd. Bright colored pinãtas swing from the ceiling and wagon wheels hang on the stucco walls. A patio with umbrella shaded tables provides alfresco dining. The staff is pronto with smiles and service. The Buckhead Rio Bravo is part of a five restaurant chain including cantinas at Powers Ferry, Roswell, Town Center and Gwinnett.

SIMON'S MESQUITE SEAFOOD GRILL
2960 Cobb Parkway
Atlanta, GA 30339
Tel. (404) 952-6042
Hrs: Sun. - Thu.   11:30 a.m. - 11:00 p.m.
      Fri. - Sat.   11:30 a.m. - 12:00 midnight
      Sunday brunch   11:00 a.m. - 3:00 p.m.
Visa, MasterCard and AMEX are accepted.
Also,
3525 Mall Boulevard
Duluth, GA 30136
Tel. (404) 476-3474

The secret to Simon's popularity is simple: fresh fish. From the time they come off the boat until the fish go on the grill or into the oven, they remain chilled to preserve freshness. Even the cutting carried out each morning by a skilled artisan is done in refrigerated rooms.

That attention to detail and quality can be seen when you enter either Simon's location. The setting is clean and fresh. From candles on the tables to the friendly folks at the bar, these restaurants are ready for customers. Pleasant music from a grand piano tinkles in the background as you look through the menu. Each day, from six to eight varieties of fish are available. The popular mesquite grilling is called for by many patrons, while others ask for Cajun style blackened frying pan method of preparation. Simon's was the first to introduce blackened fish to Atlanta. In addition to the expected Mahi Mahi, tuna and swordfish, you can find grouper, trout, and shrimp on the menu. There is also a large selection of aged prime beef, both rib and steaks, available as a single entree or served on platters with seafood. Grilled chicken is offered in three styles. There are also choices of pasta, Pirozkis, and soup and salad combination. Simon's menu of fine food is complemented by a quality wine list featuring California and some European vintages, including the best in champagne. Either location offers an invitation to elegant dining with fine food and soft music to provide just the right mood.

Atlanta and Vicinity

SMOKE FLAME WEST BAR B Q, 1371 Simpson Road Northwest, Atlanta, GA. Tel. (404) 752-6280. The Smoke Flame West Bar B Q specializes in beef and pork ribs, chicken, and Brunswick stew. Lunch and dinner are served six days a week.

TAJMAHAL
1152 Spring Street Northwest
Atlanta, GA 30309
Tel. (404) 875-6355
Hrs: Mon. - Sat.
      Lunch   11:30 a.m. - 2:30 p.m.
      Dinner   5:30 p.m. - 10:30 p.m.
Visa, MasterCard, AMEX and Discover are accepted.

Truly deserving of being named after one of the seven wonders of the world, the Tajmahal features a select menu by the world famous chef Hans Raj Kapotra, "honored by royalty, loved by V.I.Ps, admired by movie stars, applauded by food critics and praised by celebrities." Owner Bob Patel, who hails from India and was educated as an engineer in the United States, is now fulfilling his dream of bringing his country's food to his surrogate homeland.

The interior is reminiscent of the original Tajmahal with its peaceful decor and lighting and a wonderful large saltwater fish tank in the center, with specimens from all over the world. Your senses will be heightened inside the dining area, which seats one-hundred, by soft music and tempting aromas. Desires are quickly met in the form of wines, and an extensive selection of international beers and cocktails. The menu, written in both Sanskrit and English, features a traditional Indian soup made with lentils, herbs and mild spices. Appetizers include shish kabob made with lamb and onions broiled in a charcoal-filled clay oven and Vegetable Samosas, a stuffed pastry filled with potatoes and peas. Seven items are cooked in the Tandoor clay oven, including the Tandoori Chicken, marinated in yogurt and spices and baked to a succulent tenderness. A large menu features chicken, lamb, seafood, rice and vegetarian specialties. All dinners include Papadam, Dai, Raita, Pulao rice, Nan and condiments. All entrees are made to taste: mild, medium and hot.

The Tajmahal, one of the seven wonders of the world, is made of pure white marble and took twenty-two years and over twenty-thousand laborers daily to complete. The Tajmahal restaurant is made of exceptional Indian cuisine, service and atmosphere, a pleasure palace for the people of Atlanta and visiting travelers.

TROTTER'S RESTAURANT, 3215 Peachtree Road Northeast, Atlanta, GA. Tel. (404) 237-5988. Trotter's Restaurant has been recognized as an award-winning restaurant which has changed the dining experience in Atlanta. Reservations are recommended for the elegant establishment.

U.S. BAR AND GRILL, 2002 Howell Mill Road, Atlanta, GA. Tel. (404) 352-0033. The U.S. Bar and Grill features original Mexican cuisine including cabrito, fajitas, chicken and seafood, cooked over mesquite coals. Lunch and dinner are served seven days a week.

THE VARSITY
61 North Avenue
Atlanta, GA 30308
Tel. (404) 881-1706
Hrs: Mon. - Thu.   7:00 a.m. - 12:30 a.m.
     Fri., Sat.   7:00 a.m. - 2:00 a.m.

"Whaddaya have? Whaddaya have?" barks the man standing at the head of the serving line. If you say, "A hot dog with onions on the side and potato chips," he screams, "Dog sideways and a bag of rags! Next!" Before you have a chance to question your order, it has arrived and you know you are at The Varsity. The Varsity, "World's Largest Drive-In," has been a bona fide Atlanta Landmark since 1928. It ranks with many other well known Atlanta attractions and is recognized as one of the world's most unusual restaurants. The Varsity is a big, bustling, friendly place where 17,000 to 30,000 hungry people gather every day!

Atlanta and Vicinity

Newcomers enter the Varsity at their own risk at lunch time. Huge mobs pack the block long fast-food mecca. Long lines of people stand in front of fast and efficient conveyor belts which are pumping out mouth-watering hot dogs and burgers in blinks of the eye. Kitchens with glass viewing windows allow the public to see onion-ring workers tirelessly cutting and weeping. The people who serve at The Varsity have become as famous as the restaurant. One Varsity veteran is John Raiford, known affectionately as Flossie Mae. He has been with The Varsity for fifty years and at eighty-one has no intention of quitting.

The Varsity continues to make statistical history. On an average day, 17,000 hot dogs, 6,000 orders of french fries and onion rings and 5,000 hot peach and apple pies are sold. The Varsity is the ultimate fast-food experience.

"VEGGIE LAND" By Good Earth, 211 Pharr Road Northeast, Atlanta, GA. Tel. (404) 231-3111. "Veggieland" by Good Earth features a menu totally free of dairy and meat products. Delicious low calorie, low salt, no sugar vegetarian meals are served for lunch and dinner.

WICKERS
4355 Ashford-Dunwoody Road
Atlanta, GA 30346
Tel. (404) 395-1234
Hrs: Lunch   Mon. - Fri.   11:30 a.m. - 2:00 p.m.
     Brunch   Sunday   10:30 a.m. - 2:30 p.m.
     Dinner   Mon. - Sat.   6:00 p.m. - 10:00 p.m.
All major credit cards are accepted.

At Wickers, you'll stroll through the prettiest entrance in Atlanta, admire the birds and the orchid garden and marvel at the intricate detail on the restaurant's iron doors. The harpist lures you to your seat with soft music. The view of cascading waterfalls and carefully manicured gardens is stunning.

Wickers serves contemporary American cuisine in its casually elegant dining room. The menu is creative, from the Wild Boar Ravioli appetizer to the house specialty dessert,

Derby Souffle. Entrees include Rack of Lamb with Pommerey Mustard, Lobster Cantonese with Black Bean Sauce and Beef Tenderloin Medallions. Wickers boasts of fresh fish, game animals and fowl and creates daily additions to take advantage of seasonal favorites.

Wickers has a private dining room available for special occasions. Reservations are suggested. Wickers is located on the Garden Level in the beautiful Hyatt Regency Ravinia, I-285 and Ashford-Dunwoody across from Perimeter Mall.

RUGS

ALI BABBA ORIENTAL RUGS INCORPORATED, 2855 Piedmont Road, Atlanta, GA. Tel. (404) 233-0668. Certificates of authenticity are provided with the exquisite rugs from exotic places sold by Ali Babba Oriental Rugs. Three generations of experience is involved in the choices of quality hand knotted rugs.

HOUSE OF ORIENTAL RUGS
6201 Roswell Road
Atlanta, GA 30328
Tel. (404) 255-7888
Hrs: Mon. - Sat. 9:00 a.m. - 8:00 p.m.
     Sunday 11:00 a.m. - 6:00 p.m.
Visa, MasterCard and AMEX are accepted.

The delicately woven patterns of oriental rugs have been a source of beauty and pleasure from time out of mind. At one time, only the richest people could even think of owning these timeless masterpieces.

Today, with the help of the friendly staff at the House of Oriental Rugs, anyone with an eye for the graceful charm of these magnificent works of the weaver's art can have one in their home. Owners Mostafa Zamani and Mansour Kianfard are the third generation of their family in the rug business.

Atlanta and Vicinity

Their grandfather started many years ago in Iran making rugs by hand, and today Mostafa and Mansour offer the finest selection in Atlanta at incredible savings. Browsing through their showroom you can find oriental and Persian rugs in many different pastel, floral and geometric designs. There are Dhurry rugs of Persian design with their remarkable geometric patterns, and Kilimes of thin, soft wool with their deep pastel colors. Most of their rugs are handmade in small villages in such countries as Romania, China, Turkey, India and Pakistan. You can find Persian rugs up to a century old, and the older they are, the brighter the colors and the better they wear. With no middle men, their prices are the best in the city.

For those considering oriental rugs as an investment, free appraisal is available. They also feature expert hand cleaning and repairs. The House of Oriental Rugs is certainly your best choice for oriental rugs in Atlanta.

THE KILIM COLLECTION
22 Bennett Street
Atlanta, GA 30309
Tel. (404) 351-111
Hrs: Mon. - Sat. 10:00 a.m. - 5:00 p.m.

Kilims are much in demand now for decoration, because of their bold geometric patterns and vibrant colors. Atlanta's largest selection of kilims can be found at the Kilim Collection on Bennett Street, two blocks north of Piedmont Hospital. Owners Grace Sentell and Dee Cannon have assembled a fine collection of Turkish and Persian kilims with a wide variety of colors ranging from bold to soft and subtle. These flat weave rugs sold at the Kilim Collection were woven for domestic use rather than for export, and are from twenty to eighty years old.

All of the rugs have been washed and mothproofed. Grace and Dee have ingeniously adapted kilims to upholster furniture, to make screens and to create handbags. They have even turned them into wearable art, such as vests and belts. Custom upholstery and shipping are also available.

Designers looking for a unique decorative touch will want to drop by the Kilim Collection and talk to Grace and Dee.

Atlanta and Vicinity

They are quite knowledgeable and will be happy to display their collection. You can even find a perfect present for that hard to buy for person: a kilim Christmas stocking.

MANSOUR AUSARI ORIENTAL RUGS, 2293 Peachtree Road, Atlanta, GA. Tel. (404) 352-1911. New and used Oriental rugs from Persia, India, China and Turkey are just a few of the items offered by Mansour Ausari. Appraisals, repairs and restorations make this a total service company.

RUGS BY ROBINSON
22 Bennett Street
Atlanta, GA 30309
Tel. (404) 352-5161
Hrs: Mon. - Fri. 10:00 a.m. - 5:00 p.m.
The shop is open on weekends by appointment.

Rugs by Robinson offers the finest Portugese needlepoint rugs available. Betty Robinson custom designs rugs to accentuate and enhance her customers' surroundings. The exquisite design work is done by Betty here in the States, then the final rendering is completed in Portugal.

Betty's rugs are reproductions of the classic eighteenth century rugs, particularly of the Aubusson designs. Rugs up to twenty-seven feet in length can be found in Betty's store. Theme rugs are also available. The fabled needlepoint rug "Looms" as designed by Dutch artist Muiden is one of a collection offered. For years the one of a kind rugs such as "Looms" were not available, but now Betty carries an entire collection which was formerly in The Gulbelkian Museum in Lisbon. Betty will work closely with you in designing or choosing the rug which will perfectly complete your environment.

Betty is co-owner of the shop with her son Haynes. Rugs by Robinson is located in the exciting Bennett Street area, famous for its artisans and craftspeople.

Atlanta and Vicinity

WERCO PERSIAN AND ORIENTAL RUGS
3255 Peachtree Road Northeast
Atlanta, GA 30305
Tel. (404) 237-2584
      (800) 831-8585
Hrs: Mon. - Sat. 10:00 a.m. - 6:00 p.m.
      Sunday   12:00 noon - 5:00 p.m.
Visa, MasterCard and AMEX are accepted.

For nearly twenty years the name Werco Persian and Oriental Rug Gallery has represented to the Southeast a symbol of gracious hospitality and courtesy in the Oriental rug industry. As a family business, the owners of Werco value the relationship with their customers. They built their reputation on high standards, wide selection, business, and integrity.

Werco offers to you a tradition in elegance and uncompromised quality. As you enter the rug gallery showroom, a world of timeless beauty and cultural mystique appears before you. The knowledge you seek concerning these masterpieces from Persia, Pakistan, India, China and other far away countries is available to you. Their professional sales staff is one of the finest in the industry, consisting of many years of expertise in design and workmanship to enable you to chose only the best to suit your decorating needs.

Werco has always been able to provide its customers with hand picked rugs of superior quality. Owner and buyer Yasha Manzy uses years of expertise to find rugs which meet his mark of approval. Mr. Manzy provides the best value not by lowering his standards, but by knowing the rug market and only purchasing rugs which offer customers the best in artistry, craftsmanship and price. Werco invites you to visit their new gallery showroom on the corner of Peachtree Street and Piedmont.

SALONS

STAN MILTON IMAGES
721 Miami Circle
Atlanta, GA 30324
Tel. (404) 233-6241
Hrs: Tue. - Fri.   9:00 a.m.- 5:00 p.m.
      Wed.- Thu.   9:00 a.m.- 7:00 p.m.
      Saturday   9:00 a.m.- 4:00 p.m.
Visa and MasterCard are accepted.

If ever there was a place for complete hair and body care, this is it. Created by Stan Milton, Images has a complete range of services from cutting, styling and coloring hair to massage, pedicures, manicures, facials and even classes on yoga and other health related topics.

Stan Milton, who at age thirty-two has sixteen years of experience in this field, has worked under and has been in association with many stylists of international renown. Though his reputation grew over the eight years he was in his original salon, it has sky rocketed now with his new salon and concept. Hair styling is still the major focus, along with styling, make-up, skin care and massages, but corporate imaging is beginning to be much in demand. Concerned with providing the best product available for his customers, Stan took two years to find the product he uses, Aveda. Based on its pure and natural formulation, which is compatible with skin's natural chemistry, Aveda espouses the concept of Aromatherapy, which uses infusion oils to benefit and rejuvenate all skin types. All his salon stylists, most of whom have been with Stan for years, enjoy a great reputation for professionalism and innovation. Along with day packages for men and women, first time clients are given complimentary Aveda oil treatments for hair and a complimentary make-up and consultation to go with their hair style.

Atlanta and Vicinity

Not satisfied with just creating style with his clients, Stan surrounds them in it. The 7,000 square foot salon is open and flooded with natural light. White walls, pale natural wood, grey carpet and 3000 feet of tile floor all compliment the sizeable art gallery that is kept filled with rotating exhibits, some of which are in conjunction with Atlanta's best known art galleries. If you ever feel the need for a total makeover, go to Stan Milton's. He'll do it right, with style.

SYDELL SKIN AND BODY CARE SALON
99 West Paces Ferry Road
Atlanta, GA 30305
Tel. (404) 237-2505
Hrs: Mon. - Thu.   10:00 a.m. - 9:00 p.m.
      Fri. - Sat.   9:00 a.m. - 7:00 p.m.
Visa, MasterCard and AMEX are accepted.
Also,
Galleria Specialty Mall
One Galleria Parkway
Atlanta, GA 30339
Tel. (404) 955-5576
Hrs: Mon. - Thu.   9:00 a.m. - 9:30 p.m.
      Fri. - Sat.   9:00 a.m. - 7:00 p.m.
      Sunday   12:00 noon - 6:00 p.m.

The Sydell salons specialize in skin care, with a comprehensive approach to good health. Founder Sydell Harris oversees both salons with Lyn Ross as director of the Buckhead Salon and daughter Karen heading the staff at the Galleria. Services at both locations include facial treatments, body massage, manicures and makeup.

Because Sydell believes in a total approach to feeling good about yourself, there's information on diet and other aspects of personal health as part of the consultation. There are education programs in personal care giving you some of the skills practiced by the highly skilled staff. For the ultimate in personal pampering, there is a "Day with Sydell" that includes five hours of treatments customized for the client. The beauty products used, and also sold at the salons, are formulated just for Sydell, with emphasis on natural ingredients. Every time a client comes in, there is a fresh skin analysis to make sure the care is tailored to conditions at time of treatment. As an added feature, Sydell offers limousine service to and from any Atlanta area hotel. Everybody wants to look better, says Sydell, who put in years of training and preparation before going into business for herself. Now her experience is passed on to the staff of aestheticians, each certified and personally trained by Sydell.

The salons promise that you will both look and feel better when you begin a program, and there's a refund policy to back up the promise!

ZAPIEN'S
3119 Piedmont Road
Atlanta, GA 30305
Tel. (404) 231-2040
Hrs: Tue. - Fri.   8:30 a.m. - 6:30 p.m.
        Saturday   8:00 a.m. - 4:30 p.m.
Visa, MasterCard and AMEX are accepted.

Individual style, rather than trendy design, is featured at this salon. It was once a small Atlanta home. Now it is a contemporary, light and airy place closer to being an art gallery than a beauty shop.

At Zapien's, a trained staff offers hair styling and a full range of personal services, including European style facials and manicures. Erving and Norman Zapien are hair and make up consultants to corporate clients, in addition to taking care of customers by appointment at the Piedmont Road location. They urge first time clients to come in for a complimentary consultation before embarking on a new hair design and other treatments. Norman Zapien brings over twenty years of hair design experience to the salon. He jets between here and New York to take care of his customers, learning about new concepts as he travels. Consultations on make-up are a specialty for Erving Zapien. She frequently does makeup for professional models and celebrities. The shop is contemporary, not your typical line of beauty shop stations or mass production hair

Atlanta and Vicinity

design. Service is personalized, records of each consultation are kept and used when a client returns.

Zapien's works to bring out the best appearance of each person. They also offer seminars for women's groups and professional organizations interested in improving personal appearance. This "Best Choice" got that way by its attention to the changing fashion scene and to applying new techniques on an individual basis.

SCIENCE CENTER

FERNBANK SCIENCE CENTER
156 Heaton Park Drive
Atlanta, GA 30307
Tel. (404) 378-4311
Hrs: Monday   8:30 a.m. - 5:00 p.m.
      Tue. - Fri. 8:30 a.m. - 10:00 p.m.
      Saturday   10:00 a.m. - 5:00 p.m.
      Sunday   1:00 p.m. - 5:00 p.m.
Call for times for special events.

Fernbank Science Center was born out of a desire to preserve the forest while teaching others about it and the world of science. The center's purpose is to educate and inform the public and students while having fun, in the fields of astronomy, geology, oceanography, space, chemistry, physics and life science.

Learning is experiential and exciting in Exhibit Hall which offers exhibits that include an authentic Apollo spacecraft, dinosaurs, Treasures of the Earth and a saber-toothed tiger reconstruction. Self guided tours of the Fernbank Forest are excellent for identifying original vegetation of the area. For those of you who want to enhance your green thumbs, the Botanical Garden and Greenhouse provides an instructional environment for learning about horticulture, with its herb, rose and demonstration rose garden. Worlds beyond can be witnessed in the observatory through the largest telescope in the world that is dedicated primarily to public education. Daily planetarium programs are offered to adults and children five years or older; those under twelve must be accompanied by an adult.

The educational facilities of the science center include slide sets, instructional media kits and traveling exhibits which are used by schools, libraries and other interested non profit groups. The meteorological laboratory, electron microscope laboratory, human development classroom and library offer scientific marvels to the entire community. A trip to the Fernbank Science Center is an "out of this world" experience.

SHOE SHOPS

A.J.'S SHOE WAREHOUSE
1788 Ellsworth Industrial Boulevard
Atlanta, GA 30318
Tel. (404) 355-1760
Hrs: Friday   10:00 a.m. - 6:00 p.m.
     Saturday 10:00 a.m. - 5:00 p.m.
Visa and MasterCard are accepted.

The owners of A.J.'s have twenty years of experience in the wholesale shoe business and for the past four years have brought their expertise to the public by offering fine shoes, handbags and accessories at affordable prices in a high tech warehouse setting. The owners travel extensively, hand picking their stock to meet their high criteria. That decision was the answer to every shoe shopper's prayer.

A selection of fifteen thousand pairs of shoes, mostly from Spain and Italy, are displayed conveniently and are easily accessible for fitting. There's no hurry as you stroll up and down the aisles, stopping to try on whatever strikes your fancy, judging appearance in one of the many mirrors, or calling on a

Atlanta and Vicinity

nearby clerk if needed. The store even provides a basket to carry your choices in as you continue browsing. A.J.'S specializes in narrow and medium widths, with at least five hundred pairs of sample size 6B on hand at all times. The prices are a pleasant surprise: shoes that sell for $150 elsewhere may be as little as $75; you can also find styles as low priced as $9.50 (*at the time of this publication*). A recent addition to the warehouse is a large selection of jewelry, hand chosen from the work of skilled artisans.

You'll find check out as easy as shopping, with two banks of registers and several cashiers waiting to serve you. A.J.'S Shoe Warehouse is off of I-75 near Howell Mill Road, conveniently located for Buckhead and Midtown shoppers, but also well worth the trip if you're farther away.

FRIEDMAN'S SHOES
209 Mitchell Street
Atlanta, GA 30303
Tel. (404) 524-1311
Hrs: Mon. - Sat. 9:00 a.m. - 5:30 p.m.
Also,

4340 Roswell Road	223 Mitchell St. SW
Atlanta, GA 30342	Atlanta, GA 30303
Tel. (404) 843-2414	Tel. (404) 523-1134

Visa, Mastercard, AMEX and Discover Card are accepted.

People come from all over the nation to buy their shoes at Friedman's, the largest shoe store in the Southeast. Started by manager Randy Teilhaber's grandfather back in 1935, this family business has been at the same location for over fifty-three years.

One of the largest shoe stores in the country, Friedman's offers shoes in all sizes from size six to grand size eighteens. They also carry a large selection of unusual and exotic shoes made from non-traditional skins such as snake and crocodile. There is a full line of ladies shoes from the most elegant dress shoe to casual everyday shoes and sandals. Friedman's also carries a large selection of evening bags, hand bags, belts and accessories. A large selection of sports shoes, including Reebok, Nike, and NBA, attracts many sports professionals to the original shoe store. Around the wall you'll see many pictures of celebrities and sports figures, like NBA players Michael Jordan and Charles Oakley, who come to Friedman's to buy their shoes.

With a selection of adult, sports, dress, casual and fun styles, Friedman's carries everything you could think of in shoes. Even if you are hard to fit, you'll find what you need at Friedman's, a "Best Choice" for quality, selection and service at a very reasonable price.

SPORTING GOODS

OUTBACK OUTFITTERS AND BIKES
1125 Euclid Avenue Northeast
Atlanta, GA 30307
Tel. (404) 688-4878
Hrs: Tue. - Wed.   11:00 a.m. - 6:00 p.m.
     Thu. - Fri.   11:00 a.m. - 8:00 p.m.
     Saturday   10:00 a.m. - 6:00 p.m.
     Sunday   12:00 noon - 6:00 p.m.
Visa, MasterCard and AMEX are accepted.

Many people who travel want to see the country from a different point of view, and can get expert advice when they visit Outback Outfitters and Bikes in the Little Five Points neighborhood. This unique store is becoming a focal point on the East Coast for adventure.

Outback Outfitters and Bikes carries the best selection of mountain bikes in the Southeast and has an expert staff to show you how to get the most out of them. Service is what gives this store its high reputation and they're serious about their business. The store carries mountain bikes from the world's finest manufacturers. The bikes are made doubly strong in order

Atlanta and Vicinity

to withstand the punishment of traveling on off pavement trails.

Both backpackers and bicyclists will be impressed by the complete selection of accessories. Within the layout of 4,000 square feet, you'll feel as if you've begun you're adventure in the store. You'll find shelves packed with items such as ultra light and functional tents, clothing, sleeping bags, and cooking utensils. You need go nowhere else for first aid equipment or backpacking food items. The staff field tests all of the equipment and accessories personally. They can gear you with light, high performance equipment for a long expedition or a neighborhood ride.

After a productive shopping trip, relax in a comfortable rocking chair and watch the latest video describing mountain bike and touring adventures. Everything at Outback Outfitters and Bikes is geared toward making your adventure an ultimate joy.

TAVERNS

KNICKERBOCKERS
89 Park Place
Atlanta, GA 30303
Tel. (404) 688-7863
Hrs: Mon. - Fri. 11:00 a.m. - 11:00 p.m.
     Saturday   Private parties by reservation.
Visa, MasterCard and AMEX are accepted.

This is the old York's Pool and Recreation Parlor, which dates from 1910. It was once the lunch stop for Atlanta's lawyers and the competition spot for the best of the pool shooters.

Knickerbockers emerged with a change of ownership in 1983. It retains much of the old place but adds a touch of newness, too, in its conversion to a restaurant. The bar, a mahogany creation forty-eight feet long, remains in place along with the traditions of the old pool hall. Walls are graced with caricatures of the famous who have visited here. In the back room, where a huge fireplace dominates one wall, the famed Knickerbockers buffet luncheon is set out every weekday. There is also a menu of salads, soups, seafood and more. Among the dishes which get the most attention is Aunt Charley's Famous Chili, one of the least expensive choices on the moderately priced bill of fare. Also recommended, a chicken cooked in sesame ginger sauce that goes by the name of Phoenix Chicken; a strip steak served with cognac cream sauce; and rainbow trout covered with lemon butter sauce. For a sandwich that goes beyond, ask for York's Chili Dog, with or without a topping of cheese and onions. There's a feeling of history here which begins with the old terrazzo floors and extends up to the black tin ceilings. Knickerbockers is an easy walk from most downtown locations, with good food and more awaiting you.

MANUEL'S TAVERN
602 North Highland Avenue
Atlanta, GA 30307
Tel. (404) 525-3447
Hrs: Mon.-Sat. 10:30 a.m. - 2:00 a.m.
        Sunday   3:00 p.m. - 11:00 p.m.
Visa, MasterCard, AMEX and Discover are accepted.
Also,

4877 Memorial Drive	3330 Petree Corner Circle
Stone Mountain, GA 30083	Norcross, GA 30092
Tel. (404) 296-6919	Tel. 446-8250

Who sells the most draft beer in Atlanta? What is the oldest family-owned bar in the city? Where did Jimmy Carter hold a press conference to announce his run for governor? In each case the answer would be the same: Manuel's Tavern.

The *Atlanta Constitution* named Manuel's the best bar in Atlanta for three years running and the *New York Times* called it "Atlanta's quintessential neighborhood bar," whereas *Newsweek* places it among the ten best bars in the world. It is the kind of place where great ideas and neighborhood gossip are exchanged. The smoky, rustic atmosphere is home to players of Shakespeare as well as players of the gridiron. It is a sports bar where one can occasionally watch a Shakespeare play, and it's been a fixture in town for more than thirty-two years. In addition to the good brew, good company and good atmosphere, there's also the food. Manuel's serves up legendary hamburgers, some double decker, some loaded with cheese and bacon. And for die hard carnivores, there is a fine array of steaks in various sizes and cuts.

With all these qualities, you would think Manuel's would have trouble accommodating all of its customers, but the thirty-two foot bar and seating for 450 in at the main location, as well as two other community locations, enables Manuel's customers to be well served. So for a Tavern for folks of all walks of life, try Manuel's.

MOE'S AND JOE'S
1033 N. Highland Avenue
Atlanta, GA 30306
Tel. (404) 892-9231
Hrs: Mon.- Wed.   11:00 a.m.- 12:00 midnight
     Thu. - Sat.   11:00 a.m.- 1:00 a.m.

Due to the limited methods of transportation available during the early period of American history, the tavern became an important element of daily life. There, a weary traveler could satisfy his needs for food, drink and relaxation. The legacy of those public meeting places is alive and well in a contemporary version at Moe's and Joe's, where conviviality and relaxation are the order of the day.

Moe's and Joe's creates a nostalgia of its own, as it is one of the oldest neighborhood taverns in Atlanta and one of the true beer bars left. Begun in 1947, the tavern boasts Horace McKennie, the original bartender, who has become a fixture and a celebrity in his own right as he maintains his dominion over the bottles and kegs at his command. Hamburgers, hot dogs and fries comprise the tavern fare, to be washed down with a cold, frothy beer from the tap. The interior has an ambiance of the 50s and 60s. There is an old jukebox that plays your melodies for a quarter, and it is said that the phone company has been trying for years to buy the vintage phone booth on the premises.

Enjoyed by local residents and a lure to college students, the tavern has also had the distinction of having had two movies filmed there. Not too many years ago, a former President's son could be found playing pinball and drinking beer with his Security Guard while enjoying the local gossip with the customers. Moe's and Joe's invites you to step back in time, eat, drink and raise your glass to good health and pleasure.

THEATER

ACADEMY THEATRE, 173 Fourteenth Street N.E., Atlanta, GA. Tel. (404) 892-0880. Georgia's oldest theater company. Come see contemporary dramas, classic masterpieces, and regional premieres in this lovely new facility.

WINE SHOP

PHARR WINE & CHEESE SHOP
320 Pharr Road
Atlanta, GA 30305
Tel. (404) 261-4422
Hrs: Mon. - Sat. 9:30 a.m. - 6:30 p.m.
Visa and MasterCard are accepted.

Pharr Wine & Cheese Shop has been providing fine wines and cheeses, wine tasting and expert advise to its customers for more than twenty years. Owner Bob Nettles, a member of the National Wine Club, believes, "Wine for a smart buyer is as good as real estate, and they aren't making any more dirt."

It's not every store that can say it has the best selection of French wines in Atlanta; Pharr Wine & Cheese Shop can.

Atlanta and Vicinity

Pharr gives the public the chance to experience and learn about different wines and cheeses at their weekly tastings. You'll not only learn about tastes, but about what makes a wine valuable so that you can invest wisely. According to Bob, "A good vintage of an investment grade wine can triple in value in two years." He should know, as he is the purveyor and advisor for the finest wine cellars in Atlanta. Stop by Pharr the next time you're headed for an intimate picnic and pick up a gourmet meat or cheese sandwich to go along with your bottle of Bordeaux.

Pharr has developed a reputation for quality service, a variety of fine domestic and imported wines, as well as a knowledgeable staff willing to share their secrets about just the right wine to buy for investment, an intimate meal or dinner party. You may want to pick up a bottle or two of Bob's jeroboams of 1982 Chateau Mouton Rothchild of Paullican. They're on sale for $1,250 each. If what Bob says about wine is true, you may have yourself a great investment.

ATLANTA DURING THE CIVIL WAR

By

Merritt Scott Miller

It could easily be argued that the Battle of Atlanta began with the Battle of Kennesaw Mountain. It was after that ghastly Yankee loss that William T. Sherman and his 90,000 veterans, in late June 1864, outflanked Rebel general Joe Johnston's grey boys. They forced the quiet little master Confederate tactician, who fought like an Irish bantam, to pull his forces back across the Chattahoochee River and into the trenches around Atlanta itself.

The move did not please Confederate President Jefferson Davis. He himself was under incredible pressure, what with Grant's legions facing Lee's brave but weary, shoeless and half starving battalions just outside Richmond. The South needed a victory, not a Union siege, so in a last ditch effort to produce a miracle, President Davis replaced Joe Johnston with General John B. Hood.

Now Hood wasn't nearly the strategist or tactician quiet Johnston was, but he was as tough as any general the Confederates fielded. Their army was considered the bravest in the world at the time and he was thought to be as courageous and daring as Mr. Lee. One of Sherman's generals, John Schofield, warned, "He'll hit you like hell, now, before you know it."

Union forces found that out soon enough. While the Army of the Cumberland crossed Peachtree Creek, five miles from the center of Atlanta, and the Army of Tennessee went east on another of Sherman's famous flanking maneuvers, on July 20, John Hood and his Rebs let them have it. It was as good an assault as ever was made in that war, but when the Johnnies came smashing toward Peachtree Creek, they ran into the Yankees under Pap Thomas. It was Pap's artillery that broke the Confederate charge and by the end of the day, thousands of grey soldiers were dead. Hood pulled back, but he had no

Atlanta and Vicinity

intention of quitting. Instead, he let the federals keep the high ground above Peachtree Creek and turned on the flanking Army of Tennessee, catching it at Decatur. On July 22, Hood's boys, vastly outnumbered, screamed down on the blue southern flank, killed the Union general commanding, and only narrowly missed pushing the Army of Tennessee clear back on itself.

Once again, Hood pulled back, and word reached Sherman that the Confederates were just about spent. If that was true at that time, it had changed less than a week later. On July 28, Hood struck viciously again at the Army of the Tennessee, catching it this time at Ezra Church, west of Atlanta. The Union forces held their ground but they did not advance.

It was then that Sherman realized he wasn't marching into Atlanta if it meant going through Hood's boys to do it, so he settled in for a siege, setting his cannons up on high ground, bombarding them day and night and setting fire to much of the town. His troops chopped up the railroads supplying Atlanta and the skirmishes resulting from these encounters, though on a much smaller scale, gave the boys in blue more than bloody noses. And so August of 1864 wore on, with Sherman not gaining an inch but slowly strangling the jewel of the Confederate southeast, while Hood's men steadfastly manned their trenches and helped civilian brigades put out fires. It was a war of attrition. Sherman slowly surrounded the city, hoping as much, if not more, in fact, to capture Hood and his army, as to destroy Atlanta.

Hood was up against impossible odds. He was outnumbered by a vastly better equipped, clothed and certainly better fed army. Yet he managed to hold out for six weeks, the whole time of which Atlanta was under the cannon. Noble C. Willians, a boy living in Atlanta at the time, was to describe the experience thusly,

> *"Shells were frequently exploding in the main business portion of the city, and when they would come in contact with the hard paving stones, there was no calculating what course they would take. Both soldiers and citizens were maimed and killed in the streets almost daily."*

Night and day shells were constantly being thrown into the city, increasing the mortality rate. They also set fire often to the houses, which kept the firemen constantly busy extinguishing flames.

It was the Battle of Jonesboro on August 31, when Sherman moved to cut Atlanta's southern rail access, which forced Hood to finally evacuate the city. The four months of fighting had cost each side over 30,000 casualties.

On September 1, Confederate soldiers marched, but not before setting fire to some eighty carloads of ammunition they could not take with them. They had surrendered the town but they had not given up the fight. Circling to the northwest, Hood and his 40,000 remaining veterans jabbed at Sherman's supply lines and when the Union general tried to strike back, Hood pranced out of the way, prompting Sherman to observe, "I cannot guess his movements as I could those of Johnston, who was a sensible man and did only sensible things."

In mid-October, Sherman gave up, but sent part of his army back to Tennessee to checkmate any attempt on Hood's part to strike while Union forces commenced the sack and ruin of Georgia. Atlanta did not fare well under siege and when it fell, Sherman sent a messenger to Hood and the two agreed to a truce long enough to evacuate any remaining civilians who

Atlanta and Vicinity

wished to go. Sherman subsequently made evacuation an order. On November 8, 1864, he issued to his staff the following orders:

"The general commanding deems it proper at this time to inform the officers and men of the Fourteenth, Fifteenth, Seventeenth, and Twentieth Corps that he has organized them into an army for a special purpose, well known to the War Department and to General Grant. It is sufficient for you to know that it involves a departure from our present base, and a long and difficult march to a new one.

"All the chances of war have been considered and provided for, as far as human sagacity can. All he asks of you is to maintain that discipline, patience, and courage which have characterized you in the past; and he hopes, through you, to strike a blow at our enemy that will have a material effect in producing what we all so much desire, his complete overthrow."

Couched in these lines were the dictates which, from the day they were issued until the last detachment left the city on the night of November 14, turned Sherman's troops loose to destroy factories, foundries, railroads, mills and railroad property between Chattanooga and Atlanta. The sack of Atlanta itself commenced, as well, with often vicious gangs of Union soldiers pillaging private homes before setting them aflame. It was this destruction not only of Atlanta, but of the entire state along the wide swath Sherman cut through it in his march to Savannah that caused so much of the hatred which was to follow. It was, however, war, and to Sherman, the only way to win it was to destroy his enemy's capacity to wage it. Sherman set out to starve the Confederacy, to deny it manufactured goods, transportation and communication. He did not take it to the extremes of other generals in later wars, when they exercised a scorched earth policy which included machine gunning civilians or killing them in concentration camps.

Atlanta and Vicinity

Sherman is, however, credited with helping end an era characterized by honor, chivalry and the romantic gesture. In the minds of many historians, the Civil War itself, the costliest in U.S. history, was the first modern war, and Sherman's tactics provided an example of what it took to defeat the Confederacy and preserve the Union. Atlanta was the first casualty of the new age.

Atlanta and Vicinity

SWEET AUBURN

By

Merritt Scott Miller

Rarely has a street come to symbolize the hope, freedom and effort of a group of people the way Auburn Avenue has come to represent the dynamic growth and energy of Georgia's black population. This street has been a cultural, economic and spiritual center for many proud Atlantans who have come to call it 'Sweet Auburn'. A look at the history of Sweet Auburn will show that this area is a microcosm of Atlanta as a whole, complete with the same spirit of optimism and the same twin ideals of perseverance and industry.

Half of Atlanta's 2,029,660 people can trace their roots back through antebellum slavery to the African continent. The record of the struggles of these black Americans is as vital a legacy as any immigrant story in the South, and even in the nation. It is not only "black" history, but human history, and if one believes that what exists now is the result of what came before, the story of blacks in Atlanta is a tale of Atlanta, of Georgia, of the South, and of America herself.

Central to that chronicle is Auburn Avenue which, in 1957, *Fortune* magazine called "the richest Negro street in the world" and to which social activist John Wesley Dobbs referred to as "Sweet Auburn." It begins, however, with another race of Americans, those who lived and died, worked and played, loved and warred long before the Spanish and the English who discovered and settled Georgia ever arrived. Auburn Avenue was a Cherokee Indian trail to a tribal gathering site at what is now Atlanta's Five Points district. It also marked the way to a Cherokee burial ground near present day Lawrenceville.

In the mid-1800s, it took the name Wheat Street and served the German-American community. In 1847, Atlanta's first church for blacks, the Bethel Tabernacle. was established.

It was Mary Combs, in 1856, who became the first black resident. She purchased land at Wheat and Peach streets for

$250 and with the $500 for which she later sold it, she bought her husband's freedom.

For many years, Auburn Avenue co-existed with the booming commercial district to its west. Slaves and free blacks were not permitted to own businesses in antebellum Atlanta but occasionally exceptions were granted and one of them was made to a slave who saved the lives of 100 passengers of a train trapped on a burning bridge. Thus it was that in 1854, Ransom Montgomery became the first black entrepreneur when Atlanta city fathers gave him his freedom and granted him a vending concession at the train station.

It took the Civil War and Reconstruction to open Atlanta to further development. On Auburn Avenue, however, it was not commercialism, but education, which first took root. In 1865, Grandison B. Daniels and James Tate established the first school for blacks in Bethel Church. This school subsequently evolved into Morris Brown College. Established in 1881, it is the only university in the state founded entirely by black Americans. Tate, popularly considered the father of black business in Atlanta, a year later integrated Atlanta's central business district with a grocery on Walton Street.

In 1867, black education received additional impetus in the form of three white missionaries from Yale University who established the Storrs School for African Americans. This school was later to become Atlanta University. Shortly thereafter, First Congregation Church changed its name to Storrs Church, and in 1868, Big Bethel African Methodist Episcopal Church became the first black religious institution on Auburn Avenue.

The 1870s witnessed even more progress for blacks in Atlanta. In the first year of that decade, Wheat Street Baptist Church was founded. Rev. Peter J. Bryant, its pastor from 1898 to 1929, organized the Atlanta Benevolent and Protective Association, forerunner of the Atlanta Life Insurance Company. In 1870 William R. Finch was elected the first Afro-American city councilman. His home, on Edgewood Avenue, was a vital part of the Auburn Avenue residential community. In 1875, twelve black physicians founded the National Medical Association. And in 1879, Atlanta's first public school for

Atlanta and Vicinity

blacks, The Gate City Colored School, opened in the basement of Big Bethel Church.

The black community continued to grow well into the 1880s, and Auburn Avenue's residential neighborhood expanded to the east when black bank teller Wesley Redding bought a home on Jackson Street in 1884.

Two years later, Ebenezer Baptist Church, Dr. Martin Luther King, Jr.'s, first pulpit, was established on Airline Street. It moved to Auburn Avenue in 1922. It was also in this decade that David Howard started a funeral home that exists today as one of Atlanta's first successful black businesses.

By 1890, Auburn Avenue, however, still had a long way to go, for only 52 of the city's estimated 28,000 blacks lived there. This was to change dramatically over the next several decades, given impetus, no doubt, in 1891, with the establishment of the *People's Advocate*. Headquartered in the Auburn community, it was the first newspaper in Atlanta founded to serve the African American population.

That same year, bank teller Wesley Redding, former slave, and successful barber Alonzo Herndon, together with Richard Wright, established the Atlanta Loan and Trust Company and headquartered it on Auburn Avenue. In 1893, Wheat Street became, by petition to the city council, Auburn Avenue, and a year later, the Butler Street YMCA started up in the basement of Wheat Street Baptist Church. Auburn Avenue added another business in 1896, The Gate City Drug Store. Its founder, Moses Amos, was the first licensed black pharmacist in the state and went into business with several black physicians.

The 1890s also witnessed the first stirrings of Atlanta's formal civil rights movement when Booker T. Washington, in 1895, gave his Atlanta Compromise speech at the Cotton State Exposition.

By the turn of the century, Auburn Avenue had ten black businesses and two black professionals. By then the Auburn Avenue community had become a showcase for the black middle class but poorer African Americans were still relegated to "Darktown," the district bounded by Auburn, Jackson, Forrest and Piedmont.

Atlanta and Vicinity

In 1903, Benjamin Davis, ancestor of two famous black Air Force generals, became editor of *The Atlanta Independent Newspaper*, a Georgia Odd Fellows publication. In 1905, Alonzo Herndon, one of the founders of The Atlanta Loan and Trust Company, established Atlanta Mutual Insurance.

In 1911, Auburn Avenue received national attention when President William Howard Taft addressed a gathering from the pulpit of Big Bethel African Methodist Episcopal Church. That same year, North Carolina Mutual Insurance Company opened a branch on Auburn Avenue. The Silver Moon Barber Shop, which serves customers to this day, was started in 1912. A year later, Standard Life Insurance Company became the third black legal reserve company in the United States.

The year of 1917 witnessed America's entry into the First World War and The Great Fire, which many historians claim did more damage to Atlanta than Sherman's occupation and subsequent torching. The Auburn Avenue community was devastated, but even before the ashes were cold, the National Association for the Advancement of Colored People organized its Atlanta branch and opened offices in Auburn Avenue's Odd Fellows Building. A year later, the Butler Street YMCA got its own building and Ma Sutton (Mrs. Scottie B. Sutton) opened her famous restaurant on Auburn Avenue.

The 1920s were years of consolidation for the black community. The Citizens Trust Bank, the National Negro Insurance Company, Aiken and Faulkner Construction Company, Yates and Milton Drug Store, the Herndon Building, the Mutual Federal Savings and Loan Association, the *Atlanta Daily World*, and The Hopkins Book Concern and Furniture Company all got their start during this busy decade.

On January 15, 1929, Dr. Martin Luther King, Jr. , was born at 501 Auburn Avenue at the home of his grandparents, Rev. and Mrs. Adam Daniel Willams and parents Rev. and Mrs. Martin Luther King, Sr. King, who was later to become prominent in the national civil rights movements of the Sixties, was also the youngest man in history to be awarded the international Nobel Prize for Peace.

During the 1930s and 1940s, the Auburn Avenue community continued to thrive and black historians attribute segregation as the chief reason. Like the Germans, Italians, Irish, Jews and others who came to America as ethnic minorities and survived by building economically and culturally close relationships, so blacks in Atlanta had learned to depend on themselves.

Significant accomplishments during these decades include the construction of the Prince Hall Masons Georgia headquarters on Auburn Avenue; the opening of the famous Savoy Hotel in the Herndon Building (the Savoy is credited with the first neon sign in Atlanta); founding of WERD, first black-owned radio station in the country; and the development of nightclubs in the Auburn community now credited with much of the evolution which brought such greats as Nat King Cole and Cab Calloway to national prominence.

The 1950s and 1960s were times of both prosperity and strife in the black community in Atlanta. The street which *Fortune* magazine touted so highly was also the scene of a great deal of civil rights activism. It was also during the mid-Sixties that the construction of the downtown expressway changed the complexion of the Auburn community, and for a while it appeared as though this historic district would go the way of many black areas in other major cities in both the North and the South.

Ironically, many black historians credit this trying period of commercial uncertainty with the growth of new understandings between blacks and whites which made possible the subsequent representation of African Americans at the city and county level. The Auburn community's national importance was recognized in 1980, when Congress declared portions of it, including Dr. Martin Luther King, Jr.'s birth place, a National Historic District. This, in conjunction with local revitalization efforts, among them the founding of the Collections of Life & Heritage, Inc. in 1985, have restored much of the community and it continues, today, to grow.

Atlanta is now considered to be among the most racially progressive cities in the United States, thanks to efforts of such individuals as Ralph McGill, Andrew Young and former Georgia governor and U.S. president Jimmy Carter.

Atlanta and Vicinity

AVONDALE ESTATES

Those intending to spend time in Atlanta and seeking a unique lifestyle experience will want to drive east from the city center on Ponce de Leon Avenue and then take the southern fork (College Avenue) through the center of Decatur and Agnes Scott College to the community of Avondale Estates.

Fully one third of this planned community is on the National Historic Register and can easily be identified by its English Village theme, developed at the onset of the city's founding in 1924. Located approximately seven miles from downtown Atlanta and a mile and a half east of Decatur, Avondale Estates includes a commercial center, a historic portion of the town's residential area, several historic landscape features, a historic transportation corridor, two historic parks and an entry gate.

Avondale Estates contains outstanding examples of medieval Tudor motifs and was planned after the charter written in 1917 for Kingsport, Tennessee. The community is fully and attractively landscaped with spacious lawns, shrubbery, ornamental and shade trees, flower gardens and stone markers, gateposts and curbs.

Essentially what one has here, then, is a small city which has two lakes, several parks, a good variety of lodging and a shopping mall which contains a Macy's and other attractive mercantile establishments, all remaining consistent with an architectural theme both quaint and convincing.

ATTRACTIONS

• The entire community is an attraction of the highest order. **Willis Park**, designed for intensive recreation, has a poolhouse, swimming pool, tennis courts, playing fields and a playground incorporated into hilly terrain and heavily wooded areas, lending a most naturalistic effect.

Atlanta and Vicinity

• Secluded **Lake Avondale**, an artificially created lake, has landscaped banks, a clubhouse, paved walks, commemorative markers, stone gateposts and rustic benches. It is an ideal place to take a stroll and is considered one of the most romantic spots in suburban Atlanta.

For more information, contact the DeKalb Convention and Visitors Bureau, 750 Commerce Drive, Suite 201, Decatur, GA 30030; (404) 378-2525.

SPORTING GOODS - SKI

AVONDALE SKI SHOP
122 Avondale Road
Avondale Estates, GA 30002
Tel. (404) 294-5499
Hrs: Mon. - Thu.   9:30 a.m. - 9:00 p.m.
     Fri., Sat.   9:30 a.m. - 6:00 p.m.
Visa, MasterCard, AMEX and Discover are accepted.

The combination of owning a women's discount sportswear outlet and a membership in the Atlanta City Ski Club led owner Annette Ford to broaden her shop's horizons to include a full line of the best quality ski equipment in the business. The Avondale Ski Shop has developed a reputation during the past twenty-five years as "the place to go before you hit the slopes."

The English Tudor building with its chalet storefront, built in 1929, now houses 3,000 square feet of clothing, equipment and rentals for the slopes. Clothing for the entire family can be found bearing the labels Raven, Skyr, Sportcaster, Slalom, Serac, Swing West, Fera and Pedigree. Cedarwood and ski posters are a back drop for Pre, Elan, Dynamic, Olin, Salomon, Geze and San Marco ski equipment. This is the place to condition your skis as well as find out the latest conditions on the slopes. Buy, rent or tune your own equipment by certified technicians.

After twenty-five years in the business, Annette has maintained her enthusiasm for making sure her customers ski experience is the very best possible. Traditionally, the store has been open from August until April. This year, Annette may keep the shop open all year, adding water ski equipment to her repertoire.

BUFORD

This comfortable small north Georgia community is sited on the banks of the Chattahoochee River, five miles southeast of the Buford Dam. The dam creates the conditions for the 38,000 acre Lake Sidney Lanier. Buford is accessible from Interstate 85 and then west on State Highway 20, or from U.S. Highway 19 and then east on Highway 20.

Buford was incorporated on August 24, 1872 and in 1868, established as a stop on the railroad which connected Atlanta to Charlotte, North Carolina. Named for the president of that road, Col. A.S. Buford, it is pronounced bew'-ferd. Like all of Gwinnett County, the area literally radiates history.

A modern community by any standards, it nonetheless retains an undeniable southern charm, and makes a pleasant stop on the way to Lake Lanier, five miles to the north, and an outstanding complement to the local resorts.

ATTRACTIONS

• One of northern Georgia's premier resort areas lies at the outskirts of Buford, on the shores of the 38,000 acre **Lake Lanier**, which honors poet laureate Sidney Lanier. More than sixteen million travelers visit each year. (It's one of the less "best kept" secrets of native Atlantans.) These new Southerners come for the fishing, swimming, skiing, boating and just plain lazying on the lake itself and its many inlets, creeks and small bays.

Atlanta and Vicinity

Lake Lanier's four islands actually represent the summits of pine-covered mountains and are accessible via State Highway 365 north of Buford. They are connected to the mainland by causeway. Each offers different recreational facilities and includes campgrounds, cottages, houseboats and tennis courts. Imagine, if you will, blossom scented roads which wend across bridges, past trout ponds, equestrian stables, miniature golf courses, playgrounds and picnic pavilions.

One of the most exciting aspects of the Lake Lanier Islands is entertainment. Its amphitheater hosts such popular concert and recording stars as the unforgettable Roy Orbison, the delightful and ageless Brenda Lee and the irrepressible Sha Na Na.

• **The Stouffer PineIsle Resort**, an island unto itself, contains a spacious hotel with 250 rooms, each with its own patio. Thirty of these rooms are furnished with a hot tub on a private terrace, and four suites have functional fireplaces. PineIsle Resort has its own beautiful stretch of sandy beach, indoor and outdoor pool, tennis courts and an eighteen hole golf course designed by PGA star Gary Player. Dining at the hotel's Pavilion or in the less formal Gazebo is a real treat. For more information, contact Lake Lanier Islands Authority, P.O. Box 605, Buford, GA 30518; (404) 945-6701; Lanier Island Cottages, Lake Lanier Islands, Buford, GA 30518; (404) 945-8331; Stouffer PineIsle Resort, Lake Lanier Islands, Buford, GA 30518; (404) 945-8921.

CHAMBLEE

This DeKalb County community of approximately 7,000 is situated just north of the DeKalb Peachtree Airport on historic Peachtree Road about seven miles northeast of downtown Atlanta. Chamblee is known throughout Georgia for its Antique Row, the South's largest and most unusual antique area. It also boasts a community of historic old homes, churches and stores dating back to pre-Civil War times. One of the easiest ways to reach Chamblee is to take the MARTA north line train from downtown or Lenox Square and get off at the Brookhaven

Station. From there, you'll want to take MARTA bus No. 25 (North Shallowford) and that will drop you off in the heart of Chamblee Antique Row.

ATTRACTIONS

• **Chamblee's Antique Row** makes this community a definite "must see" in the greater Atlanta area. It's here that many of the film production companies come for the props they use when depicting life from the Revolutionary War period. No matter whether you're looking for furniture from the antebellum period; Victorian oak and walnut; Heisey, Cambridge, Fostoria, Limoges or Doulton porcelain; model trains from Lionel or American Flyer; old time neon signs; arts and crafts by senior citizens; clothing and accessories from 1870 through1930; crystal and fine china; antique lighting devices; specialty and old books; or quilts, textiles and folk art, you'll find it all and more in Chamblee. This community has the distinction of showcasing its impressive collections in historic shops and stores, for Chamblee was established during the period which saw the growth of many of the older communities in the Atlanta area and was spared, to a large extent, the destruction wreaked on Atlanta, Decatur and other towns which stood in the way of Union General William Sherman's march to the sea.

For more information, contact the Chamblee Antique Dealers Association, Chamblee, GA 30341; or the DeKalb Convention and Visitors Bureau, 750 Commerce Drive, Suite 201, Decatur, GA 30030; (404) 378-2525.

Atlanta and Vicinity

ANTIQUE SHOP

RUST N' DUST ANTIQUES
5486 Peachtree Road
Chamblee, GA 30341
Tel. (404) 458-1614
Hrs: Mon. - Fri. 10:30 a.m. - 5:00 p.m.
     Saturday 10:30 a.m. - 5:30 p.m.
     Sunday 1:00 p.m. - 5:00 p.m.
Visa and MasterCard are accepted.

What began in a basement on Peachtree Road fifteen years ago has grown into one of the Southwest's finest and most respected antique shops. Rust N' Dust has lived up to the slogan "if we don't have it we'll find it for you", and now finds itself with nine separate dealers and five different buildings.

The ever changing inventory at Rust N' Dust Antiques has been known to include furniture, primitives, advertising, glass, porcelain, wicker and toys. Old slot and pinball machines, linens, a large selection of sports equipment and everything else imaginable are available, along with some things unimaginable. Long known to filmmakers, designers and photographers, Rust N' Dust has provided that special antique for many well known stars including Michael Jackson, Bryant Gumble and Patricia Neal, just to name a few.

With a solid reputation for honesty and reliability, Rust N' Dust Antiques offers a variety that is seldom found in one location. Located in the heart of Chamblee's famed Antique Row, Rust N' Dust is a must stop for the antiquer or for anyone looking for southern hospitality at its best.

COLLEGE PARK

First called Atlantis City, then Manchester, College Park is a community of approximately 24,600 in south Fulton County. Sixteen miles southwest of downtown Atlanta on Main Street and four miles south of East Point, it is one of the major "bedroom" communities of the southern Atlanta suburbs. Close to 25 percent of its residents are employed in clerical positions, 14.3 percent in the service sector and 12.3 percent in the professional and technical fields. As such, then, College Park represents a residential area typical of "the New South."

The community originated with the establishment of a West Point Railroad spur track into the area. Incorporated in 1890, its residents changed the town name to College Park after Cox College, no longer in existence, opened as a music conservatory. Now, it serves the famous Hartsfield International Airport.

This beautiful community as been cited as a certified city for excellence in municipal operations. It is predominantly middle to upper middle class black, with a median educational level of 12.5 years. Nearly 35 percent of its residents have attended college. Unemployment hovers around 7 percent, and median family income is $22,000, while average family incomes are expected to reach $39,000 by 1992.

ATTRACTIONS

• **The College Park Golf Course**, at 3711 Fairway Drive, is one of the nicer courses in the area, particularly for those who elect to spend a few days using this community as a base of operations for business or pleasure in Atlanta itself. For more information, call (404) 373-0731.

• **The Georgia International Convention and Trade Center**, less than one mile from the Hartsfield International Airport, has over 40,000 square feet of exhibit space, seventeen meeting rooms and a 400 room hotel. This is where many of the

Atlanta and Vicinity

major trade exhibitions are held and this complex is known throughout the nation for its service and attention to detail.

For more information, contact the College Park Business and Industrial Development Authority, P.O. Box F, College Park, GA 30337; (404) 767-1537.

ANTIQUE SHOP

GOOD AND PLENTY ANTIQUES, 3819-3827 Main Street, College Park, GA. Tel. (404) 762-5798. Good and Plenty Antiques buys and sells furniture, glassware, collectibles and china of all types. Come in and browse for an hour or a day.

BOOKSTORE

TITAN BOOKS AND COMICS, 5436 Riverdale Road, College Park, GA. Tel. (404) 996-9129. Titan buys, sells and trades comics and has one-half million copies in stock. Games, baseball cards, miniatures and Japanese models are also featured.

HARTSFIELD ATLANTA INTERNATIONAL AIRPORT

By

Merritt Scott Miller

For well over a century and a half, the city of Atlanta has been synonymous with transportation, and this, in turn, has enabled it to survive economic reversals which have devastated less diversified cities in both the North and the South. A major rail center from its earliest years, it owes its very existence to the Western and Atlantic Railroad, which, in 1837, designated it Zero Milepost and dubbed it Terminus.

Atlanta leaped into the twentieth century in 1909, when Coca Cola president Asa Candler developed 300 acres in the village of Hapeville, ten miles south of the city center, into an auto speedway. A year later, the site witnessed the community's first air show. This sport became extremely popular, especially with Billy Hartsfield, then twenty-one years old, the man who was to become a legend as mayor of Atlanta for twenty-two years. He was entranced with airplanes and foresaw clearly the destiny they were

Atlanta and Vicinity

eventually to have, not only in Atlanta's future, but in the future of the world.

Auto racing did not catch on and the raceway and airstrip fell into disuse. This was not a time of great prosperity in Atlanta and, without taxpayer support, the handful of air transport entrepreneurial efforts did not succeed. Instead, Atlanta concentrated on a massive road construction program which complemented the still vital railroad industry and accommodated the increasing role passenger traffic and trucking played in the city's growth.

In 1924, the United States Army expressed an interest in building a network of military airfields in the greater Atlanta area. Bill Hartsfield, by then into his second year of his first term as an alderman from Atlanta's third ward, got together with other Fulton County aviation advocates and started things moving. After he won election as mayor, it became evident that Atlanta would, indeed, have an airfield. On April 16, 1925, outgoing mayor Walter A. Sims took the lease option—five years, rent free—on the Candler property in Hapeville.

Progress from that date on was swift. Two short dirt runways with night lighting were installed that same year. By 1926, two hangars had been erected and Florida Airways was flying mail and passengers to Miami. Three years later, Pitcairn Aviation, grandfather of Eastern Airways, and St. Tammany-Gulf Coast Airways established air mail and passenger service, and by 1929, the "little dirt field in Atlanta" was connected with New York, Chicago, Miami, and New Orleans. On April 3, 1929, the city purchased the site for $94,400.

The year of 1929 could well be said to mark the birth of Hartsfield Atlanta International Airport as it is known today. After the city officially went into the aviation business, it hired Princeton educated avionics engineer and pilot Jack Gray as airport manager. Conditions were still primitive. Gray operated out of a tiny shack with a staff of four and two mule-drawn wagons for grading and construction equipment. As he settled in, however, this most innovative man corralled convict labor and borrowed Fulton County construction equipment. In

Atlanta and Vicinity

1930, Hapeville Airport was rated among the top ten movers of air mail, had a small aircraft manufacturing plant, and served as maintenance and operational headquarters for Eastern Air Transport.

In 1932, American Airlines took a flier on ten years rent and the $35,000 was used to build the airfield's first administration building. Ironically, when President Roosevelt cancelled the field's air mail contracts, American left and did not return until 1983.

Others, however, perhaps motivated by Jack Gray's obvious dedication (to keep money coming in, Gray used an Eastern plane to give sightseeing tours of Stone Mountain) hung on. The air mail contracts were returned in 1934 and Delta Air Lines successfully bid the Fort Worth-Atlanta route. Roosevelt's administration also provided WPA funding of several million dollars and the field got paved runways. At the end of the decade, it also constructed a control tower.

The military again entered the picture in late 1940 and another one million dollars went into a variety of improvements, which met an air traffic demand typified by the 1,700 takeoffs and landings logged in one day in 1942. In 1942, as well, the airfield edged into the black financially, generating some two and a half million dollars more than it spent. In 1948, Atlanta Municipal Airport was home for Delta, Eastern and Southern airlines, handled over a million passengers, and logged a most impressive third of a million takeoffs and landings. A year later, it boasted 162 scheduled departures per day.

By 1955, Atlanta Municipal led the nation in sheer volume of air traffic and between noon and 2:00 p.m., it was the busiest in the world. In 1957, it finally started construction of a terminal. That magnificent monument to aviation was completed May 3, 1961, at a cost of twenty-one million dollars. A gleaming turquoise and steel structure, it had a control tower on the twelfth floor which ranged sixty miles, an incredible distance at that time.

The terminal itself included three restaurants and an architecturally awesome ticket lobby. It was designed to handle six million passengers per year. It wasn't, however,

Atlanta and Vicinity

enough to accommodate the incredible expansion of Atlanta and the demands of the industry itself. The ensuing decade was fraught with struggle as various studies were conducted, proposals were advanced and abandoned, an extremely touchy issue of minority participation was debated, and various airlines were courted. Finally, in January, 1977, construction was begun on the complex which exists today.

Once work started, however, it took just three and a half years to complete costing approximately $35,000 a day. It involved three major contractors, 250 subcontractors, eleven domestic airlines, five foreign carriers, Federal Customs, the Department of Agriculture, the Federal Aviation Administration, both state and federal departments of transportation, the Georgia state fire marshal, the Atlanta building department, two counties and three cities. Three new foreign carriers came aboard halfway through. Construction also involved an underground rapid transit system which, until 1985, boasted a higher volume of traffic than Atlanta's famed MARTA system.

The project encompassed a variety of improvements and when it was finished, on September 21, 1980, 25,000 employees moved out of the old terminal and into the new. By then, the airport had grown from a dirt track known as Hapeville Field, through the years when it was designated Atlanta Municipal Airport to its modern title of Hartsfield Atlanta International Airport.

According to the airport's 1987 annual report, 200,000 jobs in the greater Atlanta area are directly or indirectly related to the facility. Its total operating revenue for the year was $115,843,000.

The airport provides daily flights to and from 150 cities in the United States and over twenty major population centers in the United Kingdom, Western Europe, Mexico, the Orient and the Caribbean. Customers are served by twenty-five passenger/freight and fourteen cargo airlines. Thanks to a twenty-four hour security system, the number of incidents of theft is among the lowest of any major airport in the nation. The airport is also linked by an extensive truck and rail network to the Port of Savannah.

Atlanta and Vicinity

The Hartsfield Atlanta International Airport covers 3,750 acres; the terminal complex, roughly the equivalent area of eleven and a half football fields. Facilities include a full service restaurant and snack bar, with additional snack bars throughout the concourses; a variety of retail shops; a full service FDIC-member bank; full handicapped accessibility; cocktail lounges; duty-free shops and newsstands; car rentals;Traveler's Aid; mail service; a full battery of telephones and teletype connectors; a chapel and several vending areas. The USO also maintains an operation for military personnel and their families.

Airlines with operations based here include Aeromexico, Air Jamaica, American, Atlantic Southeast, Braniff, British Caledonian Airways, Cayman Airways, Continental, Delta, Eastern, Eastern Metro, Japan Air Lines, KLM, Lockheed, Lufthansa, Midway, Midwest Express, Northwest, Pan Am, Piedmont, Piedmont Commuter, SABENA, Swissair, Trans World, United, and USAir.

Off line passenger and air freight airlines include Aeroperu, Air Canada, Air France, Air India, Air Paraguay, Alitalia, British West Indies, El Al, Finnair, Hawaiian, Iberia Airlines of Spain, Korean Air Lines, Lloyd's Aero Boliviano, Qantas, Scandinavian Airlines System, Singapore, and Varig Brazilian Airlines.

The North and South Terminal parking areas can accommodate 18,500 vehicles. The airport is also served by taxis and several limousine services. The Metropolitan Atlanta Rapid Transit Authority (MARTA) has trains leaving and arriving every twelve minutes, with connections throughout Fulton and DeKalb counties. By MARTA, the airport is fifteen minutes from downtown Atlanta.

For more information, contact Director of Public Relations, Airport Commissioner's Office, Hartsfield Atlanta International Airport, Atlanta, GA 30320; (404) 530-6600.

Atlanta and Vicinity

CONYERS

This community of 6,567 lies approximately eighteen miles southeast of downtown Atlanta on Interstate 20 and is one of Atlanta's older suburbs. The community was founded shortly after the War of 1812, when the territory opened up in 1816. One of the earliest pioneers in the area, John Holcombe, built a log house where the courthouse now stands.

The town itself is named for Dr. W.D. Conyers, the Covington banker who gave the state owned Georgia Railroad Company the right of way which, by 1845, had turned the community into a reckonable station along the Augusta to Marthasville (Atlanta) line. In 1854, with 400 residents, the town incorporated.

Designated the county seat when Rockdale County was enacted in 1870, the community serves as the major trade center for an area whose present population of 49,600 is expected to reach 88,000 by the turn of this century. Growth at present is booming, due largely to housing prices which are ten to fifteen percent lower than in other metropolitan Atlanta areas.

ATTRACTIONS

In addition to many fine historical homes and charming accommodations, Conyers offers two major attractions which are at once unique and representative of the many faces of Georgia itself.

• For a prime example of the kind of industrialization which underlies the evolution of the New South, the tour of the **Warren Sherer Division of Kysor Industrial Corporation** would be hard to beat. This manufacturer of refrigerated display cases employs 350 people and offers a one hour tour of its production plant. Reservations are requested one week in advance and groups of one to fifty can be accommodated. The plant lies two miles from Interstate 20 East. For more information, contact Joann E. Hall, Public Relations, Warren

Atlanta and Vicinity

Sherer Division Kysor Industrial Corporation, 1600 Industrial Boulevard, Conyers, GA 30207; (404) 483-5600.

Conyers' second major attraction has particular appeal to those who find themselves at times overwhelmed by the stresses and the complexities of a dazzlingly accelerating technological age.

• Founded in 1944 by a group of monks specializing in self sufficiency, including growing their own food, the **Monastery of the Holy Ghost** harks back to an age when Old Testament prophets sought the solitude of the wilderness for extended periods of prayer, meditation and reflection. The monks also note that Jesus Christ Himself, as the Bible tells us, prepared for public ministry by sojourning into the desert for forty days and nights of Holy Communion.

Taking their lead from *Matthew 11:28*, "Come to me all you who labor and are overburdened, and I will give you rest.," and *Mark 6:31*, "You must come away to some lonely place...and rest for while.," the Monastery of the Holy Spirit offers informal retreats with or without the assistance of a retreat director. Experiences will, as the friars themselves say, vary according to the needs of the individual, but may include the chance to study the Scriptures; to be alone; to pray; to reflect on some unresolved problem; to share in the worship of the monks; to listen in silence to the Holy Spirit; and to establish and nurture a stronger bond with the Holy Spirit within. The usual stay is three days, but longer retreats can be arranged. Rooms are available on a non-denominational basis, but should be reserved well in advance. Conference facilities are also available. While there is no established fee for room and meals, participants are asked to give, each according to his circumstances.

From downtown Atlanta, the monastery can be reached by taking Interstate 20 East to the first (West Avenue) or second (Georgia Highway 138) Conyers exit, then following the signs. The monastery is also accessible by MARTA bus, limousine or taxi and is approximately one hour on the Southeastern Stages bus line to the Conyers Bus Station, where taxi service can then be provided. The monastery is about nine miles outside Conyers.

Atlanta and Vicinity

For more information, contact Guestmaster, Monastery of the Holy Spirit, 2625 Highway 212, S.W., Conyers, GA 30208.

DECATUR

Founded in the early nineteenth century and named for the War of 1812 naval hero Stephen Decatur, this community of about 17,800 is located six miles east of Atlanta proper, off Interstate 285 and west of Avondale Estates. Authorities once refused to allow the Western and Atlantic Railroad to come into the city because the citizens didn't want the noise and smog. It was, ironically, this rejection, in 1837, which gave birth to an alternative, Terminus, which became modern Atlanta.

Eventually, of course, the state owned Georgia Railroad did come through, buying the right of way in 1842, but the spirit which preserved the quality of life in Decatur remains very much evident today. History and education, government and light industry all blend under balmy skies, mild temperatures which can reach into the high eighties during the summer and rainfall which averages about three inches per month the year around.

ATTRACTIONS

The mild climate lends itself to one of the most enjoyable ways to get an overview of historic Decatur, particularly for those with a sense of history and the love of a good stroll.

• Start at downtown **Decatur's Courthouse Square** (also called Decatur Square) and the Old Courthouse itself. This magnificent edifice of native granite has a white marble courtroom and hand wound steeple clock. It houses an extensive Historical Society Archives, Library and Museum whose exhibits include: an impressive Civil War room; Indian artifacts; pioneer and frontier collections; memorabilia from the community's contributions to the First and Second World

Atlanta and Vicinity

Wars; a fascinating display of railroad artifacts and a striking Vietnam Memorial plaque listing all DeKalb County casualties.

- Then you'll cross to that quaint restored tavern known as **The Uncle Billy Hill Saloon**, for a trip back to Decatur's early days, when this drinking establishment was the most popular gathering place of the DeKalb county seat.
- The new courthouse, **Decatur City Hall**, and the **Decatur Downtown Development Authority** office will provide you with an excellent sense of the modern community and its plans for the future.
- Teachers and students alike will appreciate the walk down North McDonough Street to **Decatur High School** which, until 1953, educated boys and girls separately at two facilities on the same campus.
- At the corner of McDonough and Maple stands the misnamed **Marble House**, which, although it looks as though it was built of this beautiful stone, was actually an exercise in the potential of stucco. Built by a Savannah cotton broker as a refuge for his family during the yellow fever outbreak in 1880, it once served as a dormitory and dining room for the famous Agnes Scott College and has since been adapted for use as an office building.
- Through a neighborhood of later era homes, you'll walk to that famous **Agnes Scott College**. Built in 1889, it's oldest surviving structure, **Agnes Scott Hall**, has that tower which can be seen from any point in the downtown area. A private women's college, it was the first accredited college in the state and graduated Georgia's first female Rhodes Scholar. It was named for the mother of its founder, Col. George Washington Scott.
- Whenever there is talk of the Civil War in Decatur, there's always mention of the **Decatur Railroad Depot**. This one was built in 1891, but an earlier version was an important logistics center and Sherman's troops wanted it badly enough to fight for it. Its defenders put up staunch resistance and though they lost, **The Battle of Decatur** has been remembered ever since. This historical site is also a good place to stop and take a break at the restaurant in the old freight room.

Atlanta and Vicinity

- **The High House**, one of the first two story houses in the community, was built in the 1830s and it is said that it was here, during the Battle of Decatur, that Sherman watered his horse from that ivy covered well in the corner of the lot. The carefully restored antebellum home at 218 Barry Street, with its six fireplaces and cook's cabin in back, is typical of the Decatur townhouses built around 1855. The private home at 414 Sycamore was built about a quarter century earlier, and almost a century after the Battle of Decatur, weapons from the conflict were found there.
- **The Methodist Chapel** was built of Stone Mountain granite in 1897 and stands on the same lot as the first little Methodist Church, constructed in 1826. There's a Tiffany stained glass window visible from the back, overlooking the playground. One of the most moving monuments to Decatur's history is its cemetery, for here is where Mary Gay, heroine of the Battle of Decatur and author of the memorable, *Life in Dixie During the War*, now resides. (Her book, by the way, is available in the Historical Society office). An obelisk of Italian marble, run through the blockade during the Civil War, marks the grave of Charles Murphey, who, although a delegate to the Secessionist Convention, said often he hoped he'd never live to see Georgia leave the Union. As it turned out, he died before he could attend the convention, and so got his wish. And the parents of the first woman United States senator, Rebecca Latimer Felton, are also interred here.

For more information on this walking tour, contact the DeKalb Historical Society, Old Courthouse on the Square, Decatur, GA 30030; (404) 373-1088.

- **The Historic Complex of DeKalb Historical Society** has three antebellum structures dating back to 1830-40. The Swanton House, Decatur's first town house, has furniture of the period, blown glass windows and locks adorned with the English crown crest. The frontier era is recaptured by the **Biffle cabin**, with its log construction and clapboard siding, and by the **Thomas Barber cabin**, which was made of hand hewn logs and built by pioneers who came by ox cart with an iron pot of starter coals. For more information, write the Historical Society.

Atlanta and Vicinity

• **The Fernbank Science Center** includes a museum of natural history and a planetarium. Its sixty-five acres of forest are home for an impressive variety of native plants and make a relaxing afternoon wander. For more information, contact the Center at 156 Heaton Park Dr., N.E., Decatur, GA 90030; (404) 378-4311.

• For those who enjoy international food, the **DeKalb Farmers Market** is where you'll want to go. Known locally as The U.N. of Fresh Food, it caters to the culinary cultures of over thirty nationalities. Aisle after aisle of fresh fruits and vegetables are complemented by fresh seafood, meat and poultry, a deli and dairy, and a bakery which serves fresh bread, pastas and cookies made daily from scratch. There are even fresh flowers for the table. Contact the DeKalb Farmers Market, 3000 East Ponce de Leon Avenue, Decatur, GA 30030; (404) 377-6400.

For more information on Decatur's various offerings, contact the DeKalb Chamber of Commerce, 750 Commerce Drive, Suite 201, Decatur, GA 30030; (404) 378-2525.

GOLF AND TENNIS

NEVADA BOB'S GOLF AND TENNIS
3934 North Druid Hills Road
Decatur, GA 30033
Tel. (404) 321-4200
Hrs: Mon. - Fri. 10:00 a.m. - 8:00 p.m.
     Saturday   9:00 a.m. - 6:00 p.m.
     Sunday   12:00 a.m. - 5:00 p.m.
Visa, MasterCard, AMEX and Discover are accepted.
Also,

1376 S. Lake Plaza Drive	1570 Holcomb Bridge Road
Morrow, GA 30260	Roswell, GA 30076
Tel. (404) 968-8711	Tel. (404) 993-8400

When you need a little advice on your golf swing or information on which tennis racket is best suited for you, it pays to go to the best. As the world's largest chain of discount golf and tennis shops, Nevada Bob's offers everything imaginable for the golf and tennis enthusiast.

A fully trained, professional staff stands ready to greet you the moment you walk through the door. All are PGA certified, many are teaching professionals and former touring pros, and their knowledge of the game can not be beat. For the tennis buff, Nevada Bob's tennis staff are all certified by the U.S. Racket Stringers Association and are available to assist even the most discriminating player with any question. Both sections of the shop have received national recognition. Golf Shop Operations, a division of *Golf Digest*, has listed Nevada Bob's as one of the top twenty "off-course" shops in the nation, while the tennis shop was named as the official stringers of the AT&T Challenge Tennis Tournament, in addition to being named one of the top five tennis specialty shops in the nation by Tennis Buyers Guide, a division of *Tennis Magazine*. Many of the top manufacturers come to the staff for product testing, helping to keep the shop on the cutting edge of what's new in both sports. When it comes to equipment, Nevada Bob's has a huge selection of first quality clubs and rackets. From instructional aids to video rental, they offer a complete line of accessories for both sports.

You'll find the finest selection at the lowest prices backed by professional service at all three showrooms. From beginner to pro, you're sure to find everything you need at Nevada Bob's.

HARDWARE STORE

SMITH ACE HARDWARE, 601 East College Avenue, Decatur, GA Tel. (404) 373-3335. They offer the very best in hardware, service and gifts with more than 30,000 items stocked. Everything carried is top of the line.

RESTAURANT

EL TORO MEXICAN RESTAURANT
1248 Clairmont Avenue
Decatur, GA. 30340
Tel. (404) 451-8750
Hrs: Mon. - Sun. 11:00 a.m. - 10:30 p.m.
Visa, MasterCard, AMEX, Diners Club and Discover are accepted.

Bringing friends and family together for an ethnic evening is a most pleasurable experience when dining at the El Toro Mexican Restaurants. From the original location in Atlanta, a dozen restaurants now grace various counties in the state, and numerous awards of excellence are testimony to the fare and service received at the various locations.

Atlanta and Vicinity

A family owned and operated endeavor, The El Toro Restaurants are an opportunity to sample some of the finest in authentic Mexican foods. If words such as fajitas, chalupa and chilaquiles do not flow trippingly from the tongue, never fear, the pleasure to your palate will more than compensate for that lack. One of the many specialties of the house, the Nacho Chara is cheese nachos with assorted toppings of ground beef, chopped chicken and refried beans, all covered with shredded lettuce, tomatoes, and sour cream. Savor the Fajitas Tapatias, strips of beef cooked to succulent tenderness with tomatoes, onions and bell peppers. Served with rice, whole beans, a special tomatillo sauce and a tortilla, this dish is accompanied by a salad. For a crowning finish to the many offerings on the menu, indulge in a Sopapillas with ice cream or a delectable Flan. You may figuratively jump into, and drink your way out of, the forty-six ounce Monster Margarita served at the restaurant. Red, rose and white wines are available as well.

At the El Toro Restaurants attention is focused on quality and service. Even novices to the cuisine will be tempted to kick up their heels and shout, "Ole," after enjoying a most memorable meal at the restaurant; and for those who have always wanted to know—yes, "it is absolutely correct to eat tacos, tostadas, and tortillas with your fingers."

SPORTING GOODS

SMOKEY MOUNTAIN SPORTS, 1226 Clairmont Road, Decatur, GA. Tel. (404) 325-5295. Smokey Mountain Sports offers a full line of backpacking gear, outdoor clothing, canoes and kayaks. Clinics, rafting trips and rentals are available.

DULUTH

One of the major distinctions of this community, which lies four miles west of Interstate 985, about twenty miles northeast of downtown Atlanta in historic Gwinnett County, is that it is named for a Yankee town. Otherwise, however, its origins and history are typical of so many of Marthasville's outlying communities.

The Georgia legislature opened the Chattahoochee area up to settlement and created Gwinnett County the same year. A North Carolina farmer named Evan Howell moved to the site in 1821, and is credited with laying the groundwork for what was to become a major farming center consisting, primarily, of the large cotton plantations so typical of the entire county. Howell insured his town's posterity by building a road from the Chattahoochee River to Peachtree Road, then a major transportation route north to south.

Reconstruction changed Duluth dramatically by breaking the plantations into smaller farms which were owner operated or leased to tenant farmers. A major rail line replaced Howell's Road and completed the area's transformation into a bustling shipping and trading center, save for one thing, a suitably distinctive name.

From 1833 to 1871, Duluth had been known as Howell's Cross Roads, but that changed too when city leaders decided a new name was needed. The town leaders wanted something which would linger in the minds of outsiders, and they didn't necessarily consider themselves bound by tradition.

It so happened that in 1871, Congress and the nation were laughing about a speech of Kentucky Representative J. Proctor Knott, then promoting a rail line to an out of the way little village in Minnesota. Evan Howell's grandson thought the name would be appropriate for an equally out of the way little village in North Georgia and persuaded the community to accept the admittedly convoluted logic.

The town grew rapidly during this period and many of the older photographs show cotton bales lining the streets awaiting shipment. On Saturdays, Duluth was your archetypal Southern community, replete with tobacco chewing men arguing politics and farming, and women and children shopping and playing. Back then, as well, a twenty-two room hotel catered to summer guests from Atlanta.

In 1922, Duluth became the first community in Georgia to elect a woman mayor. Mrs. Alice Strickland ran on a temperance platform—appropriate enough for the Prohibition Era—and swore to "clean up Duluth and rid it of demon rum." Her home is a Duluth landmark even today.

In 1943, Duluth again captured the nation's attention with the building of the Joan Glancy hospital. The venerable *Saturday Evening Post* magazine ran a feature on it in 1950, and the story subsequently made radio and then a national television production.

For several decades, as well, a passenger train which brought commuters to and from Atlanta, "The Belle," often provided grist for the media mills.

ATTRACTION

• Southern railroad history is captured and preserved in the **Southeast Railway Museum**, an open, twenty-acre site with an impressive assortment of steam engines, passenger cars, box cars and an old trolley. It's located at 3966 Buford Highway and is open on Saturdays only. For more information, call (404) 691-4890.

EVENT

• In October, Duluth really comes to life with its annual **Duluth Fall Festival**, where the works of woodcrafters, oil painters and flea market merchants crowd several blocks of Old Peachtree Street along the railroad tracks.

For more information on this colorful little North Georgia community, contact the Gwinnett County Chamber of Commerce, P.O. Box 1245, Lawrenceville, GA 30246; (404) 963-5128.

DUNWOODY

This unincorporated area of Fulton County northeast of downtown Atlanta has excellent access to the Chattahoochee River National Recreation Area. The Recreation Area is an outstanding natural attraction which features an herbarium with a good selection of native plants. It is also a historical showcase featuring prehistoric village sites, Indian villages, an old paper mill, some antebellum homes and Civil War ruins. Hiking, swimming, picnicking, rafting, canoeing and kayaking are among the more popular past times. The Area also offers guided nature walks, lectures, and various appropriate woodland skills courses. For more information, contact the Chattahoochee River National Recreation Area, 1900 Northridge Road, Dunwoody, GA 30338; (404) 394-8324.

MARKET

EAST 48th STREET MARKET, ITALIAN FOOD SPECIALTIES
Williamsburg at Dunwoody
Jet Ferry Road at Mt. Vernon Road
Dunwoody, GA 30338
Tel. (404) 392-1499
Hrs: Mon.- Fri. 10:00 a.m. - 7:00 p.m.
      Saturday 10:00 a.m. - 6:00 p.m.

The East 48th Street Market, Italian Food Specialties, is a haven for those who like to cook as well as those who like to eat. A pleasurable assault on the senses, the store is filled with the aromas of family recipe sauces, spices, aged cheese, newly brewed coffee and the always enticing smell of freshly baked crusty Italian bread.

You might say that Charlie and Anita Augello, proprietors of the East 48th Street Market, Italian Food specialties, owe it all to family and upbringing as they were both involved with family in either restaurants or deli/bakery operations as youngsters. The owners wanted to capture the intimate appeal of a neighborhood grocery store for area residents, and so the market was carefully researched to produce some of the best traditional Tuscan, Piedmontese and Sicilian recipes and staples. Patrons can drop by and pick up imported items, recipe tips or an entire meal for one or a party.

Not to be overlooked are the mouthwatering meats displayed in the deli case, fresh braciole and mozzarella in Acqua prepared by Charlie on a regular basis, and shelves awash with antipasto items, imported oils, pasta, traditional cookies, cakes, candies and specialty items. The Augello's prepare their own sausages and fresh pasta including sheets of lasagna which need not be preboiled, ready to be clipped with a scissors to fit almost any size pan. Irresistible entrees and side dishes are prepared daily from family recipes. Delectable hero sandwiches are served on crusty rolls or Italian bread. The Stoffato, a tasty sandwich filled with layers of Genoa salami, mortadella, capicola, provolone, crisp lettuce, and topped with their own special sauce, is a favorite with many customers who like to take it home or dine "al fresco" at stone tables in front of the store.

Sample a dish or two, sip a cup of Espresso or Cappuccino and enjoy the friendliness and hospitality of the Augello's as you delight in an unusual shopping experience. They, along with their children, will help you prepare a take a long picnic or a party. Limited or full service catering, a favorite with their customers, is available for easy at-home entertaining. Their gift baskets and gift certificates make wonderful gifts. If you are an Italian food fan, or merely wish to sample authentic cuisine from Italy, your time at the East 48th Street, Italian Food Specialties will be time well spent.

RESTAURANT

HOVAN GOURMET
Perimeter Mall
4400 Ashford Dunwoody Road
Dunwoody, GA 30346
Tel. (404) 396-1770
Hrs: Mon. - Sat. 10:00 a.m. - 9:30 p.m.
     Sunday   12:00 noon - 5:30 p.m.
Also,
Lenox Square
3393 Peachtree Road
Atlanta, GA 30326
Tel. (404) 231-9018

When the American notion of slapping filling in between slices of bread was introduced to an Armenian chef, the "hovan" was born. Its originator in 1980 developed a new concept of using delicious Armenian flatbread to create an elegant on the road dining experience.

Hovan Gourmet concocts a variety of Hovan Roll Elegant Sandwiches for your take out pleasure. The Roll consists of famous unleavened Armenian bread covered with natural cheeses and a blend of fresh spices, avocados, lettuce and tomatoes, along with your choice of turkey, ham, roast beef, corned beef, pastrami, vegetarian or combination club. It is then rolled up into its sandwich form. This exotic mixture evidences a truly Armenian flavor and style, and patrons are offered samples of the Hovan roll when they arrive to acquaint them with its delicious uniqueness. A variety of sodas, iced tea, freshly squeezed lemonade, or pure Georgia mountain spring water can accompany your meal. The shop also offers American style breakfasts and wonderful syrupy baklava.

Atlanta and Vicinity

The tremendous success of the Hovan Roll soon led to the opening of a second shop in Lenox Square. Both stores are happy to serve party trays for business lunches, take-out, wedding receptions, concerts, or plain or fancy picnics.

EAST POINT

This south Fulton County community, with a population of 37,486, is located approximately nine miles from downtown Atlanta. Originally a stop of the Atlanta and West Point railroads in the 1880s, the town was chartered on August 16, 1887. It ranks as the seventh largest industrial city and tenth most populous city in Georgia. That often touted Georgia spirit of self reliance is very evident in East Point; both the water and electric systems are community owned. It is also one of the fastest growing townships in the southern Atlanta suburban area, having annexed more than 1.6 miles of acreage into its city limits over the last two years. Its wide variety of accommodations and easy freeway access make it a favorite of Hartsfield International Airport commuters.

ATTRACTIONS

• History lives in this community, as it does throughout the Atlanta area. The **Historic House on Norman Berry Drive** has been restored and placed on the site of the old "Que Grounds," a popular picnic area of the 1880s and 1890s.

• **The Atlanta Christian College**, established in 1937 and spread out on forty acres of beautiful East Point scenery, is fully accredited by the American Association of Bible Colleges and enjoys an impressive student teacher ratio of one instructor to every thirteen students. For information on its various public programs, contact Atlanta Christian College, 2605 Ben Hill Road, East Point, GA 30344; (404) 761-8861.

Atlanta and Vicinity

For more information, contact South Fulton County Chamber of Commerce, 6400 Shannon Parkway, Union City, GA 30291; (404) 964-1984.

FOREST PARK

This community of 19,000, incorporated in 1908, is one of the Atlanta vicinity's major transportation centers. Just minutes away from the Hartsfield International Airport, downtown Atlanta, and the Southlake Mall, it is served by the MARTA line and provides an excellent place to stay and shop while visiting the great Atlanta metropolitan area.

LIMOUSINE

EXECUTIVE TOWN AND COUNTRY SERVICE, INC.
5063 Georgia Highway 85
Forest Park, GA 30051
Tel. (404) 763-1000
      (800) 241-3943
Visa, MasterCard, AMEX, Diners Club and Carte Blanche are accepted.

The limousine symbolizes modern luxury, and in the Atlanta area, there is no more reasonably priced way to travel in style than with Executive. Business professionals rely on Executive for an economical way to the Atlanta Hartsfield Airport as well as for a method of entertaining clients and friends.

Executive was conceived ten years ago with one car and a dream. That dream has since become a reality and the one car has become more than one hundred Cadillac sedans and limousines. The Executive motto of: 'We consider you to be a guest, not a customer' clearly expresses their desire to meet your every want and need.

Atlanta and Vicinity

Many visitors call on Executive when they arrive at the airport. The limousine takes them to their business engagement or to their hotel. Others call on Executive for a personal tour of the city or for an evening out on the town. Let them add that special touch to your evening in Atlanta.

All vehicles are air conditioned for your total comfort, and the more deluxe limousines offer a bar, a color TV and a fine stereo system. All services are available twenty-four hours a day.

In addition to luxurious Cadillac sedans and limousines, Executive offers special luxury vans and motorcoaches for tours that visitors will long remember. The friendly, courteous staff of Executive is anxious to help you with all of your transportation needs.

RESTAURANT

THE GREAT AMERICAN HOT DOG HOUSE
5035 Jonesboro Road Southeast
Forest Park, GA 30050
Tel. (404) 361-6347
Hrs: Mon. - Thu.   11:00 a.m. - 9:00 p.m.
      Fri. - Sat.   11:00 a.m. - 10:00 p.m.

For those who want good, all American food at a great American price, The Great American Hot Dog House is the place to be. Easily located because of the bright red, white and blue colors, this traditional hot dog house serves your basic, delicious hot dog in a casual atmosphere with an all-American theme. While you are eating, look for figurines with such faces as W.C. Fields, Milton Berle and the Three Stooges.

Opened in 1979, the Great American Hot Dog House serves a variety of delicious hot dogs on a steamed bun. With choices like plain hot dogs, cheese dogs and Polish sausages served with chili, mustard, relish, onions, ketchup, kraut, slaw and mayonnaise, anyone can find something to suit their tastes.

Atlanta and Vicinity

And the toppings are free. Voted by the *Atlanta Journal and Constitution* newspaper as "the best hot dog place in town", the hot dogs that are served here are pure beef and pork. After your hot dog, finish off your meal with a mouthwatering, fresh baked pie such as German chocolate, egg custard, pecan, French coconut, lemon or apple. The smell of these delicious desserts will keep your tastebuds lively throughout your meal.

Add all of these ingredients together and you have the reason why The Great American Hot Dog House was picked as a "Best Choice" for Georgia. You can call ahead to order from one to one thousand of your favorite meaty, juicy hot dogs for any occasion. Your order will be waiting.

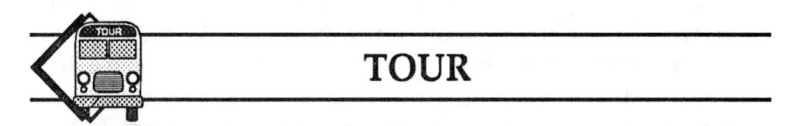

TOUR

EXECUTIVE TOUR LINES, 5036 Georgia Highway 85, Forest Park, GA. Tel. 1-800-235-9896. Elegant tour buses that are a special branch of the successful limousine service. Imported buses offer all the extras to make a memorable trip in comfort.

JONESBORO

This community of 4,000 is perhaps most famous as the general setting for Margaret Mitchell's classic best seller, *Gone With The Wind*. Located in the heart of Atlanta's southern crescent seventeen miles south of the downtown area on U.S. Highway 41 in historic Clayton County, its climate is typical of the Southern Piedmont area, with long, warm summers and winters which are short and mild. At an average of 1,000 feet above sea level, humidity is moderate and rainfall averages about forty-nine inches per year.

Once a major depot on the Central Railroad, Jonesboro is typical of the antebellum period, and because Miss Mitchell set her novel here, a replica of Tara, the O'Hara mansion, is slated for construction in 1989. The project was initiated in

Atlanta and Vicinity

response to the incredible number of inquiries received by the Clayton Chamber of Commerce asking, "Where is Tara?"

It is here and in Atlanta itself, for Miss Mitchell was faithful to the history of the period in which the novel, her only published work of the genre, is set. And if one is looking for a sequel, one need only become familiar with all that has transpired since the day Scarlett O'Hara caught the train back to Jonesboro.

Margaret Mitchell's own life was fascinating, for she was first and foremost a thoroughly dedicated writer who experienced all the trials and tribulations attending the craft. She began as a child, creating booklets for her own amusement and the entertainment of her family. Then she tried her hand at playwriting, taking popular stories of her youth and staging them for herself and her friends. As an adolescent, she attended Atlanta's Washington Seminary, where she continued to write stories and contributed to the Seminary's annual. In her twenties, she wrote for the *Atlanta Journal* magazine and attempted, unsuccessfully, to publish short stories with such chic magazines as *Smart Set*. Her "Matrimonial Bonds" was accepted by Atlanta's *The Open Door*. After an accident in which she broke her ankle, she left the *Atlanta Journal* and decided to attempt a novel.

From 1927 through 1929, she worked sporadically with an idea she described in a 1936 interview.

"I thought I would write a story of a girl who was somewhat like Atlanta—part of the Old South, part of the New south; how she rose with Atlanta and fell with it, and how she rose again. What Atlanta did to her, what she did to Atlanta—and the man who was more than a match for her. It didn't take me any time to get my plot and characters. They were there, and I took them and set them against the background which I knew as well as I did my own background."

By the end of 1929, she was discouraged and abandoned the project. Motivated by her husband, John Marsh, to continue, she took it up again in 1931 and plugged away at it stubbornly but sporadically, stashing the chapters in large manila envelopes and keeping it a secret from everyone but her husband and a few close friends.

In April, 1935, MacMillan Company vice president and senior editor Harold Latham came to Atlanta. From another editor at MacMillan, a former Atlanta resident and good friend of Mitchell, Latham had heard about this embryonic antebellum romance and inquired about it. "Peggy," as she was known to her intimates, at first denied she had a manuscript, then procrastinated by saying it wasn't ready for consideration. Again, however, John Marsh intervened and cajoled his reluctant spouse into taking it to Latham at the Georgian Terrace Hotel. The rest, to invoke the cliche, is history. Latham, one of the most astute editors in MacMillan Company's illustrious history, recognized a solid property and used his clout as vice president to see it into publication. Peggy Mitchell's own popularity seems to have had a great deal to do with it, although not due to any personal influence of her own, but rather through the support of close friends and associates.

She emerges as a touchingly modest woman who told a friend that she hoped Latham would be able to sell enough copies to pay publishing costs. The Atlanta Historical Society, on the other hand, gave her a pre-publication party in June, 1936. (Her father and her brother had served in turn as the Society's president.) Long after the book was a resounding success, and shortly before her own tragic death, she and her husband returned the favor by giving the Society a reception at its headquarters on Peachtree Street in the summer of 1948.

Peggy Mitchell never completed another novel, but she remained faithful to the essence of literature, and her own character is perhaps best reflected in the countless unpublicized charities to which she donated the considerable residuals of the novel and its film adaptation. She was faultlessly generous, as well, to other struggling writers. When she was described by a commentator as being like her character Melanie in that regard, she enigmatically responded:

"Being a product of the Jazz Age, one of those short-haired, hard-boiled young women who preachers said would go to hell or be hanged before they were thirty, I am naturally a

little embarrassed at finding myself the incarnate spirit of the Old South."

She confided to her close friends that she actually perceived herself as being more like the scandalous Scarlett, and this seems to be endorsed by those who remember her during her early womanhood in Atlanta.

There is good reason, however, to believe that she also personified deeply the shyer traits of the reclusive poetess Emily Dickinson, for when in 1939 Hollywood producer David O. Selznick decided to make the novel into a film, and offered her a handsome salary to come to the West Coast and supervise the screenwriting, she politely but firmly refused and explained her position in a letter to a relative: "The movie people offered me a good salary to come out and work on the picture, but I naturally refused. I like Atlanta too much and am too devoted to my family to leave them."

How faithful was *Gone With the Wind* to the city and period Peggy Mitchell loved so much? In her 1936 review of the novel, another authentic Southern writer, Julia Peterkin, wrote in the *Washington Post*, "It seems to me that *Gone With the Wind* is the best novel that has ever come out of the South. In fact, I believe it is unsurpassed in the whole of American writing."

A great deal of evidence supports the contention that the nation and the world agreed that it was, at the very least, a powerful and moving story.

The novel stayed on the best seller lists an unprecedented two years. It was published in thirty-seven countries in twenty-seven languages. At an autograph party held in Atlanta's famous Davison's department store (now Macy's), only eleven people showed up, but the book itself sold 173 copies, a record for Atlanta. In New York City, Macy's and Gimbels had a price war with it and sold 176,000 copies. At the end of six months, sales passed the million mark. In 1937, the novel was awarded the Pulitzer Prize for fiction.

The film version achieved similar success. Produced in 1939 and starring Clark Gable and Vivien Leigh, it won the Academy Award that year for best picture, best actress, best

Atlanta and Vicinity

supporting actress (Hattie McDaniel), and best director (Victor Fleming). In the first six months of its movie house run, an amazing 25,000,000 people saw the film. At the time, the population of the United States was slightly over 132,000,000, so almost one in twenty Americans heard Rhett tell Scarlett, "Frankly, my dear, I don't give a damn."

The film was produced entirely in Hollywood. Both Tara and Twelve Oaks mansions had no interiors. Among those who tested for the role of Scarlett O'Hara was venerable comedienne Lucille Ball.

Peggy Mitchell was born in 1900 and died August 16, 1949, five days after being struck by a speeding taxi cab in downtown Atlanta. She was buried in Atlanta's famous Oakland Cemetery. In accordance with her wishes, her husband John Marsh and her secretary Margaret Baugh destroyed all surviving manuscripts, including a completed work entitled *Ropa Carmigan*. Enigmatic to the last, Margaret Mitchell managed to immortalize the city she passionately loved while retaining her modesty to the end. Scarlett O'Hara might have found this difficult to accept, but Melanie, no doubt, would have understood.

ATTRACTIONS

• **Ashley Oaks** is typical of the historic sites so widespread in the area. Built in 1879 by Leander Carruth Hutcheson, the first elected sheriff of Clayton County, the home is a genuine Georgian House with Greek Revival influence. Over one million handmade bricks, made of clay from the banks of the neighboring Flint River, were used in the exterior construction of this fourteen room residence. It has ten working fireplaces, ceilings that are fourteen feet high, period antique furnishings, Waterford crystal, silver and oil paintings and other artifacts evocative of the period. Presently owned by Mr. and Mrs. George Baily, it is open for specifically arranged tours.

Atlanta and Vicinity

- **The Stately Oaks Mansion**, built in 1839 by Whitmell P. Allen, originally stood four miles north of the community and was a landmark to invading Northern troops. It is now the headquarters for Historical Jonesboro and located on Lake Jodeco Boulevard.
- **The Warren House**, built by Guy Lewis Warren in 1859, was used as headquarters and hospital by both Southern and Northern troops during the Battle of Jonesboro, August 31 - September 1, 1864. It is located on Main Street in downtown Jonesboro.
- **The Dickson Funeral Home**, at the corner of McDonough and Johnson Street, is one of the few buildings in the community to survive the war. Although its brick facade is modern, the building houses the old horse drawn hearse which took Confederate Vice President Alexander H. Stephens to his funeral in 1883.
- **The Patrick R. Cleburne Memorial Cemetery**, at the corner of McDonough and Spring, is the final resting place for 600-1,000 Confederate soldiers killed during the Battle of Jonesboro.
- **The Stephen Carnes House**, just down McDonough Street, was the 1850s home of a Jonesboro wagon factory owner who also made caskets for the Confederate Army.
- **Jonesboro's Old Town Cemetery**, at the corner of King and Wilburn, and the original Jonesboro Methodist Church, date back to 1845.
- **The 1869 Jail** housed the only man ever hung in Clayton County. It became a residence in 1898.
- **The 1869 Courthouse** is believed to have been rebuilt on the foundation of the original structure destroyed by Northern General Judson Kilpatrick's cavalry raid of August 19, 1864. Since 1898, it has been the Jonesboro Masonic Lodge Hall.
- **The Elliott Morrow Cottage**, at McDonough between King and Mill, was owned by James Hodge Morrow, brother of Colonel Radford E. Morrow, for whom the city of Morrow was named. The rear wing housed Jonesboro's first post office, dating from 1842.
- **The Johnson-Blalock House**, home of Col. James F. Johnson, signer of the Georgia Secession Ordinance in 1861, had

Atlanta and Vicinity

an interesting tie into the Old West. Johnson's wife, the former Martha Holliday, was the aunt of Dr. James Henry 'Doc' Holliday, the dentist, gunfighter and protege of Wyatt Earp. Confederate commissary supplies were stored in the house in 1864 and it was used as a hospital during and after the Battle of Jonesboro.

- **The 1867 Depot and Old Business District** were rebuilt after the town was burned to the ground by Yankees in 1864, just prior to the Fall of Atlanta. The material is of blue and gray Georgia granite and the structures themselves contain many period artifacts.
- **The 1898 Courthouse** was where Margaret Mitchell came to research local records while writing *Gone With the Wind*.
- **The Camp Plantation**, southwest of Jonesboro on Lake Jodeco Road, is a typical plantation plain style house and looks much as it did in 1860. The residence of one of Clayton County's largest antebellum planters, it was where citizens came to escape the fighting during the Battle of Jonesboro.
- **The Allen-Carnes Plantation**, about 1.7 miles further east, is probably the oldest surviving building in Clayton County and dates from the 1820s. During the Battle of Jonesboro, it too was a refuge for citizens of the community. Purchased in 1866 by Stephen Carnes from Colonel Allen's widow, it is still owned by the Carnes family and has been restored to its 1866 appearance.
- **Noah's Ark Church**, about a mile further east, was originally the Mount Pleasant Methodist Episcopal Church and was built in 1845. The Mount Pleasant Academy was just north of it. In 1852, the name was changed to honor Rev. Noah Smith, a popular minister of the congregation. The present sanctuary actually dates from about 1880 and includes many early style monuments in the churchyard. One of the church's original trustees was Col. Allen, of the Allen-Carnes Plantation.
- **The Sigma Chi Monument**, to the south of the church on Tara Avenue, is a 100 ton Georgia Cherokee Marble monument, built in 1939, to commemorate the Constantine Chapter of Sigma Chi, formed at the site on the night of September 17,

Atlanta and Vicinity

1864 by seven young Confederate soldiers who had been members of the college fraternity at various Southern universities before the war.

• The inspiration for Ashley Wilkes' "Twelve Oaks" plantation in *Gone With the Wind*, the **Lovejoy Plantation**, on Tara Boulevard south of the Sigma Chi Monument, was previously known as the **Crawford-Talmadge Plantation**. Built around 1835 for Mr. and Mrs. Thomas Shanklin Crawford as a gift from her father, John Dorsey, Thomas Crawford enlarged the house considerably in 1850. In September 1864, Confederate General John Hood regrouped the defenders of Atlanta there after Sherman took the city. When the Yankee forces approached Lovejoy Station, on the Macon and Western Railroad, Thomas Crawford filled the mansion's columns with grain to prevent it from being confiscated. The lawns were the scene of a major battle between the boys in grey and the boys in blue. Battle trenches are still discernible a mile from the site. For more information, contact the Clayton County Chamber of Commerce, P.O. Box 774, Jonesboro, GA 30237.

RESTAURANT

EMPIRE OF CHINA
751 Highway 138 Southeast
Jonesboro, GA 30236
Tel. (404) 473-9977
Hrs: Mon. - Thu.   11:00 a.m. - 9:30 p.m.
      Fri. - Sat.   11:00 a.m. - 10:30 p.m.
      Sunday   12:00 noon - 9:30 p.m.
Visa, MasterCard and AMEX are accepted.

The idea of combining Korean and Chinese food may seem unique to most people, but in the Yu family it is a tradition. Most of the recipes created at Empire of China are handed down from Grandfather Yu, including the secret recipe of the ever popular Mandarin beef ribs. The Yu custom began seventy-five years ago, and today, owners John and Nile Yu are sous chef and manager while John's father, Hai Jen Yu, is chef.

Freshly prepared, homemade Mandarin, Szechwan and Korean meals are served in an intimate setting of burgundy, pale pink flowered wallpaper, black lacquered chairs and linen napkins. You'll be able to relax, perusing the menu under lights softened by paper and wood Chinese lanterns. The real surprise will come when you see the moderate prices. The impressive selection of pork, fowl, beef, seafood, fish and vegetable dinners are all about $6.00, at the time of this writing. Eleven chef specials are offered. Luncheon specials include shrimp with lobster sauce, chicken with Chinese vegetables and sweet and sour pork. All luncheon specials are served with fried rice, tea, and a choice of hot and sour, egg drop, won ton soup or egg roll. Beer lovers will enjoy a glass of Tsingtao beer to go with their meal. All dishes are available for carry out and Empire of China offers full bar service as well as banquet facilities.

One meal at Empire of China will convince you that the slogan, "Quality dining at affordable prices" is an apt description of the venerable restaurant, located on the corner of Tara Boulevard and Highway 138.

THE CHATTAHOOCHEE RECREATION AREA

By

Merritt Scott Miller

When one thinks these days of Atlanta, one tends to conjure, and appropriately, a sprawling metropolitan area, rising like a technological New South phoenix from the ashes of Sherman's March, the Reconstruction and the Depression of the 1930s. This is certainly true, and it is also symbolic of that blend of gentility, awesome pride, staunch self-reliance and unfettered creative intellectualism which has made Georgia, since its very founding, a regional and national leader. Yet, the Atlanta area is also northern Georgia, with the intensely majestic Blue Ridge Mountains, backwoods country foothills, haunting marshes and the eternally beautiful Chattahoochee River.

This aspect of the Atlanta area has been preserved for posterity with the creation of the Chattahoochee River National Recreation Area. Managed by the National Park Service under the auspices of the U.S. Department of the Interior, it consists of a series of parklands along a forty-eight

Atlanta and Vicinity

mile stretch of the river, reaching north from Bowman's Island and just south of Lake Sidney Lanier to Palisades Park.

The Chattahoochee is an old river and has, for centuries, drawn humans to it for food, transportation and, in more recent times, the water and hydroelectric power for modern development.

Its parks now provide trails to hike, and meadows in which to play touch football, fly kites, toss a frisbee and engage in soccer matches. Picnic areas, complete with grills, tables and trash containers, are available in some units. The river itself is great for rafting, and the best time is from May through September. Concessionaires are located at Johnson Ferry and Powers Island and carry a limited inventory of canoes and kayaks. The rapids are gentle and easily navigable. Currents can be unpredictable around submerged rocks and snags, so a life preserver is mandatory.

Fishermen have been coming for hundreds of years, as well, to catch the trout, bream, bass and catfish, for which this great and gentle stream is known. Wildlife that calls the Chattahoochee home include beaver and muskrats, which live in burrows along the bank; fox and raccoons, which inhabit the hardwood forests and chipmunks; and squirrels and rabbits, which seem to proliferate everywhere. Turtles, snakes, salamanders, lizards, frogs and toads also call the river and its environs home. Insects include grasshoppers, dragonflies and butterflies that hop and fly among the dogwoods, redbuds, trout lilies, flame azaleas, asters, wild violets, cardinal flowers and showy scarlet sumac.

The Recreation Area consists of the following units:

1) **Palisade**—encompasses ridge trails which lead to terrific vistas of the river canyon, then descend into thick forests, and further to floodplains where rock outcroppings, sandy beaches and great expanses of shoalwater can be enjoyed.

2) **Cochran Shoals**—delights visitors with a three mile long trail, with optional loops, that is particularly appreciated by nature lovers, educators and exercise enthusiasts. Along it, some twenty-two exercise stations have been installed. It's very popular with Atlanta area joggers.

Atlanta and Vicinity

3) **Sope Creek** —leads hikers through scenic rolling hills, lush ravines and wooded areas, past old homesites, paper mill ruins and a small fishing lake.

4) **Gold Branch**—offers a secluded forest area including marshlands, open fields which were once rich farmlands and Bull Sluice Lake, the reservoir behind Morgan Falls Dam.

5) **Vickery Creek**—contains the ruins of textile mills, a dam and other structures in this gorge.

6) **Island Ford**—takes in a beautiful collection of islands and whitewater shoals.

Also within an easy drive of these parks is the Chickamauga and Chattanooga National Military Park, the Kennesaw Mountain National Battlefield Park, the Martin Luther King, Jr. National Historic Site and Preservation District and the Ocmulgee National Monument. For more information, contact Chattahoochee River National Recreation Area, Superintendent, 1900 Northridge Road, Dunwoody, GA 30338; (404) 394-7912.

KENNESAW

This community of 5,000 is found approximately twenty-one miles northwest of downtown Atlanta, on Interstate 75. Civil War history buffs have been drawn here for well over a century, for it is the site of one of the most interesting and, depending on your sympathies, courageous or most outrageous escapades of that entire conflict. It is the story of "The Great Locomotive Chase," and like any great tale, it needs a bit of set up.

Let's go back, then, to the first years of the Civil War, and to a time, as well, when there were no jetliners, no roaring eighteen wheeler diesel rigs, no automobiles. On the great rivers of the nation, steamers and barges carried passengers and freight. On land, the railroad was king, replacing, for the most part, the stage coach and other horse drawn conveyances of the earlier years of that century. Let's remember that in a war, a most important aspect is logistics. Both your army and that of the enemy needs to be supplied with replacements, food, arms and ammunition, clothing, medicines and bandages and the thousand other items which keep troops in action.

You know that if you can keep your own supplies coming in, while somehow knocking out your enemy's ability to do the same, you improve considerably your chances of victory. That is the strategy behind the blockade or capture of sea, river and lake ports. It was also what one Union Brigadier General Ormsby MacKnight Mitchel, commanding the three regiments of the Army of the Ohio's Third Division, had in mind.

The year was 1862 and Mitchel, a flamboyant West Pointer, had led his Buckeyes deep into Tennessee, and in the spring of 1862, was encamped with them at Shelbyville, about seventy rail miles from a vital Confederate railroad tie-in point at Chattanooga. The boys in grey hadn't done very well that year. Kentucky was in Union hands, along with much of northern and western Tennessee. Georgia, with its vital munitions depot at Atlanta and that state's rich cotton producing region, was threatened, while to the west, another Union army was advancing down the Mississippi and U.S.

Atlanta and Vicinity

Grant was pushing his forces south along the Tennessee River. A huge Federal war fleet was at the mouth of the Mississippi, intent on taking New Orleans.

Chattanooga was vital to the Confederacy. The Memphis & Charleston Railroad, which had been supplying rebel forces in the west, routed through the city, and the Western & Atlantic came through it from the south before continuing north through Knoxville. The fall of this rail center would paralyze logistics throughout both theaters.

Now, onto the scene comes a rather mysterious civilian named James J. Andrews. Nothing is known about him until 1859, when he showed up in Flemingsburg, Kentucky, where he worked as a house painter and clerk at the local hotel. When the South seceded, Andrews made a living smuggling medicine into the Confederacy and intelligence reports out of it. He was, in fact, a double agent in Union employ and he had done most of his scouting along the Western and Atlantic Railroad, which ran 138 mountainous miles through northern Georgia.

It should be noted at this point that the W&A was Georgia's state owned line. It was a single track, with sidings at all principal stations. Well-kept and maintained, it was considered one of the best of its kind in the South. Its course took it across several big streams on wooden covered bridges and through a long tunnel under Chetoogeta Mountain.

Andrews knew all this, of course, and appreciated how vulnerable the railroad was. His espionage had by this time earned him a reputation as a brilliant and bold thinker among the Federal high command, and since he was operating in Buckeye Brigadier General Mitchel's theater, it was natural enough that he was part of this worthy's inner circle. It was to Mitchel, then, that Andrews came with a most daring plan.

While Mitchel fought his division south across Tennessee to Huntsville, through which the Memphis & Charleston line ran, Andrews and a small party of other adventurous souls would infiltrate through northern Georgia to the W&A depot at Marietta. There they would board a northbound train, and at the village of Big Shanty, during the train's twenty-minute breakfast stop, they would steal it. They would then drive it north, burning the Western & Atlantic's bridges and the

Chetoogeta Mountain tunnel. Proceeding through Chattanooga, burning and derailing, they would meet Mitchel, who would then be able to advance on the city and take it with little difficulty.

It was precisely the kind of scheme the egotistical and publicity hungry Mitchel wanted to hear and he endorsed it heartily. On Sunday, April 6, 1862 and the next day, twenty-three volunteers were recruited from the three Ohio regiments. Three of them were sought out specifically. Wilson Brown, Martin Hawkins and William Knight had been railroad men in civilian life. They'd also seen action at Bull Run the previous summer and had fought in the several skirmishes through Kentucky.

On Monday evening, April 7, James Andrews got his little band of daring soldiers off alone and let them in on the plan. In small parties, they were to make their way through enemy lines to Chattanooga, where, at the end of the week, they would board the southbound train for Marietta. Their cover was that they were from Kentucky and were on their way to enlist with the Rebels. At Marietta, on Friday morning, they would steal the first northbound train and commence havoc on the W&A line. They set out Tuesday morning and immediately ran into trouble with the weather for, as it often does in that part of the country in the spring, it started raining heavily. Streams and rivers overflowed their banks, turning miles and miles of roads into drenched boglands. Andrews had hoped to hire wagons and local farmers to help them along the way, but instead, found himself and the others forced to go it on foot, seeking shelter among the local population or with Confederate picket posts, who believed their cover story and, apparently, welcomed them enthusiastically to the cause.

Seven of the party crossed the Tennessee River on a ferry boat west of Chattanooga and took passage on a Confederate troop train. The others were still going it on foot, and by the time they reached their first destination, they were a day behind schedule and learned that Mitchel was not. Chattanooga was in a state of panic because Huntsville had fallen. Andrews also discovered two of his party missing and much later it was learned that these men had run into some

Atlanta and Vicinity

suspicious authorities in the village of Jasper. To keep from being discovered, and with the intention of deserting at the first opportunity, they had actually enlisted in a nearby Confederate artillery unit.

Nonplused but undaunted, Andrews and his now twenty-one men surreptitiously boarded the southbound train to Marietta and when it arrived in that town, took rooms in the local hotel. In his lodgings the next morning, Saturday, April 12, he briefed his raiders one final time, noting with frustration that, once again, two of them were missing. (They overslept and missed the train.) At first light, the morning mail train pulled in. Its locomotive was the General. At that time it was only seven years old and built by one of the finest manufacturers of railroad moving stock, the Rogers, Ketchum and Grosvenor Works in Paterson, New Jersey. It was state of the art and the pride of the line. It pulled a tender, three empty boxcars reserved for food and other commissary supplies from Chattanooga, and a string of passenger cars. Andrews and his party took seats on these without incident.

The train pulled into Big Shanty at exactly 6:45 a.m. and the passengers took off for a quick breakfast at Lacy's Hotel, along with conductor William Fuller, engineer Jeff Cain, and the Western & Atlantic's machine shop's foreman, Anthony Murphy, who was along on an inspection tour. While these men departed, James Andrews and his three former civilian railroad men got off on the other side and quietly made their way to the engine, after uncoupling the train after the third empty boxcar. Swinging into the cab of The General, he signaled the rest of his men to board the third boxcar. Just fifty feet away, Confederate sentries at a large training camp watched in amazement as the abbreviated mail train, with Bill McKnight at the throttle, took off.

In the Lacy Hotel's dining room, foreman Murphy and the Rebel train crew also witnessed the departure for a few seconds, in a paralysis of shock. Then they bolted from the dining room and the chase was on, literally. Big Shanty didn't have a telegraph so there was no way to wire a warning up the line. At this point, the second hero of the tale emerges.

Atlanta and Vicinity

William Fuller, the train's conductor, was a twenty-five year old W&A man who had risen through the ranks. Loyal and dedicated both to the line and the Confederate cause, his first assumption was that his train had been stolen by deserters from the Rebel training camp. Outraged by what he took as a double insult, he set out on foot, with the foreman and the engineer doing their best to keep up with him. In truth, conductor Fuller was not expecting a long pursuit, believing instead that he would find The General abandoned a ways up the track.

That, obviously however, was not the case. The powerful engine, with its new cargo of jubilant Yankees, was barreling merrily along on schedule in order to allay suspicion further up the line. Their destination was Kingston, thirty miles north, and enroute, they borrowed a crowbar from a helpful Rebel track repair crew and stopped occasionally to take up rails and to cut a telegraph line they subsequently spotted. If conductor Fuller had no idea his train had been stolen by the hated Unionists, James Andrews was equally ignorant of the pursuit by the furious Confederate train man.

Fuller actually ran almost three miles, encountered the repair crew from which the Yankees had taken the crowbar, learned of the loan, and pieced it together very quickly. He knew then that this truly was an act of war and borrowed, for himself and his tiny pursuit party, the repair crew's pole car. When the three Western and Atlantic men found the cut telegraph wire, their deductions were confirmed and, with

Atlanta and Vicinity

redoubled vigor, they continued the chase, dragging the pole car, which was operated much as the boats which were poled up the rivers during the era, across the breaks in the line.

At the branch track at Etowah station, Fuller appropriated a tiny switching engine, the Yonah, and, after the few minutes it took to get steam up, they raced along the remaining fourteen miles to Kingston, with the Yankees about forty-five minutes ahead of them. Both parties pushed hard through pelting rain.

At Kingston, James Andrews and The General encountered their first potential disaster. Pulling off on a siding to let the southbound freight pass, they were questioned by authorities, to whom Andrews neatly palmed off another cover story. In this one, he got to be a Confederate officer under strict orders from General Beauregard, commander of the Rebel army at Corinth, Mississippi, to get munitions to him in the wake of the Battle of Shiloh.

Once again, the Rebels bought the con, but when the southbound freight arrived, it had a red flag on its last car—signaling another train following. An increasingly edgy Andrews then learned that Mitchel's victory at Huntsville had inadvertently threatened the raiders' mission. Chattanooga was evacuating military stores and trains to keep them from falling into Union hands. To Andrews' devout consternation and the growing fears of his men, the General waited a full sixty-five minutes for two additional Chattanooga-fleeing trains to pull through.

By the time the Union raiders finally pulled out, William Fuller and the little switch engine were just four minutes behind them, but faced the same jam which nearly thwarted the Yankees. On top of it, Andrews had the foresight to cut the telegraph line north from Kingston, so Fuller and his two crew had no way of wiring ahead. Totally incensed, Fuller took to his feet again, ran two miles to a branch line from Rome, Georgia and commandeered the daily train there, and continued the chase.

The Yankees, still unaware they were being pursued, rolled on toward Adairsville, ten miles up the track from Kingston, and stopped four miles south of their next destination to tear up some more track and to pile the crossties on board to serve both as tinder for The General and as fuel for the planned bridge and tunnel burning. It was during this endeavor, however, that they spotted smoke to the south and suddenly realized—with heart stopping horror, apparently—that their mission had been discovered. They jumped aboard The General and opened the throttle full out. When Fuller and his Rome engine reached the torn up track, he and his crew took up pursuit once again on foot.

Andrews and The General reached Adairsville, waited for one scheduled southbound train, and learned that another was a half hour away. He knew that if he could reach Calhoun, the next stop up the line, ahead of it, he'd have the priority to force it to a siding, and then it was a straight shot to Chattanooga. Fuller knew that as well, and began to feel absolutely desperate. Fortunately, he and his two crewmen encountered the southbound freight out of Adairsville and got their first real piece of decent luck. This train was pulled by the Texas, an engine on par with the General and fully capable of literally giving it a run for its money.

With the engine still pointed south, Fuller got the train rolling and set out in reverse. Meanwhile, back on the General, Andrews and his men encountered their first target of destruction, the trestle over the Oostanaula River, five miles north of Calhoun near Resaca. They stopped to cut the telegraph line and were in the process of prying the rail loose when the air was blasted by the loud whistle of the pursuing conductor Fuller on the Texas. At this point, James Andrews had a decision to make and many historians contend that it wasn't particularly the appropriate one. According to Stephen W. Sears, in an article for *American Heritage* magazine:

"Thus far James Andrews had been nothing short of brilliant. He had brought his nineteen men through every anticipated danger and improvised his way through dangers entirely unexpected. He had no reason to doubt that the track ahead (to Chattanooga) was clear. Of the quality and tenacity of the pursuit, he knew nothing. (The Yankees believed it was simply the last train they had passed.) The rail they were

Atlanta and Vicinity

trying to lift was well loosened, needing but a few more minutes' effort, and they would be free of pursuit and able to go about their bridge burning in comparative safety. Yet Andrews chose not to stand and fight long enough to finish the job."

Instead, the former Union spy decided to uncouple the last empty boxcar and send it barreling back down the track. The doughty conductor Fuller, however, saw the speeding rolling stock coming, adroitly reversed the Texas, met the car and continued the chase, pushing it in front of him. Andrews, watching the smoke through the rain, cursed and uncoupled a second boxcar in the middle of the covered bridge over the Oostanaula River. Fuller picked it up as well and the pursuit sped on to Resaca, where the Confederate conductor shunted his extra rolling stock off on the spur there.

Past Resaca, the country becomes very rugged, requiring more steam and hence, more fuel, of which the Yankees on the General were running low. Andrews, desperate now, began slowing at every curve to toss crossties onto the track in an attempt to derail their pursuers. Fuller took up sentinel on the tender and the Texas, with its engineer Peter Bracken at the throttle, avoided ramming each obstacle, often coming to a soft stop against it, and quickly clearing the track.

Andrews and his men did manage, eventually, to get enough lead to take on water and wood, and then made one last chance to sabotage Fuller and the Texas. While some of his raiders cut the telegraph line, others wrestled to lift the track out of its bed, and still a third party piled obstructions. The raiders pleaded with their commander to set up an ambush, but Andrews staunchly refused, and for reasons still unclear to historians. It is likely, however, that Andrews sensed the possibility of defeat and hoped that the Rebels would go easier with his men as long as they did not actually kill anyone. (He himself, fully aware that his espionage activities would be revealed in the event of his capture, labored under no illusions about his fate under those circumstances.) So when Fuller and the Texas once again hove into view, it was "all aboard" on the General, with the track still intact.

Atlanta and Vicinity

The chase thus continued, with both engines reaching the then-incredible speed of sixty miles per hour, past several prime targets, including the tunnel under Chetoogeta Mountain and the first long bridge over Chickamauga Creek. Andrews and his men tried, at one point, to set fire to the remaining boxcar, but the same rain which had plagued them when they first set out, caused the delay which put Buckeye General Mitchel in control of Huntsville and precipitated the evacuation of Chattanooga which, in turn caused the sixty-five minute delay in Kingston, prevented them now from creating a fiery diversion for the pursuing Fuller and the Texas.

Near the Georgia-Tennessee border, about a mile south of Graysville, the General began to slow down. Water was low and the tender, empty. Almost one hundred miles from where the chase began, it ended, and Andrews ordered his men to flee and do the best they could to make their way to the Union lines. In one last attempt to cause the Confederacy a little damage, the Ohioans begged Andrews permission to ambush the Texas, and again, the former spy refused. Instead, engineer William McKnight threw the General in reverse and it actually rolled slowly back down the track, where conductor Fuller gently stopped it with the rear of the Texas tender. Six hours after he watched in horror from the hotel dining room in Big Shanty as his beloved General pulled out, William Fuller had his train back.

In his summation of the raid, historian Stephen Sears concludes:

"The Andrews party would later blame their failure on the one day delay in executing the mission. They maintained that had the raid taken place on schedule, before Chattanooga was alarmed by General Mitchel's capture of Huntsville, the Western and Atlantic would have been clear of the extra trains that held them up so long at Kingston. Nor would any bridge burning efforts have been hampered by Saturday's day long rain. The theory is not improbable, considering how narrow was their margin of defeat despite all the unforeseen complications. By the same token, however, there is little reason to believe

Atlanta and Vicinity

that conductor Fuller's pursuit would have been any less vigorous twenty-four hours earlier."

Looking back, there is a rather sad aspect to this dramatic escapade, or rather several of them, actually. After General Mitchel took Huntsville, he sent a brigade east on the Memphis and Charleston line to within thirty miles of Chattanooga, ostensibly to welcome Andrews and his party coming west. Why the general ordered a bridge burned between that waiting point and the line from Chattanooga is not clearly known. It would have effectively prevented Andrews and his captured locomotive from reaching safety, unless the Buckeye raiders set off on foot, an extremely risky proposition under the circumstances. There is room to speculate that General Mitchel never really believed the enterprise would succeed to begin with, went along with it to pacify the aggressive James Andrews, then protected himself from any possible retribution from a similar Rebel raid out of Chattanooga by burning that bridge.

The raiders paid a high toll. Of the original twenty-four, only two (the pair who enlisted in the Confederate artillery unit while enroute to Chattanooga at the onset of the adventure) avoided capture. The two who failed to make the General when Andrews and his men first boarded it at Marietta were captured when they tried to enlist in a Georgia unit. So, in all, twenty-two of the raiders were caught.

Two of these escaped and were retaken. James Andrews was tried as a spy and, after a review by Confederate Secretary of War Walker and President Jefferson Davis, found guilty and on June 7, taken to a gallows near Peachtree Street in Atlanta and hung. Twelve raiders imprisoned in Chattanooga were transferred to Knoxville, where seven, selected at random, were tried for espionage, found guilty, and also hung in Atlanta.

The fourteen survivors, all imprisoned together, staged an escape. Eight made their way back to Union lines. The remaining six, recaptured, were exchanged in March 1863 and considered themselves extremely fortunate, for in December, work began on the notorious Andersonville Prison in Georgia. All fourteen were eventually awarded the Congressional

Medal of Honor. One of these was released from active duty in 1863 for medical reasons. The other thirteen served throughout the rest of the war and lived to tell about it in peacetime. General Ormsby Mitchel, their commander when the raid was staged, failed to capture Chattanooga and was transferred to ignominious duty on the North Carolina coast where, in October 1862, he succumbed to the yellow fever epidemic which swept through the southeast during the war.

And finally, the tenacious Rebel train conductor William Fuller kept his trains running for the Confederacy until the 65,000 men under General William Tecumseh Sherman marched through Georgia in 1864. Fuller did survive, however.

And now that this interesting adventure has drawn to an end, you may have another reason for visiting Kennesaw, for you see, back at the time of "The Great Locomotive Chase," Kennesaw's name was Big Shanty. It is here that still another Confederate survivor of the Civil War now resides. William Fuller's locomotive, the General, is on display at the Big Shanty Museum, which is located two miles off Interstate 75, via exits 117 or 118. The museum has a slide program and art exhibits describing the raid, and when you watch these, you might recall, as well, the Walt Disney Productions movie *The Great Locomotive Chase*, for it too was based on this incident.

Reason enough, then, for visiting Kennesaw, and if you'd like to know more about the community itself, contact the Cobb County Chamber of Commerce, P.O. Box Cobb, Marietta, GA 30065; (404) 980-2000.

APPAREL

IBIS, Town Center, 400 Earnest Barrett Parkway, Kennesaw, GA. Tel.(404) 426-7973. Women's specialties at this boutique take on a tropical note, suitable for wearing on cruises all year. Fun and funky clothing, most made of natural fibers.

Atlanta and Vicinity

THE BATTLE OF KENNESAW MOUNTAIN

by

Merritt Scott Miller

By the spring of 1864, the Civil War had dragged on for four years and the combined death toll was climbing to the half million mark, making it the costliest war in U.S. history. Americans on both sides of the Mason-Dixon Line were weary of it. From the eastern seaboard to the shores of California, from the Gulf of Mexico to upstate New York, hardly a household was untouched by it. Gone were the stirring memories of Fort Sumter. Forgotten was the elation of the crowds of Senators, Representatives and Maryland townsfolk gathered near the waters of Bull Run in anticipation of watching Brigadier General Irvin McDowell's handful of regulars and 35,000 raw recruits whip his Confederate counterpart, Brigadier General Pierre G. T. Beauregard, upstart victor of the fall of Fort Sumter.

Many, however, remembered the horror that pleasant outing turned into when 32,000 Southerners under Beauregard, Thomas J. "Stonewall" Jackson, and General Joseph E. Johnston turned a certain Union victory into a hasty retreat and then a shameful, pell mell rout which cost the overconfident Yankees some 2,500 men.

This first significant encounter was a portent, one which told both sides that the Union would either be preserved or utterly destroyed. There would be no compromise. In the spring of 1864, however, just such a compromise was in the works. Republican President Abraham Lincoln, lean, gaunt, humane, but as ruthless a commander in chief as ever America has produced, was up for re-election, but even within his own party there was talk of nominating John C. Fremont, of westward trailblazing fame.

The Democrats, as sick of it all as anyone else, turned to General John B. McClellan, one of the first Union generals in action and one subsequently replaced by more aggressive battlefield leaders. The Democrats, in an appeal to the "soft war/end the war" vote, built into their platform a plank which would have essentially ended the war and left the South a sovereign nation.

The South, pale and badly bleeding, had stopped the Union short of Richmond and its other vital center, Atlanta. Lee's boys in grey weren't winning any significant battles, but they were not losing any, either. Prevailing opinion was that if Dixie could just hold out until the election, ultimate victory, recognition and acceptance of the Confederate States of America, with the institution of slavery intact, would be theirs. That outcome was entirely feasible, given the high costs already paid and the seeming inability of Union forces to make any significant headway after the nearly 2,000 engagements it had taken to bring the see-saw course of the war itself to equilibrium.

To be sure, the South was slowly starving. The Union Navy had effectively blockaded the South's Atlantic Ocean and Gulf of Mexico ports, and although they had failed to secure those in Texas, the Confederate forces were cut off from the west by this time anyway. New Orleans' port was still operational, though, and a steady trickle of supplies made their way from Europe aboard doughty blockade runners. As long as New Orleans, Richmond and Atlanta remained in Confederate hands, the people of Dixie would continue to fight.

It was with these considerations in mind that, in May of 1864, General William T. Sherman led his 90,000 troops of tall, gangly, hardened young men from Ohio, Illinois, and other western states, out of their camps near Chattanooga and into Georgia in the general direction of Atlanta. Facing him was one of the South's ablest tacticians, the hero of Bull Run, little Joe Johnston.

Seldom in the history of warfare were two opposing generals better matched. Neither believed in squandering the lives of their men, and in an age when officers led by the mandate of their troops, rather than by force of rank alone, this was a precious quality. It meant that when Sherman or Johnston told his men they must fight, those troops did so, and with a stirring display of valor and tenacity.

Atlanta and Vicinity

As Sherman advanced into Georgia, he came through a range of hills known as Rocky Face Ridge, to a place with the ironically appropriate name of Buzzard's Roost. Here, Union scouts found Johnston's Rebels firmly and formidably entrenched. To attack would have been sheer suicide, so Sherman tried a wide flanking movement and went around Johnston's army through Snake Creek Gap toward Resaca, an important railroad station. Sherman's idea was to cut off Johnston by taking the railroad and trapping the genteel little Southerner between his troops and federal forces in Chattanooga. Once Johnson was disposed of, the way to Atlanta and through the Georgia heartland, primary food producer for the Confederacy, would have been wide open.

When Sherman flanked, Johnston, who military lore says had an almost prescient ability to escape such traps, moved swiftly off Buzzard's Roost, through Resaca and, after two days of fighting, stopped Sherman's advance. Though actually nothing more than a good defensive maneuver, word of it flashed through Dixie, reaching Richmond and causing a wave of relief and renewed determination.

Thus it went for the next few days. Sherman would flank, find Johnston facing him, skirmish, then march off and try it again somewhere else. He could not draw the Confederates out into the open and he could not get behind them. In Washington, Lincoln began to grow impatient, particularly since, in Virginia, Grant was still slugging it out, futilely for the most part, with Lee. It was the Civil War equivalent of the difference between cautious General Omar Bradley and dashing but often reckless George Patton in the Second World War.

Richmond, however, felt the same way about Johnston that Lincoln and his war cabinet were beginning to feel about Sherman. Where Sherman respectfully explained his strategy, the normally diplomatic and taciturn Joe Johnston (who distrusted and disliked Jefferson Davis ever since battle plans he'd confided to the Confederate president early in the war had wound up in the Richmond papers the next day) explained simply that while it was true that Sherman could not be permitted to take Atlanta, neither could the Confederacy afford a battle it could not win. The two generals, then, continued a ballet whose tactical intricacies are still being studied with pride and admiration at West Point and the Virginia Military Institute. Losses on both sides were light, and, in fact, Sherman was pressing steadily toward Atlanta.

Things came to a head for both sides, first during a vicious fight at New Hope Church May 25-28, and then, more dramatically, at Kennesaw Mountain on June 27.

The Battle of Kennesaw Mountain was, many historians feel, the turning point of the conquest of Georgia and, with the exception of some stout resistance during the initial siege of Atlanta, the last real battle fought in the Confederate southeast.

It was here, after New Hope Church, that Joe Johnston entrenched his troops, who manhandled their artillery up slopes so impossibly steep that horses and mules could not climb them. Grimly, the outnumbered Rebels dug in, vowing that Sherman would advance no further. The Union boys, veterans of a hundred battles and sick to death of war, grimly swore that if it took the bayonet and the sword, rifle butts, rocks, and their bare hands, they would drive Johnny Reb from the mountain, roll into Atlanta and be back across the Ohio River in time to get wood in for the winter.

It was warm that day, and even the birds were singing in the peach trees. The grass was green, the sky overhead an azure so beautiful it hurt the eyes to look at it. It was a pleasant morning, the kind that reminded men of both sides of happier, more tranquil times, and of all they had missed, and that some would never see, when, inevitably, the war ended.

In one hour, 2,500 farm boys and frontiersmen, husbands, fathers, uncles, brothers and sons lay dead. Abandoning his usual caution, Sherman ordered his men into the cannons and musket muzzles of crack Confederate troops firmly dug into deep trenches running along the parapets. The ball and shot was a nearly solid sheet and many a Rebel gunner wept openly as one wave of their brothers in blue was cut down, only to be replaced by another, silently and grimly climbing over the bodies of their comrades. It was an intense exercise in battlefield inferno which would haunt the men who fought in it for decades to come, and was summed up with chilling

Atlanta and Vicinity

understatement by Sherman's field general Pap Thomas, who told the visibly shaken commander, "one or two more such assaults would use up this army."

When it was over, General Joe Johnston sent Sherman a flag of truce and suggested that both sides take the opportunity to recover their wounded and bury their dead before continuing the slaughter. The next day, men who had been neighbors, acquaintances, or who were actually related—brothers, fathers and sons—set aside their muskets and came together on the field of battle to smoke quietly, recall better days, pass a jug and clean up the carnage. As dusk fell, and with great reluctance, both sides repaired to their earlier positions and, with heavy hearts, prepared to see it through to the end in the morning.

That, essentially, is the Battle of Kennesaw Mountain. It lasted one day and was the last really pitched battle of the war for the Union Army of the Cumberland and for the Confederate troops under Joe Johnston's command. Sherman, appalled by the bloodletting, resumed his former tactics and must have quietly cursed Lincoln's War Cabinet and himself for caving in under pressure. The South, too, mourned, for even though Johnston had shown that Johnny Reb still had a good fight in him, the gesture was empty. Sherman finally outflanked him, forced him into a defensive posture in Atlanta, and eventually took all of Georgia anyway.

For heroism and bravery, however, it would be hard to find a better example than the Battle of Kennesaw Mountain in the annals of either side.

LAWRENCEVILLE

No discussion of this interesting community of approximately 8,900, located in fascinating Gwinnett County thirty-one miles northeast of downtown Atlanta, off Interstate 85 and U.S. Highway 316 East, would be complete without some background on the county which it serves as the seat of government.

And it all starts, of course, with a man, a man with the unlikely name of Button Gwinnett.

Button was born in Gloucester, England on April 10, 1735, the son of a minister. Button grew up to be an educated merchant who married, had three daughters, and came across the Atlantic Ocean to settle, subsequently, in Charleston, South Carolina, Savannah, Georgia, and then, following a business failure, St. Catherine's Island, where he managed a plantation and got involved in parish politics. Commissioned a justice of the peace in 1767 and elected to the Commons House of Assembly two years later, he started making Revolutionary War history serving on a committee which wrote a letter to the Georgia colonial governor protesting certain taxes.

Button was not an astute businessman and withdrew from politics after his plantation failed. He emerged again in the summer of 1775, organizing what amounted to a backcountry coalition bent on removing England's Christ Church coalition from power in his part of the state. It seemed likely enough, somehow, that when the Georgia provincial congress needed a delegate to the Continental Congress, Button should get the job.

Atlanta and Vicinity

His accomplishments during the Revolution included voting for and signing the Declaration of Independence; heading the committee which drew up the first state constitution, commanding the state militia, leading it into Florida against the British, and dying honorably on May 19, 1777 in a duel with another Georgia politician with whom he did not agree.

For more information on this most interesting colonial Georgian, contact the Gwinnett Historical Society, Box 261, Lawrenceville, GA 30246. There is a wealth of material about his life at the Society's office in Lawrenceville.

Now, the county which bears Button's name was created in 1818, and the county seat was named for another figure who must be appreciated because of the lore about him in Lawrenceville.

The man's name is James Lawrence. He is the U.S. naval officer who gave the Navy its motto "Don't give up the ship." He was born in New Jersey on October 1, 1781 and served in the Barbary Wars. Admiral David Porter made him second in command in his raid on Tripoli, the same one which gave the Marine Corps a line in its hymn. Lawrence was also a first lieutenant on the *USS Constitution*, also known to historians as *Old Ironsides* , and was commander of the brig Hornet at the commencement of the War of 1812. He took the Hornet against the British brig *Peacock* and sank her with but one killed and two injured in his own command. He didn't fare nearly so well against the *HMS Shannon* and in an eleven-minute engagement, Captain Lawrence, commanding the *USS Chesapeake*, fell mortally wounded. It was when he was carried below from his quarterdeck that he uttered those immortal words.

It was for his valor that Lawrenceville bears his name. The community itself was laid out around the first permanent courthouse constructed in 1824, six years after the Georgia legislature opened up the territory and designated Gwinnett County and its boundaries. As was usual at the time, the county was developed from a land lottery and the county divided into four districts of 250 acre lots for the drawing.

The earliest Gwinnett County settlers were farmers and military frontiersmen, hence the likelihood that Lawrenceville would be named for a hero of the country's then most recent war. These folks came from the Carolinas, Virginia and eastern Georgia. Of English, Scots-Irish and Welsh Protestant descent, they valued religious freedom and formed many new church congregations. Camp meetings were one of the earliest forms of worship and Lawrenceville is near the early 1830s site of one of the most popular outdoor congregations. The courthouse followed, and then, as farmers settled in and roads were built, Lawrenceville itself prospered.

Gwinnett County is fortunate in that it was not on the direct route of Sherman's march, and that new railroad lines built during Reconstruction tied the county together. By 1871, one of the most important of these, the Danville & Piedmont line, connected Atlanta with Richmond, Virginia, and among the major stops in Georgia were the communities of Norcross, Duluth, Suwanee and Buford.

From there, the history of Lawrenceville is pretty typical of Gwinnett County and the greater Atlanta area. It continued on as the county seat, thriving quietly and preserving its history, then struggling to recover from the devastating drought and boll weevil blight which destroyed the cotton industry in the mid 1920s.

It is precisely Lawrenceville's rustic charm and its easy access to Atlanta which makes it such an interesting and charming community to visit and in which to spend leisure time.

ATTRACTIONS

- **Lawrenceville's Courthouse Square** is the oldest in the metropolitan Atlanta area. Two buildings in it date back to 1849 and historical markers do an outstanding job of depicting the county's early history. Eight Gwinnett County soldiers who fought in the Texas War of Independence are buried in the cemetery on the west side of the square and a memorial has been erected to them.

Atlanta and Vicinity

- The residence of one of Gwinnett County and Lawrenceville's earliest pioneers, the **Elisha Winn Home**, stands on Hurricane Shoals Road one mile east of the Apalachee River. The first official **Gwinnett County court** convened there.
- **The Gwinnett County Arts Council** maintains its headquarters at 383 Crogan Street and presents ten art exhibits a year. These, which include a reception and a representative performing art, highlight the works of over 200 local artists, as well as pieces from the George Williams and Steffan Thomas collections.
- **The Arts Council's Outreach Program** has also placed exhibits in such diverse locations as the cafeteria at the Humana-Gwinnett Hospital in Snellville; Little Gardens restaurant in Duluth; and at Sikes Oldsmobile in Lawrenceville. For more information on Gwinnett County art, performing art and music, contact the Arts Council at their Crogan Street address.
- Aviation history buffs will be delighted with **The Georgia Historical Aviation Museum**, housed at Briscoe Field near the city. Its collection of old warbirds includes P-51 Mustangs, DC-3's, T28B's and B-25 Billy Mitchell bombers. For more information, call (404) 979-3845.
- One of Georgia's better wineries is located at the junction of Interstate 85 and State Highway 211 east of Atlanta, near the Barrow County line. **Chateau Elan, Ltd.** is typical of the growing vineyards spreading across the hillsides of north Georgia. Visitors to this establishment can tour the production facilities and cask room, taste the fruit of the vine, and in the near future, relax in a chateau with a wine museum, conference center and restaurant. Tour and tasting room hours are Mon. - Sat., 10:00 a.m. - 4:00 p.m. Admission is free. Take Exit 48 near Braselton. For more information, contact Chateau Elan, Ltd. Vineyards, Rte. 1, Box 563-1, Hoschton, GA 30548; (404) 867-8200.
- **The Atlanta Falcons** football team maintains their headquarters in the Falcon Complex in Suwanee. That complex includes a fitness center, hotel and conference center, National Football League gift shop and more. Watching the team

practice is a popular spring and late summer pastime among native Atlantans. For more information, call (404) 945-8977.

- For those who love shopping, **Gwinnett Place**, the county's 1.1 million square foot regional mall, is hard to beat. Major stores there include Mervyn's, Macy's, Rich's and Sears. Gwinnett Place is also a vast community center and cultural complex, with exhibits and performances the year around. It's located at Interstate 85 north and Pleasant Hill Road. For more information, call (404) 476-5160.

- The site of **Old Fort Daniel**, near Hog Mountain at the eastern end of Old Peachtree Road, is definitely worth the trip, particularly for history buffs.

- **The Promised Land** was the home of planter Thomas Maguire, the cotton farmer from whom Margaret Mitchell drew for her character of Gerald O'Hara in *Gone With the Wind*. The home is the second oldest in the county and was occupied by federal forces during Sherman's conquest of George. Built during the 1820s, it is located at State Highway 124 on the Yellow River in the southern part of the county. For more information, call (404) 972-5848.

- One of the oldest churches in the county, **The Zoar Methodist Church**, is located on State Highway 124 just south of Snellville. It was built in 1811. Contact Rev. Chuck Moon at (404) 972-5905.

- The oldest church in Gwinnett County, dating back to the 1700s, is the **Mount Moriah Baptist Church**, located on Mount Moriah Road just south of State Highway 124, in the extreme northeast portion of the county. For more information, call (404) 753-6172.

EVENTS

- **Snellville Days Festival**, held each spring, attracts top name talent like comedian Jerry Clower and singers Tom T. Hall and B.J. Thomas. If you're in the area, drop by.

Atlanta and Vicinity

• Two charming smalltown fair festivals both occur in May, and are worth attending for their sheer nostalgia value alone. **Suwanee Day** and **Grayson** offer a smorgasbord of arts and crafts and some outstanding southern cooking.

• **The Elisha Winn Fair** is held in the Elisha Winn Home in Dacula in October. Activities include arts and crafts, old time culinary delights and encampments and reenactments by Civil War soldiers.

For more information on Gwinnett County, its history and its attractions, contact both the Gwinnett County Chamber of Commerce, 1230 Atkinson Road, P.O. Box 1245, Lawrenceville, GA 30246; (404) 963-5128 and the Gwinnett Historical Society, P.O. Box 261, Lawrenceville, GA 30246; (404) 962-1450.

LILBURN

This community in Gwinnett County south of Norcross at the junction of State Highway 378 and U.S. Highway 29, combines history and charm. Residents have turned its historical Main street, including the great old Railroad Place Building, into a unique collection of antique and craft shops. Each autumn, as well, the weekend long Lilburn Days Arts Festival, held in October, draws representative artists and craftsfolk from all over the greater Atlanta area. Lilburn is also the home of the Gwinnett All County Theatre Association, P.O. Box 235; Lilburn, GA 30247; (404) 923-5253; the Gwinnett Amateur Radio Society, P.O. Box 88, Lilburn, GA 30247; and the Gwinnett Ballet Theatre, 4047 Darlington Court, Lilburn, GA 30247; (404) 921-7277. All in all, Lilburn is probably the best place in the eastern Atlanta metro area to contact for cultural events in that region, and one of the most interesting places to shop, as well.

Atlanta and Vicinity

MARIETTA

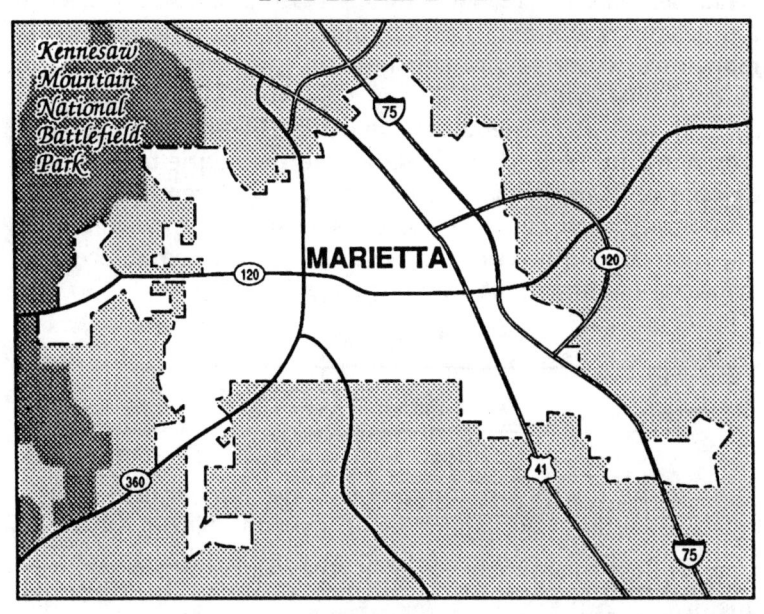

This community of 38,600, seventeen miles northwest of downtown Atlanta on Interstate 75, is a quietly thriving metropolis in the heart of some of the richest historical territory and most beautiful countryside in all of Georgia.

Originally settled by winners of the Cherokee lands lottery of 1834 and by lowland planters, the area's relative elevation of 1,118 feet had all the agricultural advantages of the swampier coastal areas and none of the drawbacks of that then-malaria and yellow fever ridden land. Marietta was also the scene and area of two of the more dramatic events of a period which seems as tragically vibrant today as it was then—well over 120 years ago.

It was here, in April, 1862 that the James Bond of the Union forces and his small band of Ohio soldiers boarded the General, the locomotive they hoped to take clear to Chattanooga, burning bridges and generally disrupting rail traffic as a presage to the subsequently long delayed capture of Chattanooga itself, and Atlanta, as well.

Atlanta and Vicinity

And when, four years or so later, Union General William Tecumseh Sherman marched through Georgia, it was at nearby Kennesaw Mountain that Confederate General Joseph T. Johnston's weary but valiant boys in grey tried to stem the federalist invasion.

It was at Marietta, as well, that Henry Cole, a local merchant, in 1866, donated land for the Marietta National Cemetery. Marietta has two such poignant reminders. The community itself evokes a more tranquil period, with its tree lined streets and beautifully preserved or restored antebellum mansions and turn of the century cottages.

ATTRACTIONS

- The town's two cemeteries have for decades drawn those of southern heritage from all over the North American continent. **The Confederate Cemetery**, established in 1863, is the final resting place for 3,000 Dixie valiants. **The National Cemetery**, Henry Cole's dream, has 10,000 Union soldiers interred, 3,000 of whom are unknown.
- **Glover Park**, in the downtown square, is a redolent expanse of brick paths which lead to a beautiful three tiered fountain, an ornate Victorian gazebo and a miniature replica of that famous "Great Locomotive Raid" engine, the General. The residential neighborhood east of Cherokee Street is one of the best places in the greater Atlanta area to recapture that historic period of southern grace and charm.
- **The Chattahoochee River** provides excellent recreational activities and White Water, a park on Cobb Parkway, has facilities to delight the youngsters, including a wave pool, waterslides, flumes and inner tube rapids courses.
- **The Marietta Welcome Center**, just off the downtown square in the old train depot, has brochures mapping out a walking and driving tour of the historic district. Sights along the route include a restaurant which served as Sherman's headquarters and a fully restored antebellum mansion.

Atlanta and Vicinity

• **Kennesaw Mountain National Battlefield Park**, located just 2.5 miles northwest of Marietta on old US 41, occupies 2,882 acres. The park offers a paved road to the summit, preserved earthworks from which Johnston's grey faced Sherman's blue, a visitor center and park headquarters, picnicking in designated areas and slide programs and exhibits recounting the battle itself.

For more information, contact the Marietta Welcome Center, 2 Depot Street, Marietta, GA 30060; (404) 429-1115 or Cobb Chamber of Commerce, P.O. Box Cobb, Marietta, GA 30065; (404) 980-2000.

ACCOMMODATION

COMPRI HOTEL, 3000 Hargrove Road Northwest, Marietta, GA. (404) 952-2555. Luxury rooms, a cooked to order breakfast and complimentary cocktails in the club or lounge are a few of the amenities available at the Compri Hotel. A steam room, an indoor pool and private exercise facilities are offered for your relaxation and fitness habits.

Atlanta and Vicinity

AMUSEMENT PARK

WHITE WATER
250 North Cobb Parkway
Marietta, GA 30062
Tel. (404) 424-WAVE
Hrs: Opens weekends April 30th
     May 28th. - Sept. 5
     Mon. - Sun. Open   10:00 a.m.
     Late summer weekends until Sept. 11th.
     Open Labor Day

Are you ready to shoot the rapids, surf the pipeline or maybe float quietly on an innertube under bridges and past gentle woods? Whatever your choice, you'll find plenty of good, safe family fun at White Water Family Water Park.

White Water is a family water park featuring more than two dozen water adventures, including white water rapids, leisurely river rambles, body flumes, the Atlanta and a special children's area. The water adventures are fun and varied. The new Bermuda Triangle is "too much fun for just one!" Two person boats wind down a water-slick flume with high banking curves and thrills. If surfing is your thing, the Atlanta Ocean at the center of the park is a 710,000 gallon pool which generates continuous four foot waves just right for body or tube surfing. The Banzai Pipeline is a totally enclosed fiberglass tube which gives riders the sensation of shooting the waves off the coast of Hawaii. Quieter times are created by the Little Hooch inner tube float, down a gently flowing river, past pretty scenery. Sunning areas near pool and "ocean" side offer more than 2,000 lounge chairs. Several restaurants offer quick snacks to full meals. Certified Red Cross lifeguards and ride attendants are on duty at all times. Safety is stressed throughout the park.

White Water was founded by the Herschend family, the same family that developed Silver Dollar City in Branson,

Missouri and Pigeon Forge in Tennessee, which later became Dollywood in honor of Dolly Parton. White Water offers good quality family entertainment in a safe and diverse setting. White Water is a great place to make a splash!

COMEDY

A COMIC CAFE
1215 Powers Ferry Road
Marietta, GA 30067
Tel. (404) 956-star
Hrs: Mon. - Thu.   One show   7:30 p.m. - 11:30 p.m.
     Fri., Sat.   Two shows 8:30 p.m. - 10:30 p.m.
     Sunday   One show   8:30 p.m.
Visa, MasterCard and AMEX are accepted.

No matter what type of comedy is your particular favorite, you'll find it at A Comic Cafe, known as the state of the art comedy club of Marietta. Owner Chris Dipetta draws from a large repertoire of talent; he's been in the business for seven years and also runs a booking agency called Snickers. The club features seasoned as well as novice acts.

If you come to the club between Tuesday and Sunday evenings, you're likely to find yourself laughing at comics such as Harry Anderson or Jay Johnson who have appeared on David Letterman and the Johnny Carson shows. No matter which of the 270 chairs you're seated in, you'll have a good view of the performer because of the four level seating arrangement, and you'll be able to hear every joke with the excellent sound system. Monday nights are improvisational, where you'll get a chance to view up-and-coming comics. Waiting for the show is almost as good as the performance. You can relax in the lounge in front of the ten foot video screen while enjoying a mixed drink, a bottle of imported or domestic beer or a glass of wine. Munchies available include fried shrimp and vegetables, buffalo chicken wings and spicy beef nachos.

Atlanta and Vicinity

If and when George Carlin visits Marietta you can bet the first place he'll visit is A Comic Cafe. It's the place to view musical, magic and every kind of adult humor you can imagine. If you feel real adventurous try one of the special Comic Atomic Punch drinks or better still come by on a Monday night and show the audience your stuff.

HARDWARE STORE

SMITH ACE HARDWARE
2133 Roswell Road
Marietta, GA 30060
Tel. (404) 973-3636
Hrs: Mon. - Fri. 7:30 a.m. - 9:00 p.m.
         Saturday   8:00 a.m. - Sun 10:00 a.m.
Visa, MasterCard, AMEX, Discover and Smith's are accepted.
Also,

601 College Avenue
Decatur, GA 30030
Tel. (404) 373-3335

5920 Roswell Road
Sandy Springs, GA 30328
Tel. (404) 256-2560

West Paces Ferry Ctr.
Atlanta, GA 30327
Tel. (404) 261-6000

8560 Holcomb Bridge Rd.
North Fulton, GA 30201
Tel. (404) 586-1800

775 Whitlock Ave.
West Marietta, GA
Tel. (404) 422-1646

When you are away from home and need a good hardware store, Smith Ace Hardware is the place to go to find what you need. You'll be certain to find just what you are looking for to make sure you are well equipped for the rest of your trip. Smith Ace Hardware/Home Center stocks over 30,000 items and has the selection you need whether it is live plants, nuts and bolts, housewares, tools or more.

Each location gives its neighborhood what it needs, be it horse feed and beekeeping supplies or gift ware. One of the more unique features of these stores is the paint section, which has a computer that reads and matches colors with the accuracy of the human eye. The store carries those reliable Honda lawn mowers and top of the line lawn furniture. There is a large garden section with gorgeous plant specimens, all guaranteed for one year, some of which are quite difficult to find elsewhere. Most of the stores have a giftware department. At the Velvet Hammer you'll find crystal, brass, wicker, pewter and even jewelry designed by Anita Mobley, Carolyn Tanner and accessories by Liz Claiborne. And some of the stores carry a full line of Hallmark products. Each store is well organized and well lit.

The helpful sales people wear red vests so that you can immediately identify them. They are very knowledgeable about their products. They can tell you what to do to get rid of June bugs or how to get red clay out of your carpet. Special services include custom threading of pipe, glass cutting, screen making and lock rekeying. The store opened in 1935 with a philosophy of giving its customers what they wanted. Although the inventory has expanded over the last fifty years, the value and service has remained first rate.

Atlanta and Vicinity

NIGHTCLUB

CHARADES
105 North Park Square
Marietta, GA 30060
Tel. (404) 422-9800
Hrs: Tue. - Thu. 5:00 p.m. - 2:00 a.m.
  Friday 4:00 p.m. - 2:00 p.m.
  Saturday 7:00 p.m. - 3:00 a.m.
Visa, MasterCard, AMEX and Diners Club are accepted.

Charades is "Your Home for Live Rock Entertainment" in greater Georgia. Tuesday through Saturday evening the old movie house turned nightclub rocks with local popular bands and entertainers.

The building still retains its movie house balcony and stage. Bands play on the old stage. Large brass fixtures surround the entrance. The bar is replete with a big brass rail and massive wood decorations. Booths and small tables near the rail provide excellent seating for viewing musical performances. A large sunken dance floor sweeps along the front of the stage and offers plenty of space to rock, roll and swing with your partner. Pictures of well known rock groups will be looking down on you from the walls.

If you work up an appetite with all your dancing activity, indulge in appetizers and snack fare including delicious chicken wings, or head for the full taco bar offered during happy hour each night until 8:00 p.m. Video games, a black jack table and free pool are available in an adjoining room of the club. Charades is the place in Marietta to catch the latest in rock and roll entertainment, and the nightclub can hold parties of up to 350 people.

RESTAURANTS

EL RANCHERO RESTAURANTE MEXICANO, 562 Cobb Parkway Northeast, Marietta, Ga. Tel. (404) 427-9737. El Ranchero serves over fifty choices of authentic Mexican cooking at reasonable prices. A few of the specialties served for lunch and dinner are hot tamales, burritos and enchiladas.

FLAMINGO JOE'S
4719 Lower Roswell Road
Marietta, GA 30067
Tel. (404) 973-0675
Hrs: Mon.- Fri. 4:00 p.m. - 2:00 a.m.
 Saturday 1:00 p.m. - 2:55 a.m.
 Sunday 1:00 p.m. - 12:00 midnight
Visa and MasterCard are accepted.

Evoking the era of the 50s and 60s, Flamingo Joe's invites you to put on your dancing shoes and strut your stuff. The atmosphere is warm, friendly and relaxed, and is a place where friends come to meet and strangers become friends.

Decorated in keeping with the 50s motif, the walls of turquoise and black are liberally sprinkled with pictures of Elvis Presley, Marilyn Monroe and James Dean in their heyday. Continuing the nostalgia, customers will be glad to know Shag dancing and Hand Jive "are spoken here." People travel for miles to dine and dance at Flamingo Joe's. Dinner is served until 9:00 p.m. and then it's party time. A DeeJay plays the "oldies but goodies," however, lovers of contemporary music are not forgotten. Dancing on the floor is desirable, but not mandatory, as some customers, lulled by the carefree atmosphere, have been known to do a quick turn on the table or bar. For those whose knowledge of dancing stopped with the two step, classes in Shag dancing are available on Sunday, and Thursdays and Sundays are designated Shag nights. A complete dinner menu is available, and two popular favorites

Atlanta and Vicinity

of the house are Baby Back Ribs and Blackened Fish. There are dinner specials on Monday and Tuesday, and Thursday is an "all you can eat" spaghetti night. They will cater weddings and banquets, and have done many birthdays conforming to the 60s theme.

Located in a strip shopping center, there is easy access and plentiful parking available. Whether you were present at the first go-around of the fifties, or wish to acquaint yourself with some aspects of that generation, an evening at Flamingo Joe's is an enjoyable experience.

MAXIMILLIAN'S CONTINENTAL AMERICAN CUISINE
1857 Airport Industrial Park Drive
Marietta, GA 30062
Tel. (404) 955-4286

Hrs: Lunch	Tue. - Fri.	11:30 a.m. - 2:00 p.m.
Dinner	Mon. - Thu.	6:00 p.m. - 10:00 p.m.
	Fri. - Sat.	6:00 p.m. - 11:00 p.m.

Visa, MasterCard, AMEX, Diners Club and Carte Blanche are accepted.

This special dinner house began life as a hunting lodge constructed for the lawyer who played a key roll in getting Dobbins Air Base located at Marietta. Now it plays a major role in the pleasure of diners. They come to this fine country place for leisurely meals in a romantic atmosphere.

Maximillian's atmosphere and food have earned awards for owner/chef Jay Mitchell and his wife Pam, who manages the restaurant and lounge. He calls it a "dining establishment," stressing freshness and quality in food. The wine list is a selection of choice vintages. Meals at Maximillian's take time to enjoy. You can choose an elegant five course dinner special that goes with the carefully selected entrees. Or you can order a less elaborate meal, and still enjoy the entrees. Among the best are stuffed flounder, double loin lamb chops, veal and Steak au Poivre. The service is quick and personal, the setting intimate, the dining room using three rooms of the original house. Just eighty diners at a time can be seated. Downstairs there is a

Atlanta and Vicinity

small lounge overlooking a pond, a place to relax and to finish off a truly enjoyable evening by trying one of Maximillian's famous coffee drinks.

Perhaps the way to sum up the magic of Maximillian's is to use Mitchell's own words. "We try to make it so that people feel they are the only ones dining," he says. It is not unusual for diners to take three hours or more to savor their five course dinners, never feeling rushed.

OSAKA JAPAN, 4400 Roswell Road NE, Marietta, GA. Tel. (404) 973-3711. Osaka Japan features hibachi cuisine cooked at your table. Steak and seafood, Osaka style, are served amid gorgeous surroundings by the courteous staff.

THE PLANTERS
780 South Cobb Drive
Marietta, GA 30061
Tel. (404) 427-4646
Hrs: Mon. - Thu.   6:30 p.m. - 12:00 midnight
     Fri. - Sat.   6:00 p.m. - 12:00 midnight
Reservations are requested.
Visa, MasterCard, AMEX and Diners Club are accepted.

Visit The Planters and dine in the luxury of the Old South. This fine restaurant is located in an 1848 Greek Revival mansion, in the heart of thirteen beautifully landscaped acres. Original furnishings and decor add to the authentic pre-Civil War experience.

Since opening in 1981, The Planters has gained fame in the pages of *Southern Living, The New York Times, The Dallas News* and many other publications. The fine food and gracious service will provide a memorable dining experience. The menu at The Planters is changed seasonally, and offers the freshest ingredients available. A variety of appetizers and soups are offered, including shrimp filled potato crepes, Salmon Terrine with Crabmeat, steamed mussels with fettuccine and wild mushroom soup. Calorie conscious guests will enjoy spinach, avocado, feta cheese and walnut salad, served with basil dressing or fresh seasonal fruit salad with honey cream

Atlanta and Vicinity

dressing. Elegant entrees include Broiled New York Steak with Sundried Tomato Butter, Honey Fried Shrimp with Ginger Lime Sauce, Sautéed Veal with Lemon Herb Butter, Roast Rack of Lamb with Mint Pesto and Roast Wisconsin Duck. Complete your meal with a tantalizing dessert, such as Chocolate Sky High Cake, Whiskey Cream Pie, Key Lime Pie or Pear Charlotte.

Listed on the National Register of Historic Places, The Planters is the perfect location for special parties, corporate lunches and wedding receptions. For creative American cuisine in a sophisticated atmosphere, The Planters is your "Best Choice" in Marietta.

TEXAS STEAK OUT
13 North Park Square
Marietta, GA 30060
Tel. (404) 422-4322

Hrs:	Lunch	Mon. - Fri.	11:00 a.m. - 3:00 p.m.
	Dinner	Mon. - Thu.	5:00 p.m. - 10:00 p.m.
		Fri. - Sat.	5:00 p.m. - 11:00 p.m.

Visa, MasterCard, AMEX and Diners Club are accepted.

If you like steak, not one of those little "petite" steaks, but something you can really "get your teeth into," then by all means head on down to the Texas Steak Out. Located in the heart of one of Atlanta's many historic districts, this fine restaurant features good ol' down home cooking in a right friendly atmosphere.

The menu is simple—just choice, hand cut steaks. Try their Steak Kabobs. Tender and juicy, each one is a taste sensation. How about a melt in your mouth, nine ounce Filet Mignon, broiled just the way you like it, or maybe an appetizing ten ounce Rib Eye. Need something a little more substantial? How about a delicious eleven ounce New York Strip. Still not enough? Then you need the Texas Steak Out's eighteen ounce T-bone. A meal truly fit for a king. Every steak comes cooked to perfection and if you request, smothered in onions and mushrooms. For a change of pace you might want to try Smothered Chicken, Sweet and Sour Chicken or the ever popular Teriyaki Chicken. With an all you can eat salad bar, fresh, warm, home baked bread and a perfect baked potato, every meal is a steak lover's delight. For dessert they feature such sumptuous offerings as homemade cherry cobbler and a hot fudge and brownie sundae. From its Texas style decor with checkered table cloths, to the seductive aroma of onions and mushrooms, the Texas Steak Out is most definitely the "Best Little Steak House in Marietta."

MORROW

Morrow, incorporated in 1943 and largely the result of Atlanta's Second World War boom, considers itself a bedroom community serving both the greater metropolitan area and those who staff and attend Clayton State College. The city park, with its track, pavilion, and picnic facilities offers a nice place to jog and to relax. Here, as well, one finds some of the friendliest people in the South. The 3,750 people living within the city limits of this Clayton County community say that their hospitality is typical of both the old and the new South.

GIFT SHOP

SIMPLY COUNTRY INC.
1560 South Lake Parkway
Morrow, GA 30260
Tel. (404) 961-0873
Hrs: Mon. - Sat. 10:00 a.m. - 7:00 p.m.
Extended holiday hours.
Visa, MasterCard and AMEX are accepted.

Simply Country is the perfect shop to pick up a token of your visit to Georgia. Almost all the items in this cozy and well-stocked store are locally made.
Along with locally crafted gifts, Owner Kay Roberts carries famous collectibles such as Anna Perenna, Raikes Bears,

Atlanta and Vicinity

Constance Collection, Glenda Turley Prints and Norman Rockwell prints. Kay will also personalize any item you choose while you wait. The shelves of Simply Country are chock full of handmade crafts and gifts. They hang on the walls, from the ceiling and are tucked into every available niche in the shop. Of special note are the hand painted wall plaques, small country furniture pieces and rag dolls. You will also find ceramic ducks, hand dipped candles, potpourri, cards with a country message and photo albums in lace and cloth. Home accessories with a country turn are also offered at Simply Country.

Kay's merchandise has a special country and personal flavor. A memento chosen from Simply Country will be a constant reminder of Georgia hospitality.

NORCROSS

This Gwinnett County community fourteen miles northeast of downtown Atlanta got its start as a major stop on the Danville & Piedmont Railroad line which connected Richmond with Atlanta, and then continued east toward the Atlantic Ocean. The community has grown considerably and now comprises an aspect of the greater Atlanta megalopolis.

ATTRACTIONS

• **Old Pinckneyville**, located at Peachtree Road and Georgia State Route 141 just north of Norcross, contains the first Norcross post office and once sited the muster ground for the local militia company, the militia district courthouse, and a stagecoach stop. History buffs will enjoy talking to local historian Harold Medlock, who can be reached at (404) 448-4787.

• **The Pinckneyville Art Center**, at Holcombe Bridge Road and the Chattahoochee River, offers a nice display of area arts and crafts. For more information, contact the Gwinnett

Atlanta and Vicinity

County Historical Society, P.O. Box 261, Lawrenceville, GA 30246; (404) 962-1450.

• **Jones Bridge Park** offers the best view of the Chattahoochee River from its pavilion. The trout fishing here is good, and swimming and sunbathing are also popular pastimes. For more information, call (404) 962-6840.

ACCOMMODATION

AMBERLEY SUITES HOTEL
5885 Oakbrook Parkway
Norcross, GA 30093
Tel. (404) 263-0515
      (800) 227-7229
All major credit cards are accepted.

Opened in December of 1985, this hotel has made leaps and bounds toward being one of the finest hotels in Georgia today. Offering quality accommodations, friendly staff and convenient services, this hotel is a must for travelers. Centrally located, the Amberley Suites Hotel is just northeast of Atlanta and is close to Lake Lanier, Gwinnett Mall, Stone Mountain, Six Flags over Georgia and Place Mall.

As a AAA Mobile Travel Club Hotel, the Amberley offers a wide variety of room types ranging from a two or three room suite to a mini suite or deluxe king. All suites offer kitchen, living and dining areas along with bedrooms and separate baths. The deluxe king offers a spacious single bedroom in the traditional hotel format. All rooms are outfitted in traditional Queen Anne furniture with a hint of contemporary decor. Kitchens are complete with full size refrigerators, microwaves and built in coffee makers with complimentary coffee. Also included are built in hair dryers, shower massages and digital alarm clocks. Other amenities include a twenty-four hour fitness center complete with whirlpool, sauna and swimming pool. There is door to door airport service, coin laundry and

Atlanta and Vicinity

Watson's Deli and Cafe and convenience store, so as to stock your refrigerator without having to leave the complex.

Guests also appreciate cable TV complete with ESPN, CNN and The Movie Channel, four conference rooms that can accommodate up to 150 people, audio-visual equipment and catering service. Built to accommodate any type of traveler, the Amberley Suites Hotel offers everything that will will make your vacation or business trip complete. Come, try a "Best Choice" and be pleasantly surprised.

GIFT SHOPS

CHINA CHASERS
3280 Peachtree Corners Circle
Norcross, GA 30092
Tel. (404) 441-9146
Hrs: Mon. - Sat.   10:00 a.m. - 4:00 p.m.
Visa and MasterCard are accepted.

China Chasers specializes in finding out of production patterns of china and crystal. The firm also has one of the largest selections of active patterns in the Southeast, and most of these are sold at twenty to forty percent off current retail. "Patterns Past and Present" are represented on the hundreds of shelves of China Chasers. All of the merchandise of China Chasers is new, including both the out of production and current patterns.

A walk along the eight foot high aisles of China Chasers can take you on a nostalgic journey to places like your grandmother's house. Familiar old patterns, from simple to ornate, line the shelves. The staff at China Chasers will search for china replacements for such brand names as Castleton, Flintridge, Franciscan, Franconia, Gorham, Johnson Bros., Lenox, Metlox, both Vernonware and Poppytrail, Minton, Spode, Royal Doulton, Royal Copenhagen, Villeroy and Boch, Wedgwood, Heinrich, Hutschenreuther and many more. China

Chasers will keep a record of your pattern of china or crystal and notify you every time your pieces become available. Everything is done by mail with no obligation and no minimum order.

China Chasers can fill an order for a gift, enclose a gift card and send it anywhere in the United States. A special shrink wrap is used for safe shipping. China Chasers is located three miles north of #285 off Peachtree Industrial Boulevard and is easily accessible from many Atlanta locations. Access to the rear warehouse and showroom, where the out of production patterns are housed, is open to the public.

GEORGIA SWEET GEORGIA, 6624 Northeast Expressway Access Road, Norcross, GA. Tel. (404) 448-3736. Georgia Sweet Georgia is a unique gift shop offering handcrafted items and greeting cards. Gnomes, wizards and pewter dragons await you amid lighted houses and the "shops of Dickens Village."

GOLF

GOLF WAREHOUSE SALES, Interstate 85 at Indian Trail, Norcross, GA. Tel. (404) 447-4653. Golf Warehouse Sales is "one of the largest pro shops in the world" with over 20,000 pairs of national brand shoes, all pro line clubs and over 3,000 pro line bags. Free swing and putting analyzers are available.

Atlanta and Vicinity

RESTAURANTS

LEE'S GOLDEN BUDDHA CHINESE RESTAURANT
2055-C Beaver Run Road
Norcross, GA 30071
Tel. (404) 448-3377

Hrs:	Lunch	Mon. - Fri.	11:30 a.m. - 2:30 p.m.
	Dinner	Mon. - Thu.	2:30 p.m. - 10:00 p.m
		Saturday	4:00 p.m. - 11:00 p.m.
		Sunday	12:00 noon - 10:00 p.m.

Visa, MasterCard, AMEX, Diners Card and Carte Blanche are accepted.
Also,
Lee's Golden Buddha
3095 Highway 20
Buford, GA 30518
Tel. (404) 945-1224

Been Chuan Lee's Golden Buddha Chinese Restaurant is an award winning restaurant featuring Szechwan, Mandarin and Hunan cuisine. A special emphasis is placed on the á la carte dishes. You will have a choice of over 100 varieties of delicious selections.

Manager Stephen Duk Lee recommends the Pu Pu Platter en Flame with chicken wings, fried shrimp, short ribs, fried won ton, pot stickers and beef cho cho. The soup menu offers the popular Hot and Sour Soup made with sliced shredded pork, bamboo shoots and egg flower in a full bodied broth and spiced with black pepper. The Sizzling Shrimp with Scallops is an irresistible dish of tender shrimp with fresh scallops and Chinese vegetables. Your choice of main courses is superb. Your meal will be prepared at your table by one of the talented chefs of The Golden Buddha Chinese Restaurant.

The restaurant surroundings are relaxed and attractive with decorative waterfalls and fish tanks. The fortune cookies from The Golden Buddha Chinese Restaurant often read, "Congratulations, you have just enjoyed a delicious Chinese meal!" Be sure and try Lee's other Golden Buddha restaurants in Gaineville, Marietta, and Duluth.

J.R.'S LOG HOUSE
6601 Peachtree Industrial Boulevard
Norcross, GA 30092
Tel. (404) 449-6426
Hrs: Mon.-Sun. 7:00 a.m.-10:00 p.m.
Visa and MasterCard are accepted.

Owner Jerry Romano, J. R. for short, is the kind of man who knows what he wants and knows how to get it. The first thing he wants is customer satisfaction. And one way he has of being sure of keeping it is posting a sign in his barbecue restaurant that reads, "If you receive any food that is not what you expected or not to your taste, please as a great service to me, ask your server to replace it with something else."

Having to replace food is not something J.R. loses any sleep over. The happy scene at the Log House is customer after customer diving into an eye-opening country breakfast or juicy barbecue plate. The Brunswick stew is so good that folks consume forty to fifty gallons of it a day. The breakfast is said to be just about the best in the Atlanta region, and late risers can order it up until 2:00 p.m. The barbecue meat is cooked slowly over an open fire for eight to twelve hours. When it's finally served, it's covered with a barbecue sauce that is a family recipe. The restaurant is known throughout the state as one of the best barbecue places in Georgia. The salad bar at J.R.'s includes thirty items and the dessert menu contains a long list of goodies, including peach and cherry cobbler, banana pudding and brownies.

Your satisfaction is guaranteed not just once, but twice. For as the sign continues, "If you are still not completely happy, please don't be embarrassed to tell your server again and he or she will gladly deduct the amount from your check. Many thanks, J.R."

Atlanta and Vicinity

LOS ARCOS MEXICAN RESTAURANT, 5050 Jimmy Carter Boulevard, Norcross, GA. Tel. (404) 368-0343. Los Arcos serves fine Mexican food cooked over a mesquite fire. Margaritas and other cocktails are offered with lunch and dinner seven days a week.

PEACHTREE YACHT CLUB
5390 Peachtree Industrial Boulevard
Norcross, GA 30071
Tel. (404) 263-9842
Hrs: Mon. - Fri. 11:30 a.m. - 10:00 p.m.
    Saturday 6:00 p.m. - 11:00 p.m.
Visa, MasterCard, AMEX and Diners Club are accepted.

You don't have to do anything to join this yacht club except call for reservations with expectations of having a fine dining experience. The Peachtree Yacht Club does a brisk lunch business five days a week, and puts out superb dinners Monday through Saturday. The atmosphere is casually elegant. The dining room combines white cloth service and rich mahogany warmth. Through beveled glass doors the adjoining bar is done in the style of an early 1900s Chicago bar. Pictures on the wall are of twelve meter sailboats in competition, which is as close to the water as owner Bob Hughes goes with his nautical theme.

The kitchen is presided over by Steve Rice, one of the best chefs in Atlanta. Those who know pick the spinach salad, an onion soup glazed with Italian cheeses, and either the Georgia quail stuffed with veal and currants, or the roasted veal chop. It, too, is stuffed with mushrooms, onions, herbs and enhanced with a wine sauce. The menu also includes nightly seafood specials and souffles. The wine list is well rounded and chosen from the best vintages from around the globe. The Peachtree Yacht Club is in Medlock Place, across from Technology Park in Norcross.

ROSWELL

This North Fulton County community of about 23,330, north of the Chattahoochee River in the Blue Ridge foothills, was founded in 1839 by an agent of the Darien Bank and developed as a pleasant New England style community whose mills processed the cotton grown around the neighboring Alpharetta, to the immediate east. Despite its proximity to bustling Atlanta, it has retained much of its antebellum serenity and, in fact, resembles far more closely a sleepy Southern community than it does a thriving suburb of one of the most progressive areas in the New South. During his March to the Sea, Sherman spared most of Roswell, crippling only its capacity to supply the Confederacy with cotton cloth, and as a result, much of the community's history has been preserved. In fact, this is one of Roswell's greatest claims to fame, for visitors can take a walking tour which includes no less than twenty-seven structures and areas which predate the Twentieth Century.

ATTRACTIONS

- The walking tour of historic Roswell begins with the **Chattahoochee River crossing**, a covered bridge built across the river and burned by Confederates fleeing Sherman's advancing cavalry in July 1864. Allenbrook, built of handmade brick in 1845, was the home and office of the Ivy Woolen Mill manager and includes the site of the Ivy Mill, a popular antebellum picnic spot called Lover's Rock, and Vickery Creek, which provided water power for the mills.
- President Theodore Roosevelt spoke from the bandstand of **Roswell Town Square**, which was built in 1840 as a part of the original town plan. **Bulloch Hall** was the home of Roosevelt's grandfather, Major James S. Bulloch, another of Roswell's founders. The hall now serves as a cultural center and

tours and event information can be obtained by calling (404) 992-1731.
- **Barrington Hall**, built in 1842, is an outstanding example of Greek architecture and was the home of one of the original founders of Roswell. The original business district, built around 1839, has remained virtually unchanged since that period. A thirty foot dam and waterfall with a wooden millrace built in the summer of 1835 ran much of the mill district and has been faithfully preserved and restored. Other homes, churches and cemeteries are included on this most outstanding tour. For more information, contact The Roswell Historical Society, Inc., 227 South Atlanta Street, Roswell, GA 30075; (404) 992-1665.
- **The Chattahoochee Nature Center**, a non-profit environmental education and wildlife rehabilitation center in the southern part of Roswell, is a beautiful way to explore Georgia's wildlife. Walking trails wind through forests and marshes along the Chattahoochee River and include exhibits of wildlife in and around that river. Classes, field trips, films, guided walks and programs are available all year around. **The Nature Store**, which serves the needs of both the amateur and the professional naturalist, offers field guides, packs, compasses, hand lenses, bird feeders and seed, and a wide variety of children's nature books. For more information, contact c/o 9135 Willeo Road, Roswell, GA 30075; (404) 992-2055.
- Roswell also serves as the western portion for the **North Fulton County shopping area**, a district which includes the antique center of Georgia, a host of art galleries, a variety of fine restaurants and much of the best cultural activity in North Georgia. For more information, contact The North Fulton Chamber of Commerce, 1025 Old Roswell Road, Suite 101, Roswell, GA 30076; (404) 993-8808.

ACCOMMODATION

HOLIDAY INN ROSWELL
1075 Holcomb Bridge Road
Roswell, GA 30076
Tel. (404) 992-9600
Hrs: Lounge   Mon. - Fri. 4:30 p.m. - 2:00 a.m.
              Saturday 7:00 p.m. - 2:00 a.m.
The restaurant serves breakfast, lunch, dinner and Sunday buffet.
Visa, MasterCard, AMEX, Diners Club and Discover are accepted.

The Holiday Inn Roswell is one of the finest hotels and restaurants in the Atlanta area. Built just a few years ago, it has received rave reviews for its service, friendly attention to detail and excellent food.

The expansive lobby is matched only by the elegance of the rooms. All rooms offer the luxury of a suite, yet the intimacy of a single. They are furnished in a magnificent 18th Century style and include such standard features as cable TV, a radio and alarm, a spacious bath, and a king or two standard beds. There is a swimming pool in the courtyard. Horsefeathers Lounge offers entertainment and dining in a polo lounge atmosphere while the Summit Cafe offers intimate and formal dining. The bountiful breakfast buffets are especially recommended. For dinner, begin with a crab stuffed mushroom appetizer, seafood strudel or the summit salad. Then move on to the club croissant, shrimp and scallop brochette or the daily special. Entrees include certified Angus beef steaks and a grilled breast of duck.

The seven story Inn sits atop the highest ridge in Roswell, providing guests a magnificent view of the city. Located on Holcomb Bridge Road at Georgia 400, the Holiday Inn is convenient to both the airport and downtown Atlanta.

Atlanta and Vicinity

ANTIQUE SHOP

ALL THAT AND VICTORIAN II
1085 Canton Street
Roswell, GA 30075
Tel. (404) 993-2900
Hrs: Tue. - Sat. 10:00 a.m. - 5:00 p.m.

If you can't find the antique of your dreams, you just haven't looked hard enough at All That and Victorian II. Owner Jackie Winecoff has filled her shop to the brim with treasure and trinkets of yesterday. She chuckles at the intriguing clutter, saying, "If you don't think of my shop as a search and rescue experience, you could miss the buy of a lifetime." All That and Victorian II is located in downtown Roswell's historic Canton Street district. There's ample parking behind the house, so plan to spend the day enjoying yourself without a worry as to how many minutes are ticking by on a parking meter!

Visitors to Jackie's shop usually like the challenge of delving into the many rooms of the old house and coming up with the perfect collectible. You may find a lovely Staffordshire plate tucked away behind a child's old doll house. Bargains abound, since Jackie believes in stocking her place with enough "as is" items to make restoration worth while. The inventory at All That and Victorian II includes an array of vintage clothing from the 1880s to the 1950s, antique dolls, oil lamps, silver, pressed glass, kitchen crockery, bowls and jugs, and knicknacks. You'll delight in the grapevine and rose thorn wreaths from North Georgia, old issues of newspapers, and cards and memorabilia of times past. Quilts showing the painstaking handiwork of women from yesterday are affordable collector's items at this fine antique shop.

If you don't see what you are searching for, ask for it! Jackie also furnishes her private home in old things, so perhaps the collectible of your desires is only a few minutes away. If you

Atlanta and Vicinity

have time, ask for directions, and enjoy a drive by Jackie's old Victorian home, also worth a trip. When visiting Roswell, be sure to include some time for a visit to the old town, and All That and and Victorian II.

APPAREL

HOLIDAY HEALTH & RACQUET CLUB, 10701 Alpharetta Hwy., Roswell, GA. Tel. (404) 587-5611. If you are looking for fine aerobic wear and accessories to go with it, you will find a great selection at Holiday Health & Racquet Club.

SMALL WORLD
10479 Alpharetta Street
Roswell, GA 30075
Tel. (404) 993-1526
Hrs: Mon. - Sat. 10:00 a.m. - 6:00 p.m.
Visa, MasterCard, AMEX and Discover are accepted.

Living up to the motto "Roswell's first and finest," comes easily to Small World, the first children's clothing store in the area. The "finest" part of their slogan is evidenced by the high quality lines they carry, made strictly for boutique shops and worn by child actors throughout the country.

Shopping for boys and girls is a pleasure in the soft grey comfortable setting of Small World, with its name brand, up-to-date clothing displayed playfully throughout the store. Boys' clothing sizes range from 0-4 toddler and girls' from 0-14 years. Children and adults enjoy choosing from name brands: Bibo, Golden Rainbow, Sarah Kent, Julie Tenant, Absorba, "Organically Grown Kids" and Camp Beverly Hills. Owner Lois Oster, who's been in the business for sixteen years, has the expertise and enthusiasm it takes to provide each of her customers with unique items just right for them. Young girls will walk out feeling like princesses in their new outfits, complete with all the accessories: socks, hair bows, jewelry and even a plush, color-coordinated stuffed animal.

The next time you and your child are in the mood for doing something different, contact Small World and find out when their next scheduled fashion show is taking place. It's a fun and easy way to plan a wardrobe for the school year and for special occasions. When the rest of the world is getting you down, stop by Small World for a whole new perspective.

ART GALLERY

THE ANN JACKSON GALLERY
932 Canton Street
Roswell, GA 30075
Tel. (404) 993-4783
Hrs: Mon. - Fri. 10:00 a.m. - 6:00 p.m.
     Saturday   10:00 a.m. - 5:00 p.m.
All major credit cards are accepted.

Located in a former Ford Motor Company car dealership in the historic Roswell Square, the Ann Jackson Gallery features investment arts for the home and office. From custom framing to interior design, this exclusive shop is ready to fill your every art need.

The crisp white walls and vintage Oriental rugs of the Ann Jackson Gallery are a perfect showcase for the dozens of beautiful oils, watercolors and mixed media paintings on display. Browse through the enchanting lithographs of Palm Beach artist Edna Hibel, the dramatic silkscreens of California's Aldo Luongo as well as the vibrant works of many of the nation's prominent artists. Landscapes, seascapes and still life compositions are arranged in classic complement to one another. Customers may order works in oil, watercolors and acrylics as well as prints and drawings by any major artist in the U.S., including such superlative masters as Chagall, Erte' and Dali.

Atlanta and Vicinity

A world traveler, owner Ann Jackson has left the day to day management in the hands of her daughter Valerie Jackson. Under Valerie's guidance the Gallery has expanded into the areas of home and office interior design and consultation. A gallery filled with the matchless beauty and passion of contemporary American art, the Ann Jackson Gallery is a must-see for anyone with an eye for the finer things in life.

GIFT SHOP

JESSICA'S ON PARK SQUARE
55 Park Square, Suite 107
Roswell, GA 30075
Tel. (404) 642-6916
Hrs: Mon. - Fri.   10:00 a.m. - 6:00 p.m.
         Saturday   10:00 a.m. - 5:00 p.m.
Hours are extended during the holiday period.
Visa, MasterCard and AMEX are accepted.

When you enter this shop you can feel the warmth and friendliness surround you. Named after the owners' daughter, Jessica's on Park Square is a unique and quaint gift shop in which you can find something for everyone on your list.

Located in the new section of historic Roswell Square, Jessica's is decorated in a traditional colonial style with Colonial Rose and Lafayette Green crown mouldings and cabinetry. A floral border and antique displays finish off this unique look. In preparation for opening in August of 1986, owner Kay Simmons filled her shop with a wide variety of gift items. Some of the more popular items are traditional brass accessories by Baldwin and Virginia Metalcrafters, English placemats, coasters and serving trays by Pimpernel and a large assortment of Colonial and Victorian accent pieces such as porcelain and brass lamps, baskets, pillows, picture frames and bookends. A custom floral design service, men's and children's

Atlanta and Vicinity

sections, and many gift items indicative of the South add appeal and variety to this well rounded gift shop.

Kay also offers her customers gift wrapping and UPS services. If you are in the mood to be charmed, come to Jessica's on Park Square; you'll be sure to find what your heart desires.

RESTAURANTS

THE GRILL, 1570 Holcomb Bridge Road, Roswell, GA. Tel. (404) 993-8733. The grill features one of the largest selections of imported and domestic beers to go with the "old-fashion style" hamburgers, steaks and hot dogs. A soda fountain dating from the 1930s lends a special flavor to this unique restaurant.

La GROTTA
647 Atlanta Street
North of the Old Roswell Square
Roswell, GA 30075
Tel. (404) 998-0645
Hrs: Tue. - Sat. 6:00 p.m. - 10:30 p.m.
Visa, Mastercard, AMEX, Diners Club, Carte Blanche and Discover are accepted.

Dining at LaGrotta is more than enjoying a good meal, it is an event. Roswell is blessed with many fine dining houses but LaGrotta tops the list. *Altlanta Magazine* rated LaGrotta as "one of the best" for its food and wine list. Housed in an 150 year old home in the historic Roswell district, the restaurant is described by its co-owner and manager, Gildo Fusinaz, as "country-European."

The atmosphere is both intimate and elegant. Floor length drapes frame full length windows, while candles flicker on the tables and the fireplace spreads its glow. The menu and wine list are extensive. Known for its veal dishes, the restaurant features five outstanding veal meals. You can choose

Atlanta and Vicinity

from Scaloppine di Vitello alla Parmigiana, a breaded veal scaloppine with Mozzarella cheese, tomato sauce and spaghetti or Scaloppine di Vitello alla Grotta, veal with artichoke bottom, fresh mushrooms, and creamy Marsala sauce. Seafood specialties are served with the daily fresh fish. A house favorite is Trota alla Livornese, pan fried trout with baby shrimp and capers sauteed in a lemon butter sauce. The sweet ending to your meal or La Dolce Fine will bring raves of Bravissimo! The Zabaglione al Spumante o Marsala comes highly recommended.

The service at LaGrotta is as smooth as the Marsala sauce. Gildo Fusinaz and his attentive staff are quick to be at your service with a smile and a menu suggestion. LaGrotta is the restaurant of choice for local residents and dignitaries.

LICKSKILLET FARM RESTAURANT
1380 Old Roswell Road
Roswell, GA 30076
Tel. (404) 475-6484
Hrs: Tue. - Sun.   5:30 p.m. - 9:45 p.m.
     Sunday brunch   11:30 a.m. - 2:15 p.m.
Visa, MasterCard, AMEX, Discover and Diners Club are accepted.

If you're looking for the perfect spot to woo a sweet young Georgia miss, you've found it. Not even Scarlett O'Hara could complain about the elegant pre-civil war farmhouse on five and one half acres, replete with a babbling brook. The Lickskillet Farm Restaurant has been serving excellent four course meals for more than twenty-five years.

Freshly prepared, cooked to order meals are served in an elegant dining atmosphere. The employees give quality service which is always on time, whether you like precision or you have all night to relax and enjoy the meal and tasteful surroundings. Full four course meals: homemade soup of the day with cracklin' cornbread, tossed green salad, two cold vegetables, two hot vegetables, assorted breads, beverage and dessert are served with the entree of your choice. Tasty filet mignon; Surf and Turf, strip steak and lobster tail with baked potato, served with mushroom, onion and cheese sauce; fish of the day; sauteed chicken livers and skillet pork chops are among the entrées available. The management invites you to select just the right bottle of wine to go with your meal from the shelves of their wine room.

If a Sunday morning drive brings you to the Lickskillet, you'll want to take advantage of one of Atlanta's finest champagne country brunches with its all you can eat fruit bar and excellent selection of meats, eggs and homemade breads. No matter what the reason: a wedding in the gazebo, an intimate dinner and stroll by the river, or a family gathering, the Lickskillet is a "Best Choice."

MAHOGANY GRILLE
900 Mansell Road
Roswell, GA 30076
Tel. (404) 594-7761

Hrs:	Lunch	Mon. - Fri.	11:00 a.m. - 4:00 p.m.
	Dinner	Mon. - Thu.	5:00 p.m. - 10:00 p.m.
		Fri., Sat.	5:00 p.m. - 11:00 p.m.
	Brunch	Sunday	11:00 a.m. - 3:00 p.m.
	Dinner	Sunday	5:00 p.m. - 10:00 p.m.

Visa, MasterCard and AMEX are accepted.

This friendly neighborhood restaurant has always been known for fresh fish, and excellent steaks and prime rib. Mahogany Grille is part of the Mansell Oaks Plaza, a new shopping center on Mansell Road. The restaurant uses mahogany in its furnishings, creating a warm feeling. There's an intimate cafe atmosphere with clay tile floors, and ceiling fans turning over the bar, but there is seating for over 180 people.

The service is good and the attention is on quality in food preparation. Only the freshest of fish, beef and poultry are accepted for preparation. Delicious desserts are made on the premises, along with a great clam chowder. Among the best items on the dinner menu is a seafood grille with shrimp and the day's fish special. Another dish that comes highly recommended is the crabmeat stuffed jumbo shrimp. There's a one pound cut of prime rib of beef, and a smaller portion, too. For family groups, there is a special children's menu with smaller portions and special desserts. There are superior salads and sandwiches for lunch, and they are also available for a lighter dinner. The seafood pasta salad is great and some of the notable sandwiches are the grilled tuna, the bacon cheddar, and the Philly cheese steak sandwich. The bar has its own menu of appetizers and sandwiches with daily specials during the happy hour from 3:00 p.m. to 7:00 p.m.

Proprietor Nick Lourick makes this place a pleasant dining experience, beginning with his greeting at the door. The neighborhood friendliness extends to everyone. The pledge is "delicious food, pure and simple."

WATERSTONE'S
Roswell-Mill Shopping Center
555 South Atlanta Street, Suite A700
Roswell, GA 30075
Tel. (404) 594-8361
Hrs: Lunch   Tue. - Fri.   11:30 a.m. - 2:00 p.m.
     Dinner   Tue. - Sat.   6:00 p.m. - 11:00 p.m.
Visa and MasterCard are accepted.

Old Historic Roswell has world class food to offer and Waterstone's is the place to enjoy it. Voted the most romantic restaurant in Atlanta, it is as elegant as an English country tea room. More than a few wedding proposals have been made there, and even a wedding ceremony or two.

The food at Waterstone's is always fresh, never frozen. Attention is paid to every detail of making your dining experience most enjoyable, from the daily food purchases at nearby markets to the fresh cut flowers on each table. The dinner appetizers are sure to tempt you. Cream of Basil Soup, a house signature item, heads the list. Also featured are steamed mussels, Duck Liver Terrine, marinated Montrechet or the Chef's Choice. The entrees are equally impressive, beginning with grilled veal chop, grilled chicken or grilled pork chop. Highly popular is the Game of the Night or the Catch of the Night, two dishes your server will gladly describe. Diners also

Atlanta and Vicinity

enjoy the blackened amberjack, sauteed scallops, Salmon Fettuccine, Beef Tenderloin, mixed grill of the night, linguini or "Henry's Favorite," a linguini with Italian sausage, tomatoes and red wine. Among the desserts, the chocolate pecan torte is quite popular with guests and will perfectly complete your dinner.

All dinners are served with pasta, house salad, a sampler bread basket and the day's fresh vegetable. Reduced portions are available for those with smaller appetites. For guests who dine or enjoy a cocktail outside, Waterstone's deck overlooking Vickery Ridge allows a sensational view of Roswell Mill and spectacular sunsets over the ridge. Come for the romance, return for the food. Reservations are suggested and proper attire is required.

SANDY SPRINGS

This large unincorporated area of approximately 72,877 is bounded by the Atlanta city limits to the south, the Chattahoochee River to the west and north and by Dekalb and Gwinnett Counties on the east. Sandy Springs has more than 30,000 households and over 5,000 businesses and is as typical of the New South as any you'll find.

It derives its name from a natural springs which flows from a 1.8 acre hollow, bordered by Sandy Springs Circles, Sandy Springs Place and Hilderbrand.

Its modern hotels, multiple access routes to Atlanta (Interstate 285 links up to Interstate 75, which sweeps south into the heart of Georgia's capital; and US 19, which runs directly to the heart of the city after becoming Peachtree Road), and its beautifully preserved historic section make it an outstanding "must see" for those vacationing or on business in the greater Atlanta area.

ATTRACTIONS

• **The Sandy Springs Historic Site**, which encloses the original springs and a community center, is surrounded by steep slopes and a wide meadow. These are laced with lush gardens of herbs, fruits, shrubs, and trees and flowers native to Georgia. Also featured is **The Williams-Payne House**, a plain style, one story farm house built around 1870. It has been restored to its original and includes authentic period furnishings. It houses a period museum and a small meeting/reception center, both of which are available for rent and free tours daily.

• Another outbuilding on the site is an 1860s **Sandy Springs milk house**, evocative of the period. **The Arbor** is an important aspect of the site, as well. An enclosed pavilion, designed to replicate a camp meeting hall which was once sited nearby, it has a capacity for 150 formal banquet diners and 250 for informal events. It includes a complete mobile catering kitchen, heating and air-conditioning, a cathedral ceiling and double restrooms with handicapped facilities.

The combination of facilities makes this one of the nicest and delightfully functional resources of its kind. Whether one is simply passing through, or planning an extended stay in the area, the Sandy Springs historic site should be experienced. For more information, contact the Sandy Springs Chamber of Commerce, 6021 Sandy Springs Circle, Suite 100, Sandy Springs, GA 30328; (404) 847-9583.

Atlanta and Vicinity

RESTAURANTS

LA PAZ
6410 Roswell Road
Sandy Springs, GA 30328
Tel. (404) 256-3555
Hrs: Sun. - Thu. 5:00 p.m. - 10:00 p.m.
         Fri. - Sat. 5:00 p.m. - 11:00 p.m.
Visa, MasterCard, AMEX and Diners Club are accepted.

La Paz in Spanish means "peace." In Sandy Springs, it also stands for good Mexican food and drink in a congenial, festive atmosphere.

This popular restaurant and bar has been a neighborhood fixture for years, offering fast, friendly service and top quality food. It has developed a loyal following with both native Atlantans and out of town visitors. Fresh ripened California avocados, chiles from Mexico and fresh meats and produce are used to create a variety of savory dishes. All sauces are made fresh daily, including the chile salsa. The extensive menu features such dishes as Zapnins, a chimichanga style burrito; La Paz, a combination plate with a King crab enchilada, a chile relleno and a beef taco; and Pacifica, a combination of a cheese enchilada, a bean burrito, and a beef taco served with rice and beans. Owner Tom Nickoloff frequently travels to Mexico to gather new recipes for the menu.

La Paz resembles a red brick "Alamo." The first floor is reminiscent of a Mexican cantina. The second floor features outdoor dining under awnings, from May to October. The bar has all your favorite drinks, and offers Margarita specials on Monday and Tuesday evenings.

S AND W SEAFOOD RESTAURANT AND MARKET, 6125 Roswell Road, Sandy Springs, GA. Tel. (404) 255-8218. The S AND W Seafood and Market boasts one of the largest offerings of seafood in the nation. All of the food in the restaurant comes from their market next door and is prepared according to your wishes, including Cajun-style.

SMYRNA

Many of those who live in this city of 30,000 proudly serve their nation as members of the armed forces stationed at nearby Dobbins Air Force Base. Originally a trade center for northwestern Atlanta cotton growers, the city also provides a small town environment for employees of Lockheed. Proud of its image as typical "New South," the community points to two of its major shopping centers. The Galleria is the home of exclusive speciality shops and the Stouffer-Waverley Hotel. The Cumberland Mall boasts Macy's, J.C. Penny, Sears, and a host of speciality shops and theaters.

APPAREL

HOLIDAY HEALTH & RACQUET CLUB, 3270 South Cobb Drive, Smyrna, GA. Tel. (404) 432-9215. Drop in at the Holiday Health & Racquet Club if you want to look over an excellent selection of aerobic wear from such firms as Dance France. You'll also find a great selection of accessories.

RESTAURANTS

AUNT FANNY'S CABIN
2155 Campbell Road
Smyrna, GA 30080
Tel. (404) 436-9026 and 436-5218
Hrs: Mon. - Fri. 11:30 a.m. - 2:30 p.m.
     Mon. - Fri. 6:00 p.m. - 10:00 p.m.
     Saturday 6:00 p.m. - 10:30 p.m.
     Sunday 1:00 p.m. - 10:00 p.m.
Visa, MasterCard, AMEX and Diners Club are accepted.

Rich in history and tradition, Aunt Fanny's Cabin is named in memory of Aunt Fanny Williams, a slave who was born and who lived in the Cabin. The Cabin was originally a part of the Campbell Plantation. Aunt Fanny was believed to have been born in the early 1850s but no one knows her age for certain. Many of the recipes served at the Cabin today are Aunt Fanny's.

The first rooms of the Cabin were built around 1840 and still stand in the front of the restaurant. The wooden planks and the brick floor are part of the original building. A big rock fireplace welcomes guests. Old copper cookware which was used in the early days of the Cabin hangs against the stones of hearth. Burn spots on the wooden plank floor show evidence of the buckets of burning charcoal used as heating in Aunt Fanny's day. Since the beginning, the restaurant has used young men who live in the area to sing-song the menu. The chanter brings a large blackboard which he is wearing as a collar around his neck and gives a friendly greeting of "what'll it be?" The blackboard has a list of the day's meals.

Aunt Fanny's is world famous for its dinners of fried chicken, Gen-U-Wine Famous Smithfield ham, charcoal broiled steaks and fresh rainbow trout. Aunt Fanny's Cabin is proud of its twenty-two employees whose combined serving experience exceeds 500 years. Aunt Fanny's Cabin has been called the Southern capital of good food and hospitality.

HOUSE OF CHAN, 2469 Cobb Parkway Southeast, Smyrna, GA. Tel. (404) 955-9444. The House of Chan has been referred to by *Atlanta Magazine* as "one of the fifty best restaurants." Other kudos include the comment "no accident that Chan's is a winner" by the *Atlanta Journal* and a rating as "one of the best in the U.S.A" by the *Times Book New York*.

STONE MOUNTAIN

Georgia's Stone Mountain is exactly that, an incredible massive dome of bald granite, rising 825 feet above surrounding forested plains to a total elevation of 1,683 feet. It is believed to be over 300 million years old, measures five miles around at the base and covers 583 acres. Its granite forms the bedrock of the surrounding area and many of Georgia's most impressive structures are constructed from the stone quarried nearby. Totally barren, save for the tenaciously cheerful Yellow Daisy which grows in the shallow soil of its crust, this strange geological configuration is older than the Himalayas.

Stone Mountain is often called Georgia's Mount Rushmore, for it is here that three of Dixie's most beloved and nearly legendary heroes are captured in bas relief on the north face.

Atlanta and Vicinity

Mounted and posed in the traditional "hat over the heart" pose so popular with artists of that period, Confederate President Jefferson Davis, General Robert E. Lee and General Stonewall Jackson stand in the sculpture, which measures 90 by 190 feet and ranks as the largest high relief art of its kind in the world. The Memorial Carving took over fifty years to finish and has drawn over six million visitors since completion. Facing north, the famous trio serve as a reminder that while Sherman may have conquered Atlanta and Grant may have accepted Lee's sword at Appomattox, Dixie herself yet lives.

The Memorial Carving can be viewed close at hand by taking the Skylift. These cable cars of Swiss manufacture rise over 825 feet and the top of the mountain features a theater, snack and gift shops, and an unforgettable panorama of downtown Atlanta and the surrounding North Georgia countryside. Stone Mountain serves as the centerpiece for a 3,200 acre state park which combines recreation, entertainment, leisure, history and education, all within sixteen miles of downtown Atlanta.

ATTRACTIONS

- To help visitors gain an appreciation of the size of this granite monolith, genuine **steam locomotive trains** are provided. A throwback to the days when steel rails united Dixie (and the rest of the continent), these trains, which are replicas of the two involved in that exciting Civil War escapade now known as The Great Locomotive Chase, chuff their way through sylvan woodlands. Passengers are transported past early settlements, granite quarries and other impressive natural and pioneer features.
- Perhaps the single most impressive display at Stone Mountain Park is the fantastic **laser light show**, held nightly at the Memorial Carving. For nearly an hour, visitors lounge across the tree bordered expanses of Lasershow lawn while colorful beams are projected onto Stone Mountain's north face,

Atlanta and Vicinity

choreographed to popular music and seemingly viewed with pride by Dixie's great men themselves. This fantasy filled production, called Night on Stone Mountain, is shown each evening, May through Labor Day, and on weekends through October.

- Stone Mountain Park has over twenty acres of natural woodlands, which are home to cougar, elk, bison and other wildlife which were once native to Georgia. Some have been domesticated and are on display in the **Traders Camp Petting Zoo**.

- For a walk through Georgia's antebellum past, you can explore a **reconstructed plantation** consisting of actual early nineteenth century buildings collected from all over the state. They have been reassembled here in a complex which includes a beautiful mansion, overseer's house, slave cabins, country store and several other structures, all furnished from the period. It is open daily from 10 a.m. to 9 p.m. during the summer and from 10 a.m. to 5:30 p.m. the rest of the year.

- For those who enjoy old cars and the nostalgia associated with the nickel jukebox, the **Antique Auto Museum** is just the thing. It features over forty restored automobiles, nickelodeons, musical instruments and associated memorabilia.

- **Stone Mountain Lake** covers 363 acres and the side wheeler *Scarlett O'Hara* offers the perfect way to cruise it. The Memorial Carving can be seen from several points on the water, and the bird and aqua life make this relaxing diversion one you won't want to miss. Anglers in particular will enjoy the park's two well stocked fishing lakes. Canoes, kayaks and other small boats are available for rental. The lake has a beautiful white sandy beach, waterslides, picnic tables and miniature golf, so this is definitely where to come for fun in the sun.

- If you're into golfing, bring your clubs to **Stone Mountain Park**. The eighteen hole course was designed by Robert Trent Jones and is rated among the top twenty-five in the country by *Golf Digest*. The greens are as scenic as any you'll find and you'll have President Davis and Generals Lee and Jackson watching just to keep your partner honest. Tee time reservations are advised and can be made by calling (404) 498-5717.

Atlanta and Vicinity

- For those who enjoy their recreation on silver blades, the **Ice Chalet** features regularly scheduled public skating, numerous competitions, exhibitions, intramural hockey and skating instruction, all across an Olympic size rink, which is open the year round.
- Stone Mountain Park certainly hasn't ignored campers either. **The Family Campground**, with over 400 sites, offers a variety of facilities, including those for RV's, and is both the largest and most complete complex of its kind in the metropolitan Atlanta area. Limited reservations can be made by calling (404) 498-5701.

EVENTS

- **April: The Old South Celebration** is staged at the Antebellum Plantation and features arts and crafts, traditional regional folk music and an authentically recreated Civil War army camp.
- **May: The Springfest** highlights arts and crafts, a barbecued pork cook off and clogging exhibitions.
- **July: The Fantastic Fourth** celebration features one of the largest fireworks displays in the South, concerts and dance exhibitions.
- **September:** That stubborn little flower which thrives happily on the otherwise barren dome of Stone Mountain is paid homage through the **Yellow Daisy Festival**, the largest arts and crafts show in the Southeast.
- **October:** For those of the kilted persuasion, the **Scottish Festival and Highland Games** are a must. Folk dancing, Scottish band competitions and athletic events are staged, replete with traditional foods and crafts.
- **December:** A month long celebration called simply **Holiday Celebration** includes a Christmas Carol Sing A Long, Carriage Rides, an Ice Skating Show, Candlelight Tours, some of the most impressive Christmas decorations around and even a chance to chat with Santa Claus.

For a complete schedule of events and a special calendar of them, call (404) 498-5633.

• One of the most hauntingly beautiful experiences one can have at Stone Mountain Park is to hear **The Bells of Stone Mountain**. The carillon, a thirteen story tower rising from the lakeshore, uses miniature bell tone rods and amplification for its 732-bell effect. Concerts are given Monday through Saturday, at noon and 4 p.m.; and on Sunday at 1 p.m., 3 p.m. and 5 p.m. This, then, is a glimpse of Georgia's Stone Mountain Park. For more information, write care of P.O. Box 778, Stone Mountain, GA 30086 or call (404) 498-5600 or (404) 498-5690.

COLLECTIBLES

THE OLD CURIOSITY SHOP
767 Main Street
Stone Mountain, GA 30083
Tel. (404) 469-8208
Hrs: Mon. - Fri.   9:00 a.m. - 6:00 p.m.
         Saturday   10:00 a.m. - 6:00 p.m.
Visa, MasterCard, AMEX and Discover are accepted.

The Old Curiosity Shop in Stone Mountain is as unusual as it is intriguing. Although its namesake, built in London in 1567, is still in operation today, curators Joe and Barbara Hurt can honestly boast that there is no other shop like theirs in all the world. It contains antiques, collectibles, works of art and items of natural history.

Charles Dickens wrote the following in the mid-1800s: "The place where he made his way at leisure, was one of those receptacles for old and curious things...treasure. Suits of mail, standing like ghosts in armour here and there. Fantastic carvings brought from monkish cloisters; rusty weapons of various kinds; distorted figures in China and wood, and iron, and ivory; tapestries and strange furniture that might have been designed in dreams." He could just as well have been speaking of the present day shop in Georgia, where you will find such rare and diverse items as a five foot Foo Dog (solid wood palace guard dogs), dolls made for the shop by women in England, a Spanish coat of armor, original oil paintings and a 3500 year old mummified cat from Egypt. Other discoveries you might make there include music boxes, hand knitted mohair sweaters and rocks, minerals and fossils. Leisurely inspect the Blue Delft from Holland, fine bone china, bronzes, rare books, a London Bobby's cap and jacket, antique swords, ostrich eggs, a seventeenth century armoire and much more.

Everything in the Old Curiosity Shop is original. Joe Hurt is a leading authority on Natural History, and has served as curator for a number of well-known natural history museums. His experience and contacts over the years have allowed this shop to become as interesting and creative as it is today. Come and find your own treasure.

NOVELTY

EDDIE'S TRICK AND NOVELTY SHOP
5203 Memorial Drive
Stone Mountain, GA 30083
Tel. (404) 296-5653
Hrs: Mon. - Sat. 10:00 a.m. - 6:00 p.m.
Visa, MasterCard and Discover are accepted.
Also,
48 South Park Square   3655 Roswell Road # 120
Marietta, GA 30060   Atlanta 30342
Tel. (404) 428-4314   Tel. (404) 264-0527

Now you see it, now you don't. Eddie's Trick And Novelty Shop is a shop full of illusions, mysteries and fun for all ages. "I want the adults to feel just like kids when they come in," Frank McKinnon says. "The adults are just as bad as the kids. Many times they tell you they are buying for their kids when you know darn well they're buying for themselves."

Professional or amateur magicians can find a host of tricks and fantasy at Eddie's: disappearing coins, magic rings, all sorts of things that appear, vanish or multiply; whoopee cushions and hand buzzers and the like are stock items. Eddie's also carries the largest selection of gag gifts to be found anywhere. Costumes of all sorts are available for rent or sale. Hundreds of masks hang from the walls and with their tremendous wig selection, you can be anyone from Lady Godiva to Snow White. A full line of theatrical makeup plus all types of costume accessories make this the most unique shop of its kind in the South.

Whether you need a shocking lighter for that smoker who refuses to quit, or you are performing *Hamlet* and need a skull, this is truly a "Palace of Magic and Mischief."

RESORT

STONE MOUNTAIN INN, Stone Mountain Park, Atlanta, GA. Tel. (404) 469-3311. Stone Mountain Inn features a resort atmosphere with classic southern hospitality and family rates for the ninety-two rooms. Country cuisine and superb service are the specialties of the fine restaurant.

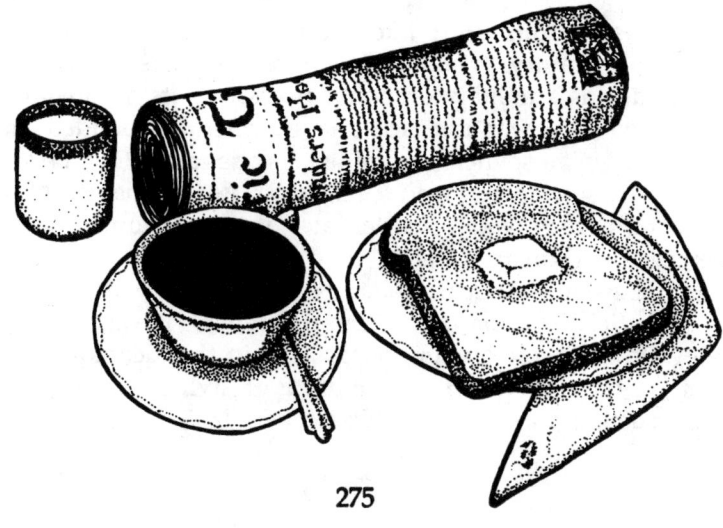

CHAPTER TWO: DAY TRIPS FROM ATLANTA

For those lucky enough to have some extra time in Atlanta, a day trip might be just the way to see a little more that this marvelous state has to offer. The following is a list compiled alphabetically that features some superior day trips. Whether you want to take in the scenic beauty of the Callaway gardens, see Old South architecture at its finest in Augusta, or visualize Civil War history at the Chickamauga and Chattanooga National Military Park, you can find it all on these trips. They are all within an easy drive of Atlanta, and are listed separately because each makes a fine excursion in its own right. Although the trips are listed individually, sometimes the different outings naturally flow together (such is the case with Athens and Augusta) so we have included information to make easy connections. Pack a picnic, get in a car and you'll be prepared to take a leisurely jaunt to any one of these fascinating areas.

ANDERSONVILLE NATIONAL HISTORIC SITE

Descriptions of it liken it to the most infamous of twentieth century prisoner of war camps. Historians have justified it as a military economic necessity. Its commandant was tried as a war criminal and executed. Wounded and captured Union soldiers committed suicide rather than be sent there. Those who survived it remember it with shame. Now, almost a century and a quarter later, it is a monument to the heroism of prisoners of war.

Its name is Andersonville.

Officially designated "Camp Sumter," it was built to alleviate the overcrowding of facilities in the Richmond area and to provide a better standard of living for inmates. Construction was begun in December, 1863, by slaves and

Confederate soldiers. The original stockade was built in the shape of a parallelogram of thick (8-12") logs sunk five feet into the ground. Nineteen feet inside this fortress, prison officials demarcated another parallel. Known as the deadline, it was not crossed, under penalty of the fate which gave it its name. The outer walls were 1,620 feet long and 779 feet wide. Sentry boxes, which the prisoners called pigeon roosts, topped the walls every thirty feet, and beyond the prison were several earthwork forts furnished with cannon. The purpose of these was dual. Their guns were intended to quell any disturbances within the walls and to be turned on any Union cavalry detachments attempting to liberate the facility. Other facilities outside the walls included two hospitals, a tiny house made of tree limbs, where the dead were brought for transportation to burial sites, and a cemetery. Prison officials maintained offices at the village of Andersonville, a quarter mile away. The tiny community, located at the end of a rail line, was the debarkation point for prisoners and served as the logistics center for the facility.

The prison camp officially opened in February, 1864. It was designed to hold 10,000. By June, two and a half times that many were confined within its pine log walls. At one time, 32,000 were held there, and during its fourteen months of operation, over 45,000 were so confined. Stockade Branch, a tributary of Sweetwater Creek, served as the water supply, augmented by small wells the prisoners dug themselves, and eventually, by an artesian spring which burst through the muddy ground during a rainstorm and which the prisoners called 'Providence Spring'.

The prisoners lived in tent shelters, provided initially by the Confederate Army. In the beginning, conditions were as good as any other such facility in the South. Georgia was not seriously affected by the Civil War until the latter years of it, and evidence strongly suggests than an appropriate share of the food and other materiel this state supplied the Confederacy at large was marked for Union prisoners of war. The camp itself was designed to provide a humane alternative to sites elsewhere. Several factors combined to give Camp Sumter its hellish reputation, and not all of the blame can be laid at the feet of the South. The war itself was not expected to last more than a few months, so there was no real reason for long range planning. Captured soldiers were generally held at first in existing jails, warehouses, and other makeshift facilities. Large numbers of them were paroled, on the promise that they would not rejoin the armed forces. In an era when a man's word was as good as a written contract, such pledges were realistic. The governments involved did not expect their parolees to fight again, and most did not.

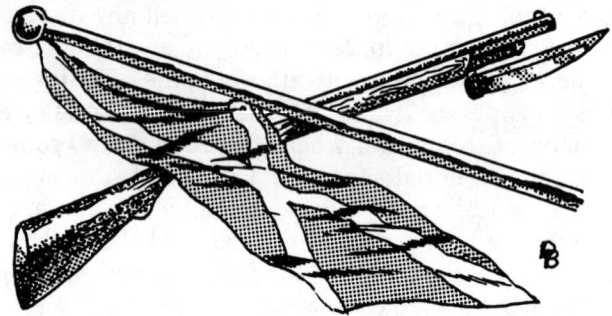

At the war's onset, the South had the agricultural and industrial capabilities to care for those few prisoners it found necessary to confine for extended periods. Its Atlantic and Mississippi River ports were fully operational and what it could not supply itself, it was still importing from Europe and elsewhere. But as the war dragged on, prime farm land and factories were destroyed, the Mississippi River fell into federal hands, and the Union blockade of ocean and Mexican Gulf ports began strangling the economic throat of the Confederacy.

As Union casualties continued to mount, public sentiment in the North changed as well, and leaders in Washington, D.C., reacted by ordering Union generals to fight a different kind of war, one which extended far beyond the battlefield and into those very sectors which kept both Confederate civilians and Union prisoners of war alike alive. Prisoner exchanges broke down as both governments felt compelled to augment recruitments with parolees.

All of these factors came home to Andersonville, particularly after Sherman invaded Georgia and began systematically destroying this Confederate agricultural, logistics and manufacturing center's capacity to make war. As the population of Camp Sumter increased, Confederate supplies decreased. Cloth for tents disappeared. Medical supplies, largely imported, virtually vanished with the closure of ports. The grounds of the prison itself, which was constructed in a clearing once dense with pine trees, became trampled and churned into mud. Stockade Creek became polluted with sewage, and the wells, too. Rations were reduced periodically and what few there were went first to ailing prisoners. A variety of disease swept through the prison population.

However, perhaps the most horrible problem of all was that older prisoners became robbers and murderers of newer ones. As fresh shipments of inmates arrived, they were permitted to keep all but their weapons. Tents, shelter halves, blankets, battle rations, clothing—especially woolen great coats and shoes and boots—and personal implements such as knives and entrenching tools, all became absolute survival essentials. These new contingents then, were listed on the roles, searched for weapons, and then marched into the stockade itself. Once the gates were closed, these men were set upon by starving skeletons blacked from the pine smoke of campfires, and robbed blind. Any who resisted were murdered outright. It became, in the strictest interpretation of the term, survival of the fittest.

Camp Sumter was the largest of all Civil War prisoner of war camps. Of the 45,000 men held there, 12,912 died in captivity. Compare this with the largest Union prisoner of war camp at Camp Douglas, Illinois, where of the 30,000 Confederates held there, 4,454 died. In stark statistics, Andersonville's casualty rate was nearly 29%, as opposed to 15% at its Union counterpart. At other Confederate prisoner of war camps, casualties were 16% at Florence, South Carolina, and 24% at Salisbury, North Carolina. Union figures contrast at 16% for Rock Island, Illinois; 24% at Elmira, New York; 16% at Camp Morton, Indiana; and 2% at Johnson's Island, Ohio.

Camp Sumter's commandant, Captain Henry Wirz, had formerly served with the Fourth Louisiana Infantry. All evidence suggests that he was a reasonably compassionate man, a capable administrator, and one well familiar with the potential consequences of conditions at Andersonville Prison. According to some sources, he petitioned Richmond often for more supplies, and that prisoners be routed to other facilities. He also attempted to keep his own inmates from turning on themselves. All this was to no avail because Richmond could not give what it did not have.

Much evidence suggests that Union authorities who dealt with him after his capture were well aware of the circumstances under which Captain Wirz operated and intended to deal with him reasonably. After conditions at Andersonville were made public, however, an outraged North called for retribution. Wirz was not tried as the soldier he was, but as a criminal of war. The verdict was a foregone conclusion and this victim of history—as much a prisoner as the inmates of Camp Sumter itself —was hanged.

The legacy of Andersonville did not die with him, however, for Clara Barton, founder of the American Red Cross and the brave nurse corps which served with such dedication during the Civil War, was ordered to Andersonville Cemetery where, with the assistance of one Dorence Atwater, a member of the Second New York Cavalry when he was sent to Andersonville at the age of nineteen and subsequently charged with keeping records of prisoners' deaths, identified and marked all Union graves. So complete were Atwater's records that of the more than 12,000 buried there, only 460 needed to be designated unknown. The prison site was purchased from a private owner in 1890 by the Georgia Department of the Grand Army of the Republic, a Union veterans organization. They, in turn, transferred it to their women's auxiliary. These ladies raised the funds to create a memorial park. The pecan trees planted there furnished income through the sale of the nuts. In 1910, the War Department purchased it, and then its successor, the Department of the Army. In 1970, Andersonville was made a national historic site and a year later, the National Park Service took it over.

Today, the Andersonville National Historic Site, which is located ten miles northeast of Americus on Georgia State Route, is a 475 acre park which consists of both a national cemetery and a prison site. The Visitors Center has various exhibits specifically dealing with the prison. These include a twelve minute slide program, a relief map, and a wide range of written informational materials.

The Andersonville National Historic Site is very special, for it commemorates the experience of all American prisoners of war. The United State Congress stated clearly their intention when it declared that the park's true purpose is to provide an understanding of the overall prisoner of war story of the Civil War, to interpret the role of prisoner of war camps in history, to commemorate the sacrifice of Americans who lost their lives in such camps, and to preserve the monuments located within the site.

In truth, that experience, like war itself, is a universal which transcends nationality and even history itself. It lingers long after the specific causes of conflict, and it impacts entire communities, through the family, friends, business and working associates of those directly affected. As the National Park Service points out:

"Of the 142,227 Americans captured and interned as prisoners of war during World War I and II, Korea, Vietnam, and the Pueblo incident, 17,026 died while in captivity, 21 refused repatriation, 1 is still officially classified as a POW, and 125,171 were returned to U.S. Military control. As of January 1, 1986, Veterans Administration records show that 83,430 former POWs are still alive."

This, then, too, is the Andersonville experience. Camping is prohibited, but there is a designated picnic area. For more information, contact Office of the Superintendent, Andersonville National Historic Site, Route 1, Box 85, Andersonville, GA 31711; (912) 924-0343.

ATTRACTIONS

- The tiny village of **Andersonville** itself, with its population of less than 300, has been virtually fully restored to its Civil War appearance. The town hall, firehouse and pavilion have all been dedicated to the period. Visitors here can experience an actual Pioneer Farm, with its century old log cabin, water- powered grist mill, mule-driven cane mill, and its cotton and peanut plantings. The farm also has livestock and other animals. Open daily, it is an especially interesting place to visit on weekends, when soap making and blacksmithing demonstrations are given.
- Andersonville village is also the home of the **Drummer Boy Civil War Museum**. This one million dollar attraction is the only one in Andersonville for which admission is charged.
- Each year, during the first full weekend in October, Andersonville stages a **Historic Fair**. A Civil War re-enactment is held at Pioneer Park. The farm there is also the site of a most impressive **arts and crafts gathering**, during which demonstrations of blacksmithing, pottery, glassblowing, quilting, chair caning and basket weaving are given. Square dancers and cloggers show their stuff, and music ranges from bluegrass and country western to traditional military. The fair begins with a parade on Saturday and includes a fine historic drama, "The Andersonville Trial," during which the trial of Camp Sumter commandant Henry Wirz is portrayed.

For more information on Andersonville village and its various attractions, celebrations and other aspects, contact the Andersonville Guild, Box 6, Andersonville, GA 31711; (912) 924-2558.

- The town of **Americus**, nine miles southwest of Andersonville, makes a great place to stay while visiting Andersonville. This community of 16,000 has several attractions in its own right.

- **The James Earl (Jimmy) Carter Library** is located on the campus of Georgia Southwestern College. This museum features photos and other memorabilia associated with the former Georgia governor and president, who grew up in Plains, not far from the campus. The college itself provides a tour of its facilities, augmented by appropriate lectures and other demonstrations. For more information, contact Georgia Southwestern College, Wheatley Street, Americus, GA 31709.
- **The Lindbergh Memorial**, at the Souther Field on State Route 49, honors his purchase and solo flight— four years before his Atlantic crossing— of his single-engine Jenny in 1923.

Americus also has an outstanding historic district comprised of Victorian, antebellum and Greek Revival structures. Bring your camera along on this one. For more information on Americus and its various offerings, contact the Americus and Sumter County Chamber of Commerce, 400 West Lamar Street, Americus, GA 31709; (912) 924- 2646.

- **Georgia Veterans Memorial State Park**, established to honor those who served, fought and died in all the wars in which this nation has been involved, is located nine miles west of Interstate 75's Exit 33, a few miles southeast of Andersonville village and Americus.

This 1,327 acre site can be easily identified by the military vehicles and aircraft sprawling across its outdoor museum. The indoor museum exhibits artifacts from the French and Indian War through Vietnam. Sited on the eastern shores of Lake Blackshear, it also provides a swimming pool and beach, eighty-five tent and trailers sites, ten rental cottages, and a winterized group shelter. Other popular activities here include model airplane flying, and boating and water-skiing. Celebrations and special events are held on Memorial and Veterans Day, and this is the park which hosts Christmas on the Flint. For more information, contact Georgia Veterans Memorial State Park, Route 3, Cordele, GA 31015; (912) 273-2190.

Day Trips from Atlanta

ATHENS AND AUGUSTA

Athens, a community of approximately 52,000 is located sixty-five miles northeast of Atlanta and makes an outstanding day trip. The largest city in the Piedmont foothills, it is centrally located near several state parks and has quite a bit to offer in itself.

Its impressive Greek revival homes are typical of the antebellum period, and the Athens-Clarke Heritage Foundation offers a set of four tours of over fifty of them along with the city's other historic sites, including the University of Georgia. For more information, contact Athens of Old Tours, 280 East Dougherty Street, Athens, GA 30601; (404) 546-1805.

Athens is also a very modern community, with several leading manufacturers represented. Westinghouse employs some 900 people at its transformer division and offers a one to two hour tour of production facilities. For more information, contact Westinghouse Electric Corporation, Transformer Division, Newton Bridge Road, Athens, GA 30607; (404) 548-3121.

Coble Dairy Products offers a half-hour tour of its bottling area and shipping department. For more information, contact Coble Dairy Products, Inc., 110 Newton Bridge Road, Athens, GA 30607; (404) 543-7383.

The oldest surviving residence in Athens is a fully restored home dating back to 1820. It houses the Athens Welcome Center and makes an outstanding tour in its own right. For more information, contact the Church-Waddel-Brumby House, 280 East Dougherty Street, Athens, GA 30601; (404) 546-1805.

ATTRACTIONS

• The **University of Georgia**, founded in 1785, spreads out across 4,000 acres and is the home of several notable attractions, not the least of which are the State Botanical

Day Trips from Atlanta

Gardens. A 293-acre cultural and recreational area on the Oconee River, it offers nature trails which meander through an impressive range of Georgia flora. This site of numerous concerts, art exhibits and lecture tours also includes a visitor center and conservatory. For more information, contact the Public Relations Department, University of Georgia, Athens, GA 30602; (404) 542-3354.

- The first garden club in America was founded in an 1857 brick house which originally served as living quarters for University of Georgia professors. The grounds spread across two and a half acres of gardens, courtyards and an arboretum. For more information, contact **Founder's Memorial Garden and Museum House**, 325 Lumpkin Street, Athens, GA 30602; (404) 542-3631.

- One of the best art galleries in Georgia is the **University of Georgia Museum of Art**. Actually comprised of five galleries, it is the permanent home of the Holbrook and Kress collections, and features traveling exhibits which are changed monthly. For more information, contact the Georgia Museum of Art, University of Georgia, Athens, GA 30602; (404) 542-3254.

- Another home which combines history and celebrity is the **Taylor-Grady House**. This is where former *Atlanta Constitution* editor Henry W. Grady lived while attending the University of Georgia; it was later purchased and kept in the family until 1872. The house is a fine example of antebellum period architecture, and tours can be arranged by contacting Taylor-Grady House, 634 Prince Avenue, Athens, GA 30601; (404) 549-8688.

- South of Athens is one of the finest golf courses in the state. Located at **Hard Labor Creek State Park**, it offers eighteen holes of challenging duffing. The park itself, named by slaves who worked a plantation in the area, spreads out across 5,805 acres and is a popular place not only for golfing, but pedal boating, canoeing and stream fishing; horseback riding; bicycling; and hiking. Fishing on the park's two lakes is considered good to outstanding. Facilities include forty-nine tent and trailer sites, one group shelter, two group camps, twenty rental cottages, four picnic shelters and one barbecue,

Day Trips from Atlanta

horse stables, a swimming beach and a bath house. Annual events here include the **Civilian Conservation Corps** reunion in the spring; a **Holiday Hayride** in November, and the **Christmas Golf Tournament**. It can be reached by taking Interstate 20's Exit 49 to Rutledge, then heading two miles north on Fairplay Road. For more information, contact Hard Labor Creek State Park, Rutledge, GA 30663; (404) 557-2863.

- Slightly northeast of Athens is **Watson Mill Bridge State Park**, accessible by taking U.S. 29 to the Georgia Highway 72 cutoff, then proceeding to Comer and taking State Route 22 south for three miles. This park's 144 acres include a beautiful five acre mill pond with an actual grist mill and old power dam. The pond has outstanding catfish and bass angling, and in July hosts a Confederate encampment and skirmish. **Georgia Indian Awareness Weekend** is also celebrated here in August, and in season day and overnight canoe trips are available. Facilities include twenty-one tent and trailer sites, three picnic shelters, a group shelter, and canoe and pedal boat rentals. For more information, contact Watson Mill Bridge State Park, Route 1, Comer, GA 30629; (404) 783-5349.

FOLLOWING SHERMAN TO AUGUSTA

The drive from Atlanta to Augusta offers a variety of recreational opportunities, beginning with Hard Labor Creek State Park (see Athens). Lake Oconee, some 19,000 acres of outstanding fresh water fishing, boating and swimming, has two campgrounds and a wealth of picnicking spots. It also includes a portion of Oconee National Forest's 109,268 acres. This one includes the Scull Shoals Historical Area, a ghost town, sites of Georgia's first paper mill, cotton gin and textile factory, and a wealth of boating, camping, fishing, picnicking and swimming opportunities. For more information, contact Oconee National Forest, P.O. Box 1437, Gainesville, GA 30501; (404) 536-0541.

Further east, the town of Crawfordville makes a great jumping off point for A. H. Stephens State Historic Park. Named for the Congressman who became first a U.S. Congressman, then vice president of the Confederacy, then

Day Trips from Atlanta

again a congressman and also a governor of Georgia, this 1,189 acre site blends history and recreational opportunities.

His home, Liberty Hall, was built in 1830 and next to it is the Confederate Museum, which houses one of the most representative collections of Civil War artifacts to be found in Georgia. The park also includes two lakes, a swimming pool and a beach. Fishing is legal and open all year long. Boating includes fishing boat rentals and private boats. There are thirty-six tent and trailer sites, four picnic shelters, a nature trail, and various educational programs. In April, the park hosts the Heritage Crafts Festival, and in December, Christmas at Liberty Hall. For more information, contact A.H. Stephens State Historic Park, P.O. Box 235, Crawfordville, GA 30631; (404) 456-2602.

Northeast of Crawfordville, at the junction of State Route 47 and U.S. Highway 78, is historic Washington. This community of 4,800 was founded in 1773, and in 1779, was the site of one of the most decisive battles of the Revolutionary War, the Battle of Kettle Creek. Here, as well, history lives, for this is also the home of the man they still refer to as "Georgia's unreconstructed rebel."

The home of this man is now The Robert Toombs House State Historic Site. Toombs was a Georgia plantation owner, lawyer, and state legislator, congressman and senator with a fiery temper and incredible ambition. The two seemed to war with each other constantly. He aspired to the Confederate presidency and tried to thwart Jefferson Davis. After a tenure as Confederate Secretary of State, he took a commission with the Army of Northern Virginia, and when he couldn't advance under General Robert E. Lee, resigned and spent the rest of the war in Washington. A rebel to the very end, he claimed, in 1880, that he was still not "loyal to the existing government of the United States and do not wish to be suspected of loyalty." The home of this controversial son of Dixie is located at 216 East Robert Toombs Avenue. For more information, contact Robert Toombs House State Historic Site, P.O. Box 605, Washington, GA 30673; (404) 678-2226.

AUGUSTA

Georgia's second oldest and fifth largest city lies two and a half hours east of Atlanta on Interstate 20 and the trip to it accesses several state parks. Like Athens, the city is a prime attraction on its own, however.

It was founded in 1737 as a British trading post and served as the state capital from 1785-1795. Tobacco plantations, cotton and the completion of the Augusta Canal underwrote its prosperity through the final days of the Civil War and, although it was on Sherman's March to the Sea, it was spared the destruction which befell Atlanta.

Now, in addition to being rich in history, it is considered one of Georgia's prime resort communities. For more information, contact the Augusta Convention and Visitors Bureau, P.O. Box 657, Augusta, GA 30913; (404) 722-0421.

ATTRACTIONS

• The **Augusta Museum**, the first boy's high school in the country when it was the home of the Academy of Richmond County, was built in 1802 and now houses extensive collections of archaeology, art, history, military science and natural science. For more information, contact the Augusta Museum, 504 Telfair Street, Augusta, GA 30901; (404) 722-8454.

• **Augusta Coca-Cola Bottling Company** offers a one hour tour of its offices and bottling facilities. This venerable Georgia native employs 267 people and compares favorably with the facility in Atlanta. For more information, contact Coca-Cola Bottling Company, 1901 North Leg Road, Augusta, GA 30909; (404) 736-2211.

• The **Augusta Chronicle-Herald** provides a one hour tour if its news building. For a glimpse behind the scenes of a daily newspaper, contact the Chronicle-Herald, News Building, Broad Street, Augusta, GA 30901; (404) 724-0851.

• The United State Army has created a tour package of **Fort Gordon** tailored to the age group of its visitors. Picnic

Day Trips from Atlanta

facilities and access to the mess hall are included. For more information, contact Joan Carter, Public Information, Fort Gordon, Augusta, GA 30901; (404) 791-6001 or (404) 691-7003. One month advance notice is required.

Augusta has several monuments definitely worth experiencing. These include:

- **Confederate Monument**: at Broad Street between Seventh and Eighth, this 76-foot marble shaft features life-size replicas of Confederate heroes.

- You'll find the **Confederate Powder Works** at 1717 Goodrich Street in front of the Sibley Mill. The 176-foot high obelisk chimney is the only remaining structure built by the Confederate government. It marks the site of a factory which produced over two million pounds of gunpowder during the Civil War.

- The **Old Slave Market Column** is on Broad at Fifth Street and marks a legend. A traveling preacher was refused permission to render a sermon in the Lower Market and swore that the Market Place would be destroyed down to every last stone save this one. An 1878 cyclone fulfilled that prophecy.

- The fifty-foot tall obelisk, known as **Signer's Monument** was sculpted from Stone Mountain granite. It honors Lyman Hall, George Walton and Button Gwinnet, signers of the Declaration of Independence. Hall and Walton are buried on the site.

Augusta is also a town for golfers and has several good public courses.

- The eighteen hole **Augusta Golf Course,** located on Highland Avenue, features two water holes, narrow fairways and has been described as "an interesting course." For more information, call (404) 733-9177.

- You'll find **Forest Hill Golf Course** located on Comfort Road. This eighteen hole course is relatively short and extremely narrow. It has sixty-three sand traps, two holes with water and nine holes with "out of bounds". For more information, call (404) 736- 8431.

- **Jones Creek Golf Club** is located at 4101 Hammonds Ferry in Evans. This newly built course has integrated such 'natural' hazards as existing vegetation and streams. Well adapted to championship play, it is considered one of the more challenging eighteen holers in the area. For more information, call (404) 860-4228.

Augusta is literally chock full of historical buildings and other sites. The Convention and Visitors Bureau publishes an excellent guide to them. There is also a trolley tour available. For more information, contact the Convention & Visitors Bureau, P.O. Box 1331, 1301 Greene Street, Augusta, GA 30913; (404) 826-4722.

Augusta has many historic homes, several of which are outstanding representatives of various periods of its history:

- **Appleby House**, located at 2260 Walton Way, dates back to 1830 and is now used as a branch library and the stage for summer garden concerts.
- The **Harris Home** is found at 1822 Broad Street and harks back to 1797 with furnishings from the colonial period.
- Built in 1794 as the home of George Walton, **Meadow Garden** is located at 1320 Nelson Street.
- Visitors discover **Ware's Folly** at 506 Telfair Street. It is so called because its $40,000 cost was considered absolutely scandalous when it was built in 1818. The structure now houses the **Gertrude Herbert Memorial Institute of Art**, one of the best art museums in Georgia.
- Located at 1112 Eight Street, the **Yerby Home** is the boyhood and adolescent home of famous black writer and novelist Frank Yerby.

NORTH FROM AUGUSTA

The drive north from Augusta is not only beautiful, but also rich in a number of recreational opportunities. Follow State Route 104 to the Highway 47/150 junction, then turn west to Mistletoe Road. At the end of it, you'll find Mistletoe State Park, a 1,920 acre facility on the shores of Clark Hill Reservoir, itself reputed to be one of the finest bass lakes in the nation. Three boat ramps access its 76,000 acres, and there is a swimming beach, as well. Facilities include 107 tent and trailer sites and ten cottages. Bicycles are available for rent and hikers will delight in the five miles of trails. The annual

Day Trips from Atlanta

Striper Extravaganza is held there in March; the Biathlon Competition and a Gospel Singing Fest in May. For more information, contact Mistletoe State Park, Route L, Appling, GA 30502; (404) 541-0321.

Elijah Clark State Park is located north of Mistletoe, just east of Lincolnton and makes another great stop on Clark Hill Lake. Its 447 acres offer 165 tent and trailer sites, a white sand beach, a bathhouse, twenty lakefront cottages, six picnic shelters, four boat ramps, and miniature golf and a playground. Elijah Clark was a Revolutionary War pioneer and the museum features not only displays of period artifacts but actual live demonstrations of colonial life. This is where the Pioneer Rendezvous is held in October and a Log Cabin Christmas. For more information, contact Elijah Clark State Park, Box 293, route 4, Lincolnton, GA 30817; (404) 359-3458.

Still further north, this time by taking Route 79 from just east of Lincolnton, one will find Bobby Brown State Park. This is a sentimental favorite, for it is named for Lt. Robert T. Brown, a World War II naval hero. It's located on the ruins of the colonial village of Petersburg, where the Broad and Savannah rivers flow into Clark Hill Reservoir. Its 665 acres offer sixty-one tent and trailer site, three picnic shelters, a pool and concessions, a boat ramp and dock, 1.9 miles of hiking trails and all the fishing, boating, water skiing and swimming one can pack into an outing on a 78,000 acre lake. For more information, contact Bobby Brown State Park, Route 4, Box 232, Elberton, GA 30635; (404) 283-3313.

North of Elberton, on State Route 77, just outside the community of Hartwell and on the shores of Hartwell Lake, is Hart State Park. This one is an angler's paradise, for in the 56,000 acre reservoir are rainbow trout, large mouth bass, black crappie, bream and wall-eye pike. Swimming, boating and water skiing are also popular activities here. The park's 147 acres encompass eighty-three tent and trailer sites, five modular cottages, three picnic shelters, two boat ramps, a swimming beach, and a playground. Activities also include music programs at Cricket Theatre, a Labor Day Music Festival, a craft show the first Saturday in October, at the hot rods at the Hart Car Show, the first Sunday in November. For

Day Trips from Atlanta

more information, contact Hart State Park, 1515 Hart Park Road, Hartwell, GA 30643; (404) 376- 8756.

From Hartwell, a drive west on U.S. 29 to Royston will bring one to Victoria Bryant State Park. The nine hole golf course here is set among beautiful rolling Piedmont hills, where facilities also include a swimming pool, five picnic shelters, two pioneer campsites, twenty-five tent and trailer sites, three playgrounds, and five miles of hiking trails distributed among the park's 406 acres. There is also a fully stocked fish pond where bank fishing only is permitted. In the spring, the Annual Jr.-Sr. Catfish Rodeo is held, while the Fourth of July witnesses the Independence Day Bluegrass Festival. This is also where Pioneer Skills Day is held, the first weekend in November. For more information, contact Victoria Bryant State Park, Route 1, Box 257, Royston, GA 30662; (404) 245-6270.

Highway 17 goes north from Royston to Interstate 85. By taking the freeway east several miles to Lavonia, then going north off Exit 58 onto State Route 17, one can follow the signs to Tugaloo State Park. This 393 acre facility sites on a peninsula around which the waters of Hartwell Reservoir lap. Fishing here is outstanding—this is large mouth bass country—and other recreational opportunities include water-skiing, swimming, bicycling, tennis, and miniature golf. Facilities include 122 tent and trailer sites, twenty cottages, two fishing ramps and nine boat docks. Mountain music programs are a specialty and in April, the park hosts Rushing Waters Pow Wow, while in October, the Harvest Festival is held there. For more information, contact Tugaloo State Park, Route 1, Lavonia, GA 30553; (404) 356-4362.

The northeastern end of this swing ends at Traveler's Rest, just off U.S. 123 near the town of Toccoa. This plantation home was built in 1833 by Devereaux Jarrett, the wealthiest man in the beautiful Tugaloo Valley. Among those who stayed there when he added an inn to it was John C. Calhoun, the South Carolina notable, and Joseph E. Brown, Georgia's Civil War governor. A National Historic Landmark, this one has been fully restored and the tour of it is outstanding. For more information, contact Traveler's Rest State Historic Site, Route 3, Toccoa, GA 30577; (404) 886-2256.

CALLAWAY GARDENS- A ONE OF A KIND RESORT

One of the most beautiful creatures in all of creation lives only about ten days in its most evolved state. It can see 9,000 times more than a human being can, however, and it tastes with its feet.

This gentle species occupies a special place in the hearts of Georgians and is, hence, celebrated in one of the most beautiful spots in the mountains of northern Georgia. The creature is, of course, the butterfly, and the sylvan paradise in which it is honored is the newly opened, but already world famous, Day Butterfly Center conservatory in the heart of Callaway Gardens.

These 2,500 acres of native flowers, woodlands, scenic drives and nature trails are situated near Pine Mountain, seventy miles south of Atlanta (thirty miles north of Columbus) on U.S. Highway 27. Each year, thousands of people living in the greater Atlanta area come here for a vacation as varied as it is relaxing and rejuvenating. This is, truly, one of the most pastoral resort areas in the state. The Gardens themselves are a horticulturist's paradise on earth.

Consider the Azalea Trails, for example. Along them, over 700 varieties of cultivated azaleas bloom from late March to May, in the company of dogwoods, rhododendrons, and numerous wildflowers. Take ten minutes or ninety, and in any season, you'll observe all manner of wildlife and birds.

Meadowlark Gardens features three walking trails. The Wildflower Trails, a twenty-five to forty minute excursion, winds gently through wildflowers and ferns. The Holly Trail, as its name implies, leads one for some forty minutes through 450 varieties of holly and, by season, daffodils, prunifolia, azaleas and camellias. Rhododendron Trail provides an incredible display of rhododendrons in late spring, as well as ferns, ground covers, and ornamental shrubs and trees. An added

Day Trips from Atlanta

attraction of the Meadowlark Gardens is the Pioneer Log Cabin, an authentic, handhewn log structure dating back to the early 1800s, and complete with a hostess who could have lived then herself, were she not so lovely.

Mr. Cason's Vegetable Garden includes seven and a half acres planted with over 400 varieties of vegetables, herbs and fruits. Here begins the paved walkway around Robin Lake. The lake's beach is the center for much of the park's entertainment and Callaway Gardens is famous for that, as well. Activities include Florida State University's "Flying High" Circus; rides on the Robin E. Lee Riverboat and the Whistlin' Dixie miniature train, and dramatic water ski shows. Recreation runs to sunbathing and volleyball, miniature golf, and badminton. The beach itself is a mile long stretch of dazzling white sand. The Mountain Creek Lake Trail is an invitation to explore the flora and fauna of a beautiful stretch of water, itself accessing the tinier lakes of Bluebird, Bobolink and Whippoorwill. The Boathouse and Gardens Restaurant and Veranda Restaurant are located on the southwestern shore. Wildlife here includes mallard ducks, green herons, turtles and squirrels, while flowers such as native azaleas, rhododendrons and wildflowers proliferate. The entire excursion takes some three hours.

The Laurel Springs Trail runs along the secluded slopes of Pine Mountain Ridge, following the edge of Laurel Springs Creek. It's a great place to experience the ageless majesty of an Appalachian hardwood forest and mountain laurel thickets. This one usually takes about forty-five minutes.

The Chapel Trail begins at the Ida Cason Callaway Memorial Chapel. This tranquil sylvan church features organ concerts throughout the year, and the strains of the pipes float out over azaleas and mountain laurel, often heard by the beautiful white tailed deer which inhabit the Gardens.

For the horticulturist, professional or dedicated hobbyist, perhaps the greatest attraction of the Gardens is the John A. Sibley Horticultural Center. A relatively recent addition, this impressive greenhouse and garden complex consists of theme gardens which flow together about a two story waterfall and beautiful expanses of lawns. Here, as well, are featured the most advanced techniques of energy conservation, including solar radiation, insulation, radiant heat, natural cooling, protective screens and folding glass doors. The Center is named for a member of the Board of Trustees of the Ida Cason Callaway Foundation. Mr. Sibley is also honorary Chairman of the Board of the Trust Company of Georgia.

But what of the butterflies? They are enshrined in the $5.3 million octagon conservatory, where they fly among the habitats from which they were transported. If you've never traveled to exotic, faraway places, you will here, for the Gardens has re-created the climates and environments of Central and South America, Malaysia and Taiwan. The butterflies live here and it is truly their home.

Day Trips from Atlanta

There are full accommodations available here, as well. These include inn accommodations, country cottages, luxurious villas and an executive lodge. There are four beautifully maintained golf courses, seventeen lighted soft and hard tennis courts, racquetball courts and instruction in all of these. Horseback riding, trap and skeet shooting and quail hunting on a 1,000 acre preserve are also enjoyed. Anglers are not neglected either, for Mountain Creek Lake offers bass and bream fishing. The other lakes feature sailing and swimming. There is also a major conference center.

In its mission statement, the founders of Callaway Gardens, Cason J. Callaway and his wife, Virginia Hand, state the intention of this beautiful resort, which is to provide a wholesome family environment where all may find beauty, relaxation, inspiration and a better understanding of the living world. They have achieved that goal. For more information, contact Callaway Gardens, Pine Mountain, GA 31822; (404) 663-2281.

CHICKAMAUGA AND CHATTANOOGA NATIONAL MILITARY PARK
LEGACIES TO A BOLD PAST

The drive northwest from Atlanta to the Chickamauga and Chattanooga National Military Park will take you through Marietta, Kennesaw, Acworth and Allatoona Lake, and several of the communities enroute are worth visiting. Marietta, Kennesaw, Acworth and Lake Allatoona are just a few interesting stops along the way, and they have been described at various other parts of this book. Also on the way, just north of Allatoona Lake, is the town of Cartersville. Cartersville is a small town that brims with history and hospitality, and it is discussed in Chapter Two. Other towns enroute to Chickamauga and Chattanooga National Military Park are featured below, and after that the Park and its ferocious place in Civil War history is discussed.

Day Trips from Atlanta

CALHOUN

The town of Calhoun lies twenty-three miles north of Cartersville. This was the heart of the Cherokee Nation until, in 1835, they were "relocated" to Oklahoma. Until 1850, Calhoun was known by its Indian name of Oothcaloga, which means place of the beaver dams. Its new designation honors Secretary of State John C. Calhoun. Now a dairy, poultry and beef center, the community saw one of the bloodier Civil War battles in the area. New Echota State Park is located four miles to the northeast.

ATTRACTIONS

- The **Confederate Cemetery** is the final resting place for some 400 rebel soldiers killed when Sherman's forces, in their march on Atlanta, attempted to outflank General Joe Johnston and were forced to flank again when they were stopped after two days of bloody fighting at Resaca, in May 1864. The cemetery includes the actual battlesite where, the third weekend in May, it is reenacted. For more information, contact Confederate Cemetery, 300 South Wall Street, Calhoun, GA 30701; (404) 625-3200.
- Aircraft buffs will enjoy visiting the **Mercer Air Museum**. This outdoor attraction has seventeen airplanes dating from 1944 and is open seven days a week. For more information, contact Mercer Air Museum, Belwood Road, Calhoun, GA 30701.
- The **Gordon County Historical Society** has its headquarters in the **Oakleigh House**. Sherman used it for his headquarters during his stay here enroute to Atlanta. The home contains a collection of over 1,500 dolls from various periods. For more information, contact the Gordon County Historical Society, Wall Street, Calhoun, GA 30171; (404) 629-1515.
- Fourteen miles east of Calhoun on State Route 140 is the town of **Fairmont**, best known for the **Sunrise Planetarium**. The

Day Trips from Atlanta

programs here, all with religious orientation, range from astrology to zoology and are offered every Sunday afternoon. For more information, contact Sunrise Planetarium, Highway 53, Fairmont, GA 30139; (404) 337-2775.

• **Salacoa Creek Park,** ten miles east of Calhoun on State Route 156, offers a 126-acre lake, electric motor boating, a picnic area, fishing, camping and a swimming area. This one hosts an annual bass tournament. For more information, write Salacoa Creek Park, Route 1, Ranger, GA 30734; (404) 629-3490.

• Calhoun hosts the internationally known **Concerts in the Country** from May through October. For more information, contact Concerts in the Country, P.O. Box 2045, Calhoun, GA 30701; (404) 629-0226.

DALTON

Eighteen miles north of Calhoun lies **Dalton,** also known as the carpet capital of the world for the 208 floor covering plants there employing 28,000 people. About sixty percent of the world's carpeting is produced in the Dalton area. In addition to being a major marketing point for floor coverings—savings of up to fifty percent are usual in the town's 200 carpet stores—this community of 21,235 has an abundance of civic pride and a cultural tradition of which it is justifiably proud.

ATTRACTIONS

• **Crown Gardens and Archives.** Constructed in 1884, this building is the hub of Dalton's creative, arts and crafts, local history and music, dance and drama activities. It's also one of the best places in town to find out what's going on. For more information, contact Crown Gardens and Archives, 715 Chattanooga Avenue, Dalton, GA 30720; (404) 278-0217.

• **West Point Pepperell** offers a limited tour of its rug manufacturing facility. For more information, contact Derek Davis, West Point Pepperell, P.O. Box 1208, Dalton, GA 30720; (404) 278-1100.

- Dalton's community center for the arts holds frequent art exhibits and is the site of Dalton's annual **Fall Festival of Arts and Crafts**, held in September. For more information, contact Creative Arts Guild, 520 West Waugh Street, Dalton, GA 30720; (404) 278-0168.
- Mothers Day and Columbus Day visitors to Dalton can see an actual working corn mill dating back to 1859 when they take in the **Whitefield County Fair**. The mill is powered by turbines built beneath the flowing waters of **Coahulla Creek**. For more information, contact Prater's Mill, 101 Timberland Drive, Dalton, GA 30720; (404) 259-5764.

CHICKIMAUGA AND CHATTANOOGA

From Dalton, continue north eleven miles on the interstate to the village of Boynton, then cut west on Georgia State Route to the eastern entrance to the historic Chickamauga and Chattanooga National Military Park.

This 8,102-acre park, the oldest in the nation administered by the National Park Service, commemorates two of the most pivotal battles of the Civil War. For a fuller appreciation of the facility itself, historical perspective might be helpful.

The time is June 1863. The 58,000 strong Union Army of the Cumberland, under the able command of General William S. Rosecrans, had been enjoying several months of relative inactivity in encampments around Murfreesboro, Tennessee. He'd tasted blood last at the Battle of Stone's River and he hadn't enjoyed it. His foe then had been General Braxton Bragg and the battleground had been wet, cold, dismal and haunting. Only the stubborn fighting of Union General Thomas "Pap" Thomas had averted a Federal rout, and Rosecrans' troops had taken the brunt of a rolling Confederate assault. He had, therefore, no desire to tangle with the Rebs again, unless the odds were clearly in his favor.

Back in Washington, however, Lincoln, Secretary of War Stanton, and Union Army commanding general Halleck were pressing for a Union victory in the southeast. Rosecrans' field commander, Ulysses Grant, was most adamant. "Old Rosy" argued that if he stayed where he was, he'd keep Bragg from coming south to link up with Joe Johnston. Grant, besieging Vicksburg, finally lost his patience and ordered Rosecrans to march. Reluctantly, Rosecrans decamped and set about clearing Bragg out of central Tennessee. In a series of skillful skirmishes, he outflanked Bragg's army of 45,000 hardened Confederate veterans, forcing them to abandon fixed positions across a defensive line in front of Nashville.

The way was open to Chattanooga, but it meant facing the legendary Bragg again, so Rosecrans, believing Bragg had been substantially reinforced, halted his advance for two weeks, attempting to persuade Grant, who had just taken Vicksburg, to reinforce him.

In fairness to him, Rosecrans was not simply faced with one of the Confederacy's most fearsome fighters, but with some of Dixie's most treacherous and inhospitable countryside. He seems to have been extremely concerned about having his army cut to ribbons between the two. Bragg, in the meantime, learning of the fall of Vicksburg, and believing that an imminent joining of Grant's army with the troops of Rosecrans would destroy whatever chances he had of holding Chattanooga, abandoned the city in favor of protecting his supply lines and the valuable resources of Atlanta and northern Georgia.

On September 9, 1863, General Rosecrans marched unopposed into Chattanooga. Bragg, meanwhile, set up defensive positions around Lafayette, Georgia, to the southwest, and sent the call to Richmond for reinforcements. Thus was the stage set for the Battle of Chickamauga.

Rosecrans, heady over an apparently easy victory at Chattanooga, foresook his characteristic caution and made plans to pursue Bragg into northern Georgia. What he could not have known was that joining Bragg were some of the fiercest troops the Confederacy fielded during the entire war, and they were commanded by equally awesome generals, including James Longstreet, D.H. Hill, and the legendary Confederate cavalryman, Bedford Forrest. As historian Bruce Catton notes, for the first time in the entire Civil War, the numerical odds favored the Confederates. Rosecrans' Army of the Cumberland, numbering some 60,000, were facing one of the finest fighting forces in the then-known world, some 70,000 infuriated, impassioned, cold-steel veterans to whom the enduring phrase damn-Yankee was a hyphenated invitation to Hell.

Even the unflappable Union General Pap Thomas was uneasy as the Army of the Cumberland advanced through the razor-edged Appalachians. Autumn had set in, with its torrential rains and sudden chilling sunsets. By then, the federals knew that Bragg, Longstreet, Hill and Bedford Forrest were waiting for them at Chickamauga Creek, and many noted that this stream had been known among the Cherokees as the "river of death". It also disturbed them to realize that because of the ruggedness of the region, their various army corps were so widely dispersed than an attack en masse was virtually impossible.

On September 19, 1863, a dozen miles south of Chattanooga, the battle was joined along a six mile front of thick woods, treacherous mountains, and the gap in Missionary Ridge, through which the road from Chattanooga wound. So dense was the terrain that between the trees and the smoke of cannon and small arms, it was a scarlet kaleidoscope of individual holocausts, often so closely joined that bayonets, musket butts, rocks and clubs were the instruments of death. Along Chickamaugua Creek itself, Bedford Forrest's dismounted cavalrymen fought like incensed and screaming banshees. By nightfall, the lines were mixed, and through the ground mist came the terrible screams of the wounded and dying. Thirst-crazed men drank from the rivulets of the river of death and found it wine red and salty with blood.

The attack was resumed the next day, with Pap Thomas receiving the brunt of it. A division sent to reinforce him got lost and when it failed to arrive, Thomas sent another request to Rosecrans. The Union commander, believing the division he'd sent had been cut down, then shifted his strength to Thomas' front and James Longstreet's rebels smashed into the depleted Union flank, there to be met by Brigadier General Thomas J. Wood's redoubtable federals. It was some of the fiercest fighting of the war and at the end of it, the Army of the Cumberland was retreating to Chattanooga.

The cost of this two-day battle was 30,000, some 16,000 casualties inflicted on the Army of the Cumberland, which lost what amounted to one-third of its effective fighting force. Thus began the Siege of Chattanooga. The Confederates held the heights of Missionary Ridge and Lookout Mountain, and the plain in between. They closed the road and set about the grim task of starving the Army of the Cumberland into submission. What Bragg had most desperately desired to do at Chickamauga Creek, destroy Rosecrans' entire army, he set about now to accomplish, and, as historian Bruce Catton has noted, not so much as a case of hardtack, a side of bacon, or a bale of hay could get into Chattanooga for the use of the Army of the Cumberland unless these Confederates consented, and they had drawn their lines on top of Lookout Mountain for the express purpose of withholding their consent. The only way into Chattanooga was by way of the Tennessee River, and the Confederates held the heights above it, as well.

As autumn of 1863 waxed into winter, the Union situation looked like this: the federals held Nashville and had built up a huge supply depot there. They also held Bridgeport, twenty-five miles to the east of Chattanooga and a terminus of the Memphis and Charleston Railroad. The Chattanooga end of that railroad was obviously closed and the only other alternative was a treacherous mountain road which made a sixty mile detour through countryside held by the Rebs. The federals, nonetheless, tried and that road became littered with the broken bodies of teamsters and horses, and the wreckage of wagons. In Chattanooga, Union soldiers went on half rations and then quarter rations. The horses were in no better shape and even tried to eat the wood of the commissary wagons.

Washington, in the meantime, grew desperate in its desire to break the siege. Sherman's Army of the Tennessee was ordered out of Vicksburg and began the long march east from Mississippi. Grant met with Secretary of War Stanton, was placed in command, and managed to make his way to Chattanooga to take personal charge. Enroute, he sent word relieving Rosecrans and replacing him with the tenacious Pap Thomas.

At Bridgeport, he conferred with Army of the Cumberland chief engineer General Baldy Smith and learned that Smith, headquartered in Bridgeport, was building a steamer, with the intention of taking a force and supplies up to Chattanooga and forcing their way in through a two mile road which led from Brown's Ferry. The plan seemed feasible because also headquartered in Bridgeport was General Joseph "Fightin' Joe" Hooker and 12,000 troops of the Army of the Potomac. Braxton Bragg, unaware of these developing plans, decided that he could hold Chattanooga with considerably fewer men and detached Longstreet to crush Union General Burnside's force, itself under siege in Knoxville. When Grant learned of this, he ordered Sherman to move as quickly as possible. Sherman's men fought their way to Brown's Ferry and reached it on November 20, 1863.

On November 24, 1863, the federals attacked and the Battle of Missionary Ridge began. While Pap Thomas' remaining 12,000 men of the Army of the Cumberland stared across the plain at the base of Missionary Ridge, Sherman hit the upper end of it and Hooker struck at Lookout Mountain.

Hooker had the easiest time of it, for he found that his forced outnumbered the defenders of Lookout Mountain by five to one. When Sherman attacked Missionary Ridge, however, he found that it was not one mountain, but a series of them, and all during that day, he came under heavy fire each time he descended one slope and tried to scale another. Night fell and his Army of Tennessee had still not secured its objective, despite heavy losses. It has been noted that the ferocity of this fighting so infuriated Sherman's forces that it set into motion the viciousness with which they conducted their general's infamous March through Georgia.

The next day, things did not appear to be going much better. Hooker's men got down the other side of Lookout Mountain and became lost in the dense woods. Sherman continued to have his own problems, as well. Pap Thomas' objective, the Chattanooga base of Missionary Ridge, was not considered a realistic one, but was planned merely to divert the rebels' attention from Sherman's attack. That's not the way it turned out, however.

During the Siege of Chattanooga, the Army of the Cumberland watched 10,000 of its number die because of starvation, disease, exposure, and attempts to break out. They were also chafing under the derision of the other two armies involved, for they had not been expected to retreat before Bragg at Chickamauga Creek. So when the order came to attack Missionary Ridge, they settled to the task with grim determination. Keeping perfect marching order, they advanced across the intervening plain into the mouths of Confederate cannon and the vicious crackling tongues of Rebel rifle and musket fire. When they reached the base of Missionary Ridge, they made short work of the Confederates entrenched there, then paused.

General Phil Sheridan commanded them and had the attack failed, he could have been court-martialed, for the Army of the Cumberland was ordered only to take the base of the ridge. Perhaps inspired by a colonel of the 104th Illinois, who vowed that his men would be first to take the summit, he pressed his assault, while, on Orchard Knob, General Grant and Pap Thomas watched, slackjawed in disbelief, as the half-starved Army of the Cumberland fixed bayonets and snarled their way, inch by inch, up the 500 foot summit.

Bragg's army crumpled and the Siege of Chattanooga was broken.

It is these two battles, then, that Chickamauga and Chattanooga National Military Park commemorates. The Chattanooga National Cemetery, established in 1863; Orchard Knob; the Crest Road along Missionary Ridge; Wilder Tower, an outstanding place to view the Chickamauga Battlefield; the Brotherton House, which marks the location where Bragg's men broke the Union line at Chickamauga; and Snodgrass Hill and Snodgrass House, site of the Union field hospital, have all been preserved.

The Chickamauga Visitor Center, nine miles south of Chattanooga on U.S. Highway 27, has a museum which includes not only an outstanding collection of battlefield paraphernalia, but an extensive display of American rifles and muskets. Multi-media presentations tell the story of the Battle of Chickamauga. Lookout Mountain's Point Park includes the Ochs Memorial Museum and Observatory, the New York Peace Monument, the Cravens House, and Umbrella Rock.

Group campsites, intended primarily for those wishing to study the historical aspects of the park, are available, and other amenities include drinking water and a camp store. For more information, contact Chickamauga and Chattanooga National Military Park, P.O. Box 2128, Fort Oglethorpe, GA 30742; (404) 866-9241.

And finally, there is the village of Chickamauga itself. This community of 1,842 lies just southwest of the park on Georgia State Route 193 and consists, in large park, of frontier and antebellum structures, many of which are on the National Register of Historic Places.

These include the Gordon Lee House, antebelleum mansion used by the federals for a field hospital during the Battle of Chickamauga. For more information, contact Gordon Lee House, 217 Cove Road, Chickamauga, GA 30707; (404) 375-4729.

CLEVELAND: HOME OF BABYLAND HOSPITAL

A few years back, one of the strangest but ultimately most endearing fads ever to tickle the hearts of Americans from the Atlantic to the Pacific was the Cabbage Patch Kids. With an irony even historians can appreciate, this phenomenon began in a tiny Appalachia community and did a kind of reverse Sherman's March north, across the Mason-Dixon Line and into the hearts of Yankee youngsters everywhere.

That little north Georgia town was Cleveland, located north of Atlanta on Interstate 85 and accessible via Exits 985 and 365. It is also centrally located some nine miles south of Helen via Georgia State Highway 75, and within reach of Dahlonega by taking U.S. 19 some fourteen miles north to U.S.

129, then slightly east and south another eleven miles (beautiful countryside the entire way, incidentally.)

Babyland General was an actual hospital constructed in 1919 as White County's only medical clinic. It came to national attention in 1978, when Xavier Roberts "delivered" his first cabbage patch baby. Millions have been born here since. If you're getting the idea that "cute" doesn't cover it, you're right.

Babyland General has doctors and nurses rushing around from the operating room to the delivery room to the nursery and the recovery room. You may be fortunate enough to see an actual "delivery" and even if you're not, you'll still be charmed out of your socks by the sheer range, variety and number of Kids and other lovable creatures.

If you decide to "adopt" a Cabbage Patch Kid, you'll be shown the newborns, interviewed, and given an Oath of Adoption. Along with your darling doll, you'll receive an Official Birth Certificate and Adoption Papers and become an actual Cabbage Patch parent. And since you'll definitely want all the accessories which go with a "baby," you'll be encouraged to visit the gift shop for clothes and other items.

There's something else very special at Babyland General. Remember back when you were a kid and had your favorite pet? Maybe it was a puppy, a kitten, a hamster, a guinea pig, rabbit, or maybe you had gold fish. Cabbage Patch Kids love bears and it's at Babyland General that you'll meet The Furskins, four adorable, huggable North Georgia bears from Moody Hollow, each with it's own tale to tell.

For more information, contact Babyland General Hospital, 19 Underwood Street, Cleveland, GA 30528; (404) 865-2171.

COLUMBUS

With a population of well over 174,348 and encompassing a greater metropolitan area of 400,000, Columbus is Georgia's second largest city. In addition to being located within easy driving distance of such attractions as Callaway Gardens,

Warm Springs and Franklin D. Roosevelt Park, it has a great deal to offer.

Columbus is an industrial and trade center whose major industries include food and food processing, machinery, metals and textiles. Federal, state and local government also accounts for a significant share of the employment, along with the military at nearby Fort Benning.

Tourism has become a major industry, as well, and while much of it is centered around the several historical districts, Columbus also boasts over 2,000 acres of parks. Offerings among these include four golf courses, twenty-five tennis courts, fourteen swimming pools, a number of fishing ponds, two ice rinks, four bowling alleys, two RV parks, and two Chattahoochee River marinas.

HISTORY

Although a major Confederate supply center during the Civil War and the scene of a significant battle in April 1865, Columbus was spared the destruction meted out to Atlanta and other communities in northern Georgia. As a result, much of the city's heritage has been graphically preserved.

Before colonial times, the Creek Indians maintained a major village on the site of present day Columbus. During the pre-Revolutionary War era, the trading post and community which grew up around it marked the edge of the frontier. The Chattahoochee River played an important role in commerce, and then, of course, the railroads which did so much to link the state and the South in general.

Much of the older residential district dates back to the early 1800s and includes a formally constituted twenty-six block Historical District. The Columbus Historic Riverfront Industrial District, divided into five zones on the eastern banks of the Chattahoochee, includes one of the oldest industrial sites in the nation. The Columbus Iron Works, which operated for 111 years between 1853 -1964 and which is now a convention and trade center, produced the first breech-loading cannon, a prototype ice-making machine, and the Confederate ironclad Muscogee.

Day Trips from Atlanta

ATTRACTIONS

• The Columbus Historic District includes much of Old Columbus and is anchored by the **Chattahoochee Promenade**, at 76 West Seventh Street. This outdoor museum, established for the national bicentennial, makes a great place to start the tour. For more information, call (404) 324-1828.

• **The Historic Columbus Foundation**, housed in a two-story Italian style villa built shortly after the end of the Civil War, offers an outstanding two-hour guided bus tour of the city. For more information, contact Historic Columbus Heritage Tour, P.O. Box 5312, Columbus, GA 31906; (404) 322-0756.

• One of the more impressive houses in this impressive city is the **Rankin House**. This mansion dates back to the French Empire period and has been beautifully restored.

• Another classic stop is a site which witnessed performances by the likes of Edwin Booth (brother of John Wilkes Booth, the man who assassinated Abraham Lincoln,) the controversial poet and playwright Oscar Wilde, the unforgettable Lily Langtry (for whom a town in Texas was named,) and songwriter Irving Berlin, the man who brought the likes of *Give My Regards to Broadway* and *White Christmas* to the world. The Springer Opera House also has a museum which exhibits belongings and other artifacts of these and other legendary artists. For more information, contact the **Springer Opera House**, 103 Tenth Street, Columbus, GA 31906; (404) 322-0756.

• What is believed to be the oldest existing home in Columbus, the **Walker-Peters-Langdon House**, was built in 1828 and is said to be a classic example of Federal style architecture. It has been faithfully restored, right down to furnishings of the era. For more information, contact the Walker-Peters,Langdon House, 716 Broadway, Columbus, GA 31902; (404) 322-0756.

• **The Columbus Ironworks Convention and Trade Center** produced a variety of implements, weapons, munitions, and machines during its century of life. Completely restored, this

Day Trips from Atlanta

venerable brick and beam structure contains over 70,000 square feet of exhibit space, sixteen meeting halls, and an outdoor amphitheater which hosts many of the city's cultural and entertainment offerings. For more information, contact the Columbus Ironworks Convention & Trade Center, P.O. Box 2768, Columbus, GA 31902; (404) 322-1613.

• The only Confederate naval museum in the world houses the ironclad gunboat Muscogee, which was raised from the bottom of the Chattahoochee River after resting there for nearly a century. The museum contains models of other period vessels and other relevant artifacts. For more information, contact the **Columbus Naval Museum**, 101 Fourth Street, Columbus, GA 31901; (404) 327-9798.

• An excellent collection of prehistoric Native Americana, a restored pioneer cabin, art work, and a separate children's museum are among the offerings of the city's major museum. For more information, contact the **Columbus Museum of Arts and Sciences**, 1251 Wynnton Road, Columbus, GA 31902; (404) 323-3617.

• The chemist/druggist who brought the world the original formula for Coca Cola lived and worked for awhile in Columbus. His home is open for group tours, by appointment. For more information, contact **Pemberton House**, 11 Seventh Street, Columbus, GA 31906; (404) 322-0756.

• The **Jubilee Riverboat**, a sternwheeler dating back to the days when such vessels plied the Chattahoochee in great numbers, offers excursions. For more information, contact the Jubilee Riverboat, Columbus Convention and Visitors Bureau, P.O. Box 2768, Columbus, GA 31902; (404) 322-1613.

• The Columbus Convention and Visitors Bureau is also a contact for the **Three Arts Theatre** at 1020 Talbotton Road. This attraction is the home of the Columbus Symphony, reputed to be one of the finest such organizations in the South.

• The Visitors Bureau will also have information on the schedule and offerings of the **Patterson Planetarium**, at 2900 Woodruff Farm Road. This one offers daily shows.

• For those interested in hydro-electric power, the **Chattahoochee electrical power generation facility** offers tours ranging from one to four hours in length. For more information,

Day Trips from Atlanta

contact William G. Head, Georgia Power Company, P.O. Box 4545, Atlanta, GA 30302; (404) 526-7848.

- Media buffs can tour a computerized newspaper production operation by contacting the **Columbus Ledger/Enquirer**, 17 West Twelfth Street, Columbus, GA 31902; (404) 324-5526.
- Those who enjoy the look and feel of denim, and have always been curious about how such garments are made, might enjoy a tour of a plant that makes them. For more information, contact **Swift Textiles, Inc.**, P.O. Box 1400, Columbus, GA 31994; (404) 324-3623.
- **Tom's Foods** offers a forty-five minute tour of its candy, shelling and peanut operations. For more information, contact Tom's Foods, Inc., 900 Eighth Street, Columbus, GA 31902; (404) 323-2721.
- The United States Army's massive infantry and airborne training center at **Fort Benning** has a museum which traces the development of warfare in North America from the French and Indian War. Artifacts include weapons, uniforms, battle flags, medals, documents and other paraphernalia. For more information, contact the **National Infantry Museum**, Fort Benning, GA 31905; (404) 545-5313.

For more information on Columbus and its various offerings, contact the Columbus Chamber of Commerce, P.O. Box 1200, 1344 Thirteen Avenue, Columbus, GA 31902; (404) 327-1566.

DAHLONEGA
A LITTLE CITY BIG ON FUN

Some twenty years before the cry "There's gold in them thar hills," was heard at Sutter's Mill, near Sacramento, California, the precious metal was discovered in the Blue Ridge Mountain foothills of northwestern Georgia, approximately seventy-five miles from Atlanta. The first major strike of any consequence in the continental U.S., it was also the one Spanish explorer Hernando De Soto had been seeking nearly three hundred years before. The treasure that

Day Trips from Atlanta

eluded him turned out to be the economic mainstay of this community well into the twentieth century.

The 1821 find proved so lucrative, in fact, that a mint was founded there in 1838 and coined more than $6 million before it ceased operation with the onset of the Civil War. When Confederate forces captured it, they turned it to the cause of secession. Mining continued in the area until the early 1900s, when the price of gold, fixed at $35 an ounce, made the enterprise unprofitable.

The Georgia state capitol dome in Atlanta, however, is gilded with the metal, donated by Dahlonega citizens and transported by boxcar on two separate occasions in 1958 and 1980. The name of the community, in fact, is a corruption of the Cherokee, *Talonega*, which means, of course, "golden." For residents, poultry production and tourism are the major industries, although there is a commercial mining operation there now and some old timers predict that the discovery of new veins could happen any day now.

Nestled in scenic forests north of Lake Lanier, Dahlonega is a charming place to visit. There is history here, of course, and a true Southern country feel. Recreational opportunities abound in the rivers and streams, set in 250,000 acres of national forests, these with numerous trails, peaks and campgrounds. Trout fishing, hunting, backpacking, canoeing, white water rafting, nature photography and mountain climbing are all popular pastimes, and Dahlonega has outfitters and guides for all of them. And because of the reasonably mild winters, these activities can be enjoyed year round. The community itself offers shops off the historic square which feature an impressive range of antiques, Appalachian crafts, unusual gifts, fried chicken and genuine country vittles. There are also several fine restaurants offering full menus, fast food outlets, sandwich shops and even a candy store. This "little" community is one of the *not* so well kept secrets in the greater Atlanta metropolitan area. It's very likely you'll find more than a fair measure of travelers there over any given weekend or holiday, which is just fine, because there's more than enough to accommodate everyone.

Day Trips from Atlanta

ATTRACTIONS

- The **Dahlonega Gold Museum State Historic Site** captures the famous historical gold rush with exhibits displayed in Lumpkin County's first courthouse. These include nuggets and gold dust, mining equipment and an impressive photographic archive. Made of bricks and mud mortar from the surrounding area, the museum's walls even glint with traces of the precious metal. For more information, contact The Dahlonega Gold Museum, 1 Public Square, Dahlonega, GA 30533; (404) 864-2257.
- **North Georgia Agricultural College** is a fully accredited, military college that offers four year, coeducational studies in Dahlonega and has been serving the greater Southern agrarian community since 1878. It has the distinction of being the only coeducational military college in the entire United States.
- The **Price Memorial Building**, on the campus of North Georgia Agricultural College, was built in 1879, on the foundations of the United States Branch Mint opened in 1838. It is named for Congressman William Pierce Price, founder of the college. The college's ten acres of land are currently owned by the state of Georgia, after transferral of custody from the federal government. For its centennial, the steeple, some 3,200 square feet, was gilded with eleven and a half ounces of gold taken from the Josephine Mine of Auria and the Crisson Mine of Dahlonega. Of particular interest is the lobby display of a rare and complete set of gold coins produced by the mint. Visitors are encouraged and the lobby is open from Monday through Friday, 8 a.m. - 5 p.m.
- One of the best restaurants in the North Georgia Blue Ridge foothills is also one of the more historic. The **Smith House Inn** dates back to 1884 and is built over a vein of gold. Captain Hall, the original owner, purchased an acre of land east of the town square and started digging his foundations. His son discovered the gold ore but when Captain Hall tried to set

up mining operations, Dahlonega city officials, fearful of what such activity would do to the quality of life so close to the town square, forbade him from mining. Captain Hall sued, of course, but lost.

When the house was completed, he used the seven upstairs rooms for living quarters; the basement, which is now the dining room, for storage of his mining equipment; and the first floor for an assay office. A columned building beside the Smith House was his carriage house, the upper part of which served as a barn, while the basement sheltered the livestock.

He moved to Atlanta eventually and when he died in 1922, Henry and Bessie Smith bought the place. They, in turn, converted it to an inn, with Captain Hall's former living quarters serving as guest rooms. Lodging and meals came to $1.50 each back in those days. Prices have gone up some since, naturally, but the tradition, quality and flavor are still very much in evidence.

- The **Pine Tree Company**, which employs over 400 residents, spins thread for rugs and carpets. For information on their industrial tour, contact Richard Moses, Pine Tree Company, Dahlonega, GA 30533; (404) 864-3311.
- For a try at a little gold panning, contact **Crisson's Gold Mine**, (404) 864-6363; or The **Smith House**, (404) 864-2348. Both are located at **Gold Miner's Camp** on Highway 60. The camp is open daily, 10 a.m. - 6 p.m., April through November. A fee is collected for these activities.

For more information, contact the Dahlonega-Lumpkin County Chamber of Commerce, P.O. Box 2037, Dahlonega, GA 30533; (404) 864-3711.

EVENT

- One of the best festivals in all of Georgia is the **Dahlonega Bluegrass Festival**, held annually on both the fourth weekend in June and the second weekend in September at Mountain Music Park, on Highway 60 South. For more information, contact Mountain Music Park, P.O. Box 98, Dahlonega, GA 30533.

HELEN: GEORGIA'S BAVARIAN MOUNTAIN TOWN

If one awakened in Helen, one would swear it was not a former Appalachian lumber community, but an alpine village deep in the heart of Bavaria. One observation most certainly would be made, however, and it would be absolutely true. A miracle happened here.

For generations yet to come, folks from all over the South will be talking about the little timber town that refused to die when its mills shut down. They will speak of the legendary Georgia crackers who loved the land, the trees, and the way of life that had sustained them since the region's earliest pioneering times. These folks fought first the Indians, then the Yankees, struggled through the Reconstruction era, and then wrestled with the woods themselves. Through it all, they hung on. When progress came to Helen and didn't treat them very kindly, they set their heels hard, shoved their hands deep in their pockets, lit their pipes and took a long look around. The most obvious attractions were the mountains and the Chattahoochee River, the incredibly beautiful natural backdrop none of them had ever taken for granted.

It was tough, at first, coming up with an idea, particularly when the most human thing to do would have been to get scared and think about moving on. Instead, these hill people started talking among themselves, then with their merchants and other business leaders. Then came the town meetings. Finally, somebody thought of the tourists who were already making the trip up to Unicoi State Park and into the Chattahoochee National Forest. An artist by the name of John Kollock said it all reminded him of time he'd spent in Germany, and he sat down at his drawing board and made a few sketches, which he showed around. What his friends and neighbors saw was their town as it might exist in Bavaria. After some more heel settin' and pipe smokin', Helen's citizens decided they liked it, nodded among themselves, and said, "Let's do 'er." Out came the hammers, saws, the paint, the muscles and the sweat.

The transformation officially started in January 1969, and by 1971, the entire town looked as though a Bavarian fairy godmother had waved her magic wand over it and created a likeness that made her devoutly homesick. Today, the storefronts, shops and many private homes have those steeply pitched roofs, gingerbread fronts, and flowerboxes so typical of the Old Country. The alleys are cobbled and there are wall murals everywhere. Many of the signs and business names are in German or Gothic lettering.

This magic, however, is more than cosmetic. Helen doesn't just look Bavarian, it acts Bavarian. Every weekend, from early September to mid-October, the townsfolk don their lederhosen, feathered caps, embroidered dirndl skirts and braids for a series of celebrations typical of Oktoberfests from Dresden to Mannheim and back to Berlin itself. Restaurants carry German cuisine, the little brass bands with their oom-pah-pah tubas and polka trumpets serenade dancers in the streets and have special exhibitions in the pavilion. That famous German dark beer flows freely as well, and an eighteen-bell glockenspiel, one of the largest in the United States, peals popular and seasonal music several times daily.

For four weekends in January and February, Helen celebrates with its Fasching Karnival. Then, the various restaurants and lounges host festive masquerade balls. Each party has a different theme. The highlight is the unmasking at the end of the evening. Fasching is a religious holiday that originated in Austria over 3,000 years ago and celebrated the New Year. Costumes and masks resemble the fierce Nordic gods who, it was believed, joined the festivities in more human form. In April, Helen holds its Trout Festival; its Maifest in May; and over the Fourth of July, a celebration which includes the famed Chattahoochee River Tube Parade. In late November, the Christmas tree lights are lit. This holiday is particularly touching and those fortunate enough to visit then will hear carols like *Oh Christmas Tree*, *Silent Night* and others rendered in the original German.

As if that was not enough, Helen is the home of the Museum of the Hills. Located on Main Street, this attraction preserves Helen's Appalachian legacy by depicting the life of the hill country people with wax figures and taped dialogue. The other half of the museum, Fantasy Dreamland, recreates settings from fairy tales and nursery rhymes. Many a child of Dixie has had sweet dreams after visiting this one. The community also abounds with craft and antique shops, and has preserved vaudeville with its River Palace revues.

Helen is centrally located, making it convenient for excursions to several state parks, including Unicoi, a mile northwest. The Richard B. Russell Scenic Highway runs through the Chattahoochee National Forest between Helen and Neel's Gap, and is particularly beautiful in autumn.

For more information, contact the Greater Helen Chamber of Commerce, P.O. Box 192, Helen, GA 30545; (404) 878-2181.

MACON

This community of 122,000 is the third largest city in Georgia and lies seventy-five miles south of Atlanta. A major transportation center, it forms the nexus of two interstates, four U.S. highways and seven state highways. It is also well served by the Macon Municipal Airport. With fifty-four structures on the National Register of Historic places, two Heritage Walking tours and a Heritage Driving Tour, it is a fine place to experience Southern history as portrayed by its architecture. It is centrally located for easy access to such attractions at Andersonville National Historic Site, Georgia Veterans Memorial State Park, Piedmont National Wildlife Refuge, Oconee National Forest, and others.

ATTRACTIONS

• The best place to start any "exploration" of Macon is the **Macon Convention and Visitors Bureau**. In addition to loads of information about this fascinating city, this is the place to pick up an outstanding brochure entitled, "Historic Macon." The Bureau is housed in the contemporary **Macon Coliseum**. This 10,000-seat capacity edifice hosts concerts, conventions, automobile and boat shows, ice shows, and sporting events. It is located on 200 Coliseum Drive, and for more information, either drop in at the Coliseum, or contact the Macon Convention & Visitors Bureau, P.O. Box 6354, Macon, GA 31208-6354; (912) 743-3401.

• **Ocmulgee National Monument** commemorates over 10,000 years of human habitation. Located seventeen miles east of the city on the Macon Plateau, the site's 683 acres consist of several mounds of different heights and circumferences. Archaeologists consider it one of the most significant finds in North America and have traced it back to several eras.

Apparently, the first natives of the region were nomadic hunters who established camps some 90 to 100 centuries ago. The Archaic people are believed to have lived in the region between 9,000-10,000 BC, and differed from their predecessors in advanced hunting technology, for remnants of a contextually sophisticated spear-thrower have been found here. The Woodland peoples, circa 1,000 BC-900 AD, were cultivators of squash, gourds, corn and beans, and it was they who established the first permanent villages.

The Mississippians are another group believed to have been "western invaders" who apparently integrated into the existing culture without warfare. These farmers planted extensively, lived in large population centers, and developed a complex culture which devoted at least a portion of its energies to the arts. They lived in the region from 900-1100 AD. Those who followed them appear to have built upon the Mississippians and may have been the predecessors of the Creek Indians. The Lamars lived in the region from about 1350-1600 AD.

The Creek Indians were the final native settlers and their large commercial center was established for trade with the British. The village was abandoned after their defeat during the Yamassee War, in 1715.

Evidence of all of these cultures is on display at the visitor center, which also provides extensive literature on the site and a short film, entitled *People of the Macon Plateau*. For more information, contact Office of the Superintendent, Ocmulgee National Monument, 1207 Emery Highway, Macon, GA 31201; (912) 752-8257.

• **The Museum of Arts and Sciences** features three major galleries devoted to changing exhibits of art, and exhibits of culture and science, fossil zygorhiza, rock and mineral displays, and a collection of reptiles, small mammals, birds, and insects. The site includes a nature trail and the turn of the century studio of Macon author **Harry Stillwell Edwards**. The museum is, as well, the home of the **Mark Smith Planetarium**, second largest in the state. Here, quadrophonic sound and several special effects projectors literally bring the universe to life. This is also a great place for a picnic. For more information, contact Museum of Arts and Sciences, 3182 Forsyth Road, Macon, GA 31210; (912) 477-3232.

• One of Macon's antebellum homes was struck by a cannonball which ricocheted off a column, smashed through a window, and came to rest in the main hallway. The damage was repaired and the home has been fully restored. Its servant quarters contains a fine Confederate museum. For more information, contact **Old Cannonball House and Macon Confederate Museum**, 856 Mulberry Street, Macon, GA 31202; (912) 745-5982.

• The **Piedmont National Wildlife Refuge**, 32,000 acres on the east bank of the Ocmulgee River, lies due north of Macon and includes the community of Gladesville. It provides an outstanding opportunity to glimpse, watch, photograph and study representative species of regional animal, bird, plant and fish life. For more information, contact Refuge Manager, Piedmont National Wildlife Refuge, Round Oak, GA 31080; (912) 986-3651.

• **The Macon City Auditorium**, site of much of the city's cultural activity, boasts the world's largest copper-covered dome. The structure, completed in 1925 and extensively restored in 1979, can be easily recognized by its limestone Doric columns. For more information, contact Macon City Auditorium, Cherry and First Street, Macon, GA 31201; (912) 744-7643.

• Those who visited Sidney Lanier Lake, north of Atlanta, might want to visit the birth home of Georgia's famous poet and the author of *The Marshes of Glynn* and *Song of the Chattahoochee*. This 1842 Victorian cottage is also the home of the **Middle Georgia Historical Society**, which hosts slide shows for tour groups, and runs the gift shop. For more information, contact **Sidney Lanier Cottage**, 935 High Street, Macon, GA 31202; (912) 743-3851.

• **The Grand Opera House** is one attraction which no visitor to Macon can leave the city without seeing. Built in 1884, it was famous throughout the South for its elegance. It seats 1057, and past audiences have witnessed performances by such legendary greats as Will Rogers, Dame Sarah Bernhardt and the Gish sisters. It has been completely restored and is open for tours. For more information, contact Grand Opera House, 651 Mulberry Street, Macon, GA 31202; (912) 745-7925.

• **Brown and Williamson Tobacco Corporation** offers tours of its production area and a film on the industry. For more information, contact Brown and Williamson, P.O. Box 1056, Macon, GA 31298; (912) 743-0561.

• Those interested in seeing how bread and rolls are mass produced and packaged will enjoy **Colonial Baking Company's**

Day Trips from Atlanta

tour. For more information, contact Russell McClain, Colonial Baking Co., 2743 Montpelier Avenue, Macon, GA 31213; (912) 746-1303.

EVENT

- Each year, during the third week in March, Macon's 50,000 blossoming Yoshino cherry trees are the centerpiece for the **Macon Cherry Blossom Festival.** This is a memorable festival, comprised of many fun activities, including arts and children's festivals, a street party, hot air rides and races, auto races, an international food fair, concerts, evening torchlight walks, historic tours, a parade, a square dance, a ball, and a fantastic fireworks display. For more information, contact the Convention and Visitors Bureau.

Day Trips from Atlanta

THE STATE PARK LOOP

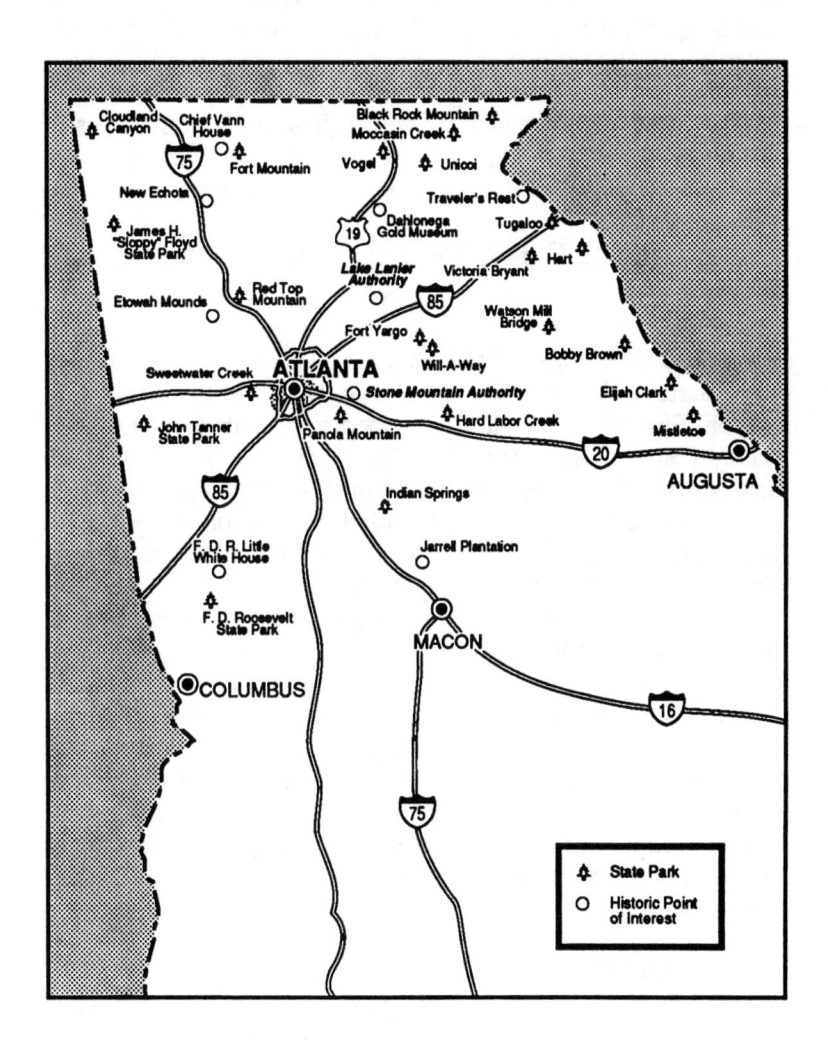

Whether your trip to the Atlanta area is for vacation or business, you will want to complete your visit by exploring at least a few of the numerous state parks and historical sites within easy driving distance. It would probably also be very helpful to be familiar with general aspects of these attractions, and what fees one can expect to pay. With this in mind, we have included a foreword detailing some factors of the parks. The following information is current for 1988 and, although subject to change, will provide a close approximation.

GENERAL INFORMATION ABOUT STATE PARKS

CAMPING AND FACILITIES

State park cottages come in one, two, and three bedroom models. Sunday - Thursday, a one bedroom rents for $35/a day; Friday - Saturday, $45/per day. Two bedrooms, $45/$55; Three bedrooms, $55/$65. Special camps for the handicapped, known as Will-a-way camps, are an added feature of many parks. These cottages are two bedrooms, $30 per day all week. There is also a $10 surcharge for one night visits.

Note: Rates for Unicoi Lodge are slightly higher, so check with that one.

Campsites vary, as well. Tent/Pop-up/RV campsites cost $8 flat rate; Walk-in campsites & Squirrel's Nest, $5; Pioneer Campsites, $1 per person, with a $10 minimum. Primitive camping is $3 per person. Reservation fee for campsites (30 days in advance only) is $5. This includes RV's, tents and pop-ups. Group camps run $3 per person per day. Each camp has a different minimum. Will-a-way group camps run $7.50 per person per day.

ACTIVITIES

Group shelters with a 50-person capacity cost $50 per day; 80-person capacity, $65; 175-person capacity, $80. Swimming pools cost $1.75 per person per day to use; beaches, $1.25 per person. Miniature golf costs $1.25 per person per round, with three games for $3; and ten games for $10. Regular golf costs $11 for greens fees; golf carts range from $12 for 18 holes for the power models and $7 for nine holes to $2.50 for the pull models for 18 holes and $1.50 for nine holes.

Fishing boats and canoes rent for $2.50 for one hour; $7 for four hours and $12 for eight hours.

For a boat, motor and one tank of gas, for four hours you'll pay $15; for eight hours, $25. Pedal boats rent by the half hour at $1.25 per person.

Bicycles are available at $1.50 for one hour; $4 for four hours and $7 for eight hours.

Tennis is $2 per one and a half hours during the day; $3 per one and a half hours at night.

HISTORIC SITES

Admission for adults runs $1-1.50; for children twelve and under, $.50-.75, and for children five and under, admission is free.

HOURS, SEASONS AND OTHER INFORMATION

All state parks are open year around from 7 a.m. - 10 p.m., except for Panola Mountain, which is open Sept. 15 - Apr. 14 from 7 a.m. - 6 p.m.; and Apr. 15 - Sept. 14, 7 a.m. - 9 p.m. Historic Sites are open Tues. - Sat., 9 a.m. - 5 p.m.; Sunday, 2 p.m. - 5:30 p.m. and are closed Mondays (except legal holidays), Christmas, and Thanksgiving.

Swimming is open June 1 through Labor Day and overnight guests must pay the regular swimming fee.

For any additional information, call the Department of Natural Resources Communications Office, toll free in Georgia at 1-800-3GA-PARK; in Atlanta, 656-3530; and from out of state you may call toll free, 1-800-5GA-PARK.

THE LOOP

For a trip which could take several days, and which will access virtually all of the Atlanta area state parks and historic sites, one might want to begin by taking Interstate 75 north to Red Top Mountain.

Day Trips from Atlanta

Some forty-seven miles north of Atlanta, on the shores of Lake Allatoona, this 1,726-acre peninsula is named for the soil, which has a high iron ore content. The countryside is hilly and leans to loblolly pines, oaks and dogwoods. These forests are home to deer, squirrels, rabbits and raccoon.

Bass and crappie make for good fishing, and boating is also popular here. The park features a marina, five docks, four ramps and a sandy beach with a bath house. Hiking is a favorite activity as well; there are some seven miles of nature trails. Other facilities include 286 tent and trailer sites, eighteen cottages, tennis courts and miniature golf. There are also some old iron mines. In October, there is an arts and crafts show. For more information, contact Red Top Mountain State Park, 781 Red Top Mountain Road, S.E., Cartersville, GA 30120; (404) 974-5182.

Almost due east of Red Top Mountain are the remains of an ancient civilization. Officially designated Etowah Indian Mounds, this historic site goes back to 1000 A.D. The mounds are the remains of worship sites and entombed within them are the nobility of the Etowah tribe.

Not much is known of this civilization, which vanished around 1500 A.D. It is known they believed in an after life and some of the artifacts buried in the mounds—and now on display at the Etowah Museum—indicate a relatively high degree of sophistication.

Several thousand Etowahs lived in the immediate area and what is preserved includes objects of stone, wood, seashells and copper. A slide show depicts what archaeologists have deduced about them and research is being conducted even today. In the spring, the site holds Indian Skills Day; in April and November, Artifacts Identification Day, and throughout the year, there are special astronomy programs. For more information, contact Etowah Mounds State Historic Site, 813 Indian Mounds Road, S.W., Cartersville, GA 30120; (404) 382-2704.

Continuing north on Interstate 75, one encounters another famous Indian historic site, New Echota State Historic Site. Particularly for those with a reverence for Native American culture, this attraction is interesting, for it was here, in 1825,

Day Trips from Atlanta

that the Cherokee nation established its capital. Yet a thriving community, much of this proud people's heritage—though they were eventually forced west on the legendary Trail of Tears in 1838-39—has been preserved.

The site consists of the reconstructed print shop, where a page of the bilingual newspaper, the *Cherokee Phoenix*, founded in 1828, some seven years after the establishment of their written language, can be read. The Supreme Court house, the original home of missionary Samuel A. Worcester, and the log Vann's Tavern are here as well. A slide show and numerous museum exhibits round out the site.

New Echota is located one mile east of Interstate 75, on Highway 225. Take Exit 131. For more information, contact New Echota State Historic Site, 1211 Chatsworth Highway, N.E., Calhoun, GA 30701; (404) 629-8151.

East of New Echota is Amicalola Falls State Park. Situated twenty miles west of Dahlonega, the best way to get there is to take State Highway 52 west at the junction of Routes 19 and 52 in Dahlonega. Amicalola features the highest waterfalls in the state. The name means, in Cherokee, tumbling waters and it describes these seven cascades which fall 729 feet. An eight mile trail from Amicalola Falls to Springer Mountain marks the southern end of that famous path from Georgia to Maine, the 2,150 mile Appalachian Trail.

This is Blue Ridge Mountain country and Amicalola is spread out over 700 acres of thick oak, hickory, maple and beech forests. In spring, the dogwood and mountain laurel along Amicalola Falls Gorge are especially beautiful.

The park features seventeen tent and trailer sites, a sixty-room lodge and meeting center, three playgrounds, five picnic shelters and rental cottages. Trout fishing is popular here, as well as hiking and camping. In April there is a Spring Wildflower Festival; in July, the Independence Arts and Crafts show; and August sports a bow hunter's rendezvous. For more information, contact Amicalola Falls State Park, Star Route, Dawsonville, GA 30534; (404) 265-2885.

Back on Interstate 75 and then east on State Route 52 is an attraction known as the showplace of the Cherokee Nation. It is, of course, the historic Chief Vann House. The beautiful, two-

Day Trips from Atlanta

story, brick and white columned and porticoed mansion was inhabited by Chief James Vann of the Cherokee Nation.

Finished in 1804, it features some exquisite examples of Cherokee carvings and in every way is a tribute to the leader who brought Moravian missionaries to his nation to teach the children. Vann was a colorful figure who killed his brother-in-law in a duel in 1808 and was himself killed a year later. Moravian Christmas is celebrated here, and in July, Chief Vann House Days.

For more information, contact The Vann House State Historic Site, Route 7, Box 7655, Chatsworth, GA 30705; (404) 695-2598.

Continuing east on State Route 52 (Interstate 75 Exit 136) is Fort Mountain State Park. This 1,930-acre site is named for a mysterious 885-foot long wall encircling the mountain and believed to have been erected in the 1100s. The wall is but two feet high and, in places, twelve feet wide. Other sources say it was built by the Spanish explorer Hernando De Soto, and still others, by the British during the Revolutionary War. The mountain itself stands 2,855 feet high and is heavily forested with oaks, mountain laurels, hickories, pines, rhododendrons, dogwoods, sourwood, red maples and wild azaleas. The park includes, slightly below the summit, a seventeen-acre lake ideal for bass and trout fishing. The lake has a beach where pedal boats are available for rent. There are twelve miles of hiking trails and other facilities include seventy tent and trailer sites, fifteen cottages, and miniature golf. In the spring,

Day Trips from Atlanta

there is a Spring Wildflowers celebration; in August, Fort Mountain Mysteries, and in October, an overnight backcountry trip. For more information, contact Fort Mountain State Park, Box 1K, Route 7, Chatsworth, GA 30705; (404) 695-2621.

Continue east on State Route 52, then catch U.S. Highway 76 north through some of the prettiest Blue Ridge country in Chattahoochee National Forest. At Blairsville, the junction of U.S. 76, U.S. 19, and U.S. 129, turn south for eight miles and there one comes upon the beautiful, truly mountainous, 250-acre Vogel State Park.

This one is forested in oaks, maples, beeches, mountain laurels, white pines and cedars. Considered the gateway to the Appalachian Trail, it includes a half-mile nature trail, seventeen miles of hiking trails, 100 tent and trailer sites, thirty-six rental cottages, and a twenty-one acre lake fronted by a swimming beach and stocked annually with 400 eight to ten inch rainbow trout.

Vogel is also known for its authentic mountain music programs. Other activities include basketball, baseball, badminton, miniature golf, pedal boat rentals, primitive camping, family group shelters and picnicking.

In April, the park hosts a Wildflower program; in August, the region celebrates Old Timers Day, and there are other seasonal festivals in the neighborhood. For a true taste of Appalachia, this is one of the best.

For more information, contact Vogel State Park, Route 1, Box 1230, Blairsville, GA 30512; (404) 745-2628.

By returning to Blairsville and continuing some twenty-four miles east on U.S. Highway 76, one can reach Moccasin Creek State Park.

This small site of thirty-two acres is tucked away on the shores of Lake Burton and is used by many as a base camp for further hiking, camping and backpacking into the high country. This park has a trout hatchery nearby, the two-mile Moccasin Trail, and stream fishing for senior citizens and children under twelve.

Facilities include fifty-three tent and trailer sites, a boat dock and ramp, a wheelchair accessible fishing pier, a playground and an open air pavilion. In June, there's a trout

Day Trips from Atlanta

program and contest, and in August, the area celebrates the Lake Burton Arts and Crafts Festival. For more information, contact Moccasin Creek State Park, Route 1, Lake Burton, Clarkesville, GA 30523; (404) 947-3194.

Continuing still a bit further east, one reaches U.S. Highway 23 and by turning north at Clayton, and driving three miles, one reaches Black Rock Mountain State Park.

The high point of this one, literally, is 3,600-foot Black Rock Mountain, so named because its summit is composed of dark granite. The view from that summit is spectacular, for this is Georgia's highest state park. The Talmadge Trail runs from Mountain City to the top of the mountain. Load up with film before starting out and take pictures of the three states you'll see from there: Georgia, South Carolina and North Carolina. The 1,500 acres of this park are forested in oaks, hickories, honey locusts, pines and tulip trees. This is also one of the better state parks for experiencing wildlife, for residents here include black bear, deer and foxes.

The park has an eighteen acre lake reserved entirely for fishing only. Hiking is also a favored activity, with some eight miles of trails. This is where the Tennessee Rock, Waterfall and James E. Edmonds trails are located.

Black Rock Mountain enjoys celebrating mountain culture with a host of programs and a Pioneer Day celebration in August. Pioneer and primitive camping are also highly favored. Facilities include fifty-four tent and trailer sites, ten rental cottages, a playground and two picnic shelters.

Day Trips from Atlanta

In May there is a wildflower fest and there is also an overnight backpacking trip every autumn. For more information, contact Black Rock Mountain State Park, Mountain City, GA 30562; (404) 746- 2141.

Well, now it's time to swing south on U.S. 23 (U.S. 441) toward, more or less, Atlanta. The next sixty miles are relaxing and very picturesque. They end at Athens, and then it's west nineteen miles on U.S. 29 to the town of Winder and Fort Yargo State Park.

This 1,850 acre Piedmont site features one of the four blockhouses the colonials built in 1792 to defend themselves against the resident Cherokees and Creeks. Facilities here include 40 tent and trailer sites, a 250-person group camp, 3 cottages, and a 260-acre lake with a beach.

This is Georgia marsh country. Wildlife programs, especially the weekend before National Wildlife Week, focus on the birdlife. Here, great blue herons, egrets, several species of ducks and red-tailed hawks make their homes. The lake is good fishing for catfish, crappie, bream and bass. The dock area has canoe and pedal boat rentals.

Fort Yargo likes its music and celebrates Bluegrass festivals on the Memorial and Labor day weekends. Picnicking is also popular here and the park has five shelters with 116 tables, and two family/group shelters. Miniature golf and tennis are also enjoyed here. Also included within the park is a recreation area with special facilities for the handicapped.

When you reach Winder, take State Highway 81, one mile south. For more information, contact Fort Yargo State Park, Winder, GA 30680; (404) 867-3489.

At this point, the loop heads west again to the junction of State Highway 316 and Interstate 85 and then, just two miles south of Sandy Springs, heads south again toward Stone Mountain Park and catches State Highway 155, off Exit 36 of Interstate 20. The destination is Panola Mountain State Conservation Park, a portion of which is a 100-acre granite monadnock which compares very favorably to Stone Mountain, except that it isn't bald. You'll enjoy this one because it has a good cross section of Piedmont plants and animals. Its nature programs and guided hikes feature these, which are set among

Day Trips from Atlanta

some beautiful forests and incredible wildflower spreads. The kids will love the educational programs on the ecology of the mountain and the forest floor. There are, in all, some six miles of hiking trails. A relatively small state park, Panola Mountain's 617 acres include a picnic area with four shelters and an interpretive center. Wildflower walks are the chief spring and autumn attractions. For more information, contact Panola Mountain State Park, 2600 Highway 155 S.W., Stockbridge, GA 30281; (404) 474-2914. This also makes a nice excursion if you're headed into Jonesboro and further south to Andersonville Prison National Park. Those going south to the National Park and Cemetery have the opportunity to visit High Falls State Park. Located 1.8 miles east of Interstate 75 from Exit 65, this 995-acre site was once a prosperous village with a grist mill, cotton gin, blacksmith shop, shoe factory and hotel. When a major railroad bypassed it, it lost its population and is today the site of a 650-acre lake and the Towaliga River. Facilities there include 142 tent and trailer sites, a swimming pool and beach, a miniature golf course, two beautiful natural and historic trails and an enchanting waterfall. For more information, contact High Falls State Park, Route 5, Box 108, Jackson, GA 30233; (912) 994-5080.

Four miles east of Jackson, on State Route 42, is Indian Springs State Park. This beautiful site offers ninety tent and trailer sites, ten cottages, a swimming beach, pedal boat rentals, fishing, and plenty of boating facilities. For more information, contact Indian Springs State Park, Indian Springs, GA 30231; (404) 775-7241.

The Jarrell Plantation State Historic Site, eighteen miles east of Interstate 75 off the Forsyth (61) Exit, and eighteen miles northwest of Macon, is a beautiful example of a Georgia plantation. It consists of twenty buildings built between 1847 and 1940. This is one of the most complete restorations of its kind in the state. For more information, contact Jarrell Plantation State Historic Site, Route 1, Box 40, Juliette, GA 31046; (912) 986-5172.

For the rest of us not headed south, however, it is time to turn north again back into the heart of Atlanta for a bit of freshening up. Then we take Interstate 20 west for the last two attractions on our tour of Atlanta area state parks.

The first of these is Sweetwater Creek, a 1,986-acre spot with a special beauty all its own. It is reached via the Thornton Road exit from I-20 and by then driving one-quarter mile, turning right onto Blairs Bridge Road, then left onto Mount Vernon Road and proceeding straight ahead until you bump into the park itself.

This one features the remnants of the New Manchester Manufacturing Company, a textile mill dating back to around the middle of the nineteenth century. Lake and stream fishing is available, and the George Sparks Reservoir has two fishing docks. The hiking, some five miles of nature trail, is hauntingly pretty, especially in the warmer months, when the wildflowers are in bloom and the trees give off their own special perfume.

As might be imagined, picnicking is popular here and Sweetwater Creek has nine shelters. This is where many Atlantans go for outdoor gatherings and a barbecue pit has been created for that purpose. The park is also the site of an annual arts and crafts show held over Memorial Day weekend, and for nature programs which run all year long.

For more information, contact Sweetwater Creek State Conservation Park, P.O. Box 816, Lithia Springs, GA 30057; (404) 994-1700.

The last stop on our tour is forty miles west of Atlanta and ten miles east of the Alabama state line. From Sweetwater Creek, return to Interstate 20 and drive west about thirty-three miles to Bowdon Junction. Here, you'll catch U.S. Highway 27 south and then head the nine miles to Carrollton. John Tanner State Park is six miles west of Carrollton just of State Highway 16. These 136 acres offer some of the finest recreation in the greater Atlanta area. Set among moderately rugged terrain—hills covered with oaks, hickories, pines, dogwood, and tulip trees—the park includes two lakes, one of which has the largest sand beach in the state park system. It includes a bath house and paddleboat and canoe rentals. The surrounding marshes are literally infested with wild birds, particularly

Day Trips from Atlanta

mallards and wood ducks, and the wildflower riots must be experienced to be believed.

Yes, this is definitely one to spend the night in, and approximately seventy-eight tent and trailer sites, a group lodge, and a six unit motor lodge make that more than feasible. A half mile nature trail provides plenty of exercise, and bicycles are also available for rent. For the little duffers, miniature golf is also featured.

With its proximity to Alabama, its May bluegrass festival is one of the best in the state, and in September, the region turns out en masse for the John Tanner Arts and Crafts show. This is also a good park any time of the year.

For more information, contact John Tanner State Park, 354 Tanner's Beach Road, Carollton, GA 30117; (404) 832-7545. For more information about the Georgia State Park system, specific festival dates, and any improvements or new facilities, contact the Georgia Department of Natural Resources, Communications Office, 205 Butler Street, S.E., Suite 1258, Atlanta, GA 30334.

Although our tour is officially over, there are two more outstanding state parks that are worth mentioning. For those wishing to take in two more of these wilderness jewels, it's time to head north again, on a route paralleling the one you took to visit Etowah Mounds and Red Top Mountain. James H. "Sloppy" Floyd State Park can be reached by taking U.S. 27 to Rome, then heading northwest to Summerville. This 269-acre recreational gem includes two lakes totaling fifty-one acres and is named for a contemporary Georgia state congressman who served from 1953 until his death in 1974. Surrounded by the Chattahoochee National Forest, it offers twenty-five tent and trailer sites, a playground, two picnic shelters, two boat ramps, two fishing docks and all the hiking the expansive Chattahoochee National Forest has to offer. For more information, contact James H. "Sloppy" Floyd State Park, Route 1, Summerville, GA 30747; (404) 857-5211.

And now, for the last of what we hope has been the outdoor experience of your life. Cloudland Canyon State Park can be reached by taking State Route 136 from U.S. 27 north of LaFayette. This 2,120-acre park is sited on the western slopes of Lookout Mountain and spreads out over a deep gorge created by Sitton Gulch Creek. Elevations here range between 800-1,800 feet. There are seventy-five tent and trailer sites, a forty-bed group camp, sixteen rental cottages, thirty walk-in campsites, a winterized group shelter, tennis courts, picnicking sites, a swimming pool and six miles of backcountry trails. The park hosts Crafts in the Clouds and a wildflower program in May, and sponsors an overnight backpacking trip in October. For more information, contact Cloudland Canyon State Park, Route 2, Box 150, Rising Fawn, GA 30738; (404) 657-4050.

UNICOI STATE PARK AND CHATTAHOOCHEE NATIONAL FOREST

If you've decided to visit Helen, you'll definitely want to spend some time in Unicoi State Park. It's located in the Chattahoochee National Forest about 100 miles northeast of Atlanta. To get there from Helen, go one mile northwest on Georgia State Highway 75, then turn east on State 356 for three miles. This will put you in the heart of 1,000 acres of that magnificent Appalachian mountain country that made Helen so inspiring.

The countryside here is wooded with pines and poplars, hemlocks and oaks, lots of mountain laurels and rhododendrons Here you'll also find sparkling Unicoi Lake, with its two serene swimming beaches and a marina which rents rowboats and canoes during the summer. The fishing here is great.

Unicoi Park has two types of lodgings. The Unicoi Lodge and Conference Center has 100 rooms arranged in four groupings, each with a common room and a fireplace. Each is suitable for a conference. The guest rooms and common rooms are modern, well appointed and cedar paneled. Some of the guest rooms have lofts; all have carpeting, individual "climate controls," a telephone and a private bath. The lodge complex has a very nice restaurant, replete with chandeliers and natural wood walls. There are also twenty-five cottages, twenty of which are set in the pines near the lake. Of teardrop, barrel or chalet design, they are set on stilts and range in size from one to three bedrooms. Twenty have a porch and fireplace and can

Day Trips from Atlanta

accommodate four to six people. The other five are on the road to Anna Ruby Falls.

Once you're settled in, you'll want to explore the area and hiking is one of the most popular ways to do it. The fishing is pretty good, too, incidentally. The Appalachian Trail runs nearby, and situated at the north border of the park is the memorable Anna Ruby Falls, on the slopes of Tray Mountain. Smith Creek, which feeds into Unicoi Lake, is itself born of two other streams which form a twin waterfall. Curtis Creek drops 153 feet; York Creek, fifty.

Anna Ruby Falls Park consists of 1,600 acres, and if you like laurel, wild azaleas, dogwood and rhododendron, you'll be in paradise.

The park also has an outstanding craft shop specializing in genuine Appalachian pieces. There are demonstrations of how these are made, and workshops and programs on Appalachian folk culture. You'll also become acquainted with the natural resources of the area, its wildlife and other aspects of the land. The park is also noted for its camping, its nature photography opportunities, and as one of the best places in northern Georgia to backpack in and truly get away from it all. For more information, contact Unicoi State Park, P.O. Box 256, Helen, GA 30545; (404) 878-2201.

Unicoi State Park is located within the vast Chattahoochee National Forest. Encompassing some 749,444 acres, a tiny portion of it was made familiar to millions of Americans who either read James Dickey's novel *Deliverance* or saw the film version starring Burt Reynolds, Jon Voigt and Ned Beatty. The forest is bordered by Cherokee National Forest in Tennessee, Nantahala and Pisgah National forests in North Carolina, and Sumter National Forest in South Carolina.

The mountains here are the southern reaches of the Appalachian and Blue Ridge. Elevations range from around 1,000 feet to Georgia's tallest mountain, 4,784-foot Brasstown Bald. From gentle hills to rugged escarpments, the land is home to pines, oaks, hickories, rhododendrons, mountain laurels and wild azaleas. There is, in fact, a greater diversity of trees here than any other single tract in the United States.

Day Trips from Atlanta

As one might expect, the lakes here are numerous. Among them are Lake Conasauga, atop a mountain; and the famous trout lake named for Mexican War hero Winfield Scott. The Chattooga Wild and Scenic River, in the northeast pocket of Georgia, is where *Deliverance* was filmed.

A seventy mile stretch of the Appalachian Trail passes through the forest from Springer Mountain to Bly Gap in North Carolina and offers eleven shelters, making this attraction one of the premier backpacking places in the entire Southeast. In all, there are twenty-one developed camping areas, fourteen picnicking areas, three wilderness areas and six swimming beaches. In season, hunting is permitted, and game includes black bear, deer, grouse, quail and wild turkeys.

Attractions within the Chattahoochee National Forest include Anna Ruby Falls; the 1,200-foot deep Tallulah Gorge; and Track Rock Gap, a well-preserved rock carving of animal figures, bird tracks, crosses, circles and human footprints.

Lake Rabun Hotel, located across the road from Lake Rabun, is a building of stone and wood dating back to 1922. Lake Rabun has twenty-eight miles of heavily wooded shoreline and a profusion of oaks, white pines, hemlocks and dogwoods. The hotel has sixteen guest rooms, six of which have semi-private baths or half baths. Ten share baths. A large stone fireplace and furniture handmade from rhododendron and mountain laurel branches dominate the lobby. For more information about the Forest, contact Chattahoochee-Oconee National Forest Recreation Area, US Forest Service, 508 Oak Street N.W., Gainesville, GA 30501; (404) 536- 0541, and for the hotel, Lake Rabun Hotel, Lakemont, GA 30552; (404) 782-4946.

CHAPTER THREE: AREAS OF INTEREST OUTSIDE ATLANTA

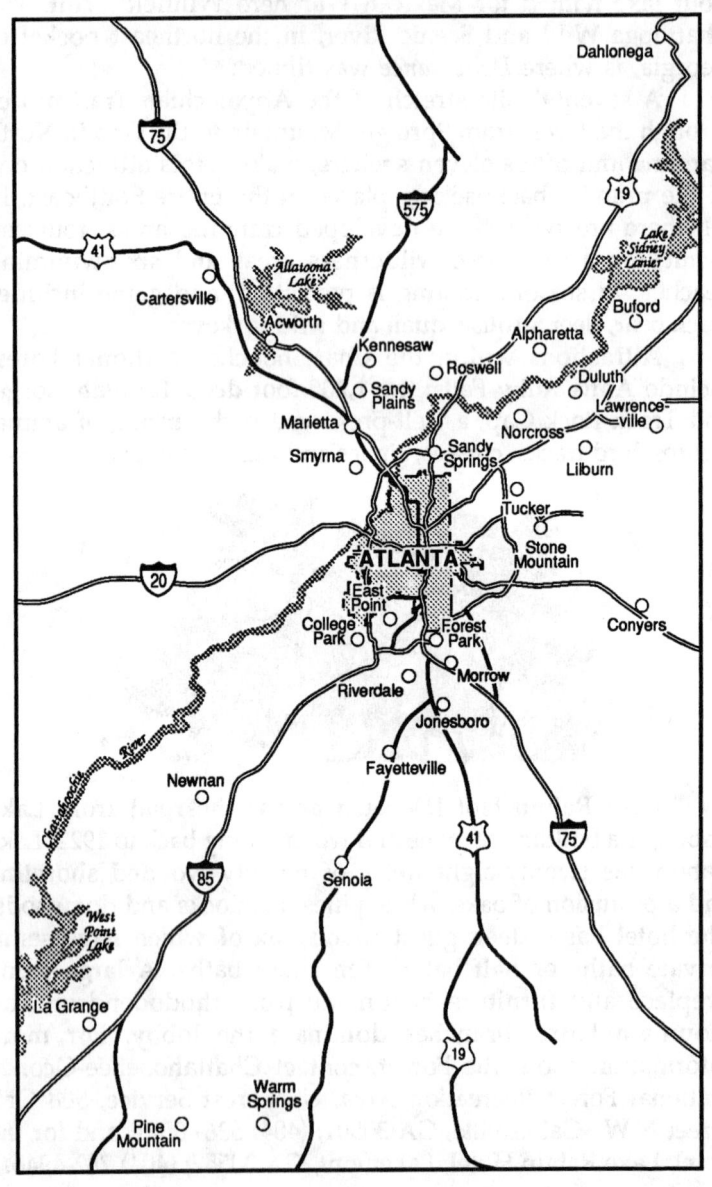

Areas of Interest Outside Atlanta

CARTERSVILLE

North of Allatoona Lake is the town of Cartersville. This community of 10,000 is centrally located to the Etowah Indian Mounds and home of Georgia governor Joe Frank Harris. This is a historical little town with about twenty restaurants and a relaxing forty acre city park. For an exploration of the surrounding area and as a place to stay while enjoying the water sports at Allatoona Lake, Cartersville is hard to beat. For more information, contact Cartersville Tourism & Industry Council, William Weinman Mineral Center and Museum, P.O. Box 1255, Culver Road, Cartersville, GA 30120; (404) 386-0576.

ATTRACTIONS

• Among the major attractions of this community is The **Etowah Arts Gallery**. This one displays extensive collections of oils, watercolors, sculpture, fabrics, pottery, and acrylics by nationally recognized artists. Exhibits rotate every two months. For more information, contact The Etowah Arts Gallery, 13 Wall Street, P.O. Box 672, Cartersville, GA 30120; (404) 382-8277.

• Cartersville is the county seat of mineral rich Bartow County and as such, is the appropriate home for the **Weinman Mineral Center**. Sited in Interchange Village, it is perhaps best known for its life-size model of a limestone cave and waterfall, which visitors can actually "explore". Hands-on exhibits cover mining and Indian history, fossils and geology. The gem collection includes the elusive amethyst. Films, slides, and other media combinations make this one a "must see" in Cartersville. A gift shop on the premises allows you to take a bit of the museum with you. For more information, contact Weinman Mineral Center, P.O. Box 1255, Culver Road, Cartersville, GA 30120; (404) 386-0576.

• Cartersville's community museum is located in the home of evangelist Samuel Porter Jones and includes manicured lawns, gardens, several outbuildings, and a spacious home dating back to the late nineteenth century. The museum is upstairs. For more information, contact **Roselawn Museum**, West Cherokee Street, Cartersville, GA 30120; (404) 386-0300.

- The **Etowah Valley Historical Society** maintains its offices and museum in the 1866-era **Wofford-Hall-White Home**, which is furnished in the period and contains a complete collection of antebellum artifacts. These folks are also the ones to contact for a full rundown on Cartersville's historical offerings. For more information, contact the Etowah Valley Historical Society, Wofford-Hall-White Home, West Cherokee Street, Cartersville, GA 30120; (404) 386-0576.

- **Georgia Power Company**'s general facility gives a one to four hour tour, replete with audio-visual presentations, lectures and slide presentations. For more information, contact Public Relations Department, Plant Bowen, Georgia Power Company, P.O. Box 4545, Atlanta, GA 30302; (404) 526-7848. Two weeks notice is required.

- There's always something going on at the **Cartersville Civic Center**. This one has seating for 700 and banquet dining for 500. Four other meeting rooms accommodate twenty to fifty. For more information, contact Cartersville Tourism and Industrial Council, P.O. Box 1255, Cartersville, GA 30120; (404) 386-0576.

RESORT

SOUTHWIND HEALTH RESORT
Route 2, Sandown Road
Cartersville, GA 30120
Tel. (404) 975-0342
      (800) 832-2622
Visa, MasterCard and AMEX are accepted.

Spend a day, a weekend or a week at this first class spa for women. Owner-Director Doreen MacAdams, a registered nurse with a Masters of Science degree from Columbia

Areas of Interest Outside Atlanta

University, offers a total rejuvenation package of gourmet low calorie meals, fitness classes on an individual level, twelve seminar topics and pampering, which includes facials, massages, make up, manicures, pedicures and much more.

The setting is a nineteenth century country Victorian home on sixteen acres overlooking Lake Alatoona. In a beautiful and tranquil environment, Southwind provides personalized attention and caring because only sixteen guests are there at a time. The gourmet low calorie meals are fabulous and Chef Mary Roegee conducts cooking classes during the programs. The Southwind Cuisine cookbook is available and offers Southwind cuisine in easy to prepare menu format.

The goal at Southwind is to motivate each person on an individual level and offer nutritional counseling and exercise guidance to help you lead a healthy, energetic life. Southwind is a unique experience because they focus on every level: physical, intellectual, spiritual and emotional. Truly "an escape from reality," this is a wonderful gift for all women so treat her with one of the gift certificates that are available.

FAYETTEVILLE

This community of 4,500 is located within easy driving distance of the Hartsfield International Airport, deep in the heart of Georgia's Piedmont antebellum country. Named after the French nobleman who served with the Continental Army during the Revolutionary War and later visited the region, the community is history itself, and the past is one of the major draws of this most charming little town.

ATTRACTIONS

- The oldest operating courthouse in the state is located in Fayetteville. For more information, contact the **Fayette County Courthouse**, Courthouse Square, Fayetteville, GA 30214; (404) 461-6041.

Areas of Interest Outside Atlanta

- Historians and writers know Fayetteville well, for the library there houses one of the most complete archives of the Civil War period, as well as notes and other memorabilia associated with the immortal novel *Gone With the Wind*. For more information, contact the **Margaret Mitchell Library**, Lee Street, Fayetteville, GA 30214; (404) 461-8841.
- When **The Fife House** housed the **Fayetteville Academy**, Scarlett O'Hara "attended it". It is considered the oldest unrenovated antebellum home in Georgia and one of the most enduring in all of Dixie. For a tour schedule and more information, contact the Fife House, 140 Lanier Street, Fayetteville, GA 30214; (404) 461-8564.

For more information on Fayetteville and its various offering, contact the Fayette County Chamber of Commerce, P.O. Box 276, Fayetteville, GA 30214; (404) 461-9983.

CRAFTS

THE STATUS THIMBLE
692 North Glynn Street
Fayetteville, GA 30214
Tel. (404) 461-3286
Hrs: Mon. - Sat. 10:00 a.m. - 5:00 p.m.
Visa, MasterCard and Discover are accepted.

Fancy needlework is an art form, practiced by women of past generations and coming back in interest as new generations discover its beauty. That discovery begins at the large window of this spacious needlework specialty shop in Fayetteville, where a variety of hand smocked dresses and samples of cross-stitching catch the eye.

Inside, you are treated to ideas by the dozens of what can be done with needlework. Julia Windham, a craftsperson who creates many of the dresses seen in the window, has gathered countless examples of needlework in the shop. There are samples of lace dresses, hand smocked clothing and antique garments. They are there for ideas, or for purchase. The Status Thimble offers classes all year long. Through patient instruction, Mrs. Windham shares her talents and the special techniques she has learned. "I have a love for what I do," she explains. It shows in the appreciation of the customers, who enjoy the needle work as much as their teacher. The shop is also a place for custom designed clothing which makes use of fancy stitches and the finest materials. There is a mail order service for folks living out of the Fayetteville area who want to take advantage of the stock. It includes a wide selection of French laces, Swiss embroideries, Irish linens, and other fabrics which are often hard to find. There are embroidery flosses, books with ideas and patterns, and about 500 smocking plates. Ribbons and lace, threads and patterns are all here at this unique specialty store.

The Status Thimble is worth traveling to if you are interested in needlework. This is the place for ideas and supplies, a place to add to your list of contacts for patterns, supplies and techniques used on heirloom work.

GIFT SHOP

GREAT TEMPTATIONS - GIFTS FOR YOU AND YOUR HOME
174 Banks Crossing Shopping Center
Fayetteville, GA 30214
Tel. (404) 461-1657
Hrs: Mon. - Sat. 10:00 a.m. - 7:00 p.m.
         Sunday   1:00 p.m. - 5:00 p.m.
Extended holiday hours.
Visa, MasterCard, AMEX and Discover are accepted.

Great Temptations - Gifts for You and Your Home carries a wide selection of collectibles for the serious collector. The shop's impressive 4,000 square feet of floor space is filled with sunlight and hundreds of delightful, sought after collectibles.

Areas of Interest Outside Atlanta

The most important collectibles of today are available at Great Temptations. An extensive collection of Tom Clark's Gnomes dance on the shelves. There are Raikes Bears, and collectible dolls by Gorham, Effanbee, Royal, World, Judith Turner, and Phyllis Parkins. Bradford Exchange plate series include the Gone With the Wind collection. Chilmark's limited edition pewter scenes are on display, as well as Andrea birds, Willet's Carousel Horses, Lladro porcelain, and Hummel figurines. There is always a large collection of Britain's David Winter's quaint cottages on display.

For those who like to Christmas shop, Great Temptations has a year round Christmas shop, featuring Byer's Choice Carolers, and Department 56's Snow Village and Dicken's Village. There are Christmas decorations of all types, including AnnaLee's elves and the beautiful Fontanini nativity figurines.

Give in to the irresistible temptation to browse for hours at Great Temptations-Gifts for You and Your Home.

RESTAURANT

DIXIE HOUSE RESTAURANT & CHOCOLATE FACTORY
445 Glynn Street South
Fayetteville, GA 30214
Tel. (404) 461-5013
Hrs: Mon. - Thu.   10:30 a.m. - 9:00 p.m.
     Fri. - Sun.   7:00 a.m. - 10:00 p.m.
Visa and MasterCard are accepted.

Where can you receive Southern hospitality, down home cooking and see delectable chocolates being hand made, all while enjoying your repast in the comfort of a rambling old six bedroom home? The answer is the Dixie House Restaurant & Chocolate Factory, the "Home of food and fun in the Southern tradition." Every day of the week you'll find all you can eat

Areas of Interest Outside Atlanta

buffets at various times throughout the day. On the weekend you can partake of the $3.99 breakfast buffet; Monday through Saturday hosts the $4.32 luncheon buffet and seven days a week the $5.49 buffet dinner is available. Those who know just how good catfish can taste can order an all you can eat catfish dinner, including soup, salad, vegetables and dessert. Dinner entrees, which range from charbroiled chicken to ribeye steak, are served with baked potato or fries, fresh baked bread, soup and salad bar. For an additional $1.29 a vegetable and dessert bar is included. All of these tasty items can be enjoyed in various front rooms or you can take your meal to the wrap around glassed-in veranda with its sunny view of passing motorists. (*Prices good at time of publication.*)

On your way out stop by and view the incredible chocolate factory where you can watch experts creating chocolate turtles, the first place winners of 1982's best piece of candy contest in the International Confectionary's Convention. You can also see the creation of seasonal molded candies and more than thirty different chocolates as they're added to cream, butternut and coconut centers. For chocolate covered Southern hospitality, take the family for a day filled with good food, sweets and atmosphere.

LAGRANGE

This community of 25,000 was named for the Old Country estate of the French soldier who fought with General George Washington's Continental Army during the Revolutionary War. The Marquis de LaFayette actually visited the area as a guest of Georgia Governor George M. Troup (for whom Troup County is named). The settlers of the area heard the French nobleman remark that their countryside bore a striking resemblance to the region just outside Paris and when the community was incorporated in 1828, it honored both the man and his flattering observation. LaGrange also has two other highly distinctive historical footnotes. This community was the only one in the United States to raise a company of women soldiers. Named after Georgia Revolutionary War heroine

Areas of Interest Outside Atlanta

Nancy Harts, this company of courageous women served admirably during the Civil War. According to local historians, they never fired a shot but displayed their courage and obvious intentions before a detachment of Union cavalry commanded by a Yankee colonel named LaGrange. Also, in nearby West Point, one of the last battles of the Civil War was fought. The Battle of West Point took place at Fort Tyler, near the present site of Hawkes Library, one week after Lee surrendered to Grant at Appomattox on April 16, 1865. Also known as the City of Elms and Roses, LaGrange is located approximately sixty miles southwest of Atlanta on Interstate 85. A blend of New South and Old, its modern industrial facilities stand beside stately antebellum homes. It is also within an easy drive of Callaway Gardens, Warm Springs, and Franklin D. Roosevelt State Park.

LaGrange has a beauty and charm all its own, and many attractions to recommend it.

ATTRACTIONS

- The cultural aspects of this city are perhaps best represented by the **Chattahoochee Valley Art Association**, located in the former Troup County Jail. The Association sponsors the annual "**Affair on the Square**," one of the oldest outdoor art festivals in Georgia, and the **LaGrange National**. For more information, contact the Chattahoochee Valley Art Association, 112 Hines Street, P.O. Box 921, LaGrange, GA 30241; (404) 882-3267.
- **The Troup County Historical Society** maintains its records, a genealogy library, and various exhibits in the renovated 1917 bank building at 136 Main Street. This is the place to contact for the various home tours the community offers. The Society also hosts the annual **History Day** in LeGrange. For more information, contact the Troup County Historical Society, P.O. Box 1051, LaGrange, GA 30241; (404) 884-1828.

Areas of Interest Outside Atlanta

- LaGrange is also enthusiastic about music. For more than forty years, the **LaGrange Mutual Concerts Association** has been bringing to town the likes of Mac Frampton, the National Opera, the Atlanta Symphony, the Ruth Mitchell Dance Company, the Columbus Brass Ensemble, and Morehouse College Glee Club. For more information and an updated schedule of events, contact the LaGrange Mutual Concerts Association, P.O. Box 1492, LaGrange, GA 30241; (404) 882-1679.
- The **LaFayette Society of Performing Arts** sponsors dance, theater, ballet and other music performances in the community. This group also sponsors the lyrical LaFayette Singers, whose Christmas concerts lend this most special of all holidays an endearing and memorable charm. For more information about this very active and most successful organization, and for an updated performance schedule, contact the LaFayette Society of Performing Arts, P.O. Box 1302, LaGrange, GA 30241; (404) 882-5253.
- Organized in 1982 under Elizabeth Turley, the **LaGrange Ballet Theatre** has been involved with members of the Ruth Mitchell Dance Company, the Atlanta Ballet, the Houston Ballet, and the New York Ballet Company in such productions in LaGrange as "The Nutcracker." For more information, contact the LaGrange Ballet Theatre Program, Price Theater, LaGrange College, LaGrange, GA 30240; (404) 882-2911.
- LaGrange has live theater and has staged such memorable shows as "The Owl and The Pussycat," and "Two by Two." For more information and an updated seasonal program, contact Mel Coe, 415 North Greenwood Street, LaGrange, GA 30240; (404) 884-0967. The **Lamar Dodd Art Center** and the **Price Theater** are both located on the campus of LaGrange College, the oldest private school in the state. The Art Center offers a permanent collection of works by famed international artists, not the least of which is the center's namesake, Georgia's legendary Lamar Dodd. There's also a superb collection of American Indian art and other various changing exhibits. The Price Theater, of course, is a legend in its own right. For more information, contact LaGrange College, LaGrange, GA 30240; (404) 882-2911.

Areas of Interest Outside Atlanta

- LaGrange is a city full of history and a great many homes are listed in the National Register of Historic Places. The city's **Broad Street District**, west of downtown, reflects a variety of nineteenth and early twentieth century architectural styles, including antebellum Greek Revival, Victorian Queen Anne, Neoclassical, Georgian Revival, Tudor Revival, and the newer Craftsman/Bungalow. One home, Bellevue, was built in the early 1850s by and for Benjamin Harvey Hill, who entertained many notable Confederate leaders there. Fully restored and furnished in the period, it is maintained by the LaGrange Women's Club, who sponsor the community's tour of homes. Located at 204 Ben Hill Street, further information can be obtained by calling (404) 884-1832.
- **The Vernon Road Historic District**, west of LaGrange College, includes the Callaway's "Hills and Dales" estate at 1200 Vernon. This one is considered among the best famed Atlanta architect Neel Reid ever designed. For more information, contact Troup County Archives, 136 Main Street, P.O. Box 1051, LaGrange, GA 30241; (404) 884-1828.
- One of the best recreational attractions in western Georgia is **West Point Lake**, located several miles west of LaGrange by a variety of routes. This huge **Chattahoochee River reservoir** encompasses 26,000 acres and over 500 miles of shoreline, and extends west into neighboring Alabama. It is reputed to have outstanding bass fishing and 52,000 acres of public recreation area. It was dedicated June 7, 1975 and its 7,000 foot dam rises nearly 100 feet above the riverbed. Facilities include three beaches, thirteen hiking and nature trails, fourteen playgrounds, five tennis courts, six softball fields, five basketball courts, 778 tent camping sites, nine group camping areas, ten individual picnic sites and thirteen pavilion sites, twenty boat launching ramps and sixteen docks. West Point Lake also includes a 9,661 acre wildlife management area which is home to, among other species, whitetail deer, grey fox, Canada geese, and bobwhite quail.

Popular activities include fishing, of course, and swimming, boating, water-skiing, hiking, and camping. The Highland Marina, just two miles outside the LaGrange City Limits, provides waterfront campgrounds, an outstanding marina, bass, pontoon and ski boat rentals, fishing guides and supervised fishing trips, overnight houseboat trips, waterfront cottages, a lakeshore restaurant, and a full range of other services. For more information, contact Jack Baytos, Highland Marina, P.O. Box 1644, LaGrange, GA 30241; (404) 882-3437.

For more information about LaGrange and its various offerings, contact the LaGrange Chamber of Commerce, P.O. Box 636, LaGrange, GA 30241; (404) 884-8671.

APPAREL

MANSOUR'S
West Lafayette Square
LaGrange, GA 30240
Tel. (404) 884-7305
Hrs: Mon. - Sat. 9:30 a.m.- 6:00 p.m.
Visa, MasterCard, AMEX and Mansour's cards are accepted.

When Nasor Mansour, a Lebanese immigrant, bought a small store selling fabric, shoes, and clothing to textile workers in 1918, little did he dream his shop would one day encompass an entire block on Lafayette Square in LaGrange. The little general store has grown to a multi-million dollar business, specializing in prestigious lines of apparel, jewelry, cosmetics and shoes. It is the only source for merchandise by Bally, Hickey-Freeman, Oscar de la Renta, Lancome and other quality lines, aside from Phipps Plaza and Lennox Square in Atlanta. It's not unusual for customers to drive 100 miles to shop at Mansour's.

The merchandise is not the only unique thing about Mansour's; when you enter the graceful structure across from the statue and fountain of the Marquis de LaFayette, you'll feel the relaxed elegance of a less hurried era that will make your shopping pure pleasure. And customers know that a Mansour is always there if you want to consult about something, or just say

Areas of Interest Outside Atlanta

hello. Nasor Mansour used to pray that his store would someday be as large as J.C. Penney, LaGrange's leading store. His grandsons believe he would be pleased to find out that his business is now supporting all three of his sons, his eight grandsons and their families. All the brothers have returned to work in the family enterprise, after obtaining degrees in finance, advertising, and marketing.

Nasor Mansour was a religious man and opened and closed each business meeting with a prayer. During the Great Depression, when other stores were cutting back, Mansour expanded, and his success has continued ever since. Employees are considered part of the family and there is no mandatory retirement age. Some sales associsiates have worked for more than thirty years, and still enjoy serving customers in the faithful Mansour tradition.

ART GALLERY

CHATTAHOOCHEE VALLEY ART ASSOCIATION
112 Hines Street
La Grange, GA 30240
Tel. (404) 882-3267
Hrs: Tues. - Fri. 9:00 a.m. - 5:00 p.m.
     Saturday 9:00 a.m. - 4:00 p.m.
     Sunday 1:00 p.m. - 5:00 p.m.
Open on all major holidays.

That imposing three story Victorian building just off the main square in LaGrange is not the county jail, it just used to be. Now it houses the Chattahoochee Valley Art Association's superb 400 piece permanent collection of contemporary American art featuring paintings, sculpture, prints, drawings, photography and crafts.

The Chattahoochee Valley Art Association was formed in 1963 to provide exhibits of contemporary art and to foster classes in the arts. Today the museum and its staff are proud to have successfully involved the community in so many diverse programs. In 1986-87 the Association provided twenty-five exhibitions, fifty-five classes and sixty-seven workshops as well as seven lectures and a number of special events. Classes span a variety of subjects including printing, photography, drawing, papermaking and crafts. The Association also hosts a major Arts Festival in late May, which draws over 100 exhibitors from all over the South, and a national competition for artists in April.

People accustomed to the High Museum in Atlanta or even the Metropolitan Museum in New York City will be impressed with the Chattahoochee Valley Art Association's museum in La Grange. The building, which is 8,700 square feet on three levels and houses four galleries, is a small artistic jewel in a small town.

GIFT SHOP

B.A. EVANS HOME HOUSE
2106 Hamilton Road
LaGrange, GA 30240
Tel. (404) 882-1184
Hrs: Mon. - Sat. 9:00 a.m. - 5:30 p.m.
Phone for special appointment.
Visa, MasterCard and Discover are accepted.
Also,
1600 Vernon Road
LaGrange, GA 30240
Tel. (404) 882-4531

B. A. Evans Home House is a country store, filled with gifts and antiques. You'll find handmade baskets, beautiful pottery, quilts, folk art and more "made in Georgia" items in this shop.

The store is located on the family farm. Inside the building is an antique furniture section. Cupboards, hutches and

Areas of Interest Outside Atlanta

chairs are the most popular items. You can find wooden swans among the hand carved wooden items, and other creatures fashioned from tin and gaily painted. Toys, pictures and kitchen items are also in the big front room. Other antiques are at the rear, including a collection of custom designed furniture chosen for its individuality, including some of the increasingly rare Georgia pine pieces sought by many collectors. Others are old wardrobes, small tables, and kitchen gadgets from a bygone era. There's another department with ornaments and decorations that make it Christmas all year long. The smell of cinnamon is in the air as you enter the Christmas shop. Here are Santas made from paper maché, cuddly Teddy bears, wooden and metal ornaments. One of the fun ways to shop at Evans Home House is with a basket in your hand and Martha Evans, the owner, at your side. You can pick out gift items, then have Martha create a basket design that includes everything, or you can commission a decorative basket for your home or someone special.

For the right touch in a home, B. A. Evans Home House has more ideas than you can imagine. It is a place for slowly strolling the aisles and dreaming.

INTERIOR DESIGN

THE MILL STORE, INC.
I-85, EXIT 3
P.O. Box 1738
LaGrange, GA 30241
Tel.   (404) 884-2674
        (800) 522-2224 GA
Hrs: Mon. - Fri.   9:00 a.m. - 6:00 p.m.
          Saturday   9:00 a.m. - 5:00 p.m.
Visa and Mastercard are accepted.

Founded in 1956, this third generation, family run business offers the best in carpets and other home furnishings at

Areas of Interest Outside Atlanta

up to half the regular cost. The size of the building itself, 45,000 square feet, says warehouse, but when you walk in, it is like you are entering a creatively displayed department store. With the gift linens attractively arranged amidst small unique gift items, it makes for an easy stroll in order for you to make your selection. Only the finest table and bed linens are offered here along with embroidered bedsheets, lace linens and floor coverings.

To make a choice for your home, continue deeper into the showroom and on your left there is a vast carpet display area with a palate of colorful carpet samples that covers the spectrum of the rainbow. Further on, there are alcoves that have beautiful flooring selections from the latest in congoleum to the beauty of hardwood floors. Pass through a pair of glass doors and you are in the actual warehouse. This area lets you see hundreds of carpet rolls in both first quality and off-goods, just waiting for your inspection.

The prices of these carpets are the best thing though; you can receive savings of up to fifty percent off on famous name brands. The Mill Store will install residentially within a seventy-five mile radius and commercially all over the country. The Mill Store will also ship your purchases anywhere in the United States. For the "Best Choice" in home furnishings come to the Mill Store. The Mill Store is the outlet for the locally made Milliken Place® carpets.

Areas of Interest Outside Atlanta

RESTAURANT

IN CLOVER
205 Broad Street
La Grange, GA 30240
Tel. (404) 882-0883
Hrs: Mon. - Sat. Lunch   11:30 a.m. - 2:00 p.m.
                  Dinner   6:00 p.m. - 10:00 p.m.
Visa, MasterCard and AMEX are accepted.

    In Clover means fine food graciously served in the Victorian elegance of a fine old house which you will find just one and a half blocks off La Grange's town square. The Queen Anne house, constructed in 1892, has seven separate dining areas, enabling it to seat about 200 persons at one time. There is also a bar called simply The Pub, which offers domestic and imported beers, mixed drinks and an excellent wine list including some of the finest sparkling wines and champagnes.
    Dining areas are decorated and arranged in the late Victorian manner. Furniture is authentic for the period; the tables are set with sparkling crystal and elegant china. Among the favorite entrees are Beef Wellington and the Red Snapper Aurora from the seafood menu. Crêpes, presented with several fillings, are popular with luncheon customers. There's a dessert menu that may present more choices than you wish, all temptations. Highly recommended are the Chocolate Amore and the Banana Almond Praline Crêpe.
    In Clover is a treat to visit. The flowers are fresh, the service is excellent. There's plenty of room, but a phone call will secure a reservation to fit into your travel schedule when you come to LaGrange.

Areas of Interest Outside Atlanta

BEHOLD THE "LOWLY" PEANUT

By

Merritt Scott Miller

Though now considered an American institution, the peanut is a lowly immigrant of mixed origins and humble beginnings. It is also the subject of much confusion and considerable slander. It belongs in any discussion of Georgia, for, while grown largely in the southern part of the state, it is extensively marketed around Atlanta and vicinity, and it also accounts, in part, for the success of a former governor and United States president. To set the record straight: In the first place, it is not a nut. Its nickname is actually much closer to the truth, for it is also called a "goober pea." The term "goober" comes from the African Congo *nguba* and is, in fact, a legume, of which peas are the most representative species.

How it came to be classed as a nut ranks with the other great mysteries of our time, for it does not grow on trees and the plant itself isn't a tree. The goober pea actually grows beneath the ground, which makes one wonder why it isn't called a goober spud, except that it isn't a potato, either. It's a subterranean pea. It's also not native to North America, but to South America, most notably Brazil. Spanish explorers are credited with spreading them to Asia, and to Africa, where the Congo natives quickly realized their value and ate them not only themselves, but fed them to their elephants, thus establishing another misunderstood tradition, the pachyderm's insatiable craving for them.

We tend to associate elephants and peanuts as being intrinsically linked since the first beginnings of both. That's not true, of course. Dumbo's ancestors didn't hear of them until about the fourteenth century. Like the humans of Africa, however, the elephants were no dummies. Even unsalted peanuts, they decided, tasted so good they had to be good for you. Peanuts, then, came to this country with the first black immigrants. They didn't catch on right away, though. Since slaves liked them, goobers were considered mostly a poor folks' food. They were also tough to cultivate and harvest, so commercial farmers left them largely alone, except during hard times.

This attitude wasn't the most enlightened in the world, for the only thing lowly about a goober is where it's grown. Legumes are valuable plants in their own right, because they return nitrogen to the soil as part of their growth process. Not only is nitrogen vital to the dirt from which most food comes from, it's a vital constituent of the air we breathe, and without it, life as most of us believe it exists on this planet wouldn't—exist, that is.

Peanuts are the seeds of the peanut bush and a typical plant has sixty to eighty of them among its roots. The goober is rich in protein. It contains eleven of the essential minerals and is an outstanding source of niacin, thiamine and other B vitamins. Most nutritionists who know their stuff will tell you that when you spread peanut butter over two sandwiches, wash it down with a glass of milk, and take on a bowl of fruit for dessert, not only are you getting a balanced meal, you're also getting about a third of the daily nutritional needs of even that most demanding of life forms, the growing human child.

What finally started turning the tide of public opinion for the peanut, then? Well, human insight and an obnoxious little insect which devastated most of the South's cotton crop in the early part of the present century.

Dr. George Washington Carver, of Alabama's Tuskegee Institute, did the nutritional research on the peanut. The boll weevil made the goober an economic agricultural necessity. And some Yankee and Dixie ingenuity when it came to turn of the century harvesting equipment accomplished the rest. Before that, to Southern farmers, it seemed like everywhere you

Areas of Interest Outside Atlanta

looked, you found the boll weevil. Now, you can't make a sandwich, visit a zoo, hit a tavern's happy hour, build a house, write a letter, blow a stump, lubricate a truck, lay a floor covering or get yourself gussied up for a night on the town without running into the peanut.

Yep, this lowly little immigrant is used as a snack, both in the shell and undressed, plain, salted and sweetened. Its oil is used in cooking and from it, other menu items like cheese, milk, coffee, flour, chili, Worcestershire sauce, fruit punch and mayonnaise can be made. When it isn't heading for the digestive tract, it is used in cosmetics, dye, axle grease, paint, ink, plastic, linoleum, medicine and explosives. And by all means, don't throw away that shell. Save it, because it's made into wallboard and added to fertilizer. Even its skin is used in making paper. The vines are plowed under to enrich the soil or bailed for livestock feed.

"Lowly?" Indeed.

The statistics are pretty impressive, too. The United States, as a whole, has less than four percent of the world's peanut acreage, but produces some ten percent of the global crop. Georgia, with 600,000 acres of the slandered pea under cultivation, produces five percent of the goobers used on the Planet Earth. In the United States, sixty percent of the peanuts grown are used for food and food products; twenty-five percent are shipped abroad; and fifteen percent is either crushed for oil and meal or used for seed.

It wasn't by accident, then, that Jimmy Carter's folks got into the goober business. Peanuts, some 17 tons of them, are consumed by Yankee fans each year, and everybody knows how smart it is to be a Yankee fan. Worldwide and nationally, goobers rank among the top ten crops. Georgia leads America's production, accounting for nearly half of the two billion pounds produced annually. It also ranks fourth on the planet.

That national brand which put the peanut in a top hat and tails had the right idea, then. There's nothing lowly about the goober at all. He's among the aristocracy and stands as a shining tribute to what's possible even for poor immigrants to America.

Behold the lowly peanut.

Areas of Interest Outside Atlanta

NEWNAN

This charming community of about 11,000 lies southwest of Atlanta, thirty-eight miles by Interstate 85, and then three miles further west on State Route 16. Established in 1828, its nickname is "The City of Homes" and this is surely the place to see antebellum Georgia at its best. The city sponsors a driving tour of twenty-three historic structures and provides an outstanding piece of literature which cannot help but enhance one's appreciation of these fine old homes. For more information, contact the Newnan-Coweta Historical Society, P.O. Box 1001, Newnan, GA 30263; (404) 253-2270.

ATTRACTIONS

- If it hasn't been completed by the time this publication reaches you, **Dunaway Gardens** soon will be. This is the site of the famous Tara estate of *Gone With the Wind* fame and will be located eight miles next to Newnan's Coweta County Courthouse. The **Male Academy Museum** is housed in an 1883-vintage boys school. A century of clothing, decorative arts and other period artifacts are showcased in a facility which includes a gift shop at which historical books can be purchased. For more information, contact Male Academy Museum, 30 Temple Avenue, Newnan, GA 30264; (404) 251-0207.

- Like its neighbor LaGrange, further south, Newnan is known for its appreciation of the arts. The **Manget Brannon Alliance for the Arts** hosts ongoing performances and exhibits. For more information, contact the Manget Brannon Alliance for the Arts, 24 Long Street, Newnan, GA 30264; (404) 251-9107.

- The **Georgia Power Company** provides a one to four hour tour of its nearby power facility. Tailored for the specific requests of its visitors, the tour includes a short slide presentation. For more information, contact William G. Head, Georgia Power Company, P.O. Box 4544, Atlanta, GA 30302; (404) 526-7848.

Areas of Interest Outside Atlanta

- Each Labor Day, Newnan plays host to the **Powers' Crossroad Bluegrass Festival**, a nationally known gathering of the best musicians the South has to offer. Festivities encompass an entire weekend and include some outstanding country cooking. For more information, contact Coweta Festivals, Inc., Newnan, GA 30263; (404) 253-2011.

- Newnan is also the site of the **Coweta County Fair**, held in September. This one includes arts and handicrafts, flowers, food products, midway rides, livestock and poultry exhibitions and various other representative aspects of Coweta County life. For more information, contact the Newnan Kiwanis Club, c/o Newnan Chamber of Commerce, P.O. Box 1103, Newnan, GA 30264; (404) 253-2270.

ANTIQUE SHOP

THE JEFFERSON HOUSE
51 Jefferson Street
Newnan, GA 30263
Tel. (404) 253-6171
Hrs: Mon. - Sat. 10:00 a.m. - 5:00 p.m.
　　　Sunday by appointment.
Visa and MasterCard are accepted.

The Jefferson House building traces its roots to 1850 when it was part of the burgeoning community of Newnan. Seven rooms of this beautifully restored old home are now packed full of treasures from times past.

The shop specializes in wedding gifts, along with many other fine items. A complete line of Gorham silver is carried, and you will also find chased silver trays and Victoria silver items. Beautiful Mottahedeh china is featured. The backs of fine china plates hold the names of respected china makers such as Haviland, Cuthbertson, Johnson Brothers, Fitz and Floyd, Longchamp and Villeroy and Boch. A wide selection of Virginia Metalcrafters and other decorative accessories is

Areas of Interest Outside Atlanta

offered. Old clocks, floral sprays, cook books, glassware, pictures, paintings, as well as personally selected antiques are but a few of the many gifts and treasures available in The Jefferson House.

A special line of Christmas decorations is shown year round. Expert assistance with your interior decorating needs is available. The friendly staff of The Jefferson House will assist you in choosing wallpaper, fabric, furniture and even garden statuary. Services include gift wrap, delivery and shipping.

RESTAURANTS

FOURTEEN SAVANNAH RESTAURANT
34 BullsBoro Drive
Newnan, GA 30264
Tel. (404) 251-3663
       (404) 253-FOOD for menu recording.
Hrs: Mon. - Sun. 11:00 a.m. - 9:00 p.m.

Just because you don't live in a palace doesn't mean you can't eat like a king on the road. The Fourteen Savannah Restaurant is a friendly, family style cafeteria restaurant where good food, fast service and reasonable prices are every day occurrences. Because of its ideal location, the restaurant is especially appealing to the hurried tourist in search of a good, wholesome meal.

This newest venture by Randall and Dianne Golden is gaining increasing popularity with locals as well as hurried visitors. The brightly lit dining area has a relaxing soft pastel background, and one is impressed by the clean, neat appointments and comfortable and efficient seating. The building itself has the friendly appearance of a country farm house, replete with shutters. The wonderful aroma of down home fried chicken seduces your senses and Meat Loaf and Baked Ham are among the variety of entrees awaiting your choice. No one will have to coerce you into eating your veggies as you sample the hearty and satisfying whipped potatoes, green beans or fried okra as only a southern cook can prepare. Don't deny yourself the pleasure of the luscious desserts. It will be hard to recall when you experienced such fine tasting Banana Pudding or Fruit Cobbler.

For the discriminating traveler, Fourteen Savannah Restaurant proves to be an entirely new dimension in "fast food," fulfilling its intent of serving tasty, wholesome food at reasonable prices.

SPRAYBERRY'S BARBECUE
229 Jackson Street
Newnan, GA 30263
Tel. (404) 253-4421
Hrs: Mon. - Sat. 7:00 a.m. - 9:00 p.m.
Closed the week of July 4th.

Barbeque lovers will be happy to follow this restaurant's motto and "pig out at Sprayberry's." No matter, whether you prefer barbequed pork or beef, chopped, sliced or with Brunswick stew, you can have your fill and top it off with delicious homemade onion rings. For those who would rather have steak or other selections, there is a menu for those selections also. The steaks are cut to order. If you're looking for a tasty dessert, you'll flip over the homemade peach and apple turnover pies, fixed the old Southern way by stewing the fruit. Traditionalists, who enjoy the small touches, are tickled pink to find they can order an old fashioned Coke, and receive it in the bottle, good and cold.

Customers feel like they're part of the family at Sprayberry's. The companionable atmosphere plus the pungent, mouthwatering aroma of barbeque roasting over a slow fire leads both natives and travelers straight to Sprayberry's front door. Once inside, you'll relish the Fifties decor, complete with shiny red-topped tables and framed pictures of pigs on the walls.

When you enter Sprayberry's you'll be in good company, because everyone from Columnist Lewis Grizzard to Beverly Sills has dropped in for a Sprayberry sandwich and a friendly

Areas of Interest Outside Atlanta

Southern welcome over the years. Even FDR was known to drive over from his Warm Springs Little White House for a taste of some Sprayberry's barbeque and delicious sauce that has become legend in these parts. For those culturally impoverished souls who can't make it to Sprayberry's for lunch time break, all is not lost. All the choice barbeques and picnic foods can be ordered for takeout and delivery.

TWELVE SAVANNAH RESTAURANT
12 Savannah Street
Newnan, GA 30264
Tel.   (404) 253-1108
         (404) 251-2181 Menu Recording
Hrs: Buffet Lunch   Mon. - Sun. 11:00 a.m. - 2:30 p.m.
         Dinner   Sun. - Thu. 5:00 p.m.- 9:00 p.m.
                                     Fri., Sat.   5:00 p.m. - 10:00 p.m.
Visa and MasterCard are accepted.

A beautifully restored Victorian home built in 1892, with ornamental columns and lacy curtains, houses one of the area's most unusual restaurants. Twelve Savannah Restaurant is a complex of three dining facilities that runs the gamut from catering, to those who wish to dine with leisure in elegant surroundings, to those observing a more hectic schedule and requiring cafeteria or take out service.

The comfortable seating, soft lighting and a general air of Victorian gentility makes dining at Twelve Savannah a memorable occasion. A host of delicious seafood specialties, rib eye steak or Chicken Savannah will delight your palate. Choose a fine wine and complete your meal with a tantalizing and luscious homemade dessert. The establishment continues its fine food and excellent service in a relaxing atmosphere during the luncheon hours as well, and you may choose from their famous buffet or delicious seafood offerings. The Back of Savannah features excellent home style cooking where you will find made from scratch salads and such favorites as fried chicken, barbecued pork and roast beef. The restaurant prepares their perfectly baked yeast rolls and mini corn muffins daily, and the satisfying and delectable homemade cakes, cobblers and puddings will have you going back for more. Breakfast is also served at Back of Savannah. Be sure to try the best doughnuts in town. One of the more popular items the restaurant offers at their Friday and Saturday night Buffet is the catfish—all you can eat—and seafood lovers will also enjoy the crab legs, fresh raw oysters and the cold boiled shrimp. Salad bar, coffee and tea as well as some inspired choices for dessert are also included in the reasonable price.

Twelve Savannah will cater your special social functions, and effortlessly live up to their slogan, "A place of delightful difference, where dining is a pleasure."

PINE MOUNTAIN

At an elevation of slightly more than 1,000 feet, this village of 1,000, located due north of Columbus twenty miles, was a significant rail center during the latter half of the nineteenth century. It draws heavily on nearby Callaway Gardens for its economic base, from whose mountain site the community received its name. That peak has been a major source of granite since 1883 and also provides visitors to Franklin Roosevelt State Park, Warm Springs, and the Gardens with good accommodations, shopping, and that relaxing, small town environment so enjoyed by tourists the region over.

Areas of Interest Outside Atlanta

ACCOMMODATION

CALLAWAY GARDENS INN
Highway 27
Pine Mountain, GA 31822
Tel. (404) 663-2281
      (800) 282-8181
Hrs: 365 days a year, 24 hours a day.
Visa, MasterCard, AMEX, Diners Club and Discover are accepted.

The difference is outstanding at Callaway Gardens Inn. Gracious hospitality, luxurious accommodations and a wealth of recreational opportunities all blend into a natural woodland and garden setting to create the famous Callaway Gardens Inn. Courteous, professional staff is ready to provide you with personalized service, exceptional dining and a world of amenities. Callaway Gardens Inn has earned the Mobil Four Star and AAA Four Diamond ratings.

The sleeping accommodations at Callaway Gardens Inn are varied and designed to give you the ultimate in comfort and exposure to the beauty of the botanical gardens surrounding the Inn. The rooms contain two double beds and a comfortable sitting area for relaxing. Many of the rooms have adjacent parlors for entertaining. The Gardens View Inn rooms have front and back entrances and overlook the Great Lawn. Three Roof Garden suites are located on the top floor of the Inn and each have a wet bar and a terrace. Seclusion and privacy are found in the Mountain Creek Villas. These rustically elegant villas are built of red cedar, native Georgia stone and blend into the beauty of the landscape. The villas come equipped with kitchens and luxurious baths. The Executive Lodge is perched on top of Pine Mountain and is ideal for exclusive entertaining. Callaway Country Cottages are two bedroom cottages featuring kitchens, woodburning fireplaces and screened porches. All of

Areas of Interest Outside Atlanta

the accommodations are richly appointed and immaculately serviced.

The dining opportunities at Callaway Gardens Inn are as varied as the accommodations. You may choose an elegant, continental meal with a tuxedoed waiter, a hearty Southern breakfast in a country kitchen or anything in between. Callaway Gardens Inn is on U.S. Highway 27 in Pine Mountain, seventy miles south of Atlanta and thirty miles north of Columbus, both towns being served by major airlines. By car, take I-85 south from Atlanta to I-85 and continue south to exit 14, turn left on Highway U.S. 27 and continue eleven miles to the Callaway Gardens Inn.. Callaway Gardens/Harris County Airport is a few minutes from the Inn and has a 5,000 foot lighted airstrip for light aircraft.

Areas of Interest Outside Atlanta

GIFT SHOP

CALLAWAY GARDENS COUNTRY STORE
Highway 27
Pine Mountain, GA 31822
Tel. (404) 663-5100
       (800) 282-8181
Hrs: Mon. - Sun. 8:00 a.m. - 5:00 p.m.
Longer hours in summer and during special events.
Visa, MasterCard, AMEX, Diners Club and Discover are accepted.

Also,
Peachtree Plaza Hotel   Georgia World Congress Ctr
210 Peachtree St., NW   285 Intl. Blvd. NW
Atlanta, GA 30343   Atlanta, GA 30313
Tel. (404) 524-1151   Tel. (404) 588-1545

301 East River Street
Savannah, GA 31401
Tel. (912) 236-4055

Hidden deep in the lush Callaway Gardens is the Callaway Gardens Country Store, the home of tantalizing, and unusual edibles in rich Georgian country flavors. Opened in 1952, the Callaway Gardens Country Store includes a gift shop, restaurant and food shop. If you love Southern food and good cooking then you will want to be sure to stop at Callaway Gardens Country Store.

The store carries the famous Muscadine products made from sweet Muscadine Georgian grapes and the restaurant serves the true Southern delicacy of Speckled Heart Grits. Mixed in amongst the cookies, preserves and homemade bread you'll find needlework pieces, wooden toys, spices, soaps, cookbooks and dolls and a whole lot more. There are Georgia cured hams aged and cured the old fashioned way, red pepper jellies, peach butter and sorghum syrup. All of these tantalizing treats are available in the store and through the store's catalogue. The catalogue is a perfect way to bring a bit of Callaway Gardens Country Store home so you can continue to enjoy these special items.

The rustic Country Kitchen Restaurant is at the back of the store. The Country Kitchen affords a view of pine covered mountains and clear blue skies. Country Kitchen Restaurant is famous for its "Feed Bag Picnic Lunch". Plan your picnic by calling ahead to the restaurant and you will have prepared for you a fabulous lunch of your choice of ham, turkey or fried chicken with potato salad, deviled eggs, pickles, carrots, a biscuit, a roll and butter with two chocolate chip cookies. You'll find the unusual at Callaway Gardens Country Store and Country Kitchen Restaurant. You can come home with your basket full of Southern treasures, beautiful keepsakes and delicious edibles.

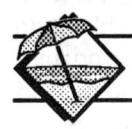

RESORT

CALLAWAY GARDENS
Highway 27
Pine Mountain, GA 31822
Tel.   (404) 663-2281
         (800) 282-8181
Hrs: Open 365 days a year, 24 hours a day.
Visa, MasterCard, AMEX, Diners Club and Discover cards are accepted.

Tucked away in the foothills of West Georgia's Appalachian Mountains there lies a lush green clearing away from the crowded world, a resort like no other, Callaway Gardens. The dream of industrialist Cason Callaway in the 1930s, the Gardens were created to preserve the native plant life of the region in its natural setting . Since then it has become much more than a place apart; this fabulous year round botanical garden and highly acclaimed resort now attracts more than 750,000 visitors annually. Visitors come to soothe their senses and refresh their souls. They also come for the wide range of recreational facilities including golf, tennis, racquetball, swimming, horseback riding, hiking, bicycling, hunting and much, much more.

Each season at Callaway Gardens offers a beauty all its own. The Gardens were created in part to preserve the prunifolia azalea, a bright red summer flower that is native only within 100 miles of the Gardens. More that 700 varieties of azaleas bloom along the drives and meandering nature trails each spring. Fall brings a splendid display of nature's colors, and English, Oriental and American varieties of holly paint the winter landscape green and red. Mr. Callaway once said: "Every child ought to see something beautiful before he is six years old." By setting aside these luxuriant surroundings, he has made that wish a possibility.

An exciting addition to Callaway Gardens, the John A. Sibley Horticultural Center opened in March, 1984. This state of the art greenhouse and garden complex introduces technological advances that allow visitors to feel indoors and outdoors simultaneously. Unique from other conservatories, the center encourages visitor involvement, permitting close interaction with plants and flowers. You also will want to see Mr. Cason's Vegetable Garden, where guests find tips and techniques for growing flowers, fruits and vegetables to take home to their own backyards. Various fruits and vegetables cover seven and a half acres of perfection and beauty. It was the filming site for *The Victory Garden South*, and has been a feature of the popular PBS television program *The Victory Garden*.

In the heart of Callaway Gardens you will find two exceptional restaurants. The first, the Gardens Restaurant, has an English country feeling, with exposed beams, and a huge, native flagstone fireplace. Indoors for dinner, try the fresh pan-fried trout, aged steaks cooked to perfection, shrimp, or Christine's special barbecued ribs. Following dinner, the talented Musicana Singers entertain. Outdoors for lunch, on the porch overlooking the scenic Lake View Golf Course, enjoy fried shrimp, a variety of salads, or a spicy Brunswick Stew served with light, tender biscuits and hearty nature fries.

Below the Gardens is the Veranda Restaurant, decorated in romantic peach pastels, inlaid woods, and French doors opening onto a flagstone patio and the golf course beyond. Enjoy a fine selection of wines and beers with your lunch or dinner while being served your favorite dishes from around the world.

Another family favorite is The Flower Mill. Located in the Country Cottage Complex, this 1950s style ice cream soda fountain and grill recreates the look and feel of a bygone era. It features naturally blended ice creams and homemade snacks, juicy jumbo hamburgers and specialty sandwiches. Great barbecued chicken, pizza, a children's menu and a vintage juke box are also big hits to be enjoyed here.

"What we try to do," says G. Harold Northrop, president of Callaway Gardens, "is give people a serene place with educational and inspirational qualities, plus all the recreational facilities. We want to give people a feeling of being close to the earth. After they've visited Callaway Gardens, we want people to take home with them consolation for the heart, nourishment for the soul, and inspiration for the mind."

Callaway Gardens covers 14,000 acres, 2,500 of which have been developed for the full service resort and garden complex. There are thirteen miles of restricted roads, thirteen lakes and miles of walking trails. The complex is owned by the Ida Cason Callaway Foundation, a public not-for-profit foundation. It is open twenty-four hours a day, every day of the year. For reservations, free brochures or more information, call (800) 282-8181.

SENOIA

This Coweta County community north of Newnan is often referred to as "a city of historic homes and friendly people." Founded shortly before the Civil War, this typical small Georgia town is the home of Southern Mills, a manufacturer of

Areas of Interest Outside Atlanta

fireproof fibers, and a plastics plant. With plenty of accommodations, shopping, and recreational facilities, it makes a great place to stay while visiting the greater Atlanta area. It has a public golf course, Brown Bell, which is a nine hole/par 36, ideal for an afternoon's relaxation. For more information, contact the Coweta County Chamber of Commerce, P.O. Box 1103, 1 Savannah Street Newnan, GA 30264.

BED & BREAKFAST INN

THE VERANDA
252 Seavy Street
Senoia, GA 30276-0177
Tel. (404) 599-3905
Visa, MasterCard and Discover are accepted

If you are looking for a Bed and Breakfast because you enjoy being away from hotel crowds and conventions, and wish to relax and easily blend into the local scene, then look no further than The Veranda.

Spacious rooms are furnished with antiques and fascinating collections of unusual memorabilia. Old quilts and comforters adorn the queen size beds and continue the ambiance of yesteryear. There are two charming parlors, a library where you will find fine old books and etchings, a dining room and gift shop. The Boals, who are the proprietors of the Veranda, are long time collectors of kaleidoscopes, and an extraordinary variety from wooden to marbleized styles can be found at the shop. Another item of interest is the selection of handmade walking canes as part of their display of beautiful and unusual gifts. Overnight guests are treated to a deluxe, home cooked breakfast. Specialties include fresh fruits, strawberry waffles, cheese omelettes, sausage, sourdough French toast, beef hash, seasoned grits, poached eggs and freshly baked hot breads. The Veranda restaurant also serves lunch and dinner by reservation, for individuals and groups, when popular regional dishes made from old family recipes are prepared and savored.

The Inn began its life in 1907 as the Hollberg Hotel. The establishment's background is intertwined with such historical figures as presidential hopeful William Jennings Bryan, and Senoia residents say that Margaret Mitchell interviewed Civil War veterans on the columned front porch as part of her research for *Gone With The Wind*. The personal warmth and graciousness of Jan and Bobby Boal, in a delightful atmosphere reflecting the past, makes The Veranda an easy choice for that special getaway.

WARM SPRINGS

Perhaps the most beloved United States president of the twentieth century thus far was not a native Georgian, but was, instead, born in Hyde Park, New York. Franklin Delano Roosevelt loved Georgia, for it gave him his life. When this robust, energetic, dynamic national leader was stricken with infantile paralysis in 1921, he searched the country over for a place which would, if not cure him, at least ease the agony of this dreadful disease.

Long before FDR came to Warm Springs in 1924, however, the curative powers of its waters were known. Wounded Indian warriors sought them out hundreds of years before the first white man came. Native Georgians who trace their ancestry back to the terrible yellow fever epidemics around Savannah in the late 1700s have no doubt read of this place in family Bibles. By 1832, the community had become a popular summer health resort. It survived Sherman's bonfires only to be leveled by another fire in 1865. By the turn of the century, the resort was again flourishing. In 1893, the town of Bullochville was established.

The name of the village was officially changed to Warm Springs in 1924 and a few years later FDR established the Warm Springs Foundation for the treatment and care of other polio victims who could not afford such medical assistance on their own.

Areas of Interest Outside Atlanta

There is no doubt that Roosevelt loved Warm Springs, for in 1932 he built a modest home here. He selected its design personally. The three-bedroom house thus reflects his feelings. The structure, though small, blends comfort, practicality and taste. When it came to landscaping, FDR permitted only that which was absolutely necessary, preferring, instead, what was there for centuries. That he loved the countryside is also obvious, for he commissioned a specially built 1938 Ford convertible with hand controls and, anonymously, spent many restful hours simply driving around in it.

FDR died in 1945, shortly before the end of World War II, but his home has been preserved and is now a national treasure. Visitors are encouraged to spend as much time as they like walking the grounds and poking about the home itself. On its living room shelves are his ship models (he was once Assistant Secretary of the Navy), and the leash of his favorite dog Fala still hangs in the closet, along with his riding quirt. Here, as well, is Elizabeth Shoumatoff's unfinished portrait of him, hanging above simple early American maple furniture and hooked rugs. The kitchen dates back to the 1930s, and is typical of the simple frame cottage itself. Sun still filters through the trees beyond the semi-circular sun deck and roses are planted around the columns at the front entrance.

The grounds include his 1938 Ford convertible and another of his favorite cars, a spritely 1940 Willys roadster. There is the guest house, where so many historic figures of the era stayed, and the servant quarters. The Walk of States has flags and stones leading to the Franklin D. Roosevelt Museum.

This museum is worth the entire trip, for it contains rare items of memorabilia and a visit to it includes a twelve minute film entitled *FDR in Georgia*. It is maintained by the Georgia Department of Natural Resources, which also operates nearby Franklin D. Roosevelt State Park. Ample parking is available, and a gift shop and snack bar are included in a complex not far away.

The Summer White House is centrally located within easy driving of Pine Mountain and Callaway Gardens.

For more information, contact the Georgia Department of Natural Resources, Communications Office Suite 1258, 205 Butler Street S.E., Atlanta, GA 30334; 1-800-3GA-PARK or, outside Georgia, 1-800-5GA-PARK.

POINTS OF INTEREST

THE LITTLE WHITE HOUSE
Georgia 85 West
Warm Springs, GA 31830
Tel. (404) 655-3511
Hrs: Mon.-Sun. 9:00 a.m. - 5:00 p.m.
Last tour starts at 4:15 p.m.
No credit cards or personal checks are accepted.

To follow in the footsteps of FDR is as simple as a visit to Warm Springs, Georgia. Just an hour from the Hartsfield International Airport in Atlanta is the charming little village of Warm Springs, barely changed since the days Roosevelt ventured south to get away from the pressures of public office and to take treatments available for his polio affliction.

Areas of Interest Outside Atlanta

Roosevelt's restful little retreat, just south of town, was to be called The Little White House, and the fact that he loved this cozy cottage was well known.

Franklin Delano Roosevelt was born to wealth and power. He spent his youth cloistered in a lavish Victorian society that catered to the privileged few. He lived in the grandest manor house, but never owned one of his own until he built The Little White House in 1932. These rustic surroundings were to be the place where he found happiness and true solitude.

Franklin D. Roosevelt died on April 12, 1945. As he sat at his desk in his small but comfortable living room, he suffered a cerebral hemorrhage and died five hours later. Just a few feet from him on that morning sat artist Elizabeth Schoumatoff concentrating on the now famous unfinished portrait of FDR. The portrait is there for you to see, left as it was that spring morning as a final tribute to one of America's finest sons.

WARM SPRINGS VILLAGE
Main Street
Warm Springs, GA 31830
Tel. (404) 655-2609
     (404) 655-2263
     (404) 655-2558
Major credit cards are accepted in most shops.

The village of Warm Springs has long been known for the restorative powers of its waters. For centuries Native Americans came here looking for healing. President Roosevelt came here in 1924, seeking a cure for his polio, and later chose it as the site of his "Little White House." There is little doubt that Roosevelt revered this sleepy little town. He was drawn, just as visitors are today, to the beautiful Pine Mountain forests and the peace and tranquility of the area.

Present day Warm Springs, with its charming hotel, shops and restaurants, looks much the same as when FDR first arrived. There are sixty shops along Main Street, specializing in antiques, collectibles, folk art, quilts, wooden crafts, antique furniture, books, custom jewelry and souvenirs. Visitors should plan to spend an entire day here, shopping and browsing along the wooden sidewalks. You need that much time to see all the shops and attractions. The village hosts a number of seasonal events featuring sidewalk vendors, decorations and entertainment. The most important are Spring Fling, held the last weekend of April each year, and the Candlelight tour, held annually the weekend before Thanksgiving day.

Warm Springs offers a wonderful combination of southern hospitality and fine products at reasonable prices. It is located one mile from The Little White House (now a museum) and twelve miles from Callaway Gardens and Roosevelt State Park.

Areas of Interest Outside Atlanta

SO YOU'D LIKE TO BE A TOURIST?

Or
"How to steer your cruise ship through smooth waters and avoid the stormy seas."

By

Merritt Scott Miller

As many a weary traveler has learned, being a tourist is not as easy as it first seems. If you're like most vacationers, you have worked hard for those magical weeks of leisure. Your holiday looms ahead like a trip to Heaven itself and chances are you have been dreaming of it for months.

It might be a fantasy you fall back on when the boss growls at you, the casserole burns or somebody forgets it was his turn to carpool your kids to school. It starts out as a pleasant thought, becomes a coping device, and by increasing degrees builds into a preoccupation. You find yourself gritting your teeth just to get through the days.

By the time the magic day arrives you are frazzled, but relief is imminent. You've spent all night packing the car, poring over road maps and doing those thousand and ten things that seem to crop up at the last minute.

"Did we remember to stop the paper?"
"Are you sure the hotel has our reservations?"
"Where's that stack of travel books and brochures?"

At the appointed hour, or perhaps a few hours later, everyone rushes out to load up the car. Invariably—usually about fifty miles from home—those nagging doubts about whether somebody left the water running or forgot to lock the back door assail you like so many mosquitoes at an ill-chosen campsite. It's enough to send your blood pressure straight through the roof of the car.

And then, when you finally arrive at your destination, you're either lost or overwhelmed. You discover you can't possibly see all the attractions listed in the mound of brochures.

Areas of Interest Outside Atlanta

Your stress escalates. You learn some attractions have changed their hours, are no longer operating, or have increased their admission prices. It begins to dawn on you that you have successfully turned your two week dream vacation into a fourteen day nightmare. And still you have the strenuous task ahead of convincing neighbors, friends, relatives and co-workers that you had a *fantastic* time on your trip.

If this scenario has ever happened to you, you're probably wondering if there is a way to exchange these problems for a successful vacation. We want to help. Here are a few thoughts on how to prepare for a terrific, exciting, relaxing trip.

HEADING FOR THE HIGH SEAS

First, choose the kinds of things to do and see that will prove relaxing to you. What kind of vacation are you planning?

"Ah-ha!" we hear you say. "What do you mean, what *kind* of vacation?"

Well, your lifestyle makes a difference. What kind is yours? What do you do for a living? Your job may involve a great deal of physical activity. Or like many Americans today, your occupation may entail sitting at a computer, attending sales conferences, spending time behind a counter or on the telephone. Your job may require substantial out-of-town traveling or long daily commutes in and out of the city.

Does that make a difference? It sure does! Have you ever heard the expression "busman's holiday"? It's a vacation that involves the same activities you normally do on your job. For a bus driver, it means being on the road visiting different towns. For a teacher, it's an educational tour of museums, libraries and cultural exhibits. For a businessman, it's time spent in cities. For a logger, it's a camping trip. In short, if your vacation looks like what you do the other fifty weeks of the year, you aren't "getting away from it all."

Ideally, people confined to an office should leave the city and head for a spot offering a variety of recreational and cultural opportunities. That's the best kind of vacation for the majority of Americans. But be sure to decide whether you want a vacation that is primarily active or primarily relaxing. And figure out whether you're the type of person who needs to structure every moment or the type who wants to loll around and let whatever happens, happen.

Don't forget the needs of your spouse and children. A vacation should allow families to play together as well as pursue activities fun for each and all. Make sure your schedule includes something for everyone. Here's where "Best Choices" comes in to help you do just that.

CHARTING THE COURSE

1. Decide how much you can afford to spend and what type of vacation fits in with your finances. Two weeks at the Riviera? One on the Oregon Coast?

2. Make a list of the things you and those you are sharing the vacation with are interested in. Include cultural and recreational activities you genuinely enjoy but don't often get to do.

3. Based on these considerations of interest and affordability, pick a vacation spot and figure out how much

time you can spend there. List at least three reasons why your spot is appealing. These might include:

a. It's the perfect place to get away from it all.
b. You've always wanted to go there.
c. Somebody you know went and raved about it.

Include everyone in the planning. Discuss and then decide on your destination and date. Once you've gotten this far, you're ready to delve into the details of getting ready to go.

4. Firm up your ideas of how you're going to manage and spend your precious vacation time. Study this book and write down attractions and places that match your list. Don't worry about the list being too long. You can always trim it.

5. Put first things first. This is really important. You might give each item a ranking of 1-10, with 10 the most enjoyable.

6. Write down the address and phone number of your selected sites. Check on opening and closing times, entrance fees and other important details. Occasionally these details change after your "Best Choices" book has been published. Double check if you like by using its listed phone number to call the place in question.

7. You now have the basic outline for your vacation. Spread out a map and start grouping your choices by specific areas. Doing this will move you into the next phase: scheduling.

8. Rough out a vacation calendar. Your kids can help. Make the squares for each day big enough to allot the time you plan to spend at each attraction, activity or restaurant. Be sure to include unstructured time and perhaps time for family members to split up and do different things.

There. Your vacation is mapped out. Check to see if you have made reservations where you need them. Finally, total up how much the entire venture is going to cost. Add at least ten percent to take care of unexpected expenses.

Areas of Interest Outside Atlanta

BATTEN DOWN THE HATCHES

Once you know where you're headed, turn your planning attention to the homefront to ensure the safety and sanctity of your home while you're on the road.

1. Arrange to have someone watch your house or check up on it every few days. That should include watering the lawn (or shoveling the walks), picking up mail and collecting and forwarding any messages left on the door. Consider a housesitter if necessary.

2. Arrange a timer for a few lights and at least one radio. Design and coordinate a system that will create the impression while you're gone that someone is home but too busy to answer the door.

3. If you use a telephone answering device, make your "greeting" as noncommittal as possible. ("Sorry, we can't come to the phone right now because we're in the yard feeding Killer, our purebred pit bull.") Police strongly advise against giving any information that you are leaving town or how long you will be away.

4. Replace or repair any insecure windows and doors.

5. If you have pets, make arrangements well in advance to board them at a kennel or with a friend.

6. Make a check list of last minute things to do: closing drapes, turning off sprinklers, locking doors and windows, shutting off gas and appliances, setting furnace controls and any timers, etc. After ensuring that your list is complete, post it where it will be the last thing you look at and check off, item by item.

7. Make an itinerary of locations and phone numbers where you plan to stay. Leave a copy with anyone who might have to get in touch with you, such as your employer (if you must!), a close relative, friend or your house watcher.

8. Buy travelers' checks and, if you feel the need, make arrangements with a friend or your bank to forward emergency funds. Your credit cards or bank automatic teller machines are your handiest source of emergency cash.

Areas of Interest Outside Atlanta

SET SAIL

Your vacation is charted to the minute and the cent. So relax. Throw on your Hawaiian print shirt, dangle the camera around your neck and shove off. By all means don't be afraid to be the tourist that you are. Enjoy it. Revel in it! Let the locals appreciate and help you enjoy the area they live in and are no doubt proud of. And remember that a vacation is a time to do the wild, the wacky and the unexpected.

Best wishes for the Best vacation with the "Best" of all guides!

INDEX

A Comic Cafe 238
A.J.'s Shoe Warehouse 151
Abbadabba's 86
Abstein Gallery 70
Acacia 105
Academy Theatre, The 26, 157
Acworth/Lake Allatoona, City of 7
Addis Ethiopian Restaurant 106
Adeline Turman 73
Agnes Scott College 185
Alfredo's 106
Ali Babba Oriental Rugs, Inc. 143
All That and Victorian II 256
Allen-Carnes Plantation, The 205
Alliance Theatre, The 26
Alonzo F. Herndon, home of 37
Alpharetta, City of 7-8
   Antique Shop 9-10
   Hardware Store 10
   Photography 10-11
Amberley Suites Hotel 247
Americus 282
Andersonville 282
Ann Jackson Gallery, The 258
Antique Auto Museum 271
Appleby House 290
Ariel Gallery 73
Arts Festival of Atlanta 46
Ashley Oaks 203
Atkins Park 107
Atlanta Antiques Exchange, The 54
Atlanta Art Gallery 70
Atlanta Ballet 27
Atlanta Botanical Garden 26,85
Atlanta Cabana Hotel 49
Atlanta Chamber Players 27
Atlanta Christian College, 196
Atlanta, City of 16-46
   Accessories 47-49
   Accommodations 49-54
   Antique Shops 54-56
   Apparel 56-69
   Art Galleries 70-74
   Bakeries 75-77
   Balloons 78

Bookstore 79
Collectibles 79
Comedy 79-80
Education 80-81
Entertainment 81-82
Fabric Shop 82-83
Florist 83-84
Furniture Store 84-85
Garden 85-86
Gift Shops 86-91
Hair Salon 91-92
Hardware Store 92-93
Jewelry Stores 94-95
Kitchen Supplies 96-97
Market 97-98
Museum 98-99
Music 99-100
Nightclub 100-101
Pottery 101-102
Pubs 102-103
Raceway 104
Restaurants 105-143
Rugs 143-146
Salon 147-150
Science Center 150-151
Shoe Shops 151-153
Sporting Goods 153-154
Taverns 154-157
Theater 157
Wine Shop 157-158
Atlanta Civic Center 27
Atlanta College of Art 27
Atlanta Dogwood Festival 46
Atlanta During the Civil War 159-163
Atlanta Falcons, The 230
Atlanta-Fulton County Stadium 29
Atlanta-Fulton Public Library 27
Atlanta Gas Light 27
Atlanta Golf Classic 46
Atlanta Hilton and Towers 49
Atlanta Historical Society 28, 98
Atlanta International Raceway, The 28
Atlanta Jazz Theatre 29
Atlanta Journal and Constitution 29
Atlanta Life Insurance Company 29

381

Index

Atlanta Market Center 41
Atlanta Museum, The 29
Atlanta Newspapers 29
Atlanta Preservation Center 30
Atlanta State Farmers' Market 45
Augusta Chronicle-Herald, The 288
Augusta Coca-Cola Bottling Company 288
Augusta Golf Course 289
Augusta Museum, The 288
Aunt Charley's 108
Aunt Fanny's Cabin 268
Australian Body Works 56
Avanzare 109
Avondale Estates, City of 169-170
　Sporting Goods-Ski 170-171
Avondale Ski Shop 170
B.A. Evans Home House 349
Baby Doe's Matchless Mine 110
Backstage Ltd. 91
Balloons By The Bunch 78
Barrington Hall 254
Battle of Kennesaw Mountain, The 222-226
Behold the Lowly Peanut 353-355
Bells of Stone Mountain, The 273
Bitty Herlihy 72
Black American heritage 31
Bones Steak and Seafood 110
Bosco's 110
Boston Sea Party 111
Boutique Physique 56
Broad Street District 346
Brown and Williamson Tobacco Corporation 319
Buford, City of 171-172
Busy Bee Cafe 112
Bygone Era Architectural Antiques 55
Cable News Network Center 31
Cafe Lawrence 115
Café De La Place 113
Café Intermezzo 114
Calhoun, City of 297-298
Callanwolde Fine Arts Center 31
Callaway Gardens 365
Callaway Gardens Country Store 364
Callaway Gardens Inn 362
Cameron-Cobb Ltd. 73

Camp Plantation, The 205
Capo's Cafe 116
Carl Ratcliff Dance Theatre, The 26
Carlson & Lobrano Galleries Ltd. 70
Carolyn Wicher 73
Carter Presidential Center 30
Carter, James Earl (Jimmy), Library 283
Cartersville, City of 337-338
　Resort 338-339
Cartersville Civic Center 338
Cast Ocean 117
Center for Puppetry Arts 30
Center Stage Theatre 30,81
Chamblee's Antique Row 173
Chamblee, City of 172-173
　Antique Shop 174
Chantilly's Uptown Grill 117
Charades 240
Chastain Park 45
Chateau Elan, Ltd. 230
Chattahoochee Electrical Power Generation Facility 309
Chattahoochee Nature Center 254
Chattahoochee Promenade 308
Chattahoochee Recreation Area, The 208-210
Chattahoochee River Crossing 253
Chattahoochee River, The 234
Chattahoochee Valley Art Association 344, 348
Chefs' Grill 117
Chequers Bar & Grill 118
China Chasers 248
Chopstix 118
Christa Frangiamore 73
Clark College 80
Clayton Cameracraft 10
CNN Cinema 6 44
Coach and Six 109
Coca-Cola Bottling Company, The 31
Collections of Life and Heritage 32
College Park, City of 175-176
　Antique Shop 176
　Book Store 176
College Park Golf Course, The 175
Colonial Baking Company 319

Index

Columbus Ironworks Convention and Trade Center, The 308
Columbus Ledger/Enquirer 310
Columbus Museum of Arts and Science 309
Columbus Naval Museum 309
Compri Hotel 235
Concerts in the Country (Calhoun) 298
Confederate Cemetery (Calhoun) 297
Confederate Cemetery (Marietta) 234
Confederate Monument 289
Confederate Powder Works 289
Conyers, City of 182-184
County Cork Pub 102
Coweta County Fair 357
Crisson's Gold Mine 313
Crossroads Seafood and Lounge 120
Crown Gardens and Archives 298
Custom Clothing by H. Stockton, Inc. 57
Cyclorama, The 32
Dahlonega Bluegrass Festival 313
Dahlonega Gold Museum State Historical Site, The 312
Dalton, City of 298-299
David Westmeier 73
Day Trips from Atlanta
  Andersonville National Historic Site 276-283
  Athens and Augusta 284-292
  Callaway Gardens 293-296
  Chickamauga and Chattanooga National Military Park 296-305
  Cleveland 305-306
  Columbus 306-310
  Dahlonega 310-314
  Helen 314-316
  Macon 316-320
  The State Park Loop 321-333
  Unicoi State Park and Chattahoochee National Forest 333-335
Decatur City Hall 185
Decatur, City of 184-187
  Golf and Tennis 188-189
  Hardware Store 189
  Restaurant 189-190
  Sporting Goods 190

Decatur High School 185
Decatur Railroad Depot 185
Decatur's Courthouse Square 184
Dekalb Farmers' Market 187
Delta Airlines 33
Dessert Place, The 75
Diane McPhail 73
Dickson Funeral Home, The 204
Dixie House Restaurant & Chocolate Factory 342
Don Juan's Spanish and Continental Restaurant 120
Donatelli 101
Doubletree Hotel 49
Drummer Boy Civil War Museum 282
Duluth 190-192
Duluth Fall Festival 192
Dunaway Gardens 356
Dunwoody 193
  Market 193-194
  Restaurant 195-196
Dusty's Barbecue 121
E. Rooks 47
East 48th Street Market 193
East Point, City of 196-197
Eat Your Vegetables 122
Eddie's Trick and Novelty Shop 274
1867 Depot, The 205
1869 Courthouse, The 204
1869 Jail, The 204
1898 Courthouse, The 205
El Ranchero Restaurante Mexicano 241
El Toro Mexican Restaurant 189
Elisha Winn Fair, The 232
Elisha Winn Home 230
Elliott Morrow Cottage, The 204
Embassy Suites Hotel (Akers Mill) 49
Embassy Suites Hotel (Crown Pointe) 50
Emory University's Museum of Art and Archaeology 33
Empire of China 206
Empress of China III 123
Encore Restaurant 123
Etowah Arts Gallery 337
Etowah Valley Historical Society 338
Executive Tour Lines 199

Index

Executive Town and Country Service, Inc. 197
Executive Villas Hotel 51
Fairmont 297
Fall Festival of Arts and Crafts (Dalton) 299
Family Campground (Stone Mountain) 272
Fancy Delancey 58
Fantasia Flowers Limited 83
Fayette County Courthouse 339
Fayetteville, City of 339-340
   Crafts 340-341
   Gift Shop 341-342
   Restaurant 342-343
Fernbank Science Center, The 35, 150, 187
Fife House, The 340
56 East Restaurant and Desserts 123
Fisherman's Cove 124
Flamingo Joe's 241
Folk•Art Imports 87
Forest Hill Golf Course 289
Forest Park, City of 197
   Limousine 197-198
   Restaurant 198-199
   Tour 199
Fort Benning 310
Fort Gordon 288
Fort Peachtree 36
Founder's Memorial Garden and Museum House 285
Fourteen Savannah Restaurant 358
Fox Theatre 36
Fragile 88
Frances Aronson Gallery 71
French Quarter Suites 51
Friedman's Shoes 152
Gabbies Fashion and Gift Boutique 89
Gallery South 71
Georgia Department of Archives and History 36
Georgia Governor's Mansion 37
Georgia Historical Aviation Museum, The 230
Georgia International Trade and Convention Center 175
Georgia On My Mind 2-7
Georgia Power Company 338, 356
Georgia Renaissance Festival 46
Georgia State Capitol 37
Georgia Sweet Georgia 249
Georgia Veterans Memorial State Park 283
Gifts Extraordinaire Ltd. 89
Glover Park 234
Golf Warehouse Sales 249
Good and Plenty Antiques 176
Gordon County Historical Society 297
Grand China 125
Grand Opera House, The 319
Grant Park 37
Great American Hot Dog House, The 198
Great Temptations-Gifts For You and Your Home 341
Gretchen's Children's Shop 59
Grill, The 260
Guffey's of Atlanta, Inc. 60
Gwinnett Arts Council's Outreach Program 230
Gwinnett County Arts Council, The 230
Gwinnett Place 231
Hard Labor Creek State Park 285
Harris Home 290
Hartsfield Atlanta International Airport 177-181
Hemingway's Terrace 110
Henri's Bakery 76
High House, The 186
High Museum at Georgia-Pacific Center, The 38
High Museum of Art, The 38
Highland Hardware 92
Historic Columbus Foundation, The 308
Historic Complex of DeKalb Historical Society, The 186
Historic Fair (Andersonville) 282
Historic House on Norman Berry Drive 196
Holiday Celebration (Stone Mountain) 272
Holiday Health & Racquet Club 257, 267

Index

Holiday Inn Roswell 255
Hospitality House 89
Hotel Ibis 51
House of Chan 269
House of Denmark's Butikken Gift Gallery 90
House of Oriental Art, 143
Hovan Gourmet 195
Hyatt Regency Atlanta 41
Ibis 61, 221
Ice Chalet 272
In Clover 352
Indigo Coastal Grill 125
Inman Park Trolley Barn 39
J.R.'s Log House 251
James Earl (Jimmy) Carter Library 283
Jeanne's Body Tech 62
Jefferson House, The 357
Jessica's on Park Square 259
Jody 94
Johnny Rockets 126
Johnny's Hideaway 100
Johnson-Blalock House 204
Joli-Kobe 77
Jones Bridge Park 247
Jones Creek Golf Club 289
Jonesboro, City of 199-206
  Restaurant 206-207
Jonesboro's Old Town Cemetery 204
Jubilee Riverboat, The 309
Judie Jacobs 72
Junkman's Daughter, The 62
K. Hartwig Dahl 73
Kate Pendleton 74
Katherine Panhorst Smith 73
Kennesaw Mountain National Battlefield Park 235
Kennesaw, City of 211-221
  Apparel 221
Kilim Collection, The 144
King, Martin Luther Jr., Center, The 39
Kitchen Fare 96
Kleinberg Sherrill 48
Knickerbockers 154
La Grotta 260
La Paz 266
LaFayette Society of Performing Arts 345

LaGrange Ballet Theatre 345
LaGrange, City of 343-347
  Apparel 347-348
  Art Gallery 348-349
  Gift Shop 349-350
  Interior Design 350-351
  Restaurant 352
LaGrange Mutual Concerts Association 345
LaGrotta 127
Lake Acworth 7
Lake Avondale 170
Lake Lanier 171
Lamar Dodd Art Center 345
Lanier Plaza Hotel 52
Lark and the Dove, The 128
Laser Light Show (Stone Mountain) 270
Lawrenceville's Courthouse Square 229
Lawrenceville, City of 227-231
Lee's Golden Buddha Restaurant 250
Lickskillet Farm Restaurant 261
Lilburn, City of 232
Lindbergh Memorial, The 283
Lindy B's 129
Lindy's 129
Little White House, The 371
Lone Star Steaks 130
Los Arcos Mexican Restaurant 252
Lovejoy Plantation 206
Lovett Marie Gallery 71
Lyn Perry 74
Ma Maison Restaurant 130
Macon Cherry Blossom Festival 320
Macon City Auditorium, The 319
Macon Convention and Vistors Bureau 317
Macon Museum of Arts and Sciences 318
Mahogany Grille 262
Manget Brannon Alliance for the Arts 356
Mansour Ausari Oriental Rugs 145
Mansour's 347
Manuel's Tavern 155
Marble House 185
Marcy Turk 72

Index

Margaret Mitchell Library 340
Margo Owens 74
Marietta, City of 233-235
   Accommodation 235
   Amusement Park 236-237
   Comedy 237-238
   Hardware Store 238-239
   Night Club 240
   Restaurants 241-245
Marietta Welcome Center, The 234
Marra's 131
Marriott Suites-Atlanta/Perimeter 52
Martin Luther King, Jr. Center, The 39
Maximillian's Continental American Cuisine 242
Mayfair Suites Hotel 53
Mc Kinnon's Louisane and Grill Room 132
Meadow Garden 290
Melting Pot, The 133
Mercer Air Museum 297
Mercer University 40
Methodist Chapel, The 186
Metropolitan Atlanta Rapid Transit Authority 39
Middle Georgia Historical Society 319
Middleton and Lane Jewelers, Inc. 95
Mill Store, Inc., The 350
Minoo Fine Bakery and Restaurant 134
Mitchell, Margaret, Library 340
Mitzi and Romano 63
Modo Sushi 135
Moe's and Joe's 156
Monastery of the Holy Ghost 183
Mooncake 64
Morris Brown College 40
Morrow, City of 245
   Gift Shop 245-246
Mount Moriah Baptist Church 231
National Cemetery, The 234
National Infantry Museum 310
Nevada Bob's Golf and Tennis 188
New Georgia Railroad 43
Newnan, City of 356-357
   Antique Shop 357-358
   Restaurants 358-361
Next City Comedy Theatre, The 79
Nexus Gallery, The 40

Noah's Ark Church 205
Norcross, City of 246-247
   Accommodation 247-248
   Gift Shops 248-249
   Golf 249
   Restaurants 250-252
North Fulton County 8
North Fulton County shopping area 254
North Georgia Agricultural College 312
Oakland Cemetery 40
Ocmulgee National Monument 317
Old Cannonball House 319
Old Curiosity Shop, The 273
Old Fort Daniel 231
Old Pinckneyville 246
Old Slave Market Column, The 289
Old South Celebration (Stone Mountain) 272
Old Spaghetti Factory, The 135
Omni Coliseum 40
Omni International 45
Original Pancake House, The 135
Osaka Japan, 243
Outback Outfitters and Bikes 153
Outdoor Activity Center 41
Oxford Book Stores 79
Partners Morningside Café 136
Partners Pantry 136
Patio by the River, The 137
Patrician Galleries South 71
Patrick R. Cleburne Memorial Cemetery, The 204
Patterson Planetarium 309
Peachtree Center 41
Peachtree Playhouse, The 41
Peachtree Yacht Club 252
Pemberton House 309
Pharr Wine and Cheese Shop 157
Phyllis Alterman Franco 74
Piedmont National Wildlife Refuge 319
Pierremont Plaza Hotel 53
Pinckneyville Art Center, The 246
Pine Mountain, City of 361
   Accommodation 362-363
   Gift Shop 364-365
   Resort 365-367

Index

Pine Tree Company, The 313
Planters, The 243
Poppy's 65
Powers' Crossroad Bluegrass Festival 357
Price Memorial Building, The 312
Price Theater 345
Promised Land, The 231
Providence Park Outdoor Recreation Center 8
Ramada Renaissance Hotel 53
Rankin House 308
Raven's Nest/The Friendly Toad 9
Reconstructed Plantation 271
Residence Inn, The 53
Rexer-Parkes 66
Rhodes Hall 42
Rio Bravo 138
Road Atlanta 104
Roswell, City of 253-254
    Accommodation 255
    Antique Shop 256-257
    Apparel 257-258
    Art Gallery 258-259
    Gift Shop 259-260
    Restaurants 260-264
Roswell Historical Society, The 42
Roswell Town Square 253
Rugs By Robinson 145
Rust N' Dust Antiques 174
S and W Seafood Restaurant and Market 266
Salacoa Creek Park 298
Sandi Grow 74
Sandy Springs 264-265
    Restaurants 266-267
Sandy Springs Historic Site, The 265
Sandy Springs Milk House 265
Scan Des 84
Scientific Atlanta, Inc. 42
Scottish Festival and Highland Games 272
Scrub-A-Dub Pub 103
Senoia, City of 367-368
    Bed & Breakfast Inn 368-369
Sevananda 97
Sidney Guberman 72
Sigma Chi Monument, The 205
Signer's Monument 289
Simon's Mesquite Seafood Grill 139
Simply Country 245
Six Flags Over Georgia 12-15
Small World 257
Smith Ace Hardware 10, 189, 238
Smith House Inn, The 312
Smoke Flame West Bar B Q 140
Smokey Mountain Sports 190
Smyrna, City of 267
    Apparel 267
    Restaurants 268-269
Snappy Turtle 67
Snellville Days Festival 231
So You'd Like to be a Tourist? 374-379
Southeast Railway Museum 192
Southern Bell Center's Telephone Museum, The 42
Southern Christian Leadership Conference 44
Southwind Health Resort 338
Sprayberry's Barbecue 359
Springer Opera House 308
Stan Milton Images 147
Stately Oaks Mansion 204
Status Thimble, The 340
Steam Locomotive Trains 270
Stefan's, Inc. 68
Stephen Carnes House, The 204
Stone Mountain 269-273
    Collectibles 273-274
    Novelty 274-275
    Resort 275
Stone Mountain Carving Museum 45
Stone Mountain Inn 275
Stone Mountain Lake 271
Stone Mountain Park 271
Stone Mountain Springfest, The 272
Stouffer PineIsle Resort, The 171
Studio Theatre, The 26
Susan Marple 72
Suwanee Day 232
Swan House, The 28
Sweet Auburn 164-168
Swift Textiles, Inc. 310
Sydell Skin and Body Care Salon 148
Tajmahal 140
Taylor-Grady House 285

Index

Terrace Garden Inn 54
Texas Steak Out 244
Theatrical Outfit, The 44
Three Arts Theatre 309
Titan Books and Comics 176
Tom's Foods 310
Traders Camp Petting Zoo 271
Tritt Gallery 71
Trotter's Restaurant 141
Troup County Historical Society 344
Tula Showrooms/Studios 72
Tullie Smith House, The 28
Twelve Savannah Restaurant 360
U.S Sixth District Federal Reserve Bank 35
U.S. Bar and Grill 141
Uncle Billy Hill Saloon, The 185
University of Georgia 284
University of Georgia Museum of Art 285
Varsity, The 141
"Veggie Land" 142
Veranda, The 368
Vernon Road Historic District, The 346
Victorian Playhouse, The 28
Vivian Gray of Atlanta 69
Walker-Peters-Langdon House 308
Walter J. Penny Fine Fabric 82
Ware's Folly 290
Warm Springs, City of 369-371
    Points of Interest 371-373
Warm Springs Village 372
Warren House, The 204
Warren Sherer Div. of Kysor Industrial Co. 182
Waterstone's 263
Watson Mill Bridge State Park 286
Wax 'N' Facts 99
Weinman Mineral Center 337
Werco Persian and Oriental Rugs 146
West Point Lake, 346
West Point Pepperell 298
Westin Peachtree Plaza, The 54
White Water 236
Whitefield County Fair 299
Wickers 142
Willis Park 169
Wills Park Equestrian Center 8

Woodruff Arts Center, The 44
World Wide Coin Investments 79
Wrecking Bar, The 55
Wren's Nest, The 41
WSB Radio and Television 44
Yellow Daisy Festival 272
Yellow River Wildlife Game Ranch 44
Yerby Home 290
Zapien's 149
Zoar Methodist Church, The 231
Zoo Atlanta 42

NOTES

NOTES

NOTES

NOTES

NOTES

NOTES

NOTES

NOTES